EXCEL INSIGHTS

A MICROSOFT MVP GUIDE TO THE BEST PARTS OF EXCEL

24 EXCEL MVPS

Holy Macro! Books

PO Box 541731

Merritt Island FL 32954

USA

Excel Insights

Printed in USA by Hess Print Solutions.

First Printing: January 2020.

Authors: Jon Acampora, Liam Bastick, Leila Gharani, Michael Girvin, Roger Govier, Frederic le Guen, Mathieu Guindon, Tim Heng, Wyn Hopkins, Ian Huitson, Bill Jelen, Tony de Jonker, Gašper Kamenšek, John MacDougall, Dave Paradi, Jon Peltier, Jan Karel Pieterse, Ken Puls, Oz du Soleil, Hervé Thiriez, Mynda Treacy, Henk Vlootman, and Charles Williams.

Lead Editors: Liam Bastick and Ingeborg Hawighorst

Technical Editors: Liam Bastick, Tim Heng, Bill Jelen, Jan Karel Pieterse and Charles Williams.

Indexer: Nellie Jay.

Compositor: Jill Cabot.

Cover Design: Shannon Travise.

Screen Reader Captions: Jon Acampora, Liam Bastick, Leila Gharani, Roger Govier, Frederic le Guen, Mathieu Guindon, Wyn Hopkins, Ian Huitson, Bill Jelen, Gašper Kamenšek, John MacDougall, Dave Paradi, Jon Peltier, Jan Karel Pieterse, Ken Puls, Oz du Soleil, Mynda Treacy, Henk Vlootman, and Charles Williams.

Published by: Holy Macro! Books, PO Box 541731, Merritt Island FL 32954.

Distributed by Independent Publishers Group, Chicago, IL.

ISBN 978-1-61547-067-9 Print, 978-1-61547-153-9 Digital.

Library of Congress Control Number: 2019952976.

Excel examples used in this book can be downloaded from: https://mrx.cl/mvpfiles.

Table of Contents

Smart Uses of Custom Number Formatting

by Leila Gharani

Number formatting is ideal for manipulating data in presentations without actually "touching" the source data. Most people normally use it to show numbers with a thousand separator or as percentage, or even to show green for positive and red for negative values, but they hardly go beyond that.

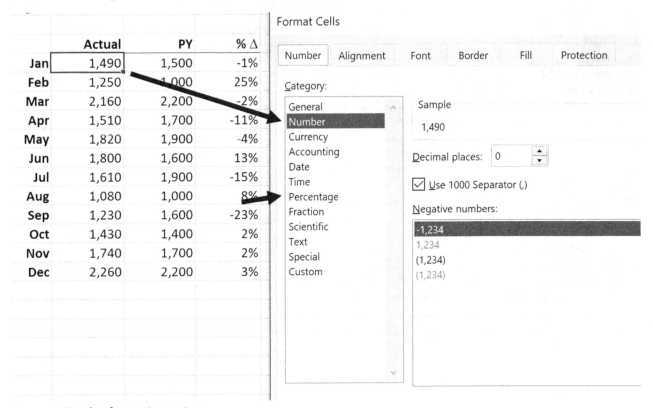

Common Number formatting options.

The image below shows how you can extend the usual number formatting options to create impressive reports. You can even use dynamic thresholds to control the formatting.

	Actual	PY				Threshold	5%	
					Actual	PY		
Jan	1,490	1,500	▼	Jan	1,490	1,500	-1%	
Feb	1,250	1,000	▲	Feb	1,250	1,000	25% ▦	
Mar	2,160	2,200	▼	Mar	2,160	2,200	-2%	
Apr	1,510	1,700	▼	Apr	1,510	1,700	-11% ■	
May	1,820	1,900	▼	May	1,820	1,900	-4%	
Jun	1,800	1,600	▲	Jun	1,800	1,600	13% ▦	
Jul	1,610	1,900	▼	Jul	1,610	1,900	-15% ■	
Aug	1,080	1,000	▲	Aug	1,080	1,000	8% ▦	
Sep	1,230	1,600	▼	Sep	1,230	1,600	-23% ■	
Oct	1,430	1,400	▲	Oct	1,430	1,400	2%	
Nov	1,740	1,700	▲	Nov	1,740	1,700	2%	
Dec	2,260	2,200	▲	Dec	2,260	2,200	3%	

Flexible Threshold

Custom number formatting to emphasize deviations.

I will take you through the necessary steps to create reports like these. It's easy. The catch is, you first need to understand the rule behind custom number formatting. Once you do, it'll open up your eyes to all the opportunities to improve the presentation of your reports.

Rule Behind Custom Number Formatting

To access custom number formatting, right-click on any cell, click 'Format Cells…' or use the shortcut key Ctrl + 1. In the window that appears, in the Number tab, go to Custom.

The Custom option allows you to create your own customized formats. You can choose how to display positive and negative numbers, as well as how you'd like zero values and text entries to be formatted.

Proper use of custom number formatting requires you to follow a special syntax which is comprised of four parts (when all four parts are specified):

Positive number; Negative number; Zero; Text

Each segment is separated by the semicolon (;) symbol, known as a delimiter.

Excel doesn't require all four parts though. If your formatting includes only two parts, Excel assumes the first part of the formatting to be for positive values and zeros while the second part will be used to format negative values. If you specify only one format segment, i.e. the semi-colon is entirely left out from the syntax, then Excel ignores positive and negative but applies the same formatting to all four parts.

In the 'Custom Format Cells' dialog box, you have over 30 different number formats available:

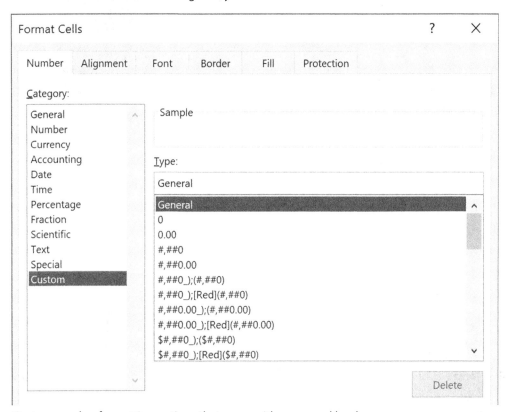

Custom number formatting options that come with every workbook.

If you scroll through these, you come across symbols like #, 0, ?, [Red], etc. The below list explains the uses of the most common symbols:

- **0** *(zero)* is a fixed placeholder for values. It is commonly used to define the number of decimal places.
- **#** *(pound / hash)* is a digital placeholder as in 0. The difference is # doesn't force trailing zero values. For example, if you have ## as a custom number format and the value in the cell is 2, you will see a 2. Whereas, if you have 00 as the custom number format, you will see 02 shown in the cell instead. A common format for the thousand separator is #,##0. This means commas are displayed for every three (3) digits.
- **,** *(comma)* displays the thousand separator. Note that this can be different depending upon your regional settings. For example, if your regional settings are German, you'll need the "." Instead of the ",".
- **.** *(period)* displays decimal digits. As with the thousand separator, this is dependent upon your regional settings. Again, for the German setting, you'll need the "," instead of "." for decimal places.
- **_** *(underscore)* adds a space the size of whatever the next character is, so "_)" would make a space the same size as a closing bracket. This is typically used so the value input is not stuck to the cell border. This aligns positive numbers correctly below negative values in parentheses.

- * *(asterisk)* repeats the next character until the width of the cell is filled. For example, you'd like the currency symbol on the left-hand side of the cell, followed by blank space and then the number. The wider the column width, the wider the blank space in between the dollar symbol and the number.
- @ ('at sign') is a placeholder for text.
- **[Red]** changes the color of the values to red. Excel custom number formatting has a certain number of color codes available which can be used here. In English, the names recognized are [Black], [White], [Red], [Green], [Blue], [Yellow], [Magenta] and [Cyan]. For example, the standard [Green] is quite bright for reports. [Color 10] can be used for a darker green. They all need to be entered with square brackets. There are 57 colors available, [Color 0] (the one everyone always forgets about!) through [Color 56]. You can find the link to the complete list of color index and values in the downloadable workbook.

Hiding Zero Values in Reports

A practical use of custom number formatting is to hide zero values in reports. Follow these steps to add a custom number format:

- Select the data range to be formatted
- Right-click / format cells or use shortcut Ctrl + 1
- Click on category 'Custom' and under 'Type' write the custom number format string: '#,##0;-#,##0;'
- Click OK

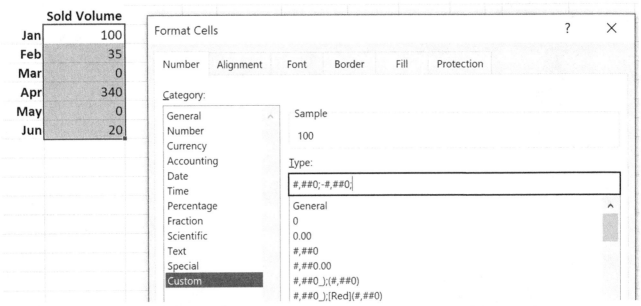

Custom number formatting to hide zero values.

Zero values are now shown as empty cells, because the third argument (after the second delimiter) is blank.

Remember custom number formatting is like applying make-up. It changes the visible appearance but not the actual content.

If you click on one of the newly formatted empty cells and look at the formula bar, you will see a zero value in there.

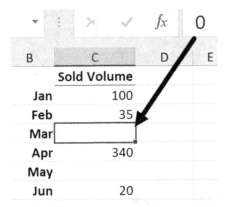

Zero values disappear (but they are still there).

Showing Values in Millions

Let's assume your task is to show the following monthly sales data in millions. Instead of 30,000,000, you'd like to show it as 30 M:

	A	B	C
4			**Sales**
5		J	30,000,000
6		F	40,000,000
7		M	20,000,000
8		A	25,000,000
9		M	32,000,000
10		J	35,000,000
11		J	36,000,000
12		A	37,000,000
13		S	40,000,000
14		O	42,000,000
15		N	43,000,000
16		D	44,000,000

Monthly sales data.

One option is to add an extra calculation step by dividing the data by 1,000,000 and adding an "M" to this with the following formula:

```
=C5/1000000 & " M"
```

Please don't do this!

	A	B	C	D	E	F	G	H
4			**Sales**			**Sales**		
5		J	30,000,000		J	30 M	=C5/1000000 & " M"	
6		F	40,000,000		F	40 M		
7		M	20,000,000		M	20 M		
8		A	25,000,000		A	25 M		
9		M	32,000,000		M	32 M		
10		J	35,000,000		J	35 M		
11		J	36,000,000		J	36 M		
12		A	37,000,000		A	37 M		
13		S	40,000,000		S	40 M		
14		O	42,000,000		O	42 M		
15		N	43,000,000		N	43 M		
16		D	44,000,000		D	44 M		

Showing the data in millions by adding text to the value is something you should avoid!

Changing formatting using this approach converts each cell value into a text cell because text added to a number converts the final value to a text string. Excel automatically left-aligns these because it doesn't recognize them as numbers. Your values might "look" like millions, but the actual values in the cells are not numbers. They are *text*. This means you can't perform any mathematical operations on them.

Formatting the data as millions is the more efficient and practical approach. To do this, highlight the raw data and go to custom number formatting. Apply this format:

```
0,," M";-0,," M";-
```

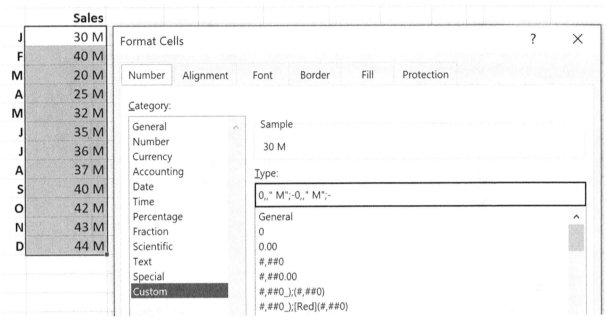

Custom number formatting to show data as millions followed by the "M" abbreviation.

"0,," says to Excel, "display this number in millions". One comma represents thousands and two commas denote millions. The second "M" adds text to the formatted number, *but it remains a number*. Notice the text is inside quotation marks and there is a space before it. This way the "M" doesn't stick to the number.

The part after the first semi-colon is identical to the positive number format but displays negative values with the minus sign. The "-" after the second semi-colon replaces zero values with a dash sign. Text formatting in this example has been ignored. Only positive, negative and zero values have been modified.

Without looking at the values in the formula bar, one would think the cell value to be "30 M".

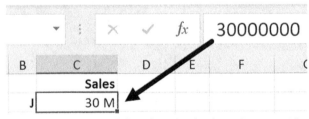

We see 30 M in the cell, but the actual value is "30000000".

The actual value in the cell is "30000000". You can continue to perform mathematical operations on this value, and it will behave accordingly.

Creating a chart on this data is also neater and easier to read than the one created on the original data set, which uses a standard number formatting with a thousand separator and zero decimal places.

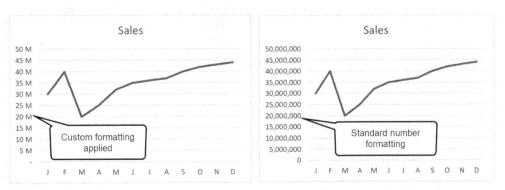

Custom number formatting for the chart axis looks neater and better organized.

Showing Deviations as Symbols

Let's take this a step further and disguise values as symbols. This way, you can show deviations with up and down arrows or any other symbol of your choice.

You might have done this in the past with conditional formatting. After going through this section, I think you will find the custom number formatting method much easier to apply. I personally prefer custom number formatting over conditional formatting whenever I can, for the following reasons:

- I can choose any symbol (I'm not a big fan of the existing conditional formatting symbols, although it is possible to customize these too, admittedly)
- There is no duplicating of the formatting rules, which is a common issue with conditional formatting
- Custom number formatting is faster to implement
- Custom number formatting is not volatile (i.e. it recalculates every time you do anything in Excel) unlike conditional formatting. This makes calculations faster and spreadsheets more stable
- It's less resource intensive in general, as compared to conditional formatting when used on large data sets

As a first step, you need to select the symbols. Click on an empty cell. Go to the Insert tab on the ribbon and select Symbol. Select the symbol you'd like to use in your report and click on Insert. Choose more symbols if you like. This inserts them in the active cell. For this example, I will use the up and down arrows found under Arial in the subset 'Geometric Shapes'.

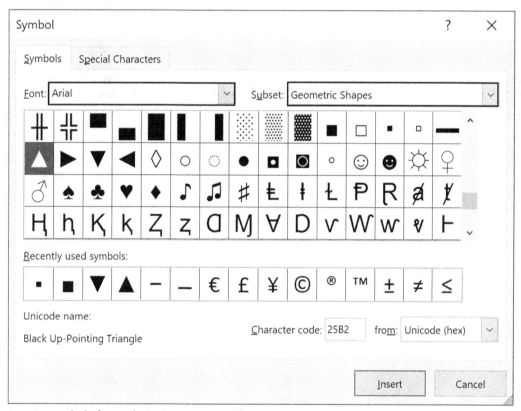

Insert a symbol of your choice in an empty cell.

Remember: to use custom number formatting, you need numbers in the cells.

In the following example, we can calculate the change from Actual to 'Previous Year' (PY) as follows:

    =C7−D7

E7			×	✓	fx	=C7-D7	

	A	B	C	D	E	F
6			Actual	PY		
7		Jan	1,490	1,500	-10	
8		Feb	1,250	1,000	250	
9		Mar	2,160	2,200	-40	
10		Apr	1,510	1,700	-190	
11		May	1,820	1,900	-80	
12		Jun	1,800	1,600	200	
13		Jul	1,610	1,900	-290	
14		Aug	1,080	1,000	80	
15		Sep	1,230	1,600	-370	
16		Oct	1,430	1,400	30	
17		Nov	1,740	1,700	40	
18		Dec	2,260	2,200	60	

Calculate the deviation by deducting Previous Year (PY) values from Actual values.

Now that you have numbers, you can disguise them as you'd like. Copy the arrow symbols you previously inserted. Highlight the values in the deviation column (column E), right- click, 'Format Cells', go to Custom and apply the following formatting:

▲;▼;

The values in the deviation column are shown as up and down arrows. Remember the first argument before the semi-colon is how positive numbers should be formatted. These are now shown as an up arrow. Negative numbers are formatted as a down arrow, and zero values are hidden.

	A	B	C	D	E
6			Actual	PY	
7		Jan	1,490	1,500	▼
8		Feb	1,250	1,000	▲
9		Mar	2,160	2,200	▼
10		Apr	1,510	1,700	▼
11		May	1,820	1,900	▼
12		Jun	1,800	1,600	▲
13		Jul	1,610	1,900	▼
14		Aug	1,080	1,000	▲
15		Sep	1,230	1,600	▼
16		Oct	1,430	1,400	▲
17		Nov	1,740	1,700	▲
18		Dec	2,260	2,200	▲

Values disguised as symbols.

Now let's add some color to the symbols. With the values selected, go back to custom number formatting (press Ctrl +1) and edit the arguments to:

[Green]▲;[Red]▼;

Press OK and the arrows now have colors. Personally, I find the standard green too bright. My preference is [Color 10] for a darker green or [Color 43] for a lighter version. The below image uses [Color 10] for the up arrows.

	Actual	PY	
Jan	1,490	1,500	▼
Feb	1,250	1,000	▲
Mar	2,160	2,200	▼
Apr	1,510	1,700	▼
May	1,820	1,900	▼
Jun	1,800	1,600	▲

See the figures on this page in color. Scan here.

[Color 10] is used for the up arrows.

The custom number formatting box is language sensitive. If you're using Excel in another language, translate "color" to your language. The index numbers are identical in all versions.

Up and Down Arrows with Percentage Deviation

What if you wanted to show the percentage value together with the symbol in the same cell? No problem. First calculate the percentages by (Actual – PY)/PY, or alternatively Actual/PY -1.

Highlight the values and go to custom number formatting. Type the following format:

[Color 10]0% ▲;[Red] -0% ▼;

Your result will show both the cell value formatted as a percentage, followed by the symbol.

	Actual	PY	
Jan	1,490	1,500	-1% ▼
Feb	1,250	1,000	25% ▲
Mar	2,160	2,200	-2% ▼
Apr	1,510	1,700	-11% ▼
May	1,820	1,900	-4% ▼
Jun	1,800	1,600	13% ▲
Jul	1,610	1,900	-15% ▼
Aug	1,080	1,000	8% ▲
Sep	1,230	1,600	-23% ▼
Oct	1,430	1,400	2% ▲
Nov	1,740	1,700	2% ▲
Dec	2,260	2,200	3% ▲

Custom number formatting to show percentage values and symbols in the same cell.

If you'd like to align the symbols to the right-hand side of the cell and the values to the left-hand side, you can take advantage of the asterisk sign. The asterisk sign repeats the next character to fill up the cell. If the next character is a space, it will repeat the space. This ensures the breathing space inside the cell, is proportional to the width of the cell. Now let's update the custom number formatting to be:

[Color 10] 0%* ▲;[Red] -0%* ▼;

	Actual	PY		
Jan	1,490	1,500	-1%	▼
Feb	1,250	1,000	25%	▲
Mar	2,160	2,200	-2%	▼
Apr	1,510	1,700	-11%	▼
May	1,820	1,900	-4%	▼
Jun	1,800	1,600	13%	▲

Symbols are aligned to the right-hand side and numbers to the left-hand side.

This aligns the symbols under one another. I find the report easier to read this way.

Conditional Number Formatting Using the Custom Number Format Option

Up until now, I shared the major rule behind custom number formatting: first comes positive numbers, then negative values, then zero, then text.

What many people don't know is that custom number formatting also allows for conditions. It has more limitations than Excel's conditional formatting feature, but it can be utilized to create a high, low and other case scenario. To define conditions, you need to include them in square brackets [ ], similar to colors. The syntax then works as:

```
{format1}[Condition 1];{format2}[Condition 2];{format3}
```

This works like a nested IF formula: if the first condition holds, do the first number format; if the second condition holds (but not the first) do the second format; otherwise go with the third format.

Let's take the example above, but this time add conditions based on absolute differences.

If the difference between Actual and PY is more than one hundred, I'd like to have a green up arrow. If the difference is less than zero, a red down arrow and for values between zero and one hundred, I'd like an orange rectangle.

Update the custom number formatting arguments to be:

[Color 10][>100] ▲ ;[Red][<0] ▼ ;[Color 45]━

Left-align the values in the E column to get the symbols closer to the data.

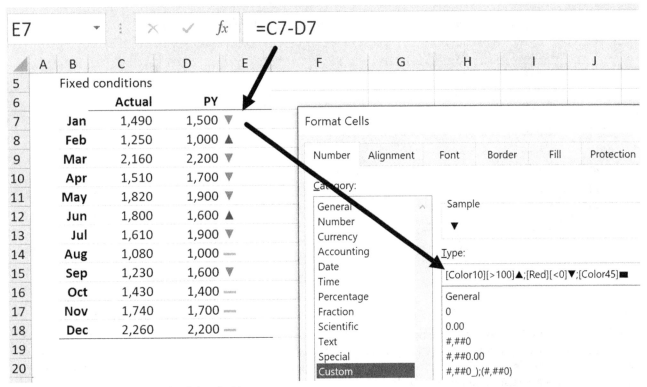

Conditional formats based on fixed thresholds.

This generally works fine. However, if you define the second condition to be <-100 instead of <0, you will see a minus sign beside the symbol for the values between 0 and -100.

A better way around this is to use the technique shown below.

Dynamic Thresholds with Custom Number Formatting

This time, in addition to defining conditions for the threshold, I'd like to input the threshold value in a cell. Unfortunately, you don't have the option to apply cell references in the Custom Number Format dialog box.

A way around this to take advantage of the first rule of custom number formatting. The fact that I can format positive, negative, zero and text values in different ways gives me four conditions I can control. These conditions are pre-defined based on the number and type (text or number) of the value entered in the cell. Let's use this to our advantage.

This time, I'd like to add a 5% threshold. A green arrow should appear for the rows where the difference is above 5%. Any value that's below -5%, should appear as a red arrow. Other values should be invisible.

I've placed the threshold value in a cell (cell E22 in the image below) and formatted it as percentage. I've also calculated the percentage difference between Actual and PY in column E. In column F, I would like to use symbols for the cells where the deviation is greater than the threshold.

I can use the IF function to assign three different types of flags to the cells. For the cases where the percentage change is greater than the threshold, I'd like a 1. If the percentage change is lower than the negative value of the threshold, I'd like a -1. If it lies in between, I'd like a zero (0). Therefore, I can use the following formula:

```
=IF(E24<-$E$22,-1,IF(E24>$E$22,1,0))
```

This way each cell has either a value of 1, -1 or 0.

	A	B	C	D	E	F	G	H	I
22				Threshold	5%				
23			Actual	PY					
24		Jan	1,490	1,500	-1%	0	=IF(E24<-$E$22,-1,IF(E24>$E$22,1,0))		
25		Feb	1,250	1,000	25%	1			
26		Mar	2,160	2,200	-2%	0			
27		Apr	1,510	1,700	-11%	-1			
28		May	1,820	1,900	-4%	0			
29		Jun	1,800	1,600	13%	1			
30		Jul	1,610	1,900	-15%	-1			
31		Aug	1,080	1,000	8%	1			
32		Sep	1,230	1,600	-23%	-1			
33		Oct	1,430	1,400	2%	0			
34		Nov	1,740	1,700	2%	0			
35		Dec	2,260	2,200	3%	0			

Using the IF function to get three types of values (0,1 and -1).

Next step is to apply custom number formatting. This time I will use a square symbol (also available in Symbols, under Arial / Geometric Shapes).

Insert the symbol in an empty cell. Copy the symbol, then highlight the data in column F, go to custom number formatting and apply the following format:

[Color 43]■;[Color 53]■;

I picked Color 43 for a lighter green and Color 53 for a darker red. Zero values will be hidden.

	Actual	PY	Threshold	5%
Jan	1,490	1,500	-1%	
Feb	1,250	1,000	25%	■
Mar	2,160	2,200	-2%	
Apr	1,510	1,700	-11%	■
May	1,820	1,900	-4%	
Jun	1,800	1,600	13%	■
Jul	1,610	1,900	-15%	■
Aug	1,080	1,000	8%	■
Sep	1,230	1,600	-23%	■
Oct	1,430	1,400	2%	
Nov	1,740	1,700	2%	
Dec	2,260	2,200	3%	

Custom number formatting with dynamic thresholds.

Now if I change the threshold to 15%, my report automatically updates as shown below.

	Threshold	15%	
	Actual	**PY**	
Jan	1,490	1,500	-1%
Feb	1,250	1,000	25% ▪
Mar	2,160	2,200	-2%
Apr	1,510	1,700	-11%
May	1,820	1,900	-4%
Jun	1,800	1,600	13%
Jul	1,610	1,900	-15% ▪
Aug	1,080	1,000	8%
Sep	1,230	1,600	-23% ▪
Oct	1,430	1,400	2%
Nov	1,740	1,700	2%
Dec	2,260	2,200	3%

Symbols are allocated based on the threshold specified.

That's how easy it is to "connect" custom number formatting to a cell value. You can of course expand on this. For example, instead of inputting the threshold manually, you could define it with a formula. You could calculate the average deviation and use this as a basis for the IF formulas.

With this method, you can also have a fourth condition.

Let's assume my conditions are as follows:

- >10%: dark green symbol
- 5-10%: light green symbol
- 2-5%: yellow symbol
- <2%: red symbol

Notice all the conditions are based on positive values. That's okay, because I will use a formula to get the appropriate flags.

	A	B	C	D	E	F	G
3			Condition	Lower	Upper	Color	
4			More than	10%		Dark green	
5			Between	5%	10%	Light green	
6			Between	2%	5%	Yellow	
7			Below		2%	Red	
8							
9			**Actual**	**PY**			
10		Jan	1,490	1,500	-1%	t	=IF(E10>=$D$4,1,IF(AND(E10>=$D$5,E10<$E$5),-1,IF(AND(E10>=$D$6,E10<$E$6),0,"t")))
11		Feb	1,250	1,000	25%	1	
12		Mar	2,160	2,200	-2%	t	

Setting up the flags for custom number formatting with four conditions.

The formula I've used for column F is:

```
=IF(E10>=$D$4,1,IF(AND(E10>=$D$5,E10<$E$5),-1,IF(AND(E10>=$D$6,
    E10<$E$6),0,"t")))
```

Value 1 is assigned for the first condition, -1 to the second, 0 to the third and "t" for the fourth condition. I will custom number format column F values as follows:

[Color 10]▪;[Green]▪;[Yellow]▪;[Red]▪

That's it! My report is complete.

	Actual	PY	
Jan	1,490	1,500	-1% ▪
Feb	1,250	1,000	25% ▪
Mar	2,160	2,200	-2% ▪
Apr	1,510	1,700	-11% ▪
May	1,820	1,900	-4% ▪
Jun	1,800	1,600	13% ▪
Jul	1,610	1,900	-15% ▪
Aug	1,080	1,000	8% ▪
Sep	1,230	1,600	-23% ▪
Oct	1,430	1,400	2%
Nov	1,740	1,700	2%
Dec	2,260	2,200	3%

Custom number formatting with four conditions.

Scan here to see this image in color:

There are different functions you can use here depending on your knowledge and experience. For example, if you're comfortable with VLOOKUP, you could use the following formula:

```
=VLOOKUP(E30,$D$24:$F$27,3)
```

The formula is shorter but if you use this method, you must organize your condition table correctly. The lower boundaries need to be sorted in ascending order otherwise the approximate match of VLOOKUP will return errors or wrong results.

Adjust the conditions depending on the data and your requirements.

	A	B	C	D	E	F	G	H	I
23			Condition	Lower	Upper	Value	Color		
24			Below	-100%		t	Red		
25			Between	2%	5%	0	Yellow		
26			Between	5%	10%	-1	Light green		
27			Above	10%		1	Dark green		
28									
29			Actual	PY					
30		Jan	1,490	1,500	-1%	t	=VLOOKUP(E30,$D$24:$F$27,3)		
31		Feb	1,250	1,000	25%	1			
32		Mar	2,160	2,200	-2%	t			

VLOOKUP function as an alternative to the nested IF function

Once you have the flags in place, apply the number formatting specified above.

Get Creative with Custom Number Formatting

I hope the seven examples in this chapter have given you some ideas for your own reports. Custom number formatting can be a bit scary to work with if you don't understand the syntax. Now that you do, there's nothing stopping you. Take advantage of this simple but powerful feature to optimize your reports.

Ctrl + Enter
by Gašper Kamenšek

This chapter will introduce you to **Ctrl + Enter** and then through three real-life scenarios show the added value of using it. So, without further ado, let's start with something really simple. We want to put today's date in cell A1 and format it so that we can see the name of the day next to the date.

Here is a step by step progression:

- select cell A1
- press Ctrl + semi-colon (;) to get today's date
- press Ctrl + Enter
- press Ctrl + 1 to activate 'Format Cells' dialog
- choose Custom format and type DDDD, MM/DD/YYYY

The key here is the third step. Did you notice how pressing Ctrl + Enter instead of pressing Enter or Tab has confirmed the cell entry, but in a way that still left A1 the active cell so that we could jump straight to formatting? Pretty impressing right? Let's take it a step further.

Now we want to put today's date into the first 5,000 cells of column A. The key takeaway in this example will be that we can use Ctrl + Enter to enter the same entry into multiple cells at once. Here are the necessary steps:

- enter A1:A5000 into the Name Box and press Enter (do not click anywhere after this step!)

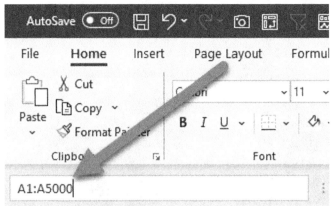

The Name Box.

- use Ctrl + semicolon (;) to get today's date
- press Ctrl + Enter, and you should see today's date in all 5,000 cells

Now we know that with Ctrl + Enter we can enter the same entry into multiple cells at once. For our next scenario, we are going to use Ctrl + Enter together with another Excel gem. This one is called 'Go To Special'. For this scenario, we start with this sample data:

	A	B	C	D	E	F
1	January	February	March	April	May	June
2	1,436.24 $	1,243.25 $	694.87 $	1,718.68 $	267.69 $	1,962.09 $
3			3,447.94 $	234.01 $		1,278.84 $
4			1,938.99 $		346.21 $	
5	1,007.92 $	493.77 $	2,375.89 $	1,259.56 $	1,345.46 $	943.72 $
6	2,563.94 $		647.59 $	44.21 $		750.82 $
7		562.18 $	243.92 $	1,518.08 $	89.01 $	2,144.65 $
8	450.49 $	1,766.52 $		1,095.87 $	452.11 $	
9	3,054.13 $	1,007.62 $	4,184.76 $	333.49 $	2,097.38 $	1,546.65 $
10	664.32 $	80.71 $	326.38 $	1,125.15 $	759.66 $	2,618.70 $

Sample data with blank cells.

As you can see, we have a few blank cells. All we want to do is to put a zero (0) into those blank cells. Here is a step-by-step breakdown:

- select the entire table (Ctrl + A)
- press F5 (or Ctrl + G) and press 'Special...'

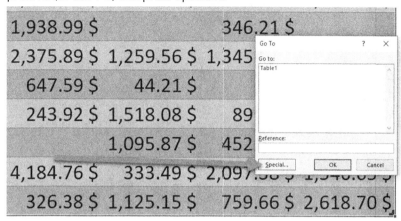

The 'Go To Special' window.

- choose Blanks and press OK

The 'Go To Special' dialog box.

- now that you have only blank cells selected, type zero (0) and press Ctrl + Enter

'Go To Special' and Ctrl + Enter is one of the strongest combinations of two different Excel "tools" coming together, to empower you to do great things. Just think about using the 'Visible cells only' to add a certain comment to rows derived by filters...

This brings us to our final scenario. This one will show you that Ctrl + Enter is even more versatile than you thought. For this scenario, we will start with a file that has its cell formats pre-designed.

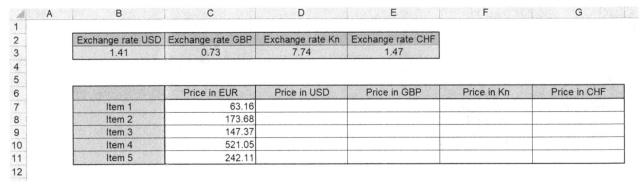

Example with pre-designed cell formats.

All we need to do is to calculate the desired prices in range D7:G11. If Ctrl + Enter did not exist this would be a venture full of pasting only formulas, copying without formats and other special ways excel offers for copying formulas. However, with Ctrl + Enter, it's just three simple steps:

- select the range D7:G11
- write the formula **=$C7*B$3**

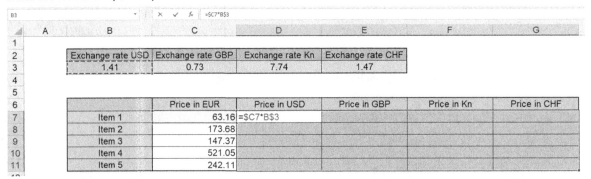

Example having typed in the formula.

- press Ctrl + Enter

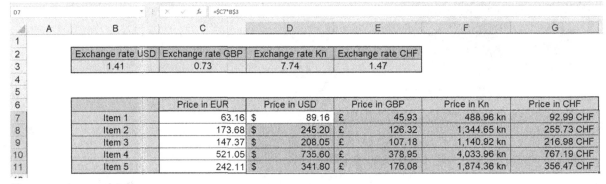

The example completed.

Et voila, we have all the formulas copied, and not a single format has been overwritten.

Auto-Magically Master INDEX MATCH (and Other Formulas)
by Wyn Hopkins

INDEX MATCH isn't easy. After you learn the magic technique in this chapter it's simple!

What Does INDEX MATCH Do?

Imagine a company that supplies parts for various vehicles, and we have a price list like the one below.

	A	B	C	D	E	F
1	Vehicle Group	Vehicle Section	Product Code	Product Name	Product Cost	Product Selling Price
2	Car	External	C1-164	Wiper	$ 1.50	$ 1.78
3	Car	External	C2-992	Wheel	$ 20.00	$ 23.12
4	Car	Internal	C3-666	Indicator	$ 8.00	$ 9.48
5	Car	External	C4-562	Bumber	$ 30.00	$ 33.33
6	Car	External	C5-693	Petrol cap	$ 5.00	$ 5.87
12	Aeroplane	Internal	A1-404	Joystick	$ 1,500.00	$ 1,725.00
13	Aeroplane	Internal	A2-727	Life Vest	$ 60.00	$ 69.36
14	Aeroplane	External	A3-478	Wiper	$ 40.00	$ 44.32
15	Aeroplane	External	A4-26	Wing Lights	$ 10.00	$ 11.53
16	Aeroplane	Internal	A5-884	Table	$ 100.00	$ 117.70
17	Aeroplane	Internal	A6-198	Seat Belt	$ 30.00	$ 35.16
22	Boat	External	B1-433	Rudder	$ 200.00	$ 228.60
23	Boat	Internal	B2-832	Life Vest	$ 40.00	$ 46.76
24	Boat	Internal	B3-775	Radar	$ 400.00	$ 448.00

INDEX MATCH is perfect for finding information in a table based on a reference.

The INDEX MATCH formula combination allows you to look up a product code and return a corresponding value from any other column. I'll explain how this works shortly. The result is time saved from manually searching / filtering and greater accuracy as searching manually can lead to mistakes.

If we had 10 different products, we could just copy the formula 10 times:

```
=INDEX(PartsList!D:D, MATCH(D2, PartsList!C:C, 0))
```

	D	E	F	G
	Code	Looked Up Name		
	C5-693	Petrol cap		
	B1-433	Rudder		
	A9-679	Headphone Jack		
	C5-693	Petrol cap		
	B1-433	Rudder		
	B1-433	Rudder		
	C7-80	Glove Box		
	A10-894	Window Blind		
	A4-26	Wing Lights		
	B8-255	Oar		

The formula =INDEX(PartsList!D:D, MATCH(D2, PartsList!C:C,0)) is not easy to write.

While the result is great, the formula itself is very unfriendly to write. Firstly, it's not one but two functions INDEX and MATCH. Secondly, you have to remember the order to use them which isn't easy for occasional users. This is often why VLOOKUP is a preferred alternative to INDEX MATCH, but we'll address that later in the chapter.

A Bit of Background - How Does INDEX MATCH Work?

Before we jump into the nice and simple solution, let's understand how INDEX MATCH works. If you don't care, then just skip this section; it's OK, I won't tell.

We need to break INDEX MATCH down into its 2 parts. The **MATCH** part is used to find which row contains a matching item

```
=MATCH("C4-562",C:C,0)
```

| G5 | ▼ | : | × | ✓ | fx | =MATCH("C4-562",C:C,0) |

	A	B	C	D	E
1	Vehicle Group	Vehicle Section	**Product Code**	Product Name	Product Co
2	Car	External	C1-164	Wiper	$ 1.5
3	Car	External	C2-992	Wheel	$ 20.0
4	Car	Internal	C3-666	Indicator	$ 8.0
5	Car	External	C4-562	Bumper	$ 30.0
6	Car	External	C5-693	Petrol cap	$ 5.0
7	Car	External	C6-236	Wing Mirror	$ 60.0

MATCH example.

For example, looking at the screenshot above, if we choose to find a MATCH for C4-562 we will get the answer five (5) as this is the fifth row of the selected range.

> **Note**: the final argument of zero (0) is required to look for an exact match.

INDEX is then used to return the nth item from a column:

```
=INDEX(D:D,5)
```

| D1 | ▼ | : | × | ✓ | fx | =INDEX(D:D,5) |

	A	B	C	D	
1	Vehicle Group	Vehicle Section	Product Code	Product Name	F
2	Car	External	C1-164	Wiper	
3	Car	External	C2-992	Wheel	
4	Car	Internal	C3-666	Indicator	
5	Car	External	C4-562	Bumper	
6	Car	External	C5-693	Petrol cap	

Identifying the product code is in the fifth row.

This formula would result in the word "Bumper" because it is the fifth item in the list.

Finally, you replace the typed in 5 with the MATCH Formula to give

```
=INDEX(D:D,MATCH("C4-562",C:C,0))
```

This is a tricky formula to write from memory.

AutoCorrect

If you skipped or didn't really understand the last section, don't worry. The title of this chapter is Auto-Magically Master INDEX MATCH, so let's get on with the magic part. The first part of this requires AutoCorrect.

To introduce AutoCorrect, we'll discover how typing "„" (two commas) can AutoCorrect to a bullet point. You can set up AutoCorrect to do all sorts of magical things – that's a hint as to what's coming…

- Insert a bullet point into Excel using the Symbol icon (on the Insert tab of the ribbon)
  - o do

Click on the Insert Ribbon and then click the Symbol icon.

- Pick Arial font and subset Geometric Shapes (it's near the bottom of the list)

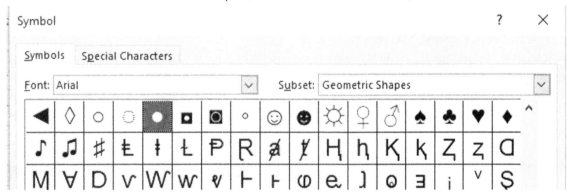

Choose something that looks like a bullet point, e.g. under Arial, Geometric Shapes.

Double-click on the bullet point and click Close. You should now have a bullet point in one of your cells. Don't press Enter just yet

Highlight your bullet point (by double clicking on it) and press Ctrl + C to copy it

Important: Don't copy the entire cell, just the bullet point itself within the cell.

After copying press Escape and then check it's worked by pasting the bullet point into another cell. We are now ready to paste this bullet point into Excel's AutoCorrect library.

Click on File followed by Options (or press Alt + F + T) then Proofing and finally AutoCorrect Options…

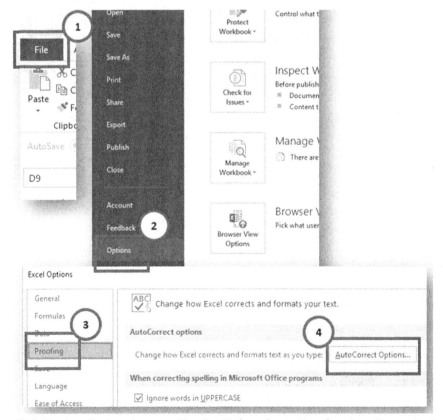

Click File then Options (or press Alt + F + T) then choose Proofing, AutoCorrect Options…

You now can type "„" (two commas) in the 'Replace:' box and then click in the 'With:' box and press Ctrl + V to paste the bullet point in there as pictured:

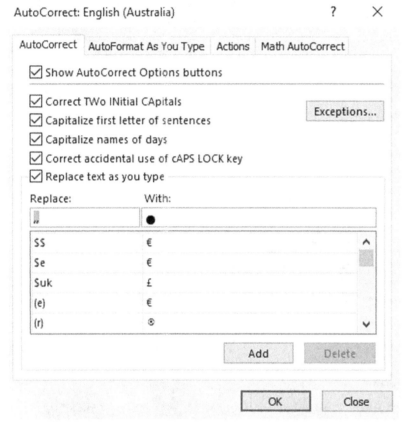

Using two commas to create a bullet point.

Click Add followed by OK and then OK again.

Now in any cell simply type "„" followed by a space and your commas auto-magically correct to a bullet point. Excellent! If you happen to not want AutoCorrect to occur, you can always press Ctrl + Z or click Undo.

As you can see from the previous screenshot you could use "$$" to automatically create a "£" or a "€" symbol. Also, any long name you type regularly could be abbreviated here.

> **Note**: If you've ever been caught out by typing (c) and it autocorrecting to © then you can delete that in this AutoCorrect Options… window too.

> **Note**: If you have a recent version of Excel and a numeric keypad on your computer, the Excel team made it easier to insert a bullet by using Alt+7 on numeric keypad.

With Great Power Comes Great Responsibility

I'm not suggesting you are the sort of person who likes to play practical jokes on colleagues and family members, but if someone does leave their computer unlocked you could, *and I'm not saying should*, quickly use File -> Options -> Proofing -> AutoCorrect… to change the word "the" to "idiot".

> **Warning**: This AutoCorrect dictionary is shared across ALL OFFICE PRODUCTS so this change will affect Word, Outlook, and Power Point etc.

Pre-build Your INDEX MATCH Formula Using AutoCorrect

Finally, here's the technique to quickly master INDEX MATCH and make it easy to use, even easier than its close rival VLOOKUP. Type the following formula into your AutoCorrect Options window, or copy it and then paste it from the downloadable sample file:

```
=INDEX(Step3ResultColumn,MATCH(Step1LookupCell,Step2LookupColumn,0))
```

Remember, it's File -> Options -> Proofing -> AutoCorrect Options…

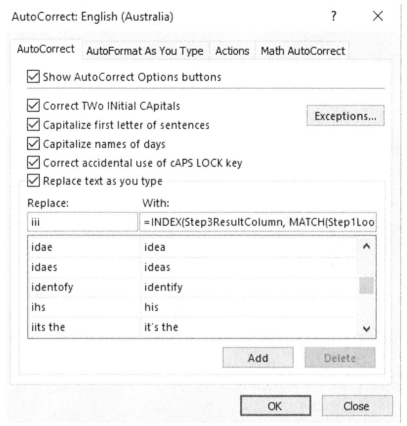

Getting AutoCorrect to create your INDEX MATCH formula template.

In the replace box type "iii" or something of your choosing that won't trigger AutoCorrect accidentally.

> **Warning**: If you use the letter "i" just twice then when you write the word "skiing" the two letters will be replaced by your entire formula!

Using Your Pre-built Formula

Now we have our formula built we can try it out in our earlier example. To do this, type "iii" into the cell F2 on the sheet named 'Using the AutoCorrect trick' then press Space:

E	F	G	H
Code	Whole Column	Used Range	Table
C5-693	iii		
B1-433			
A9-679			
C5-693			

Using your pre-built formula.

Then double click on the phrase 'Step1LookupCell' so that it highlights:

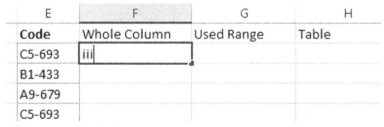

Highlighting the first argument of MATCH.

Follow this by clicking on the cell you want to look up a value for. In this case, it is Cell E2:

	E	F	G	H	I	J
	Code	Whole Column	Used Range	Table		
	C5-693	=INDEX(Step3ResultColumn, MATCH(E2, Step2LookupColumn, 0))				
	B1-433					
	A9-679					

Replacing the first argument of MATCH.

Next, double-click on the phrase 'Step2LookupColumn' to highlight it.

	E	F	G	H	I
	Code	Whole Column	Used Range	Table	
	C5-693	=INDEX(Step3ResultColumn, MATCH(E2, Step2LookupColumn, 0))			
	B1-433				
	A9-670				

Double-click on the formula element 'Step2LookupColumn'.

Go to the column labelled 'Product Code' in the 'Parts List' sheet and click on column C to select the entire column.

C1	▼	⋮	✕	✔	*fx*	=INDEX(Step3ResultColumn, MATCH(E2, PartsList!C:C, 0))

	A	B	C	D	E	F
1	Vehicle Group	Vehicle Section	Product Code	Product Name	Product Cost	Product Selling Price
2	Car	External	C1-164	Wiper	$ 1.50	$ 1.78
3	Car	External	C2-992	Wheel	$ 20.00	$ 23.12
4	Car	Internal	C3-666	Indicator	$ 8.00	$ 9.48
5	Car	External	C4-562	Bumper	$ 30.00	$ 33.33
6	Car	External	C5-693	Petrol cap	$ 5.00	$ 5.87

Click on column C to select the entire column.

Then in your formula bar, double-click on 'Step3ResultColumn' to highlight it.

⋮	✕	✔	*fx*	=INDEX(Step3ResultColumn, MATCH(E2, PartsList!C:C, 0))

	B	C	D	E	F
	Vehicle Section	Product Code	Product Name	Product Cost	Product Selling Price
	External	C1-164	Wiper	$ 1.50	$ 1.78
	External	C2-992	Wheel	$ 20.00	$ 23.12

Double-click on 'Step3ResultColumn'.

Finally, select whichever column you'd like to return, in this case click on column A, to return the corresponding 'Vehicle Group'.

A1	▼	⋮	✕	✔	*fx*	=INDEX(PartsList!A:A, MATCH(E2, PartsList!C:C, 0))

	A	B	C	D	E	
1	Vehicle Group	Vehicle Section	Product Code	Product Name	Product Cost	Product Se
2	Car	External	C1-164	Wiper	$ 1.50	$
3	Car	External	C2-992	Wheel	$ 20.00	$
4	Car	Internal	C3-666	Indicator	$ 8.00	$
5	Car	External	C4-562	Bumper	$ 30.00	$

Click on column A to select the entire column.

Press Enter to complete the process. Your answer should be 'Car'. Try and repeat this process for the next item in the list.

1. To do this, in cell F3 type "iii" followed by a space:

	E	F	G	H	I	J	K
	Code	Whole Column	Used Range	Table			
	C5-693	Car					
	B1-433	=INDEX(Step3ResultColumn, MATCH(Step1LookupCell, Step2LookupColumn, 0))					
	A9-679						
	C5-693						

Beginning again in cell F3.

Then do the following steps:

- Double-click 'Step1LookupCell' and then click on the cell containing the code you are looking up
- Double-click 'Step2LookupColumn' and go to the 'Parts List' sheet and select column C
- Double-click 'Step3ResultColumn' and select column A from the 'Parts List' table

Success!

You can now simply copy the formula down for the rest of the items in the list.

Improvements, Tips and Tables

It's best practice not to highlight entire columns as it can impact performance on more complex spreadsheets as you are referencing 1 million rows with your MATCH and your INDEX. One option would be just to highlight the used ranges so your formula would change from

```
=INDEX(PartsList!A:A,MATCH(E2,PartsList!C:C,0))
```

to

```
=INDEX(PartsList!$A$2:$A$31,MATCH(E2,PartsList!$C$2:$C$31,0))
```

That is a really ugly looking formula.

Note: The $ signs are there to lock the references in place as you copy your formula down.

Also, if new data is added to the bottom of your 'Parts List' table, then your formula will need to be manually changed to pick up the new data. This is not ideal. The best solution is to turn your Parts List into a Table. An Excel Table is a "thing" and is so useful in many ways. INDEX MATCH and Tables work together beautifully:

- It makes your formulas more "readable"
- As you add more data your formulas will automatically pick up the data

To turn your 'Parts List' into a Table, simple click in the 'Parts List' and press Ctrl + T followed by clicking OK (the check-box, 'My table has headers', should be ticked).

	A	B	C	D	E	F
A1		fx	Car			
1	Vehicle Group	Vehicle Section	**Product Code**	Product Name	Product Cost	Product Selling Price
2	Car	External	C1-164	Wiper	$ 1.50	$ 1.78
3	Car	External	C2-992	Wheel	$ 20.00	$ 23.12
4	Car	Inter			$ 8.00	$ 9.48
5	Car	Exter			$ 30.00	$ 33.33
6	Car	Exter			$ 5.00	$ 5.87
7	Car	Exter		ror	$ 60.00	$ 68.88
8	Car	Inter		x	$ 20.00	$ 22.98
9	Car	Exter		t	$ 35.00	$ 39.52
10	Car	Inter		e	$ 26.00	$ 30.37
11	Car	Internal	C10-880	Tow Bar	$ 80.00	$ 92.16

Create Table ? ×

Where is the data for your table?

=$A$1:$F$31

☑ My table has headers

OK   Cancel

Converting the 'Parts List' data into a Table.

Then you should give your Table a name such as tblParts.

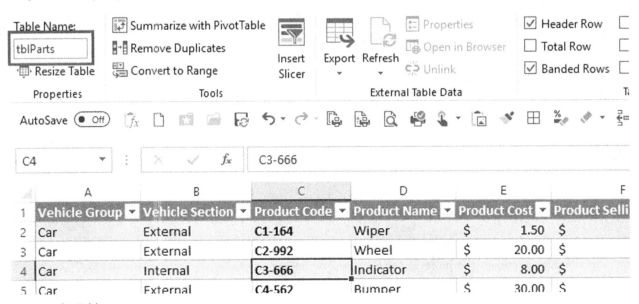

Renaming the Table.

Now you can try out our "iii" AutoCorrect Magic trick as before. Go to cell H2 of the page you were adding formula to then type "iii" followed by pressing Space. Then, double-click 'Step1LookupCell' and then click on cell E2.

E	F	G	H	I	J	K	L	M
Code	Whole Column	Used Range	Table					
C5-693	Car	Car	=INDEX(Step3ResultColumn, MATCH(E2, Step2LookupColumn, 0))					
B1-433	Boat	Boat						
A9-679	Aeroplane	Aeroplane						

Editing 'Step1LookupCell' and replacing it with cell E2.

Double-click 'Step2LookupColumn' and go to the 'Parts List' sheet and click on any cell in the tblParts 'Product Code' column then press Ctrl + Space to highlight the column.

| C5 | ▼ | : | ✕ | ✓ | *fx* | =INDEX(Step3ResultColumn, MATCH(E2, tblParts[Product Code], 0)) |

	A	B	C	D	E	F
1	Vehicle Group ▼	Vehicle Section ▼	Product Code ▼	Product Name ▼	Product Cost ▼	Product Selling Price ▼
2	Car	External	C1-164	Wiper	$ 1.50	$ 1.78
3	Car	External	C2-992	Wheel	$ 20.00	$ 23.12
4	Car	Internal	C3-666	Indicator	$ 8.00	$ 9.48
5	Car	External	C4-562	Bumper	$ 30.00	$ 33.33
6	Car	External	C5-693	Petrol cap	$ 5.00	$ 5.87

Clicking in a cell and pressing Ctrl + Space highlights an entire column.

Double-click 'Step3ResultColumn' and click in any cell in the 'Product Name' column then press Ctrl + Space.

| D5 | ▼ | : | ✕ | ✓ | *fx* | =INDEX(tblParts[Product Name], MATCH(E2, tblParts[Product Code], 0)) |

	A	B	C	D	E	F
1	Vehicle Group ▼	Vehicle Section ▼	Product Code ▼	Product Name ▼	Product Cost ▼	Product Selling Price ▼
2	Car	External	C1-164	Wiper	$ 1.50	$ 1.78
3	Car	External	C2-992	Wheel	$ 20.00	$ 23.12
4	Car	Internal	C3-666	Indicator	$ 8.00	$ 9.48
5	Car	External	C4-562	Bumper	$ 30.00	$ 33.33
6	Car	External	C5-693	Petrol cap	$ 5.00	$ 5.87

Completing the formula.

The formula reads as follows

```
=INDEX(tblParts[Product Name],MATCH(E2,tblParts[Product Code],0))
```

Now press Enter and your result should be 'Petrol Cap'. This formula is much more meaningful than the alternative

```
=INDEX(PartsList!$M$2:$M$31, MATCH(E2,PartsList!$C$2:$C$31,0))
```

If you would rather bring back 'Selling Price' just backspace out the word 'Product Name' and select 'Product Selling Price' instead:

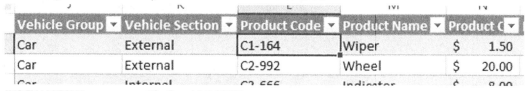

It's easy to change your mind!

Advantages over VLOOKUP

Those of you that know VLOOKUP may not immediately see the benefit of using INDEX MATCH since the formulas produce the same result. However, INDEX MATCH has three key advantages.

- INDEX MATCH can look to the left to return results, e.g. we could not return 'Vehicle Group' or 'Vehicle Section' data using VLOOKUP as they are to the left of 'Product Code'

Vehicle Group ▼	Vehicle Section ▼	Product Code ▼	Product Name ▼	Product C ▼
Car	External	C1-164	Wiper	$ 1.50
Car	External	C2-992	Wheel	$ 20.00
Car	Internal	C3-666	Indicator	$ 8.00

INDEX MATCH is more versatile than VLOOKUP.

- INDEX MATCH doesn't return the wrong answer if you insert or remove columns, whereas VLOOKUP may give the wrong answer when the data set it's referencing has columns inserted or removed
- You don't have to count columns with INDEX MATCH, you just pick the two you want to use. With VLOOKUP you manually count across the number of columns and type that number in as the column you want to return.

The BIG advantage VLOOKUP used to have was that it was easier to write than INDEX MATCH – not anymore! Now that you know how to Auto-Magically generate your INDEX MATCH formula it's a simple case of "iii" and a few double clicks.

If I haven't convinced you of the benefits of INDEX MATCH, then setup a shortcut for VLOOKUP using "vvv" instead:

```
=VLOOKUP(Step1LookupCell,Step2TableOfData,Step3TypeColumnNo,FALSE)
```

Relative Named Ranges –
When Named Ranges Go Walkabout

by Mynda Treacy

Named Ranges is a vast topic that includes some simple techniques that we all can – and should – use to make our spreadsheets easier to build and maintain. There are also some more advanced techniques, like relative named ranges, which are good to know. They are especially useful for that occasion when you inherit a workbook from an Excel super user who thinks you'll have no hope deciphering their file.

Relative References

A **relative named range** returns a result that is relative to the cell in which you use it.

To understand this, let's take a moment to revisit a concept that every Excel user should know very well and that is the way a relative cell reference automatically updates as it's copied from one cell to the next.

For example, cell B7 in the image below contains a SUM formula that uses relative cell references B2:B6:

◢	A	B	C	D	E
1	Product/Year	2015	2016	2017	2018
2	Product A	637	802	788	377
3	Product B	252	920	996	398
4	Product C	653	144	768	967
5	Product D	171	320	547	130
6	Product E	527	144	840	713
7	Total Product Sales	2,240	2,330	3,939	2,585
8		↑	↑	↑	↑
9	Formula in row 7:	=SUM(B2:B6)	=SUM(C2:C6)	=SUM(D2:D6)	=SUM(E2:E6)

Formulas containing relative cell references.

When we copy the formula in cell B7 (shown in the image above) across to cells C7, D7 and E7 it automatically adjusts the column reference relative to its new location, i.e. copying the formula in B7 across one column to cell C7 will result in =SUM(C2:C6), and so on.

> **Note**: if I were to copy the formula down a row the row references would also adjust as they are relative to both rows and columns.

Relative named ranges work in the same way, and we can use them to replace the individual SUM formulas in row 7 of the example above.

Example

For example, in the image below, row 7 contains the formula =Total_Sales. The Edit Name dialog box shows that the name Total_Sales, which is displayed for the active cell, B7, is referring to the formula:

```
=SUM(Sheet2!B2:B6)
```

B7	▼	:	×	✓	f_x	=Total_Sales

◢	A	B	C	D	E
1	Product/Year	2015	2016	2017	2018
2	Product A	637	802	788	377
3	Product B	252	920	996	398
4	Product C	653	144	768	967
5	Product D	171	320	547	130
6	Product E	527	144	840	713
7	Total Product Sales	2,240	2,330	3,939	2,585
8		↑	↑	↑	↑
9	Formula in row 7:	=Total_Sales	=Total_Sales	=Total_Sales	=Total_Sales
10					

Edit Name ? ✕

Name: Total_Sales

Scope: Workbook ⌄

Comment: ⌃ ⌄

Refers to: =SUM(Sheet2!B2:B6) ⬆

OK   Cancel

Total_Sales Named Formula.

Total_Sales is, in essence, a named formula, and I'll refer to it as such going forward.

> **Warning**: Don't try to use spaces (" ") in a range name. They are not accepted, as space is actually the inter-sect operator in Excel (e.g. trying to use 'Total Sales' would make excel seek the intersection of a range name called 'Total' with one called 'Sales'). The use of underscores is a common convention in separating words in range name definitions.

Also notice that the named formulas in cells B7, C7, D7 and E7 are all the same:

```
=Total_Sales
```

However, if I edit the name while the cursor is set in cell C7 you can see in the image below that the named formula, Total_Sales, is now referring to cells C2:C6:

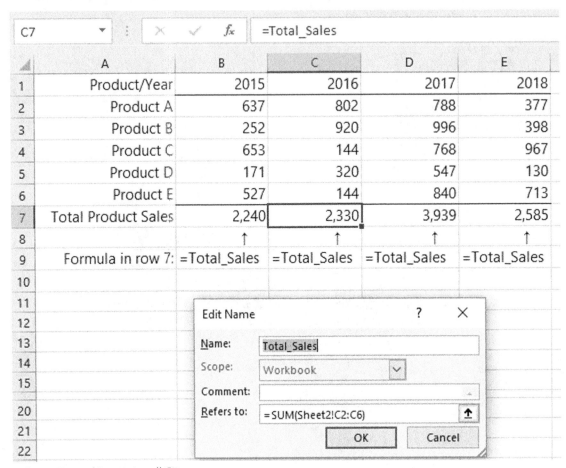

Relative Named Range in cell C7.

Likewise, if you edit the names while cells D or E are selected, you'll find they reference D2:D6 and E2:E6 respectively. In other words, the named formula Total_Sales will always sum the five cells immediately above the cell in which you place it. It does this because the cell references in the 'Refers to' field are relative.

Scope of Relative Named Ranges

The named formula, Total_Sales, has the scope of the workbook, meaning I can use it on any sheet, however the 'Refers to' specifies that it will always sum cells on Sheet2:

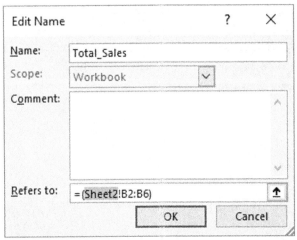

Relative range references Sheet2 in 'Refers to' field.

For example, if I enter =Total_Sales in cell B7 on Sheet1 it will sum cells B2:B6 on Sheet2.

If I want to use this named formula relative to any sheet, I can change the 'Refers to' to:

```
=SUM(!C2:C6)
```

Omitting the sheet name and leaving the exclamation mark in front of the cell references results in a dynamic sheet reference. Therefore, while the named formula will have the scope of the workbook, it will refer to the active sheet.

For example, if I now enter =Total_Sales in cell B7 on Sheet1 it will sum cells B2:B6 on Sheet1.

In other words, I have a truly relative named formula, i.e. relative to both the cells and the sheet.

> **Warning**: This use of an exclamation mark in named ranges has been known to cause Excel to crash and can create problems when used with VBA (e.g. creating an action like Application.CalculateFull), so use it with caution. That said, I've never experienced any problems, so it may be resolved in more recent versions of Excel (or I'm more careful these days!).

Creating Relative Named Ranges

Location, location, location. It's the cliché that should be front of mind when creating relative named ranges.

When you create a relative named range, you should first select the cell that you want the range to be relative to. For example, to create the Total_Sales named formula, I first selected cell B7. Then, from the Formulas tab > Define Name:

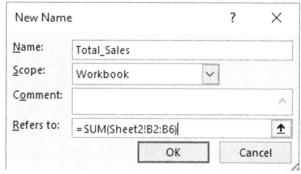

◢	A	B	C	D	E
1	Product/Year	2015	2016	2017	2018
2	Product A	637	802	788	377
3	Product B	252	920	996	398
4	Product C	653	144	768	967
5	Product D	171	320	547	130
6	Product E	527	144	840	713
7	Total Product Sales				

Select the cell that you want the range relative to before defining the name.

This will open the New Name dialog box where you can give your named range or formula a name (no spaces allowed, see earlier). Then, select the scope and enter the cell reference or formula in the Refers to field:

New Name dialog box.

Other Uses for Relative Named Ranges

So far, the example we've looked at is a relative named formula, but you can also create a relative named range. For example, with cell B7 selected we can name the cells B2:B6 Product_Sales:

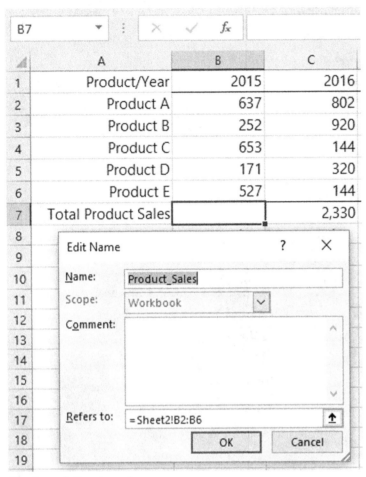

Create a relative named range.

We may then use the relative named range in a SUM formula (or any other formula):

B7		fx	=SUM(Product_Sales)		
	A	B	C	D	E
1	Product/Year	2015	2016	2017	2018
2	Product A	637	802	788	377
3	Product B	252	920	996	398
4	Product C	653	144	768	967
5	Product D	171	320	547	130
6	Product E	527	144	840	713
7	Total Product Sales	2,240	2,330	3,939	2,585

Using relative named ranges in formulas.

Relative Dynamic Named Ranges

Dynamic named ranges are a staple for the intermediate / advanced Excel user. They allow us to return a range that adapts to ever changing data or criteria. For example, we might use a dynamic named range as the source for a PivotTable.

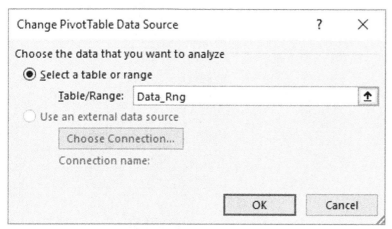

Using dynamic named ranges as the source of a PivotTable.

As new rows are added to our source Data_Rng, the dynamic named range also increases to include the new data, thus eliminating the need for us to update the PivotTable source cell references.

Maybe you're using a PivotTable as the source data for a regular chart. You may use a dynamic named range for the chart source allowing it to automatically pick up changes in the PivotTable size.

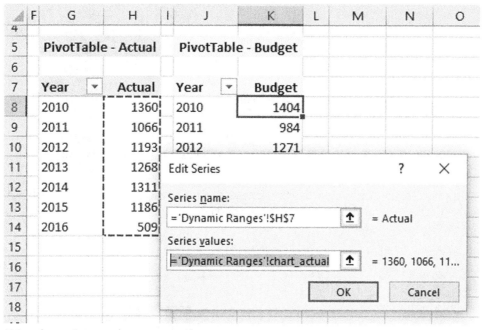

Using dynamic named ranges as a chart source.

However, typically these dynamic named ranges aren't relative.

An area where relative dynamic named ranges will come in handy though, is for Sparklines. In the image below, I've inserted a group of Sparklines in column A and you can see the Data Range is hard coded C2:I9:

▲	A	B	C	D	E	F	G	H	I
1			Jan	Feb	Mar	Apr	May	Jun	Jul
2	_▪_▌▪_▪	ACT	25,292	33,711	27,904	36,694	30,791	28,846	34,459
3	_▪▪▌▪▪▪	NSW	778,994	897,425	1,021,715	1,184,557	907,704	1,006,080	1,145,990
4	_▪▪▌▪_▪	NT	51,834	57,425	58,122	75,391	51,418	58,080	63,150
5	_▪▪▌▪_▪	QLD	473,078	529,565	558,611	661,046	529,353	557,546	605,544
6	_▪▪▌▪_▪	SA	88,702	104,214	106,254	120,261	91,163	102,657	120,934
7	_▪▪▌▪_▪	TAS	49,100	50,562	55,922	68,062	49,233	53,043	59,664
8	_▪▪▌▪_▪	VIC	477,519	556,682	651,431	778,445	571,022	686,695	824,849
9	_▪▪▌▪_▪	WA	196,579	231,758	245,125	282,654	230,084	251,258	328,987
10									

Edit Sparklines ? ✕

Choose the data that you want

Data Range: C2:I9 ⬆

Choose where you want the sparklines to be placed

Location Range: $A$2:$A$9 ⬆

OK   Cancel

Fixed Sparkline ranges.

This means that when new data is added for future months in column J onward, we'll have to edit the Sparkline Data range and update it MANUALLY! That 'M' word is enough to make an advanced Excel user queasy.

Now ideally, we'd use a dynamic named range for the Sparkline data range, but you can't enter a dynamic named range for a group of Sparklines, only for individual Sparklines. I don't fancy creating seven separate dynamic named ranges, one for each row. That's way too much work.

Luckily, we can create one dynamic named range that is relative to the cell it's in and use that for each individual Sparkline (it's a lot quicker to copy and paste seven Sparklines). With the Sparklines removed, I'll start with cell A2 selected and then go to the Formulas tab > Define Name.

I'll call my relative dynamic named range sparkline_rng, and use an INDEX MATCH formula like so:

```
=$C2:INDEX($C$2:$O$9,MATCH($B2,$B$2:$B$9,0),COUNTA($C$1:$O$1))
```

Scan the QR code at right to see the formula in color.

In English the formula reads

- Start the range in cell C2
- find the last cell in the range C2:O9 using INDEX
- find the row INDEX by MATCHing the value in cell B2 to the cells in B2:B9
- find the column that INDEX should use by COUNTAing the columns that contain text in the range C1:O1 to find the last column containing values

Tip: The MATCH component of the formula above could be replaced with any other function that will return the row number argument for INDEX, e.g. COUNTA($B$2:$B2) or ROWS($B$2:$B2) will also work.

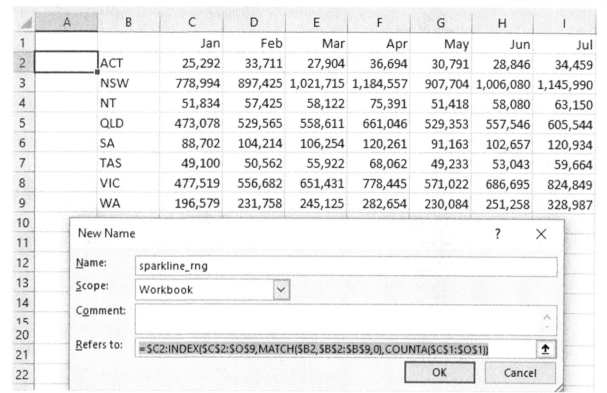

Define the Sparkline dynamic named range making sure to select the cell that will contain the first Sparkline.

I can check the formula is evaluating correctly by inspecting it in the Name Manager (CTRL+F3).

For example, in the image below, you can see I've selected cell A3 and in the Name Manager I've selected the sparkline_rng. To see the marching ants around the cells returned by the formula, I simply click anywhere in the 'Refers to' field:

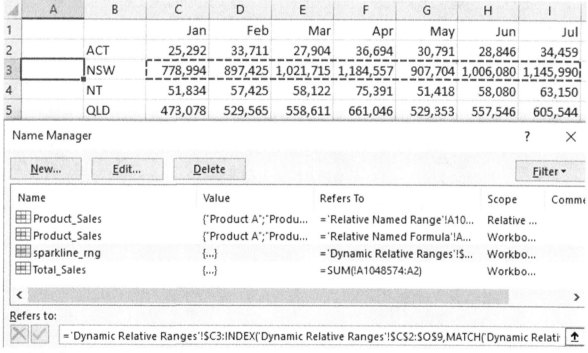

Check the dynamic relative named range formula is evaluating correctly.

Now that I know my named range is working correctly, I can insert the Sparklines. Simply enter the first one and in the Create Sparklines dialog box enter the relative dynamic named range in the Data Range field:

▲	A	B	C	D	E	F	G	H	I
1			Jan	Feb	Mar	Apr	May	Jun	Jul
2		ACT	25,292	33,711	27,904	36,694	30,791	28,846	34,459
3		NSW	778,994	897,425	1,021,715	1,184,557	907,704	1,006,080	1,145,990
4		NT	51,834	57,425	58,122	75,391	51,418	58,080	63,150
5		QLD	473,078	529,565	558,611	661,046	529,353	557,546	605,544
6		SA	88,702	104,214	106,254	120,261	91,163	102,657	120,934
7		TAS	49,100	50,562	55,922	68,062	49,233	53,043	59,664
8		VIC	477,519	556,682	651,431	778,445	571,022	686,695	824,849
9		WA					4	251,258	328,987
10									
11									
12									
13									
14									
15									
16									
17									
18									

Create Sparklines   ?   ✕

Choose the data that you want

Data Range: sparkline_rng   ⬆

Choose where you want the sparklines to be placed

Location Range: $A$2   ⬆

OK   Cancel

Create the first Sparkline.

Then copy and paste the Sparklines *one at a time,* so they remain ungrouped:

▲	A	B	C	D	E	F	G	H	I
1			Jan	Feb	Mar	Apr	May	Jun	Jul
2		ACT	25,292	33,711	27,904	36,694	30,791	28,846	34,459
3		NSW	778,994	897,425	1,021,715	1,184,557	907,704	1,006,080	1,145,990
4		NT	51,834	57,425	58,122	75,391	51,418	58,080	63,150
5		QLD	473,078	529,565	558,611	661,046	529,353	557,546	605,544
6		SA	88,702	104,214	106,254	120,261	91,163	102,657	120,934
7		TAS	49,100	50,562	55,922	68,062	49,233	53,043	59,664
8		VIC	477,519	556,682	651,431	778,445	571,022	686,695	824,849
9		WA	196,579	231,758	245,125	282,654	230,084	251,258	328,987

Copy and paste the Sparkline to the remaining rows.

A big thanks to Christopher Mangels for the Sparkline example.

Limitations

Relative named ranges cannot be used in hyperlinks because cell A1 is always the hyperlink anchor for a defined named:

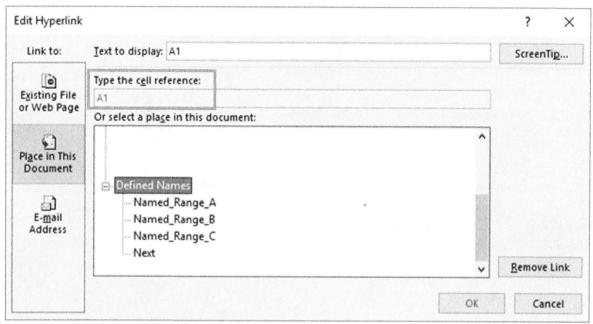

Hyperlinks will not work with relative named ranges.

Using absolute named ranges with Hyperlinks isn't an issue, but for relative named ranges it essentially renders them absolute, or always relative to A1 when used with hyperlinks.

Get the Workbook

The workbook for this chapter (from https://mrx.cl/mvpfiles) contains the examples covered and further tutorials on topics covered including:

- Relative and Absolute References
- Absolute Named Ranges
- INDEX and MATCH formulas
- Dynamic Named Ranges
- Sparklines
- Creating Regular Charts from PivotTables

An Introduction to Excel's New Data Types

by John MacDougall

Since the start of Excel, one cell could only contain one piece of data. With Excel's new rich data type feature, this is no longer the case. We now have multiple data fields inside one cell!

When you think of data types you might be thinking about text, numbers, dates or Boolean values, but these new data types are quite different. These are really connections to an online data source that provides more information about the data.

At present there are two data types available in Excel; **Stocks** and **Geography**.

For example, with the new Stock data type our cell might display the name of a company, but will also contain information like the current share price, trading volume, market capitalization, employee head count, or year of incorporation for that company.

The connections to the additional data are live, which is especially relevant for the stock data. Since data like the share price is constantly changing, you can always get the latest data by refreshing the connection.

Caution: The stock data is provided by a third party. Data is delayed, and the delay depends on which stock exchange the data is from. Information about the level of delay for each stock exchange can be found here: mrx.cl/aboutsources

The data connection for the Geography data type is also live and can be refreshed, but these values should change very infrequently.

Converting Data

Whichever data type you want to use, converting cells into a data type is the same process. As you might expect, the new data types have been placed in the Data tab of the Excel ribbon in a section called 'Data Types'.

At present the two available data types fit nicely into the space. However, you can click on the lower right area to expand this space, which seems to suggest more data types are on their way!

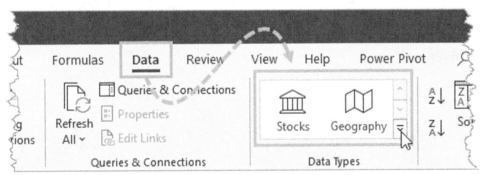

Data Types in the Data tab.

You will need to select the range of cells with your text data and go to the Data tab and click on either the Stock or Geography data type. This will convert the plain text into what is known as a **rich data type**.

Warning: You can't convert cells containing formulas to data types.

You can easily tell when a cell contains a data type as there will be a small icon on the left inside the cell. The federal hall icon indicates a Stock data type and the map icon indicates a Geography data type.

	A	B	C			A	B	C
1					1			
2		Amazon			2		🏛 Amazon.com (XNAS:AMZN)	
3		Apple			3		🏛 Apple (XNAS:AAPL)	
4		Facebook			4		🏛 Facebook (XNAS:FB)	
5		Microsoft			5		🏛 Microsoft (XNAS:MSFT)	
6		Google			6		🏛 Alphabet (XNAS:GOOG)	
7					7			

Convert to Stock data type.

The right click menu has a contextual option which is only available when the right-click is performed on a cell or range containing data types. This is where you'll find most commands relating to data types.

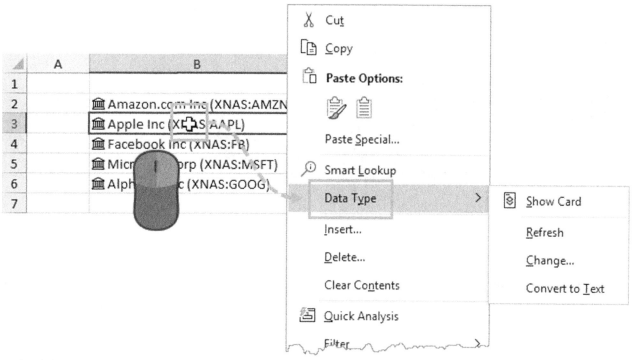

Right-click menu Data Type options.

If you want to add to your list of data type cells, all you need to do is type in the cell directly below a data type and Excel will automatically convert it to the same data type as shown here.

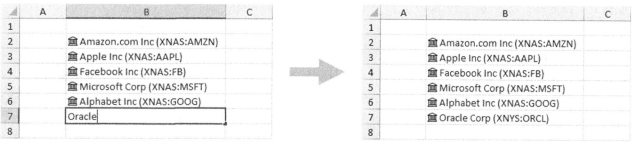

Automatically convert to Data Type.

Excel will try and convert your text with the best match, but it might not always find a suitable match or there might be some ambiguity. When this happens, a question mark icon will appear in the cell. You can click on this icon to help Excel find the best match.

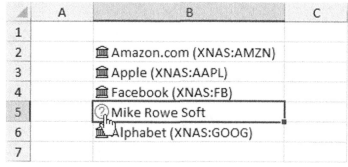

Data type not recognized.

Click on the question mark icon and this will open the 'Data Selector' pane. You can use the search bar to try and locate the desired result and then click on the Select button to accept one of the options presented.

In case Excel made the wrong choice, you can also change a data type. You simply right-click on the data and choose 'Data Type' then Change from the menu. This will also open the 'Data Selector' pane.

Data Selector pane.

Currency and Cryptocurrency Data

With the Stock data type, you can get more than just stocks from a company name. The Stock data type can also be used for currency and cryptocurrency conversions.

You can convert pairs of currencies into data types to get exchange rates.

	A	B	C			A	B	C
1					1			
2		AUDUSD			2		🏛 AUD/USD	
3		CADUSD			3		🏛 CAD/USD	
4		GBPUSD			4		🏛 GBP/USD	
5		EURUSD			5		🏛 EUR/USD	

Currency conversion.

You can convert cryptocurrency / currency pairs into data types too. However, do note that exchange rates between cryptocurrencies are currently not supported.

	A	B	C			A	B	C
1					1			
2		BTCUSD			2		🏛 BTC/USD	
3		ETHUSD			3		🏛 ETH/USD	
4		XRPUSD			4		🏛 XRP/USD	
5		BCHUSD			5		🏛 BCH/USD	

Cryptocurrency conversion.

Country, State, Province, County and City Data

The Geography data type supports most types of geographies. Countries, states, provinces, counties and cities will all work. The fields available for each type of Geography will vary. For example, a country, state, province, or county might have a capital city field, but this field will not be available for a city.

	A	B	C	D	E	F	G
1							
2		Country		State		County	
3		🗺 England		🗺 California		🗺 County Clare	
4		🗺 Ireland		🗺 Texas		🗺 County Cork	
5		🗺 France		🗺 Florida		🗺 County Galway	
6							
7		Province		City			
8		🗺 Ontario		🗺 Paris			
9		🗺 Quebec		🗺 London			
10		🗺 Alberta		🗺 Amsterdam			
11							

Geography Region Types.

Data Cards

There is a pretty cool way to view the data contained inside a cell. When you click on the icon for any data type a **Data Card** will appear. This is also accessible through the right-click menu. Simply right-click then choose 'Data Type' from the menu and finally, 'Data Card'.

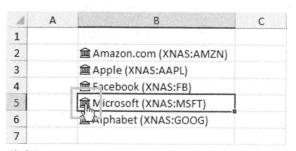

Click Data Type icon.

Data cards will show all the available data for that cell and may also include a picture related to the data such as a company logo or a country's flag. Each piece of data displayed in the card also comes with an 'Extract to grid' button that becomes visible when you hover the mouse cursor over that area. This will extract the data into the next blank cell to the right of the data type.

In the lower right corner of the card, there's a flag icon. This allows you to report any bad data that might be displayed in the card back to Microsoft.

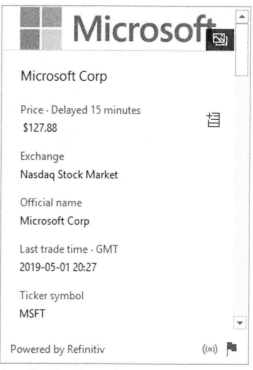

Data Card for Microsoft.

Extracting Data

The data cards are nice for viewing the data inside a cell, but how can you use this data? There are 'Extract to grid' buttons for each piece of data inside the data cards, but these will only extract data for one cell. What if you want to extract data from many cells?

When you select a range of cells containing data types, an 'Extract to grid' icon will appear at the top right of the selected range. When you click on this, Excel will show a list of all the available data that can be extracted. Unfortunately, you'll only be able to select one piece of data at a time.

A handy feature with extracting data, is that Excel takes care of the number formatting. Whether you're extracting a percentage, number, currency, date or time, Excel will apply the relevant formatting.

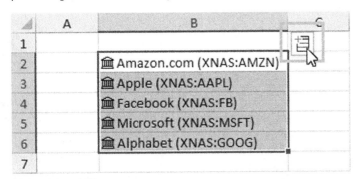

'Extract to grid' icon.

Dot Formulas and the FIELDVALUE Function

'Extract' is probably not the best word to use for the 'Extract to grid' button. If you check the contents of the extracted data, you'll see it's a formula reference to the data type cell. In fact, you don't need to use the extract to grid button to create these formulas. You can write them just like any other Excel formula:

    =B3.Population

The above formula will return the population of Canada.

    =B3.Population/B3.Area

This formula will give us a density calculation and return 3.7 people per square kilometer (at the time of writing).

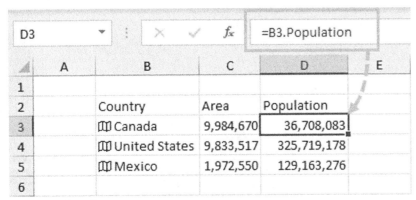

Dot Formula Reference.

Thankfully, Excel's formula IntelliSense will show you all the available fields when you create a cell reference to a data type cell followed by a period. This makes writing data type formulas easy!

Note: When the field name contains spaces, the field reference needs to be encased with square brackets.

Dot formula will AutoComplete.

It should also be noted that formulas only support one dot:

```
=B3.Capital
```

The above formula will return the capital of Canada, which is geographical data.

```
=B3.Capital.Population
```

However, the above formula won't return the population of the capital city of Canada. To get this information, you would need to extract the capital, then copy and paste the result as a value, then convert that value to a data type, then extract the population.

The **FIELDVALUE** function was introduced with data types and can be used to get the exact same results from a data type cell.

```
=FIELDVALUE(Value, Field)
```

This new function has two arguments:

- **Value** is a reference to a data type
- **Field** is the name of a field in the data type

Warning: The FIELDVALUE function does not have IntelliSense for the available fields in a data type.

The previous example to return the population of Canada can be written using the FIELDVALUE function.

```
=FIELDVALUE(B3, "Population")
```

FIELDVALUE formula.

The previous example to return the population density can be written using the FIELDVALUE function.

```
= FIELDVALUE(B3, "Population")/FIELDVALUE(B3, "Area")
```

A new **#FIELD!** error has been added to Excel for the dot formulas and FIELDVALUE function. This error can be returned for several reasons:

- The field does not exist for the data type
- The value referenced in the formula is not a data type

- The data does not exist in the online service for the combination of value and field

#FIELD! Error.

Ireland is returning a #FIELD! error for the abbreviation because this data is missing online.

Refreshing Data

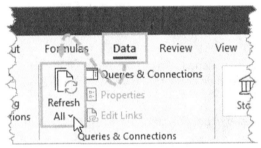

Refresh command in the Data tab.

How do you refresh data? Using the 'Refresh' and 'Refresh All' commands found in the Data tab will refresh any data types you have in your spreadsheet. This means you can use the keyboard shortcuts Alt + F5 (Refresh) and Ctrl + Alt + F5 (Refresh All) to refresh data types. Using the Refresh command will refresh all cells in the workbook that are the same data type as your active cell. The Refresh All command will refresh all cells of any data type.

> **Warning**: Refresh All will also refresh all other connections in the workbook such as PivotTables and Power Queries.

There is also a refresh method that is particular to data types. If you select a cell with a data type, you can right-click and choose 'Data Type' from the menu then choose Refresh. This will refresh all cells in the workbook that are PivotTables tables or Power Query.

Unlinking Data

If you no longer want your data connected, you can unlink the data by converting it back to regular text. The only way to do this is to right-click on the selected range of data then choose 'Data Type' from the menu and select 'Change to Text'.

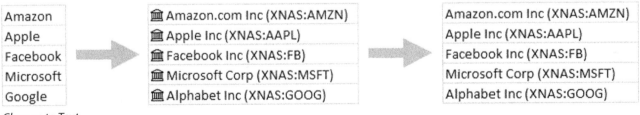

Change to Text.

> **Warning**: Linking and unlinking data might change your data.

When you convert text to a data type and then convert it back to text, you might not get your original text back exactly as it was. It's best to create a copy of any text data before converting to a data type so you always have the original text.

Using Tables with Data Types

You don't need to use Excel Tables with data types, but there is a nice bonus feature with Tables when extracting data. Excel will create the column headings for you!

> **Note**: You can create an Excel table from the Insert tab with the Table command or using the keyboard shortcut Ctrl + T.

The 'Extract to grid' button will appear anytime the active cell is inside a table containing data types. The active cell does not need to be on a cell containing a data type. When there are two or more columns with data type inside a table, the 'Extract to grid' button will be based on the right most column. Unfortunately, this means you can't extract from any other columns.

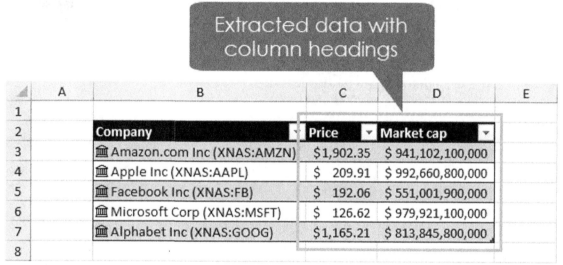

Extracted data with column headings

	A	B	C	D	E
1					
2		Company	Price	Market cap	
3		🏛 Amazon.com Inc (XNAS:AMZN)	$1,902.35	$ 941,102,100,000	
4		🏛 Apple Inc (XNAS:AAPL)	$ 209.91	$ 992,660,800,000	
5		🏛 Facebook Inc (XNAS:FB)	$ 192.06	$ 551,001,900,000	
6		🏛 Microsoft Corp (XNAS:MSFT)	$ 126.62	$ 979,921,100,000	
7		🏛 Alphabet Inc (XNAS:GOOG)	$1,165.21	$ 813,845,800,000	
8					

Extracted data in a Table.

Using Sort and Filter with Data Types

Sorting and filtering data types has a nice feature that allows you to sort and filter based on any field even if it hasn't been extracted.

> **Note**: Turn on the sort and filter toggles for any table or list by using the Ctrl + Shift + L keyboard shortcut.

When you click on the sort and filter toggle of a column of data types, you will be able to select a field from a drop down at the top of the menu. This will change the field, which sorting and filtering is based on. For example, we could select the 'Year incorporated' field and sort our list of companies from oldest to newest or filter out any company incorporated after the year 2000.

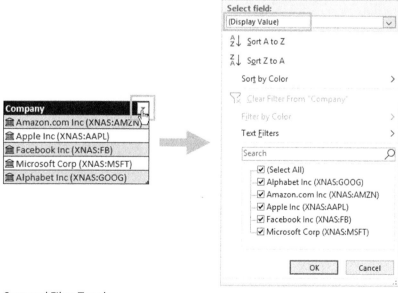

Sort and Filter Toggle.

Finding Data Types in a Workbook

Data types are visually distinct because of the icons in cell, so distinguishing between a regular cell and a data type cell is easy. But what if you want to locate all the data type cells in a large workbook? Visual inspection might not be practical. Since data types are not supported by earlier versions of Excel, the easiest way to locate them in a workbook is with Excel's check compatibility feature.

Note: Check compatibility can be found in the **File tab > Info > Check for Issues > Check Compatibility**.

The Compatibility Checker will list out all the features in the workbook that are not backwards compatible with prior version of Excel. To find any data types, you can look for the words "This workbook contains data types…" in the summary. Each summary will also have a 'Find' hyperlink that will take you to the location and select those cells.

Note: Selecting only **Excel 2016** from the 'Select versions to show' button will reduce the results in the compatibility checker and make finding the data types easier.

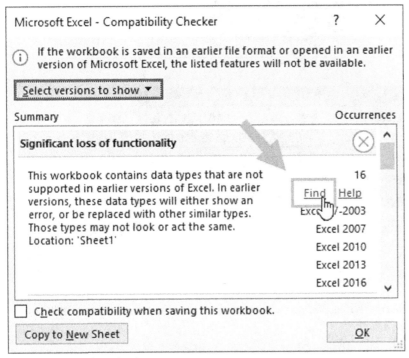

Excel Compatibility Checker.

A Look to the Future – Dynamic Arrays
by Liam Bastick

Every now and then there is a step change in Excel. Excel 2007 saw the dawn of the ribbon, Excel 2010 saw PowerPivot and Power Query – now Office 365 will soon introduce another game changer: dynamic arrays.

Dynamic Arrays

It's late September 2018 and Microsoft's Calc team has been busy behind the Excel scenes rearranging the furniture, for they are about to unleash a new calculation engine which will deal with Excel formulas in a whole new and exciting way.

But there's a catch.

There are new toys to be had, but they will neither be available in Excel 2016 nor Excel 2019. You will need Office 365 – and even then, you'll need the Insider Fast version for the time being:

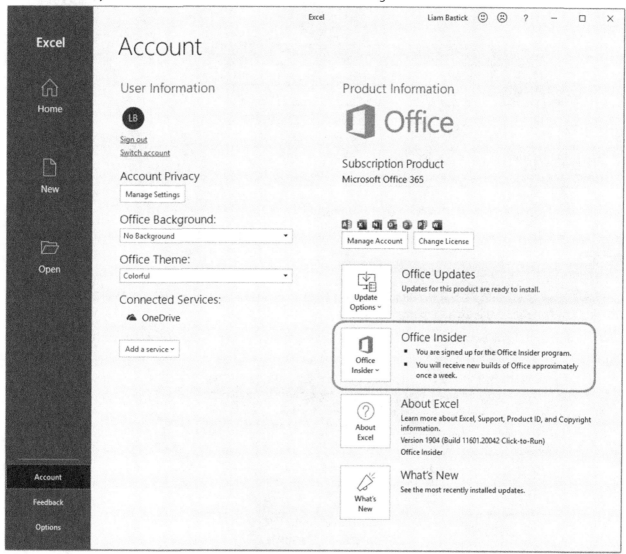

Office Insider Fast is required.

So what is the big deal? Let me explain. Consider the following table:

	A	B	C
1		**Existing Market**	**New Market**
2	**Existing Product**	Organic growth	Market development
3	**New Product**	Product development	Diversification
4			

Data Table displaying Ansoff's Matrix in Excel.

Imagine I wanted to copy this table. I could copy it in the usual way by selecting a cell and then typing

    =A1

and then copying this formula across two columns and down two rows. Alternatively, I could use an array formula:

A5	▼	:	✕ ✓	*fx*	{=A1:C3}

	A	B	C
1		**Existing Market**	**New Market**
2	**Existing Product**	Organic growth	Market development
3	**New Product**	Product development	Diversification
4			
5		Existing Market	New Market
6	Existing Product	Organic growth	Market development
7	New Product	Product development	Diversification
8			

Copying the table using an array (Ctrl + Shift + Enter) formula.

Here, I have highlighted the cells A5:C7 (three rows and three columns to mirror the dimensions of the original table), then typed in the formula

    =A1:C3

and then pressed Ctrl + Shift + Enter to add the braces ({ and }) which generates an array formula as pictured above, duplicating the original table, excluding the formatting.

It's overkill doing it this way, but it causes problems too. For example, imagine I tried to insert a row between rows 6 and 7 (above). That would not be allowed:

	A	B	C
1		**Existing Market**	**New Market**
2	**Existing Product**	Organic growth	Market development
3	**New Product**	Product development	Diversification
4			
5		Existin	
6	Existing Product	Organi	
7	New Product	Produc	
8			
9			
10			
11			

Microsoft Excel ✕

⚠ Only Chuck Norris can change part of an array.

OK

Rows, columns and cells may not be inserted into part of an array.

Well, maybe I *might* have changed the error message, but the lesson learned remains the same. These "old school" arrays were useful for working with groups of cells, but they were cumbersome and inflexible. This is where dynamic arrays come in.

This time, I go back to cell A5 and simply type in

 =A1:C3

and just press Enter (no Ctrl + Shift required!):

| A5 | ▼ | : | ✕ | ✓ | _fx_ | =A1:C3 |

◢	A	B	C
1		**Existing Market**	**New Market**
2	**Existing Product**	Organic growth	Market development
3	**New Product**	Product development	Diversification
4			
5		Existing Market	New Market
6	Existing Product	Organic growth	Market development
7	New Product	Product development	Diversification
8			

Example of a dynamic array spilling.

There was no pre-selection of a 3x3 grid. I just typed the formula into cell A5 and it automatically extended to the requisite number of rows (three) and columns (three). It simply *spilled*. This is new; in the past, Excel would have returned an *#VALUE!* error as it would not have known how to deal with the representation of nine cells in one cell. Now the calculation engine has matured.

Consider cell A6:

| A6 | ▼ | : | ✕ | ✓ | _fx_ | =A1:C3 |

◢	A	B	C
1		**Existing Market**	**New Market**
2	**Existing Product**	Organic growth	Market development
3	**New Product**	Product development	Diversification
4			
5		Existing Market	New Market
6	Existing Product	Organic growth	Market development
7	New Product	Product development	Diversification
8			

Formulas are greyed out in the dependent spilled range.

Do you see how the formula is greyed out in the formula bar? This is to highlight that whilst the formula has propagated into this cell, this is not where the formula was originally typed (it will always emanate from the top left-hand corner of the spilled range). If I were to type "Blockage" into this cell I would get the following:

◢	A	B	C
1		**Existing Market**	**New Market**
2	**Existing Product**	Organic growth	Market development
3	**New Product**	Product development	Diversification
4			
5	#SPILL!		
6	Blockage		
7			
8			

Non-blank cells cause #SPILL! errors.

Here, if a formula cannot spill, you get the brand new *#SPILL!* error at the origin instead. However, this is not the only reason an *#SPILL!* error could occur:

- **the spill range is not blank:** as in my example (above), this error occurs when one or more cells in the designated spill range are not blank and thus may not be populated.

◢	A	B	C
1		**Existing Market**	**New Market**
2	**Existing Product**	Organic growth	Market development
3	**New Product**	Product development	Diversification
4			
5	#SPILL!	! ▾	
6	Blockage		
7		Spill range isn't blank	
8		Help on this Error	
9		Select Obstructing Cells	
10		Show Calculation Steps	
11		Ignore Error	
12		Edit in Formula Bar	
13		Error Checking Options...	
14			
15			

Select Obstructing Cells.
When the formula is selected, a dashed border will indicate the intended spill range. You may select the error "floatie" (believe it or not, this is what Microsoft call these things!), and choose the 'Select Obstructing Cells' option to immediately go the obstructing cell. You can then clear the error by either deleting or moving the obstructing cell's entry. As soon as the obstruction is cleared, the array formula will spill as intended.

- **the range is volatile in size:** this means the size is not "set" and can vary. Excel was unable to determine the size of the spilled array because the formula may be volatile and / or return different dimensions such as =SEQUENCE (RANDBETWEEN (1,10)). (The SEQUENCE function is explained below; **RANDBETWEEN (1,10)** merely generates a random number between one (1) and 10.)
- **the range extends beyond the worksheet's edge:** in this situation, the spilled array formula you are attempting to enter will extend beyond the worksheet's range. You should try again with a smaller range or array.
- **Table formula:** Tables (generated by Ctrl + T) and dynamic arrays are not yet best friends. Spilled array formulas aren't supported in Excel Tables. Try moving your formula out of the Table, or go to Table Tools -> Convert to range.
- **out of memory:** I have forgotten what this one means. Sorry, I couldn't resist that. The spilled array formula you are attempting to enter has caused Excel to run out of memory. You should try referencing a smaller array or range.
- **spill into merged cells:** spilled array formulas cannot spill into merged cells. You will need to un-merge the cells in question or else move the formula to another range that doesn't intersect with merged cells.
- **unrecognized / fallback error:** the "catch all" variant. Excel doesn't recognize, or cannot reconcile, the cause of this error. Here, you should make sure your formula contains all of the required arguments for your scenario.

Just having the ability to spill formulas without using IF statements and other complex calculation logic might be good enough, but Microsoft has also let out six new dynamic range functions into the wild to support this cool new feature.

However, it may be an alliteration and sound like something you can get arrested for, but dynamic arrays do come at a small price…

Implicit Intersection Implications

There aren't many users out there who used them, but there are some legacy calculations affected by the new calculation engine.

In the past, if you entered

=A$2:A$11

anywhere in rows 2 through 11, the formula would return only the corresponding value from that row (i.e. the **implicit intersection** of the formula reference and the row or column where the formula resides). However, in the brave new world of Office 365 (eventually!), typing this formula would create a spilled array formula. To protect existing formulas, we need a new – if not instantly breathtaking – syntax: ladies and gentlemen, please meet the @ symbol:

▲	A	B	C	D	E
1	Data		@		Without @
2	Alpha				Alpha
3	Bravo		Bravo	=@A$2:A$11	Bravo
4	Charlie				Charlie
5	Delta				Delta
6	Echo		Echo	=@A$2:A$11	Echo
7	Foxtrot				Foxtrot
8	Golf				Golf
9	Hotel				Hotel
10	India				India
11	Juliet		Juliet	=@A$2:A$11	Juliet
12					

Using the @symbol to protect the legacy calculations.

Be prepared to meet the @ symbol when you least expect it. If you have created these sort of implicit intersection formulas in earlier versions of Excel, to ensure backwards compatibility, the calculation engine will "throw in" @ symbols into legacy formulas to ensure calculations opened in Office 365 will still calculate as originally intended. Microsoft doesn't want you to cry over spilt spills (sorry, I am milking the joke here).

Dynamic Array vs. Legacy Array Formulas

Prior to this new functionality, if you wanted to work with ranges in Excel, you used to have to build array formulas, where references would refer to ranges and be entered as Ctrl + Shift + Enter (legacy) formulas. The main differences are as follows:

- Dynamic array formulas may spill outside the cell bounds where the formula is entered. The dynamic array formula technically only exists in the cell in the top left-hand corner of the spilled range, whereas with a legacy Ctrl + Shift + Enter formula, the formula would need to be entered into the entire range.
- Dynamic arrays will automatically resize as data is added or removed from the source range. Ctrl + Shift + Enter array formulas will truncate the return area if it's too small, or return #N/A errors if too large.
- Dynamic array formulas will calculate in a 1 x 1 cell context.
- Any new formulas that return more than one result will automatically spill. There's simply no need to press Ctrl + Shift + Enter.
- According to Microsoft, Ctrl + Shift + Enter array formulas are only retained for backwards compatibility reasons. Going forward, you should use dynamic array formulas instead (well, for those who have access to them).
- Dynamic array formulas may be easily modified by changing the source cell, whereas Ctrl + Shift + Enter array formulas require that the entire range be edited simultaneously.
- Column and row insertion / deletion is prohibited in an active Ctrl + Shift + Enter array formula range. You first need to delete any existing array formulas that are in the way.

Everybody clear? I think we are finally good to start introducing the new functions…

SEQUENCE Function

I mentioned there were six functions added to the Office 365 version of Excel (presently just Insider Fast, but they will come through eventually). The first cab off that rank is the **SEQUENCE** function. Its syntax is given by:

```
=SEQUENCE(rows, [columns], [start], [step])
```

It has four arguments:

- **rows:** this argument is required and specifies how many rows the results should spill over. This should be a positive number greater than or equal to 1 (a negative value returns *#VALUE!* and a non-negative number less than 1 returns the mysterious *#CALC!* error). If a non-integer is entered, the value is truncated to the integer part.
- **columns:** this argument is optional and specifies how many columns the results should spill over. If omitted, the default value is 1; otherwise, the numerical entry requirements for **columns** are the same as for **rows.**

- **start:** this argument is also optional. This specifies what number the SEQUENCE should start from. If omitted, the default value is 1.
- **step:** this final argument is also optional. This specifies the amount each number in the SEQUENCE should increase (the "step"). It may be positive, negative or zero. If omitted, the default value is 937,444. Wait, I'm kidding; it's 1. They're very unimaginative down in Redmond.

Therefore, SEQUENCE can be as simple as SEQUENCE(x), which will generate a list of numbers going down a column 1, 2, 3, …, x. Therefore, be mindful not to create a formula where x may be volatile and generate alternative values each time it is calculated, e.g.

=SEQUENCE(RANDBETWEEN(10,99))

as this will generate the *#SPILL!* range is volatile in size error.

A vanilla example is rather bland:

B11	▾	⋮	×	✓	*fx*	=SEQUENCE(D3,D4,D5,D6)

◢	A	B	C	D	E	F
1	Inputs					
2						
3		No. of Rows		3		
4		No. of Columns		4		
5		Start		5		
6		Step		6		
7						
8						
9	Outputs					
10						
11		5	11	17	23	
12		29	35	41	47	
13		53	59	65	71	

Simple SEQUENCE example.

Where SEQUENCE comes into its own is when it is integral to other functions in a financial model (say). For example, no budget or forecast tool would be complete without having the dates for each period specified. SEQUENCE can make those dates dynamic with such simple formulas:

◢	A	B	C	D	E	F	G	H
1	Start date	1 Jan 20						
2								
3	# Periods to model	5						
4								
5	Period No	1	2	3	4	5		=SEQUENCE(1,B3)
6	End Date	Jan 20	Feb 20	Mar 20	Apr 20	May 20		=EOMONTH(B1,B5#-1)

Creating date headers simply using SEQUENCE.

The formula in cell B5 is simply

```
=SEQUENCE(1,B3)
```

which produces a counter from 1 to whatever the value in cell B3 is, going horizontally across the row.

The formula in cell B6 is not much more sophisticated, once explained:

```
=EOMONTH(B1,B5#-1)
```

The function EOMONTH(date, number_of_periods) provides the date at the end of the month a number_of_periods from now. For example,

```
=EOMONTH("1 Jan 20", 0)
```

would be 31 Jan 20 (end of the month in question), whereas

```
=EOMONTH("1 Jan 20", 1)
```

would be 29 Feb 20, as this is the end of the next month (one month from now) and February is in a leap year.

The formula

```
=EOMONTH(B1,B5#-1)
```

does not use the SEQUENCE function explicitly, but B5# means "the complete spilled array" starting in cell B5 (which was caused by the SEQUENCE function). In this instance, this would be cells B5:F5. If the number of periods to model (cell B3) were to change to seven (7), then this range would become B5:H5, and so on. How cool is that? You can refer to a dynamic range in a formula and it will automatically resize. Modelling is going to become so much easier.

RANDARRAY Function

One of the great things about signing up to the Insider Fast program in Office 365 is seeing how things evolve. Sometimes, Microsoft changes its mind, and RANDARRAY is a case in point. The syntax has been extended from what it was when originally released into the wild. This function now generates an array of random numbers as follows:

```
=RANDARRAY([rows],[columns],[min],[max],[integer])
```

The function has five arguments, all supposedly optional (but upon testing, I am not quite as convinced):

- **rows:** this specifies how many rows the results should spill over. If omitted, the default value is 1.
- **columns:** this specifies how many columns the results should spill over. If omitted, the default value is also 1.
- **min:** this is the minimum value that may be selected randomly. If this is not specified, it is assumed to be zero (0).
- **max:** this is the maximum value that may be selected randomly. If this is not specified, it is assumed to be 1.
- **integer:** if this is set to TRUE, only integer outputs are allowed; the default value (FALSE) provides non-integer (decimal) results.

Other points to note:

- if **rows** or **columns** refers to a blank cell reference, this will generate the new *#CALC!* error.
- if **rows** or **columns** are entered as decimals, the values used will be truncated to the number before the decimal point (e.g. 3.9999999 will be treated as 3).
- if **rows** or **columns** is a value less than 1, *#CALC!* will be returned.
- if **integer** is set to TRUE and either **min** or **max** is not an integer, this will generate an *#VALUE!* error.
- **max** must be greater than or equal to **min**, else the error *#VALUE!* is returned.

As an example, consider the following:

B12	▼ :	✕ ✓	f_x	=RANDARRAY(D3,D4,D5,D6,D7)		

◢	A	B	C	D	E	F	G
1	Inputs						
2							
3		No. of Rows		3			
4		No. of Columns		5			
5		Start No.		1			
6		End No.		20			
7		Integer		TRUE			
8							
9							
10	Outputs						
11							
12		15	13	16	4	1	
13		8	16	18	9	1	
14		16	20	7	14	4	
15							

Simple RANDARRAY example.

This function is useful for creating datasets for statistical analysis or running simulations, for example. Oh, if I had more pages allocated, I'd provide you with some great examples, but alas, I need to move on.

SORT and SORTBY Functions

Two of the new functions, SORT and SORTBY, are similar. Let me begin with the former:

```
=SORT(array,[sort_index],[sort_order],[by_column])
```

It has four arguments:

- **array:** this is required and represents the range that is required to be sorted.
- **sort_index:** this is optional and refers to the position of the row or the column in the selected array (e.g. second row, third column). 99 times out of 98 you will be defining the column, but to select a row you will need to use this argument in conjunction with the fourth argument, **by_column**. And be careful, it's a little counter-intuitive! The default value is 1.
- **sort_order:** this is also optional. The choices for **sort_order** are 1 for ascending (default) or -1 for descending. It should be noted that you might not want to hold your breath waiting for 'Sort by Color' (sic), 'Sort by Formula' or 'Sort by Custom List' using this function.
- **by_column:** this final argument is also optional. Most people want to sort rows of data, so they will want the value to be FALSE (which is the default value if not specified).

This is a function people have been crying out for, for years. Enterprising spreadsheets gurus have developed array formulas and user-defined functions that have replicated this functionality, but you don't need it anymore! SORT is coming to a theater near you very soon.

To show you how devilishly simple it is, consider the following data:

⊿	A	B	C
1	**First Name**	**Last Name**	**Points**
2	Ivan	Idea	717
3	Amanda	Hugankiss	885
4	Artie	Detoo	976
5	Blake	Seven	508
6	Piper	Pied	978
7	Ivana	Tinkle	508
8	Artie	Chokes	300
9	Mike	Stand	778
10	Shelley	Ack	954
11	Blade	Runner	203
12	Sheikh	Spear	711
13	Mike	Robe	305
14	Daley	News	839
15	Hugo	There	611
16	Mimi	Selfish	197
17			

Sample data for SORT.

There is no need to RANK, INDEX, MATCH, VLOOKUP, and half a dozen other functions modelers have so diligently employed in the past. It's much simpler now:

| A19 | ▾ | ⋮ | ✕ ✓ | *fx* | =SORT(A2:C16,3,-1) |

⊿	A	B	C	D	E
18	**First Name**	**Last Name**	**Points**		
19	Piper	Pied	978		
20	Artie	Detoo	976		
21	Shelley	Ack	954		
22	Amanda	Hugankiss	885		
23	Daley	News	839		
24	Mike	Stand	778		
25	Ivan	Idea	717		
26	Sheikh	Spear	711		
27	Hugo	There	611		
28	Blake	Seven	508		
29	Ivana	Tinkle	508		
30	Mike	Robe	305		
31	Artie	Chokes	300		
32	Blade	Runner	203		
33	Mimi	Selfish	197		

SORT-ing data in seconds.

How easy was that? All I have done is type the formula

```
=SORT(A2:C16,3,-1)
```

into cell A19. This takes the data table (excluding the headers) and orders data by the values in the third column (second argument is 3) in descending order (final argument is -1). Done. Next.

Sorting by more than one column (or row) requires using those braces I mentioned earlier ({ and }), but this time by typing them in – *not* by typing Ctrl + Shift + Enter:

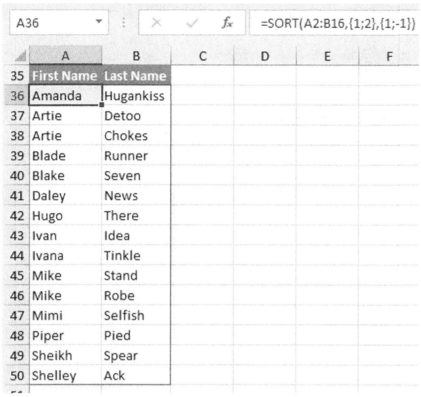

	A	B	C	D	E	F
35	**First Name**	**Last Name**				
36	Amanda	Hugankiss				
37	Artie	Detoo				
38	Artie	Chokes				
39	Blade	Runner				
40	Blake	Seven				
41	Daley	News				
42	Hugo	There				
43	Ivan	Idea				
44	Ivana	Tinkle				
45	Mike	Stand				
46	Mike	Robe				
47	Mimi	Selfish				
48	Piper	Pied				
49	Sheikh	Spear				
50	Shelley	Ack				

Sorting on two columns.

This formula is still short:

> =SORT(A2:B16,{1;2},{1;-1})

but perhaps needs a little more explanation:

- SORT will only bring back first and last names this time (cells A2:B16 specified).
- The data will be sorted on column 1 (First Name) first and column 2 (Last Name) second. This is why {1;2} is the second argument the "1" specifies column 1 and then "2" is for column 2.
- The first column will be sorted in ascending (1) order; the second column will be sorted in descending (-1) order, hence the final argument is {1;-1}.
- Remember: you use semi-colons (;) for separating columns as in this example, but you would use commas (,) if you were separating rows.

SORT is worth one more example, which provides a crossover between the old and the new:

A53 ▾ ⋮ ✕ ✓ *fx* {=SORT(A2:C16,3,-1)}

	A	B	C	D	E
52	**First Name**	**Last Name**	**Points**		
53	Piper	Pied	978		
54	Artie	Detoo	976		
55	Shelley	Ack	954		

Reporting only the Top 3 (say).

See how I reported just the top three? Perhaps Microsoft did not intend for this accident of circumstance, but hey, that's what I'm here for. I have used the same formula as in the first example,

> =SORT(A2:C16,3,-1)

but before I typed it, I selected cells A53:C55 and then, after typing the formula, I pressed Ctrl + Shift + Enter rather than merely Enter. This prevented the formula spilling outside the designated range, *et voila!* I have the top three.

Let's now turn our attention to SORTBY. The SORTBY function sorts the contents of a range or array based on the values in a corresponding range or array, which does not need to be displayed. The syntax is as follows:

```
=SORTBY(array,by_array1,[sort_order1],[by_array2],[sort_order2], …)
```

It has several arguments:

- **array:** this is required and represents the range that is required to be sorted.
- **by_array1:** this is the first range that array will be sorted on and is required.
- **sort_order1, sort_order2, …:** these are optional. The choices for each **sort_order** are 1 for ascending (default) or -1 for descending.
- **by_array2, …:** these arguments are also optional. These represent the second and subsequent ranges that array will be sorted on.

There are some important considerations to note:

- the **by_array** arguments must either be one row high or one column wide.
- all of the **by_array** arguments must be the same size and contain the same number of rows as **array** if sorting on rows, or the same number of columns as **array** if sorting on columns.
- if the sort order argument is not 1 or -1, the formula will result in an *#VALUE!* error.

It's pretty simple to use. As an example, see the names from page 52 sorted by score, without showing the score.

| A19 | ▼ | : | ✕ | ✓ | *fx* | =SORTBY(A2:A16,C2:C16,-1,B2:B16,1 |

	A	B	C	D	E	F	G
18	**First Name**						
19	Piper						
20	Artie						
21	Shelley						
22	Amanda						
23	Daley						
24	Mike						
25	Ivan						
26	Sheikh						
27	Hugo						
28	Blake						
29	Ivana						
30	Mike						
31	Artie						
32	Blade						
33	Mimi						
34							

Simple SORTBY example.

Here, using the formula

```
=SORTBY(A2:A16,C2:C16,-1,B2:B16,1)
```

I have sorted the 'First Name' field (A2:A16) on the 'Points' column (C2:C16) in descending (-1) order and then used the second sort on 'Last Name' (B2:B16) in ascending (1) order. No need for those pesky array references in multiple sorts with the SORT function (as detailed above).

FILTER Function

The FILTER function will accept an array, allow you to filter a range of data based upon criteria you define, and return the results to a spill range.

The syntax of FILTER is as follows:

```
=FILTER(array,include,[if_empty])
```

It has three arguments:

- **array:** this is required and represents the range that is to be filtered.
- **include:** this is also required. This specifies the condition(s) that must be met.
- **if_empty:** this argument is optional. This is what will be returned if no data meets the criterion / criteria specified in the include argument. It's generally a good idea to at least use " " here.

For example, consider the following source data:

	A	B	C	D
1	Item	Shape	Color	Sides
2	1	Triangle	Red	3
3	2	Rectangle	Amber	4
4	3	Circle	Green	1
5	4	Triangle	Red	3
6	5	Square	Blue	4
7	6	Rectangle	Blue	4
8	7	Rectangle	Amber	4
9	8	Circle	Amber	1
10	9	Triangle	Red	3
11	10	Square	Green	4
12	11	Circle	Blue	1
13	12	Square	Amber	4
14	13	Triangle	Blue	3
15	14	Circle	Green	1
16	15	Rectangle	Blue	4

Data for the FILTER examples.

FILTER is a formulaic interpretation of applying data filters to a source table. For example:

A22			f_x	=FILTER(A2:D16,B2:B16=B19,"Not located.")			

	A	B	C	D	E	F	G
19	Shape	Triangle					
20							
21	Item	Shape	Color	Sides			
22	1	Triangle	Red	3			
23	4	Triangle	Red	3			
24	9	Triangle	Red	3			
25	13	Triangle	Blue	3			

Filtered results for the Triangle shape.

Here, I have used the formula

```
=FILTER(A2:D16,B2:B16=B19,"Not located.")
```

where A2:D16 is my source array, from which I only wish to report shapes (B2:B16) that are Triangles (B19). If there are no such shapes, then "Not located." should be returned instead.

A22			f_x	=FILTER(A2:D16,B2:B16=B19,"Not located.")			

	A	B	C	D	E	F	G
19	Shape	Jellyfish					
20							
21	Item	Shape	Color	Sides			
22	Not located.						

Using the third argument of FILTER when there is nothing to return.

You don't need to play with this function for long to appreciate you might want more complex filters, e.g.

	A	B	C	D	E	F
19	Shape	Triangle				
20	Color	Red				
21						
22	**Item**	**Shape**	**Color**	**Sides**		
23	1	Triangle	Red	3		
24	4	Triangle	Red	3		
25	9	Triangle	Red	3		
26						
27	=FILTER(A2:D16,(B2:B16=B19)*(C2:C16=B20),{"-","None","N/A","N/A"})					

FILTER with two conditions (AND).

The formula

```
=FILTER(A2:D16,(B2:B16=B19)*(C2:C16=B20),{"-","None","N/A","N/A"})
```

looks overwhelming, but it's not quite as bad as it appears. The include argument,

```
(B2:B16=B19)*(C2:C16=B20)
```

contains two conditions. Firstly, B2:B16=B19 means that the Shape (cells B2:B16) has to be a Triangle (cell B19). Similarly, C2:C16=B20 stipulates that the Color (cells C2:C16) must be Red (cell B20). The multiplication operator (*) is used to denote AND. The Excel function AND cannot be used with arrays – this is nothing special to dynamic arrays; AND does not work with Ctrl + Shift + Enter formulas either. This syntax is similar to how you would create AND criteria with the SUMPRODUCT function, for example.

The final argument is similar to the syntax in SORT: {"-","None","N/A","N/A"}. The braces are again typed in and used to create an array argument that specifies what should be written in each column should there be no record that meets both criteria, e.g.

	A	B	C	D
19	Shape	Square		
20	Color	Red		
21				
22	**Item**	**Shape**	**Color**	**Sides**
23	-	None	N/A	N/A

FILTER formula with two conditions, but with nothing to return.

If you would prefer an OR condition the '*' should simply be replaced with '+':

```
=FILTER(A2:D16,(B2:B16=B19)+(C2:C16=B20),{"-","None","N/A","N/A"})
```

	A	B	C	D	E	F
19	Shape	Square				
20	Color	Red				
21						
22	**Item**	**Shape**	**Color**	**Sides**		
23	1	Triangle	Red	3		
24	4	Triangle	Red	3		
25	5	Square	Blue	4		
26	9	Triangle	Red	3		
27	10	Square	Green	4		
28	12	Square	Amber	4		
29						
30	=FILTER(A2:D16,(B2:B16=B19)+(C2:C16=B20),{"-","None","N/A","N/A"})					

FILTER with two conditions (OR).

UNIQUE Function

The hilarious thing about UNIQUE is that it does two things(!). It details unique items (i.e. provides each value that occurs with no repetition) and also it can return values which occur once and only once in a referred range. I understand that Excel users may welcome the former use with open arms and that database developers may be very interested in the latter. I still think there should have been two functions though.

The UNIQUE function has the following syntax:

```
=UNIQUE(array,[by_column],[occurs_once])
```

It has three arguments:

- **array:** this is required and represents the range or array from which to return unique values.
- **by_column:** this argument is optional. This is a logical value (TRUE / FALSE) indicating how to compare. If you wish to compare by row, the argument should be FALSE or omitted (since this is the default). To compare by column, you will need to select TRUE.
- **occurs_once:** this argument is also optional. This requires a logical value too: TRUE (only return unique values that occur once) or FALSE (include all distinct values), which is the default if omitted.

It's probably clearer with some examples. Let's give it a go. As always, first I need some source data:

	A
1	List
2	19
3	2
4	6
5	15
6	16
7	14
8	2
9	18
10	15
11	2
12	13
13	14
14	7
15	6
16	8
17	17
18	10
19	3
20	5
21	18

List of random numbers for the UNIQUE function.

Now, let's consider four different UNIQUE formulas. (I've repeated the source data on the left so you can see it.)

	A
1	List
2	19
3	2
4	6
5	15
6	16
7	14
8	2
9	18
10	15
11	2
12	13
13	14
14	7
15	6
16	8
17	17
18	10
19	3
20	5
21	18

	A	B	C	D	E	F	G	H
24	Unique		Distinct		Sorted Unique		Sorted Distinct	
25	19		19		3		2	
26	16		2		5		3	
27	13		6		7		5	
28	7		15		8		6	
29	8		16		10		7	
30	17		14		13		8	
31	10		18		16		10	
32	3		13		17		13	
33	5		7		19		14	
34			8				15	
35			17				16	
36			10				17	
37			3				18	
38			5				19	
39								
40	=UNIQUE(A2:A21,,TRUE)							
42			=UNIQUE(A2:A21,,FALSE)					
44					=SORT(UNIQUE(A2:A21,,TRUE))			
46							=SORT(UNIQUE(A2:A21,,FALSE))	

Four examples of UNIQUE formulas.

For simplicity, I have only looked at one column in all of the above formulas.

The first formula,

   `=UNIQUE(A2:A21,,TRUE)`

only reports data where the values occurred once and only once in the list. This excludes values such as 2, which occurred three times in the list, in cells A3, A8 and A11.

This should be compared and contrasted with

   `=UNIQUE(A2:A21,,FALSE)`

which showed all of the values that were in the list, whether they appeared once or more than once. In this instance, these values are only reported – there are no duplicates in either result.

Both of these formulas do exactly what they say on the tin. Neither have sorted the results – something I think many would expect of the UNIQUE function. Therefore, the other two formulas replicate these calculations but wrap them neatly in the SORT function from earlier. This is what you will do as you become more familiar with these new functions – you'll realize just how powerful they are in combination. This leads me neatly into our final example…

Advancing Further: Automatically Refreshing PivotTables

It won't take you long before you realize how powerful these functions and features are when combined with everything else Excel has to offer. I'd love to finish with 612 advanced examples, but would you believe, in brief, my brief is to keep my topic brief.

Consider the following dataset:

	A	B	C
1	Business Unit	Item	Sale Price
2	Foxtrot	Furniture	$ 133.28
3	Echo	Phone	$ 608.69
4	Delta	Phone	$ 667.74
5	Alpha	Laptop	$ 576.73
6	Alpha	Furniture	$ 415.27
7	Bravo	Phone	$ 382.76
8	Alpha	Furniture	$ 889.82
998	Alpha	Furniture	$ 588.45
999	Foxtrot	Phone	$ 583.80
1000	Echo	Furniture	$ 727.68
1001	Charlie	Phone	$ 494.83
1002			

Table of sales data.

If you look at the example closely, you will see 989 rows (rows 9:997 inclusive) have been collapsed in the Table I have created using the keyboard shortcut Ctrl + T (or Insert > Table). I have imaginatively called this Table 'Sales_Results'.

I have then created what appears to be a PivotTable from this dataset:

	F	G	H	I	J	K
1		Furniture	Laptop	Phone	White Goods	
2	Alpha	$ 25,469.98	$ 22,653.65	$ 25,538.27	$ 25,102.44	
3	Bravo	$ 24,067.59	$ 25,312.80	$ 23,109.49	$ 23,023.31	
4	Charlie	$ 20,885.62	$ 23,193.19	$ 16,410.58	$ 24,235.47	
5	Delta	$ 26,423.16	$ 18,914.46	$ 22,465.80	$ 25,296.14	
6	Echo	$ 19,722.97	$ 26,605.40	$ 23,081.47	$ 23,645.37	
7	Foxtrot	$ 23,137.96	$ 22,948.87	$ 19,300.13	$ 22,961.15	
8						
998	F2: =SORT(UNIQUE(Sales_Results[Business Unit]))					
999	G1: =TRANSPOSE(SORT(UNIQUE(Sales_Results[Item])))					
1000	G2: =SUMIFS(Sales_Results[Sale Price],Sales_Results[Business Unit],F2#,Sales_Results[Item],G1#)					

Pseudo-PivotTable using dynamic arrays.

This is *not* a PivotTable: it's three dynamic array formulas in cells F2, G1 and G2.

Consider the formula in cell F1:

```
=SORT(UNIQUE(Sales_Results[Business Unit]))
```

This simply sorts the unique list of business unit names in the Business Unit column of the Sales_Results table. If more business units were to be added, the list would extend automatically.

The formula in cell G1:

```
=TRANSPOSE(SORT(UNIQUE(Sales_Results[Item])))
```

is similar to the one in cell F1, but instead provides a sorted list of the items sold. TRANSPOSE is used to extend the list across row 1 rather than down column G. Usually, this would require the formula to be entered using Ctrl + Shift + Enter, but no more in Office 365 Insider Fast. It's dawned on me that a New Age has indeed dawned.

The final formula in cell G2,

```
=SUMIFS(Sales_Results[Sale Price],Sales_Results[Business Unit],F2#,
Sales_Results[Item],G1#)
```

is a "standard" SUMIFS formula with a dynamic array bent. All three columns of the Sales_Results Table are referenced, but what makes the formula a dynamic array formula are the two criteria: F2# (which is presently F2:F7) and G1# (which is presently G1:J1). Again, this formula will extend automatically should circumstances necessitate.

Why the big deal? If I had created a PivotTable, every time my data changes, the PivotTable would have to be refreshed. That's not needed here: all aspects of this crosstab query are formulaic: no refresh is necessary!

In Summary

Dynamic arrays may only be available in Office 365 Insider Fast at the time of writing, but they will be coming to Office 365 soon, although no timeframe has yet been cited by Microsoft. They will not be in Excel 2016 or Excel 2019. This has been made very clear.

The functionality and functions are game changers. If you are not already using Office 365, if any of the above is relevant to you, you might want to re-think your Excel strategy sooner rather than later.

Get the Workbook

The workbook for this chapter contains the examples covered including:

- Table using legacy array formulas
- Spilled dynamic arrays and blockages
- Implicit intersection
- SEQUENCE
- RANDARRAY
- SORT and SORTBY
- FILTER
- UNIQUE
- Pseudo PivotTable

XLOOKUP Debuts in Excel
by Tim Heng

Late August 2019 and Microsoft has added two new functions, **XLOOKUP** and **XMATCH**.

It's well known I hate **VLOOKUP** with a passion and if anything can come along and hurry its demise, well, I shall welcome it with open arms. Ladies and gentlemen, may I present the future of looking up for the masses – XLOOKUP. Hopefully, it will make an "ex" of VLOOKUP!

Why I Loathe VLOOKUP

Just as a recap, let me just summarise the resident incumbent:

    VLOOKUP(lookup_value, table_array, column_index_number, [range_lookup])

To show my disdain, VLOOKUP always looks for the lookup_value in the first column of a table (the table_array) and then returns a corresponding value so many columns to the right, determined by the column_index_number.

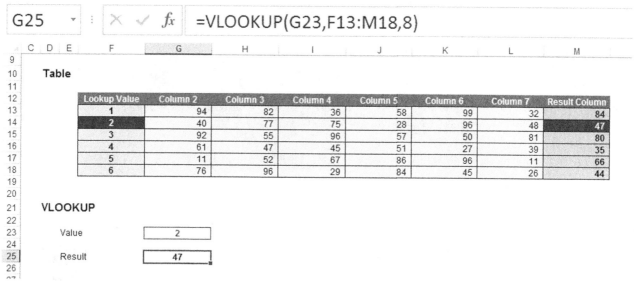

The formula in cell G25 seeks the value 2 in the first column of the table F13:M18 and returns the corresponding value from the eighth column of the table (returning 47).

Pretty easy to understand; so far so good. So what goes wrong? Well, what happens if you add or remove a column from the table range? Adding (inserting) a column gives us the wrong value:

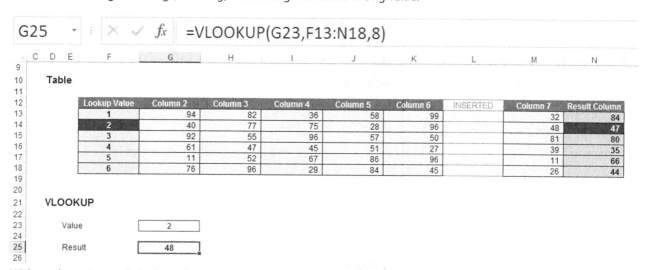

With a column inserted, the formula contains hard code (8) and therefore, the eighth column (M) is still referenced, giving rise to the wrong value.

Deleting a column instead is even worse:

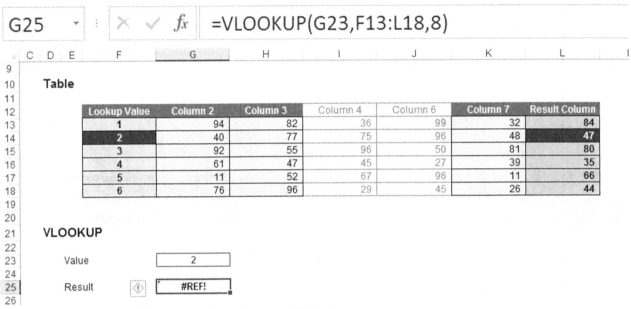

Now there are only seven columns so the formula returns #REF! Oops.

Many people will resort to using the COLUMNS function instead of hard-coding the column number. But there are more problems. In the following, VLOOKUP cannot find 2.

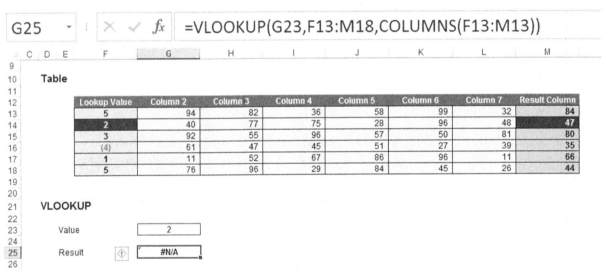

The dreaded #N/A error.

So what's going on? The problem – and common modelling mistake – is that the fourth argument has been ignored:

> **VLOOKUP (lookup_value, table_array, column_index_number, [range_lookup])**

[range_lookup] appears in square brackets, which means it is optional. It has two values:

- **TRUE:** this is the <u>default</u> setting if the argument is not specified. Here, VLOOKUP will seek an approximate match, looking for the largest value less than or equal to the value sought. There is a price to be paid though: the values in the first column must be in <u>strict ascending</u> order – this means that each value must be larger than the value before, so no duplicates. This is useful when looking up postage rates for example where prices are given in categories of pounds and you have 2.7lb to post (say). It's worth noting though that this isn't the most common lookup when modelling.
- **FALSE:** this has to be specified. In this case, data can be any which way – including duplicates – and the result will be based upon the <u>first</u> occurrence of the value sought. If an exact match cannot be found, VLOOKUP will return the value *#N/A*.

And this is the problem highlighted by the above examples. The final argument was never specified so the lookup column data has to be in <u>strict</u> ascending order – and this premise was continually breached.

VLOOKUP is not the simple, easy to use function people think it is. So what should modellers use instead?

Introducing XLOOKUP

There's a new boss in town, but it's only in selected towns presently. This function has been released in what Microsoft refers to as "Preview" mode, i.e. it's not yet "Generally Available" but it is something you can try and hunt out. Presently, just like dynamic arrays, you need to be part of what is called the "Office Insider" program which is an Office 365 fast track. You can register in File -> Account -> Office Insider in Excel's backstage area.

Even then, you're not guaranteed a ticket to the ball as only some will receive the new function as Microsoft slowly roll out these features and functions. Please don't let that put you off. This feature <u>will</u> be with all Office 365 subscribers soon.

XLOOKUP has the following syntax:

```
XLOOKUP(lookup_value, lookup_vector, results_array, [if_not_found],
    [match_mode], [search_mode])
```

On first glance, it looks like it has too many arguments, but often you will only use the first three:

- **lookup_value:** this is required and defines what value you want to look up.
- **lookup_vector:** this reference is required and is the row or column of data you are referencing to look up lookup_value.
- **results_array:** this is where the corresponding item is you wish to return and is also required (even if it is the same as lookup_vector). This does <u>not</u> have to be a vector (i.e. one row or one column of cells): it may be an array (with at least two rows and at least two columns of cells). The only stipulation is that the number of rows / columns must equal the number of rows / columns in the column / row vector – but more on that later.
- **if_not_found:** a value to be returned if no match is found. This is optional.
- **match_mode:** this argument is optional. There are four choices:
  - **0:** exact match (default).
  - **-1:** exact match or else the largest value less than or equal to lookup_value.
  - **1:** exact match or else smallest value greater than or equal to lookup_value.
  - **2:** wildcard match. You should use the special character ? to match any character and * to match any run of characters.

  Certain selections of search_mode <u>don't</u> need you to put your data in alphanumerical order!
- **search_mode:** this argument is also optional. There are again four choices:
  - **1:** search first to last (default).
  - **-1:** search last to first.
  - **2:** what is known as a binary search, first to last (requires lookup_vector to be sorted). Just so you know, a binary search is a search algorithm that finds the position of a target value within a sorted array. A binary search compares the target value to the middle element of the array. If they are not equal, the half in which the target cannot lie is eliminated and the search continues on the remaining half, again taking the middle element to compare to the target value, and repeating this until the target value is found.
  - **-2:** another binary search, this time last to first (and again, this requires lookup_vector to be sorted).

XLOOKUP compares favorably with VLOOKUP

While VLOOKUP is the third most used function in Excel (behind SUM and AVERAGE), it has several well-known limitations which XLOOKUP overcomes:

- **it defaults to an "approximate" match:** most often, users want an exact match, but this is not VLOOKUP's default behaviour. To perform an exact match, you need to set the final argument to FALSE (as explained earlier). If you forget (which is easy to do), you'll probably get the wrong answer.
- **it does not support column insertions / deletions:** VLOOKUP's third argument is the column number you'd like returned. Since this is a hard-coded number, if you insert or delete a column you need to increment or decrement the column number inside the VLOOKUP – hence the need for the COLUMNS function (and the corresponding ROWS function for HLOOKUP).
- **it cannot look to the left:** VLOOKUP always searches the first column, then returns a column to the right. There is no way to return values from a column to the left, forcing users to rearrange their data.
- **it cannot search from the bottom:** If you want to find the last occurrence, you need to reverse the order of your data.
- **it cannot search for next larger item:** when performing an "approximate" match, only the item less than or equal to the searched item can be returned and only if correctly sorted.
- **references more cells than necessary:** VLOOKUP's second argument, table_array, needs to stretch from the lookup column to the results column. As a result, it typically references more cells than it truly depends on. This could result in unnecessary calculations, reducing the performance of your spreadsheets.

Let's have a look at XLOOKUP versus VLOOKUP:

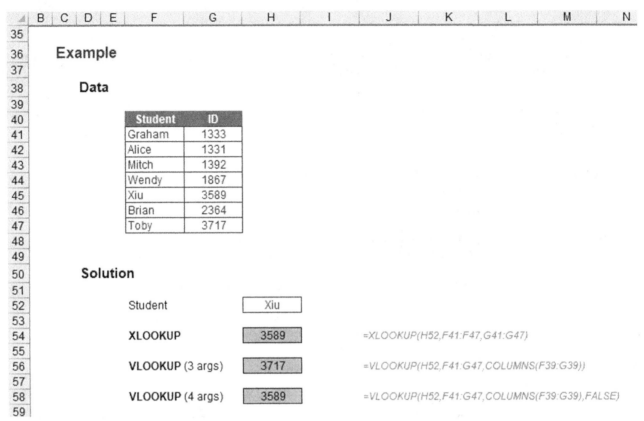

Comparing XLOOKUP and two versions of VLOOKUP.

You can clearly see the XLOOKUP function is shorter:

```
=XLOOKUP(H52,F41:F47,G41:G47)
```

Only the first three arguments are needed, whereas VLOOKUP requires both a fourth argument, and, for full flexibility, the COLUMNS function as well. XLOOKUP will automatically update if rows / columns are inserted or deleted. It's just *simpler*.

Indeed, things get even more interesting when you start considering XLOOKUP's final two arguments, namely match_mode and search_mode, as shown here.

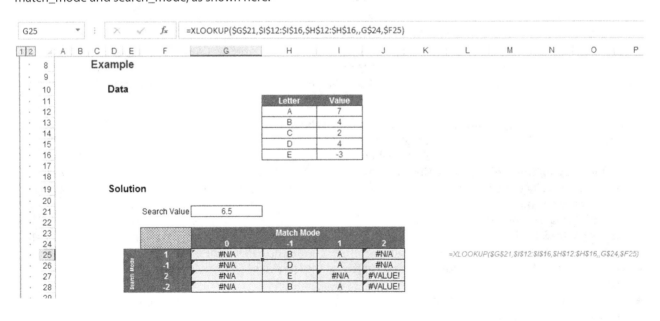

Sixteen ways to combine match_mode and search_mode.

Notice that I am searching the 'Value' column, which is neither sorted nor contains unique items. However, I can look for approximate matches – impossible with VLOOKUP.

		Match Mode			
		0	**-1**	**1**	**2**
	1	#N/A	B	A	#N/A
	-1	#N/A	D	A	#N/A
	2	#N/A	E	#N/A	#VALUE!
	-2	#N/A	B	A	#VALUE!

Do you see how the results vary depending upon match_mode and search_mode?

The match_mode zero (0) returns *#N/A* because there is no exact match.

When match_mode is -1, XLOOKUP seeks an exact match or else the largest value less than or equal to lookup_value (6.5). That would be 4 – but this occurs more than once (B and D both have a value of 4). XLOOKUP chooses depending upon whether it is searching top down (search_mode 1, where B will be identified first) or bottom up (search_mode -1, where D will be identified first). Note that with binary searches (with a search_mode of 2 or -2), the data needs to be sorted. It isn't – hence we have garbage answers that cannot be relied upon.

With match_mode 1, the result is clearer cut. Only one value is the smallest value greater than or equal to 6.5. That is 7, and is related to A. Again, binary search results should be ignored.

The match_mode 2 results are spurious. This is seeking wildcard matches, but there are no matches, hence *N/A* for the only search_modes that may be seen as credible (1 and -1).

Clearly binary searches are higher maintenance. In the past, it was worth investing in them as they did return results more quickly. However, according to Microsoft, this is no longer the case: apparently, there is "…no significant benefit to using the binary search options…". If this is indeed the case, then I would strongly recommend not using them going forward with XLOOKUP.

To show how simple it now is to search from the end, consider the following:

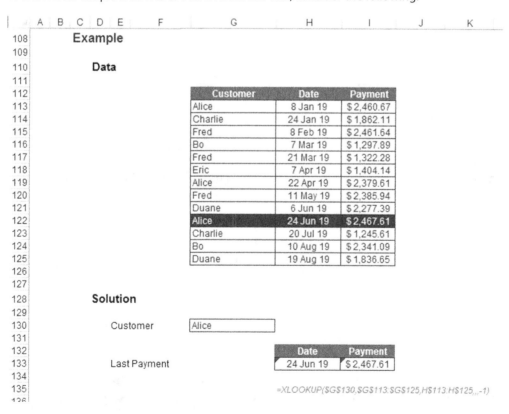

Searching for the last match.

This used to be an awkward calculation – but not anymore! The formula is easy:

```
=XLOOKUP($G$130,$G$113:$G$125,H$113:H$125,,,-1)
```

It's a "standard" XLOOKUP formula, with a "bottom up" search coerced by using the final value of -1 (forcing the search_mode to go into "reverse").

Useful Features of XLOOKUP

XLOOKUP can be used to perform a two-way match, similar to INDEX MATCH MATCH:

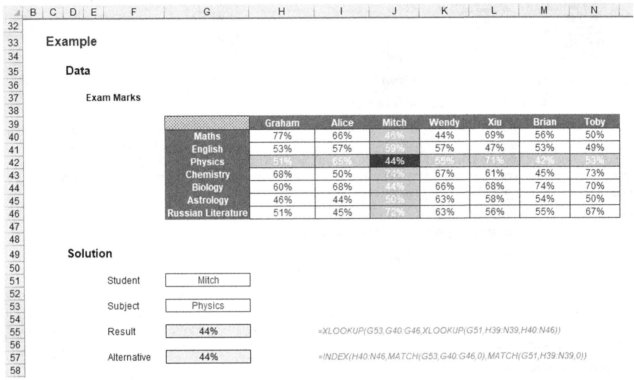

Many advanced users might use the formula

=INDEX(H40:N46,MATCH(G53,G40:G46,0),MATCH(G51,H39:N39,0))

where:

- **INDEX(array, row_number, [column_number])** returns a value or the reference to a value from within a table or range (list) citing the row_number and the column_number.
- **MATCH(lookup_value, lookup_vector, [match_type])** returns the relative position of an item in an array that (approximately) matches a specified value. It's most commonly used with match_type zero (0), which requires an exact match.

Therefore, this formula finds the position in the row for the student and the position in the column of the subject. The intersection of these two provides the required result.

XLOOKUP does it differently:

=XLOOKUP(G53,G40:G46,XLOOKUP(G51,H39:N39,H40:N46))

Welcome to the wonderful world of the *nested* XLOOKUP function! Here, the internal formula

=XLOOKUP(G51,H39:N39,H40:N46)

demonstrates a key difference between this and your typical lookup function – the first argument is a cell, the second argument is a column vector and the third is an array – with, most importantly, the same number of rows as the lookup_vector. This means it returns a column vector of data, not a single value. This is great news in the brave new world of dynamic arrays.

> **Caution**: Returning an array of values with XLOOKUP assumes that Microsoft releases the dynamic arrays feature at the same time as XLOOKUP. If XLOOKUP gets released first, these examples will require Ctrl+Shift+Enter.

In essence, this means the formula resolves to

=XLOOKUP(G53,G40:G46,J40:J46)

as J40:J46 is the resultant vector of =XLOOKUP(G51,H39:N39,H40:N46). This is a really powerful – and virtually new – concept to get your head around, that admittedly SUMPRODUCT exploits too. Once you understand this, it's clear how this formula works and opens your eyes to the power of nested XLOOKUP functions.

To show you how dynamic arrays can make the most of being able to create resultant vectors, consider the following example:

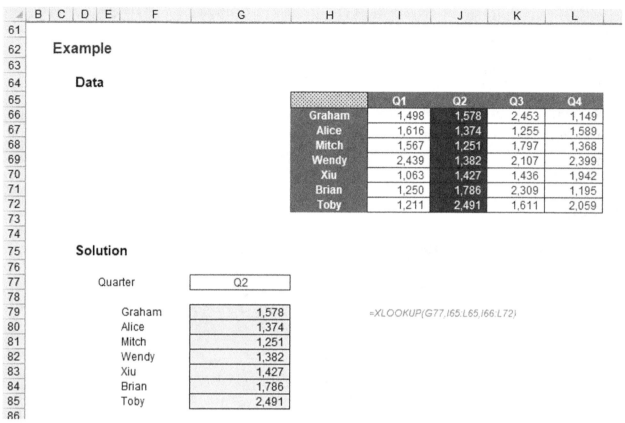

One formula returns all of the results for Q2.

The formula

```
=XLOOKUP(G77,I65:L65,I66:L72)
```

again resolves to a vector – but this time is allowed to spill as a dynamic array. Obviously, this will only work in Office 365, but it's a very useful tool that might just make you think it's time to drop that perpetual licence.

Once you start playing with the dynamic range side, you can start to get imaginative. For example:

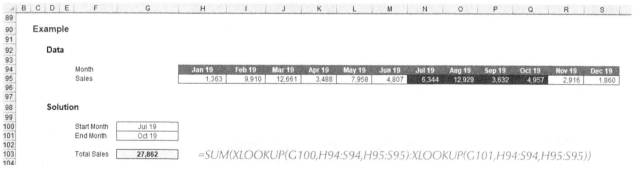

Calculate the sales between two periods:

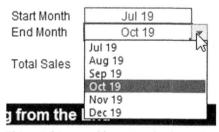

This might seem like a simple drop-down list using data validation (ALT + D + L), but XLOOKUP has been used in determining the list to be used for the end months.

Let me explain. I have hidden the range of relevant dates in cell H101 spilled across

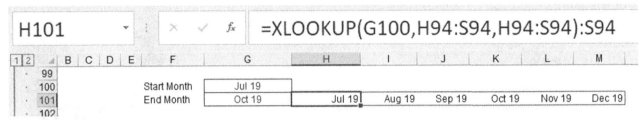

XLOOKUP can return a reference, so the formula

   `=XLOOKUP(G100,H94:S94,H94:S94):S94`

evaluates to the row vector **N94:S94** (since the start month is July). This spilled dynamic array formula is then referenced in the data validation:

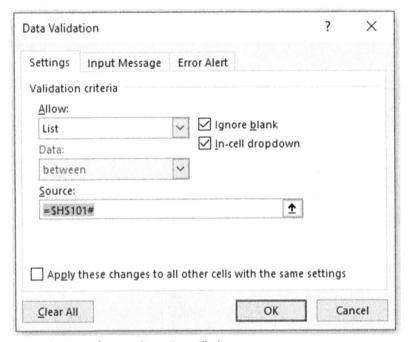

Using the # to reference the entire spilled range.

(You may recall **$H$101#** means the spilled range starting in cell **H101**.) It should be noted that the formula =XLOOKUP(G100,H94:S94,H94:S94):S94 may not be used directly in the 'Data Validation' dialog, but this is a neat trick to ensure you cannot select an end month before the start month (assuming you are a rational human being that selects the start before the end!).

The formula to sum the sales then is

   `=SUM(XLOOKUP(G100,H94:S94,H95:S95):XLOOKUP(G101,H94:S94,H95:S95))`

Again, this uses the fact XLOOKUP can return a reference, so this formula equates to

   `=SUM(N95:Q95)`

Easy! Now I am combining two XLOOKUP formulae with a colon (:) to form a range. This joins other illustrious functions used this way such as CHOOSE, IF, IFS, INDEX, INDIRECT, OFFSET, SINGLE, SWITCH and TEXT.

Word to the Wise

XLOOKUP and XMATCH open up new avenues for Excel to explore, but it must be remembered they are still in Preview and may only be accessed by a lucky few on the Insider track.

WHY THE LOVE / HATE FOR PIE CHARTS?

Why the Love / Hate for Pie Charts?

by Jon Acampora

Pie charts are the most controversial topic in the world of data visualization. Some people love them, most people seem to hate them. Why is this?

Well, I believe it comes down to their common misuse. If not constructed properly, **pie charts can easily distort the truth and be difficult to read**. Most analysts (including myself) never had formal training on data visualization principles for pie charts.

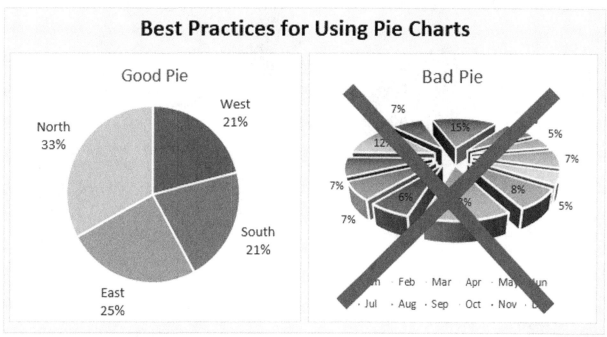

Best practices for using pie charts.

You might have heard that you shouldn't use pie charts, but your boss is demanding that you put one on a report or dashboard. If you've found yourself in this jam before, then don't worry. In this chapter, I'm going to explain best practices for using pie charts. This will help both keep you out of trouble and the boss happy.

I will cover the following topics on pie charts:

- What are pie charts?
- When to use pie charts – it's all about the story.
- When NOT to use pie charts.
- Never use 3D pie charts, ever!
- How to pick the best slice of pizza / pie.
- Formatting tips for effective pie charts.
- Why do we love circles?

What Are Pie Charts?

Pie charts are used to display the percentage of total. All the slices (segments) must add up to 100%. Any individual slice will display its proportion of the whole.

The following chart shows the revenue for each region as a percentage of total revenue. The sum of all regions should always equal 100%.

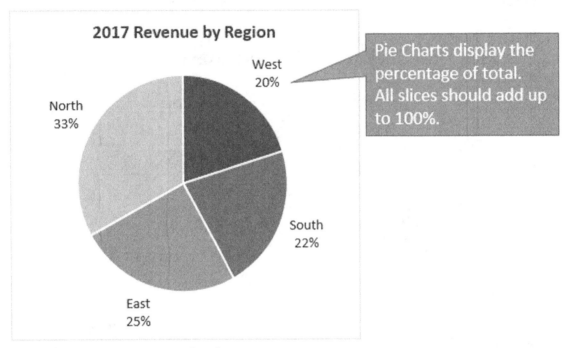

Pie charts display the percentage of total.

The circular shape of the pie quickly conveys this message to the reader. We are **dividing the pie into slices and can't have more / less than 100%.** When using a bar / column chart for percentage of total, it is sometimes more challenging to quickly determine that all the bars add up to 100%.

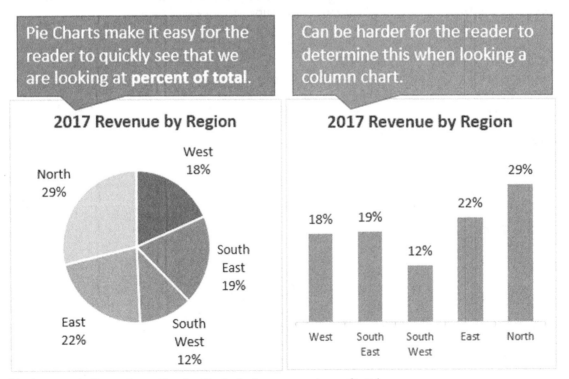

Pie charts make it easy to see the chart is displaying a percentage of total.

This seems like a good use for a pie chart, but there's more to the story…

When to Use Pie Charts – It's All About the Story

So now that we know what a pie chart is, the next question is, *"when should we use them?".*

The goal of any chart is to quickly and accurately tell a story about the data. Each chart type can tell different stories. Some tell stories of what happened over time (line chart), which category performed best / worst (bar / column chart), or relationships between variables (scatter chart).

Pie charts tell the story of how the data is divided by category. This definition alone can still lead us to tell ineffective stories. The reader should be able to quickly understand the chart's message without using too much brain power. We don't want to make them study the chart for a long time and be forced to draw their own conclusions. Our job as chart creators is to do this work for the reader.

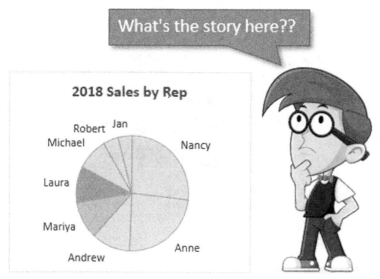

The goal of any chart is to tell a story about the data.

So, let's look at two different ways to tell stories with pie charts.

Story #1: the Even Split

The story with this chart is that there is a fairly even split between categories. All categories performed about the same. There's no clear winner and no clear loser. Yes, there is a winner and loser, but that's not the story this chart is telling:

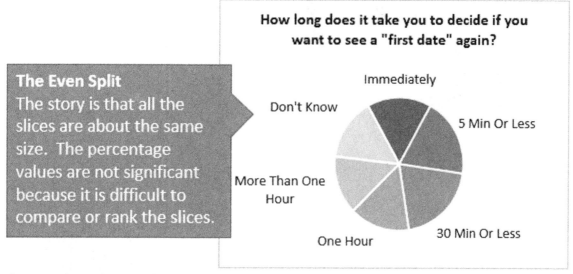

The Even Split pie chart tells the story of all categories performing similarly.

If you did want to **show the ranking** of the categories, then a **bar / column chart is a better alternative**. It is much easier for the reader to quickly make comparisons between the sizes of the bars when they share a common baseline.

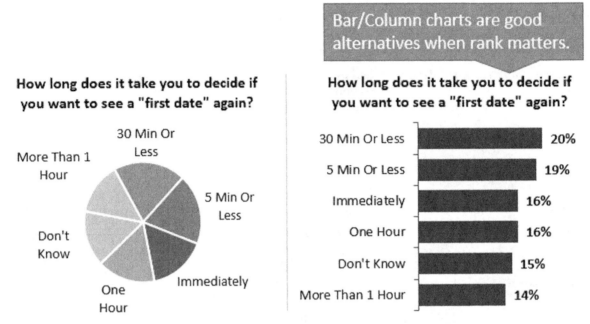

Use a bar / column chart when rank or details matter to the story.

Our **brains are not able to easily compare the size of slices in a pie**. We'll look at this in more detail in the next section.

Story #2: the Clear Winner(s)

This pie chart tells a story of a clear winner. The amount of each of the smaller slices is **not significant**. Therefore, they do NOT need data labels. That would clutter the chart. We just want to show that the winning slice made up the biggest portion of the whole.

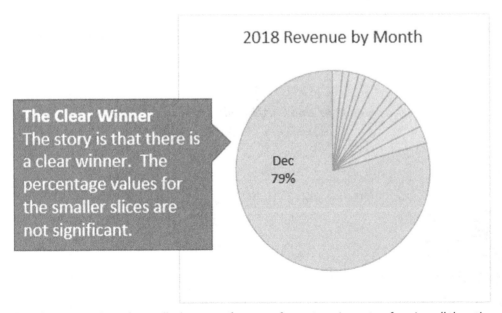

The 'Clear Winner' pie chart tells the story of one or a few categories outperforming all the others.

Sometimes we can regroup the data to tell a better story. This is an example of a pie chart I saw in a magazine on results from a survey. The story it was telling is that each of the categories performed about the same in the survey. This was an Even Split. However, we could **group the categories** to tell a different story.

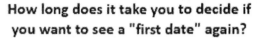

Regrouping the same data changes the story and shows a **clear winner.**

How long does it take you to decide if you want to see a "first date" again?

More Than 1 Hour 14%

Don't Know 15%

30 Min Or Less 20%

5 Min Or Less 19%

One Hour 16%

Immediately 16%

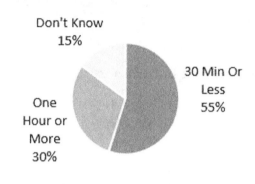

How long does it take you to decide if you want to see a "first date" again?

Don't Know 15%

30 Min Or Less 55%

One Hour or More 30%

Regrouping the same data can change the story to show a clear winner.

The chart on the right now tells a story of a clear winner. In this case it also makes the chart easier to read and helps us make decisions about dating. Be on your very best behavior in the first half hour!

It's important to note that the word "story" can make it sound like we are distorting the truth. This is NOT the case at all. We are just trying to find meaningful data insights that can help us make better decisions.

How Many Slices?

The examples above had four or more categories. However, pie charts are a great choice for making comparisons when you only have two or three categories. In this case it is easy to tell either the 'Clear Winner' or 'Even Split' story.

It's easy to tell the **Even Split** or **Clear Winner** story when pie charts have fewer categories.

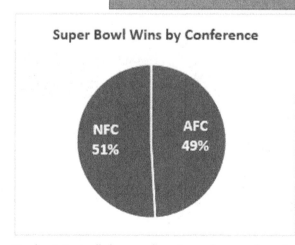

Super Bowl Wins by Conference

NFC 51%

AFC 49%

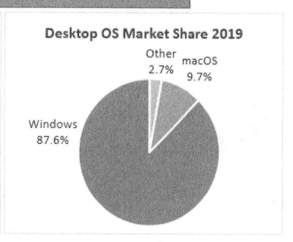

Desktop OS Market Share 2019

Other 2.7%

macOS 9.7%

Windows 87.6%

Pie charts typically have a clear story when you have two or three categories.

The general rules will tell you to not use too many categories, maybe between four and six in total. However, this isn't always true. You can have **more than six slices IF it makes sense for the story** you are trying to tell. We saw that in the example above where the month of December was a clear winner versus the other 11 months. I explain where this can go wrong in the next section.

When NOT to Use Pie Charts

The 'Even Split' and 'Clear Winner' stories are two good use cases for pie charts. This leaves us with a lot of scenarios where a pie chart will not be the best choice.

Too Many Slices Clutter the Chart

We typically want to avoid pie charts with too many slices. A case can be made if you want to tell the story of an even split. However, most readers will be confused by this and spend time trying to rank the slices. Which one is biggest, which is smallest? Does that even matter?

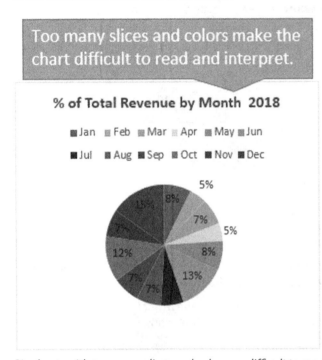 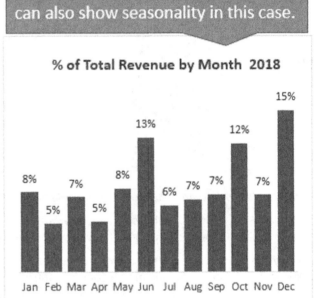

Pie charts with too many slices and colors are difficult to read.

My recommendation is to use a bar / column chart OR regroup the data to show a clear winner.

Comparisons over Time

Sometimes we want to tell the story of how proportions changed over time. For example, the image shows four pie charts. These are a percent of total vehicle sales by model for each year for Tesla (*source: Wikipedia*).

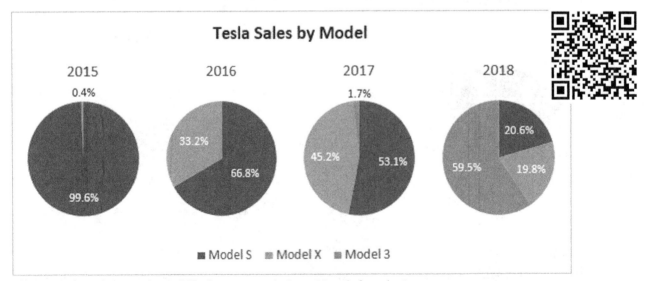

The series of pie charts makes it difficult to see trends. Scan QR code for color image.

Although this panel chart is readable, it takes time to make sense of the data. If you are not familiar with the company, then it will take time to figure out the story the data is trying to tell.

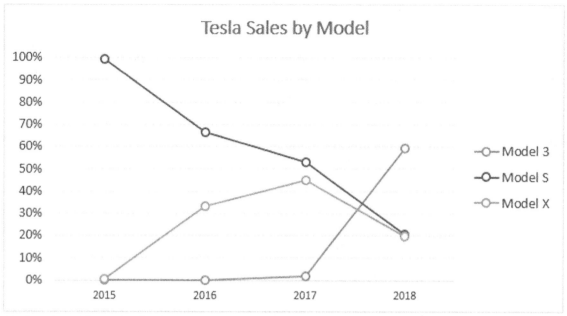

The line chart is better for displaying the percentage of total changes over time.

In this case a **line chart is much more effective**. We can see the quick spike in Model 3 sales in 2018 that made up almost 60% of sales. The line chart makes it easier to see the story for each of the models. This will be even more true as Tesla adds more models to its lineup in the future. There will be too many pie charts with too many slices, making it very difficult to read.

When Rank and Details Matter

Pie charts are generally best for high level summaries, where the details and rankings don't matter as much. It is **difficult for our brains to make comparisons between similar size slices**, and then try to reorder the slices to rank them (first, second, third, etc.). If you have more than four slices and rank is important to your story, then you should consider a bar / column chart instead of pie.

Let's look back to the sales performance chart. The image shows how close in size the slices are for 10% and 11%. Without this overlapping comparison, it's **nearly impossible** for us to tell a difference without adding data labels.

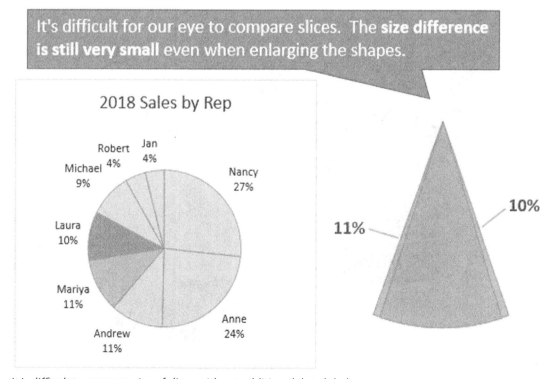

It is difficult to compare size of slices without additional data labels.

Never Use 3D Pie Charts, Ever!

Data visualization experts will tell you never to use any type of 3D chart. I agree! When we create a 3D chart, we are now using a three-point perspective and a diminishing horizon. This means the **objects in the foreground are BIGGER** than the objects in the background, even if the values aren't actually bigger.

This is especially true with pie charts. Here's a little test to prove my point. Which slice do you think represents the larger data point, #1 or #2?

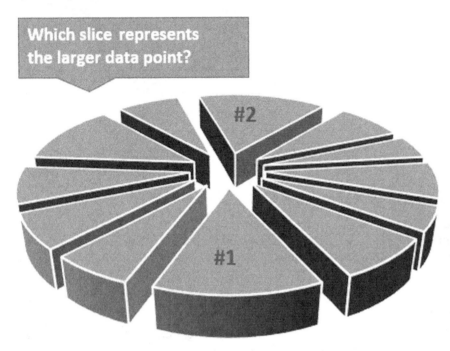

Guess which slice represents the larger data point: #1 or #2?

I'll give you a hint. The surface area of slice #1 is much larger.

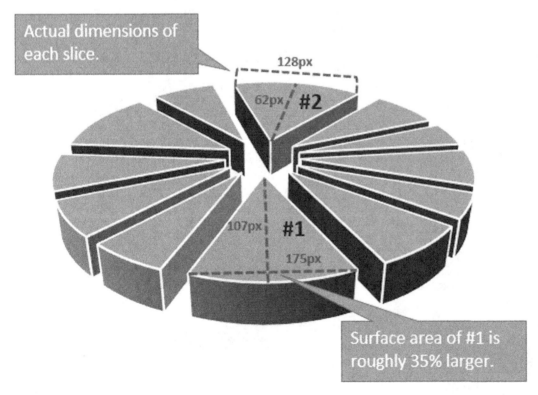

Hint: The surface area of #1 is much larger.

Did you guess #1? Unfortunately, **#2 is the winner** here. But it's stuck in the back and looks much smaller due to the perspective and diminishing horizon.

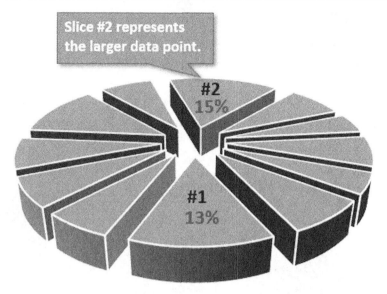

Slice #2 is the winner but looks smaller because it's in the back.

The slice in the foreground is smaller in terms of the size of the data. However, the shape that represents the data measures larger than the "bigger" slice in the back. The more you angle the chart, the worse this distortion gets. Exploding 3D pies only make this worse, as the foreground pieces get farther from the background ones.

Therefore, you are doing your audience a disservice by serving them 3D pie charts. They require extra data labels to accurately tell the story. This leaves us with cluttered charts that are slow and difficult to read.

How to Pick the Best Slice of Pizza / Pie

To further explain the issue with 3D pie charts, I want to share a life lesson that will prove invaluable next time you are at a party or office gathering. Have you ever had an argument with a friend on who gets to pick the first slice of pizza? This is an age-old battle, and sometimes a lot of the fun of sharing a pie. There is a lot of pressure on the person that gets to go first. Will they be able to figure out which slice is the biggest?

As we saw in a previous example with comparing similar slices, this is an extremely difficult task. You would have to lay the slices on top of each other, or get out a ruler and calculator, to really figure out the winner.

However, one tip that will give you an edge up is to **be directly over the pie**. If you are sitting at the table and looking at the pie at an angle, then the slices closest to you will look the biggest. The 3D perspective distorts the true size of the slice.

Pick your slice standing up, it's worth the extra calorie burn. (Photos: Alan Hardman / Rahul Upadhyay on Unsplash)

So, always stand up to pick your slice. And never use 3D pie charts!

Formatting Tips for Effective Pie Charts

Pie charts are all about presentation. As I've mentioned, we want to make it as easy as possible for the reader to consume and digest the data. So here are some quick formatting tips for creating effective pie charts.

Tip1: Remove the Legend

In the following example the legend is below the chart. This is really going to slow the reader down. Our **eye must travel back and forth** between each slice and the legend.

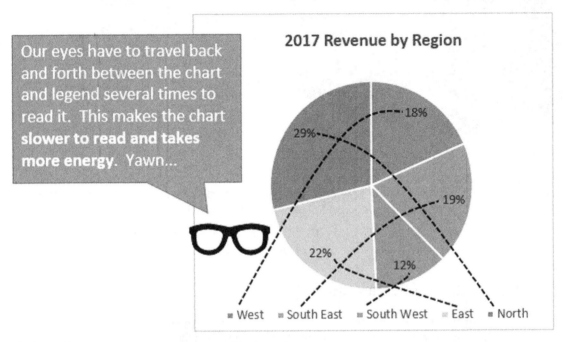

The legend can cause unneccessary eye and brain strain.

It's better to put the category name in the label. This is easy to do in Excel.

The legend is typically added when we use a lot of slices and don't have room on the chart to display them. If this is the case, then it's a good indication you should NOT be using a pie chart. A bar chart might be a good alternative.

Tip 2: Use Data Labels Sparingly

When your story is a Clear Winner pie chart, you might not need data labels on every slice. In this example the story is that sales in December made up 79% of total sales for the year. We don't need data labels for the other months. It is **not significant and clutters the chart**.

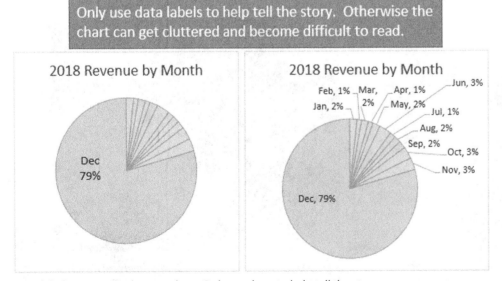

Data labels can easily clutter a chart. Only use them to help tell the story.

Tip 3: Keep the Colors to a Minimum

This tip goes along with keeping the number of slices to a minimum. However, we might have a Clear Winner chart with a lot of slices. Using a lot of different colors makes the chart difficult to read. We want to **use color to help bring attention to the message (slice) of the story**.

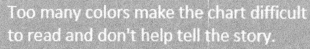

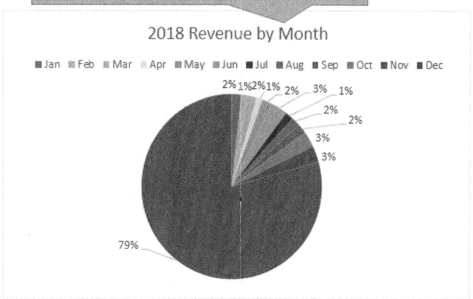

Too many colors take away from the story.

Tip 4: Tell the Story with a Text Box

You can also add some text within the chart to quickly summarize the story. This helps the reader quickly understand if the story is a Clear Winner or Even Split.

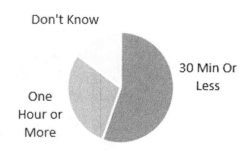

Adding text to the chart can help the reader quickly understand the story.

Tip 5: Don't be Afraid to Iterate

Charting is part art and part science. You don't have to be an artist or scientist to create charts, but both disciplines use testing and failure to succeed. The same is true with charting. **It may take several iterations** of modifying your chart **to get it right**. I encourage you to approach this as a fun exercise. One that usually leads to discovering even more insights about your data.

You can share drafts with your boss and co-workers to gather feedback. Ask them what story they see when looking at your chart. There are also plenty of online data visualization communities where you can post your work and get great feedback.

Why Do We Love Circles?

With all this controversy over pie charts, why do we like them so much? Why not just throw them out all together and use the alternatives?

Well, it turns out that we humans are **naturally attracted to circles**. In his article on "Why Do We Find Circles So Beautiful", Manuel Lima explains this phenomenon. He boils it down to three main reasons:

- Circles give us a feeling of safety. It's harder for someone to hide in a dark corner of a circular room.
- We are drawn to the round shape of the human faces. The more round and symmetrical features, the better. Think cute baby pics.
- The eye itself is round. And for that matter, so is the planet we live on and the sun that provides us energy.

Manuel has written an entire book on the topic, titled "The Book of Circles".

I also feel like **circular shapes drive curiosity and exploration**. For example, balls roll, bounce, and can be unpredictable in movement. Try golfing, bowling, or any other sport! This leaves us with a sense of wonder, and that these shapes can both defy and create gravity.

Our charts and dashboards are typically made up of a lot of rectangular shapes that are laid out on a grid (Excel sheet). So, it makes sense that we might want to add some circles to our dashboards to give them a little life.

Conclusion

In this chapter we looked at what a pie chart is, and the best practices for using them in our reports and dashboards. Most of us never received formal training on the principles of data visualization and pie charts. Don't feel bad if you've made some of these mistakes before. I have too! So, I encourage you to not get upset when you see a pie chart used ineffectively in the future. This is an opportunity to teach others and share your knowledge. To make the world of pie a better place.

I have included a one-page pdf guide in the downloads for this workbook that you can print to help remind you of the general guidelines for effective pie charts. Please feel free to share this with others. I hope it helps the next time you have a discussion with your boss on adding a pie chart to a report.

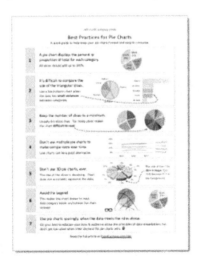

One-page guide on the Best Practices for Pie Charts.

Remember that **charts are subjective and can take several iterations to get right**. This is what makes creating charts fun and can help us discover valuable insights in the process. So, don't be afraid to explore. Happy charting!

Intermediate Charting in Excel
by Jon Peltier

Excel offers a rich charting environment for illustrating your workbooks. This chapter assumes you have at least a passing familiarity with charting in Excel, and you don't need a basic tutorial about formatting objects in Excel. I'll start with a discussion of what makes good chart source data, then I'll show how to manipulate the data in your chart. I'll describe chart types and formatting. Finally, I'll finish up with some tricks to show how flexible charts can be. Along the way I'll try to include techniques that will make your work with Excel charts more efficient and even fun.

Good Chart Data

In this section I will describe what makes "good" chart data, and how to arrange your data to make charting easier. I will then discuss problems you may encounter and how to avoid them. In the next section, I will show many of the ways you can manipulate the data in your chart.

What Makes Good Chart Data?

Excel is often smart enough to figure out how to create a chart with even the most irregular data layout. But you will get better results by using uniform data ranges when you create charts.

A uniform data source contains the data in a single contiguous range, with no blank rows or columns dividing the data. You should remove all formatting except for number formats. My preferred orientation, below left, has Y values in columns, X values (category labels) in the first column, and series names in the first row. An alternative orientation, below right, has Y values in rows, X values in the first row, and series names in the first column.

My Data	Series 1	Series 2	Series 3
Category 1	3	2	1
Category 2	6	4	2
Category 3	4	3	2
Category 4	7	5	3

My Data	Category 1	Category 2	Category 3	Category 4
Series 1	3	6	4	7
Series 2	2	4	3	5
Series 3	1	2	2	3

Two uniform data ranges, arranged by column (left) and by row (right).

Excel likes plotting fewer series with more points, so if you have more rows than columns, Excel will parse the data as if series are in columns. If you have more columns than rows, Excel will parse the data as if series are in rows. If there is a tie, Excel plots series in rows, despite my preference for series in columns.

> **Note**: If Excel plotted your series by row and you wanted series in columns, or vice versa, you can easily change this by clicking the 'Switch Row / Column' button on the 'Chart Design' tab, or the 'Switch Row/ Column' button on the 'Select Data Source' dialog.

Discontiguous Chart Data

You may not have control over the arrangement of your data. There may be blank rows and columns which you cannot remove (though you should try), or you may not want to plot every row or column of the data. Instead of selecting a single rectangular range (top left example below), you can select multiple ranges by holding down the Ctrl key, while selecting additional ranges (other examples below). You will have best results if the range you select looks like a "good" range as defined above, separated by complete unselected rows and columns. Don't forget to select the top left cell, which is not strictly plotted as X or Y value or series name.

My Data	Series 1	Series 2	Series 3
Category 1	3	2	1
Category 2	6	4	2
Category 3	4	3	2
Category 4	7	5	3

My Data	Series 1	Series 2	Series 3
Category 1	3	2	1
Category 2	6	4	2
Category 3	4	3	2
Category 4	7	5	3

My Data	Series 1	Series 2	Series 3
Category 1	3	2	1
Category 2	6	4	2
Category 3	4	3	2
Category 4	7	5	3

My Data	Series 1	Series 2	Series 3
Category 1	3	2	1
Category 2	6	4	2
Category 3	4	3	2
Category 4	7	5	3

Contiguous (top left) and several discontiguous ranges which Excel will chart correctly.

Problem: Numbers as Category Labels

If your data has numbers as X values, Excel may plot the X values as the first set of Y values, and use the counting numbers 1, 2, 3, etc. as X axis labels. This happens commonly if you are plotting yearly data, using years as category labels. This behavior affects Line, Column, Bar, and Area charts, but usually not XY Scatter charts.

Despite the "nice" data layout as described above, the chart below has a series of Y values near 2000, which are the years intended for the X axis.

Year	Sales
2015	1400
2016	1750
2017	1925
2018	2175
2019	2500

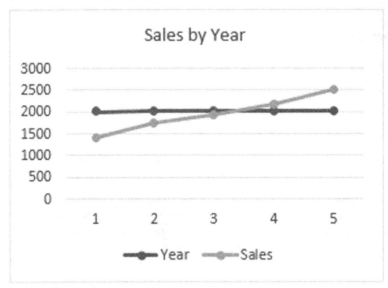

Numerical category (X axis) labels are plotted as Y values.

You can change your charting protocol to avoid the problem in several ways. You must make the first row and column of the data range *different* from the rest.

Solution 1: Plot the Y Values, then Add the Category Labels

Select just the Y values and series names and insert the chart. (The categories don't need to be separated by a blank column or row as in the figure below, that was done just for clarity.) The values are plotted correctly (see first chart below), and Excel uses the counting numbers 1, 2, 3, etc., for the X axis labels.

Then, you need to add your category labels. Right-click on the chart and choose 'Select Data' from the dialog. Click the Edit button under 'Horizontal (Category) Axis Labels', and in the 'Axis Labels' dialog, select the range containing the category labels. The labels appear as desired (second chart below).

Year	Sales
2015	1400
2016	1750
2017	1925
2018	2175
2019	2500

 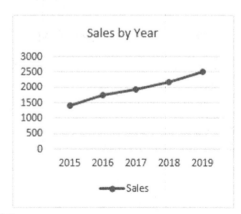

Chart made with Y values only (left) and chart with added category labels (right).

The category labels here are *different* from the Y values because you haven't included them when you selected the chart data. The need to add them later makes this approach rather tedious.

Solution 2: Use Text for Category Labels

If the first column (or row) of the data range contains text, Excel recognizes the *different* formatting and uses these text values as category labels.

Label	Sales
AAA	1400
BBB	1750
CCC	1925
DDD	2175
EEE	2500

Chart with text category labels.

You can convert numbers to text by inserting a single quote before the number at the beginning of each cell, and Excel successfully uses the numbers as X values. However, this may cause problems if those cells are used in calculations. **If you use the Text number format for the cells containing numbers, however, Excel will plot the numbers as Y values, not as X values.**

You could put dummy labels in the worksheet, create your chart, then replace the dummy labels with the numeric labels you want to use. This is almost as tedious as the previous approach.

Solution 3: Format the Category Labels as Dates

If your dates in the first column (row) are formatted as dates, Excel recognizes the *different* formatting and successfully uses these dates as category labels.

Year	Sales
1/1/2015	1400
1/1/2016	1750
1/1/2017	1925
1/1/2018	2175
1/1/2019	2500

Chart with dates as category labels.

Note: You can enter dates for your X values, and format the dates using a custom number format of YYYY, so only the year numbers will be displayed. Excel will successfully use the year-formatted dates as X values.

Solution 4: Keep the Top Left Cell Blank

The easiest way to ensure that Excel knows how to parse the data into X values, Y values, and series names is simply to leave the top left cell of the data range completely blank. The blank cell makes the first row and column *different* from the rest. You don't have to worry about formatting or data types, just overcome your compulsion to put a header above every column in the data set.

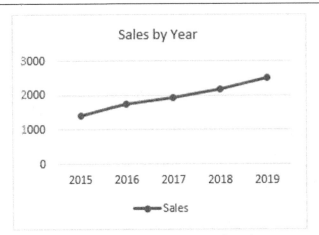

	Sales
2015	1400
2016	1750
2017	1925
2018	2175
2019	2500

A blank top left cell (shaded gray) helps Excel parse the data into X and Y values.

The blank cell must be completely empty. It cannot contain a formula that returns "" or any non printing characters.

Extended Use of Blanks to Create Multi-Tier Category Axes and Series Names

You can extend the use of blank cells to produce multi-tier category axes and series names.

In the figure below, the two blank cells at the top left tell Excel to combine the first two columns into multiple layers of category labels. Where it encounters additional blanks in the first column, it centers the previous non-blank label under the second column categories. This results in the arrangement of years and quarters along the X axis.

		Sales
2018	Q1	368
	Q2	395
	Q3	483
	Q4	509
2019	Q1	445
	Q2	545
	Q3	495
	Q4	595

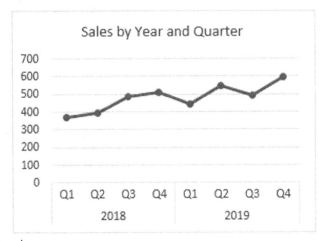

Multi-tier category labels from multiple columns.

In the figure below, the two blank cells at the top left tell Excel to combine the first two rows into compound series names. Where it encounters blanks in the first row, it uses the previous non-blank cell with the second row cell to create a series name.

	Group A		Group B	
	Internal	External	Internal	External
2015	350	500	1450	1760
2016	400	700	1250	1520
2017	550	875	1225	1600
2018	600	950	1100	1340
2019	800	1150	1000	1275

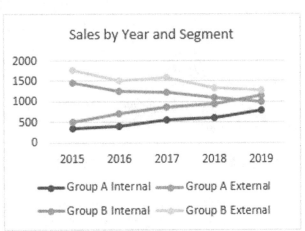

Multi-tier series names from multiple rows.

This technique is very flexible. You can combine multi-tier category labels and multi-tier series names. Each can use two or more rows or columns to create extended multi-tier elements. Below is a three-tier category axis: the three blank cells in the top left corner tell Excel to use three columns for the layered category axis labels: year, quarter, and month.

			Sales
2019	Q1	J	116
		F	188
		M	205
	Q2	A	207
		M	261
		J	274
	Q3	J	274
		A	293
		S	337
	Q4	O	346
		N	407
		D	406

Three-tier category axis.

Manipulating Chart Data

There are numerous ways to adjust which source data is displayed in your charts. I've already discussed the 'Select Data Source' dialog, but here are some methods which you may find easier.

Select Data Source Dialog

The Select Data Source dialog (shown below) is used to manipulate data in a chart. To access this dialog, click the 'Select Data' button on the 'Chart Design' tab of the ribbon, or right-click on the chart and choose 'Select Data' from the pop-up menu.

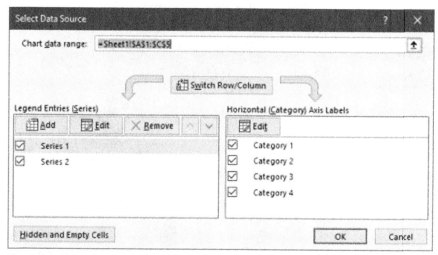

The Select Data Source dialog.

At the top of the dialog is a box showing the Chart Data Range, if that range is not too complicated for Excel to display. That means it is a well-defined rectangular range like the "Good Chart Data" described above. Below that is a Switch Row / Column button, which lets you switch whether your data is plotted by column or by row.

The dialog has a list of all series (legend entries) in the chart. You can add a series, edit the data of a series (see 'Edit Series' dialog, below left), remove a series, and change the order of series. You can also edit the axis labels for the chart (see 'Axis Labels' dialog, below right). The checkboxes allow you to filter out one or more series or categories without removing them altogether.

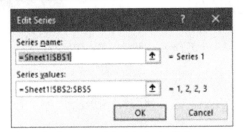
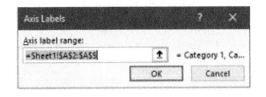

The Edit Series and Axis Labels dialogs.

For an XY Scatter chart, the Edit Series dialog (below) also includes X values.

The 'Hidden and Empty Cells' dialog provides some additional options:

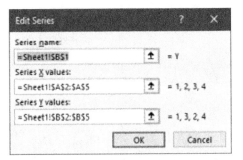
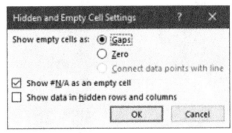

The Edit Series dialog for an XY Scatter chart.

The Hidden and Empty Cells dialog.

Series Formulas

A series is uniquely defined by a SERIES formula, of the form

or

```
=SERIES(Series Name,X Values,Y Values,Series Number)
```

Excel generates this formula automatically when the chart is created or data is added, but you can edit the formula like any other Excel formula.

In the figure below, a chart series is selected. You can see the series formula in the Formula bar, and you can also see the cell references in the formula highlighted in the worksheet, just like any other formula highlights its cell references.

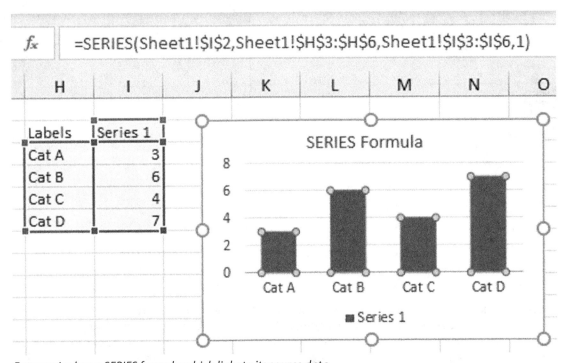

Every series has a SERIES formula which links to its source data.

Chart Data Highlights

The data highlighting shown above is a powerful way to modify the data in a chart. When the Chart Area or Plot Area of a chart is selected, the chart's source data range is highlighted (see figure below left).

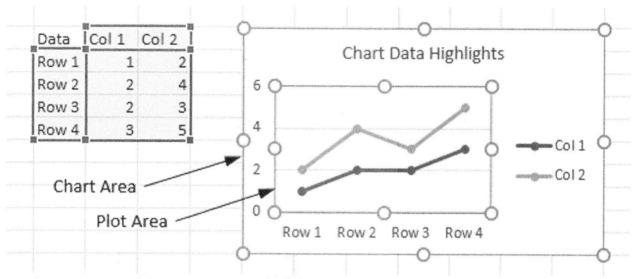

A chart's source data range is highlighted when the Chart Area or Plot Area is selected.

When a single series is selected, the source data for that series is highlighted (see below).

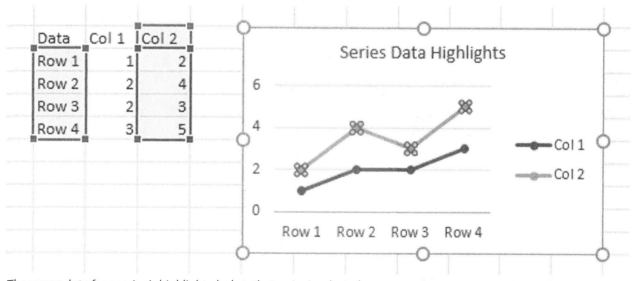

The source data for a series is highlighted when that series is selected.

The chart data highlights are color-coded: the series names are red, the categories are purple, and the Y values are blue. You can click and drag the highlight's handles (the small squares on the corners) to stretch or shrink it in any direction, adding or removing points or series. You can click on the edges of a highlight, then drag it in any direction to change which data is being plotted.

> **Note:** Sometimes the 'Select Data Source' dialog will warn that "The data range is too complex to be displayed". This means the source data is not a uniform range, as described under Good Chart Data above, or the series are plotted out of order, or data from somewhere else has been added to the chart. The whole chart data will not be highlighted, but the single series data will.

Copy-Paste

To add new data to an existing chart, you can copy the new data (Ctrl + C), select the chart, and paste (Ctrl + V).

If the data is aligned with the categories and series values in the chart, Excel will paste the copied data as new points (categories Row 5 and Row 6 in the chart below).

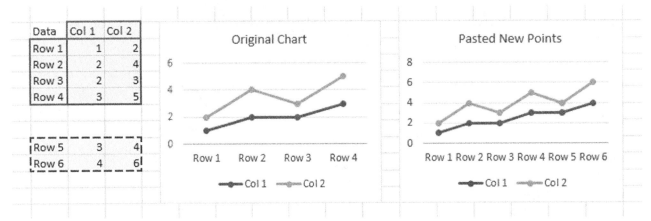

Copied data (highlighted with dashed outline, left) adds points to the original chart.

If the data is parallel to the series values in the chart, Excel will paste the copied data as new series (series Col 3 in the chart below).

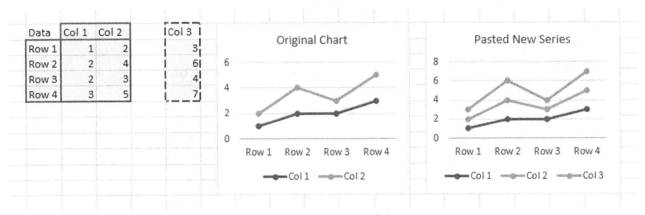

Copied data (highlighted with dashed outline) adds series to the original chart.

To ensure Excel pastes the copied data the way you want, you can use 'Paste Special' from the Home tab of Excel's ribbon (see below), or use the shortcut key combination Alt + E + S (unfortunately the Ctrl + Alt + V shortcut doesn't work if a chart is selected). Then, select the appropriate settings in the Paste Special dialog.

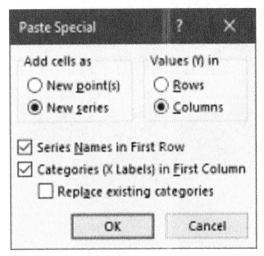

The Paste Special dialog.

Using Data in Tables

A Table in Excel is a powerful data structure with sorting, filtering, and other capabilities. When any feature in Excel refers to data in a whole row or column of a Table, and the size of that Table changes, the feature updates to reflect the new size of the Table. This includes Excel formulas, Pivot Tables, and yes, Excel charts.

In the figure below, we see a chart (left) which is based on the Table above it. By typing in new data for Cat 5 and Cat 6 in the rows just below the Table (right), the Table expands to include this new data, and the chart includes the Cat 5 and Cat 6 data in the added rows. We didn't even have to touch the chart.

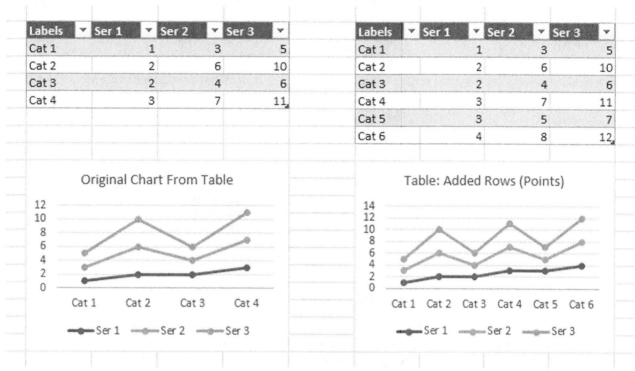

When rows are added to a chart's source data Table, the chart adds new points.

Starting with the same original Table and chart (left) in the figure below, type in a new column of data for Ser 4 in the column next to the Table. The Table expands to include the new column, and the chart includes a new series for Ser 4.

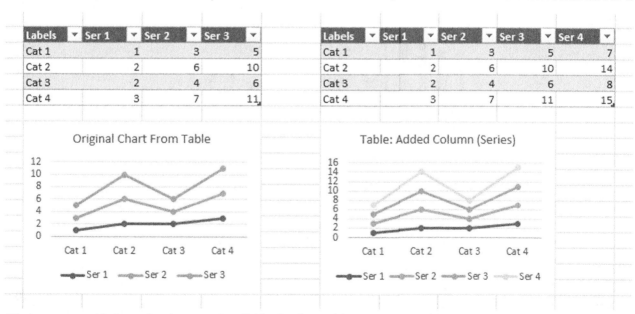

When rows are added to a chart's source data Table, the chart adds new points.

Chart Types

Rather than diving into a long discussion about each of Excel's chart types, I will describe the types of X axis values you may encounter, and discuss which common chart types work well with each. I'll add implementation notes as I describe the chart types.

Categorical X Values

The X axes of Line, Area, Column, and Bar charts all function in the same way, and work well with categorical X values, that is, text with no inherent numerical values.

When the X axis values consist of categorical labels, it is best to use column or bar charts, which show discrete values. Line charts may unintentionally imply intermediate values which don't exist.

While labels in a column chart may be angled to prevent overlap, a horizontal bar chart allows more room for easier-to-read, untilted labels.

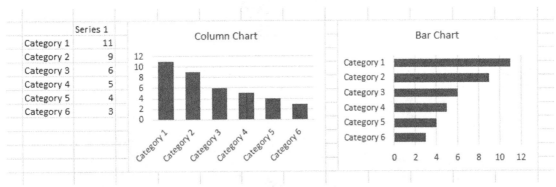

Horizontal bar charts allow for labels which are easier to read.

All column and bar charts should include zero in their Y axis scale. If the axis doesn't begin at zero, the bars have been truncated, and the apparent length of the bars no longer relate directly to their values. In the chart below right, it looks like sales tripled from January to February, then doubled again by April or May. Even though we can read the axis tick marks, our eyes detect the visible length of the bars.

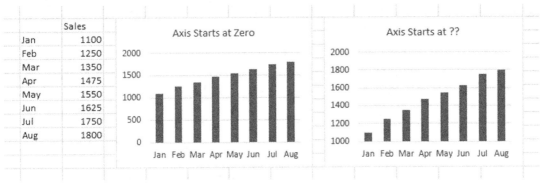

Start your bar and column chart axes at zero, or truncation of bars will distort their values.

XY Scatter charts are not suited to categorical X values: Excel can't convert the text into numbers, so it plots the data using the counting numbers 1, 2, 3, etc., for X values.

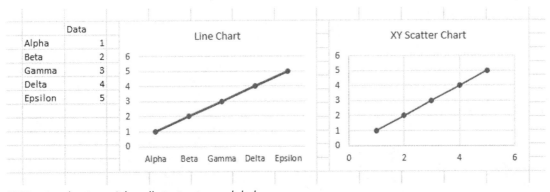

XY Scatter charts can't handle text category labels.

Sequential X Values (Timelines)

Sequential data can be actual numerical values formatted as dates, or can be text labels that convey a sequence, like January-February-March, Q1-Q2-Q3-Q4, Spring-Summer-Fall, etc.

Always plot time (date) along the horizontal axis, to avoid confusing your readers. Use Line charts to emphasize trends, to show the direction and magnitude of changes. Column charts are good when you want to emphasize individual values.

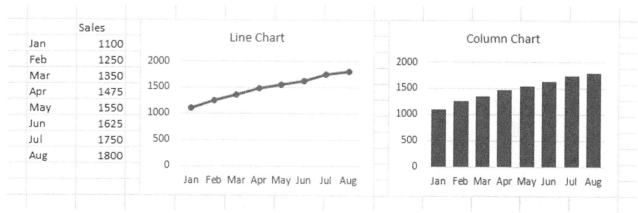

Line charts emphasize trends in sequential data, while columns emphasize the values of the discrete points.

A Line chart is perfect when actual dates are plotted along the X axis. Points are spaced proportionally according to the numerical dates, and Excel can provide nice axis labeling, such as the first of each month in the left-hand chart below, despite the different lengths of each month. If you measure the left chart below, you can see that 2/1/2019 (1 Feb 2019) is closer to 3/1/2019 (1 Mar 2019) than to 1/1/2019 (1 Jan 2019).

In addition, Excel sorts the dates internally before plotting them in the Line chart, so the line always in order goes from left to right. The XY Scatter chart shown below right also plots proportional to the dates, but the axis tick labels are not so nice to read. Those arbitrary dates on the axis make sense to a Scatter chart (the axis scale is actually 43450 to 43600 in steps of 50). Also, the data is not sorted by date, so the line goes back and forth.

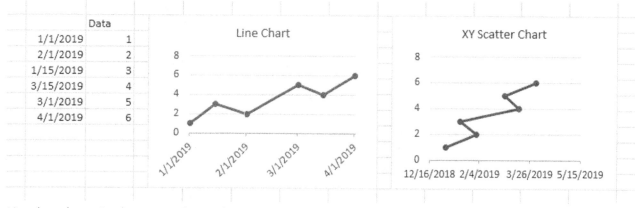

Line charts have nice date axis scaling and sorted data.

Numerical X Values

If your X values are numerical, you need to use an XY Scatter chart. In an XY Scatter chart, both X and Y axes treat their values numerically, and plot points proportionally along the axis scale according to the values. Line, Area, Column, and Bar charts don't understand numerical X values, and simply treat these numbers as non-numeric text labels.

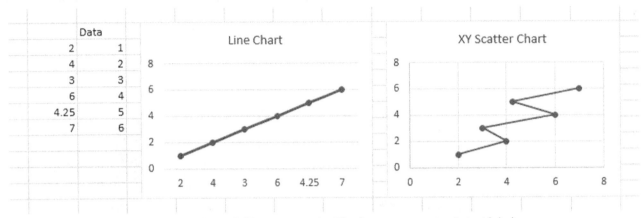

Unlike XY Scatter charts (right), Line charts (left) treat numerical X values as non-numeric text labels.

Shared versus Unique X Values

All series in Line, Column, Bar, and Area charts share the X values of the first series, even if you are able to define different X values for subsequent series. Each series in XY Scatter charts is plotted independently using its own uniquely defined X values.

Which Axis Is Which?

On most chart types, the X axis is the horizontal axis, usually along the bottom of the chart, and the Y axis is the vertical axis, usually along the left edge of the chart. However, in horizontal bar charts, the X axis is the vertical axis, usually along the left edge of the chart, and the Y axis is the horizontal axis, usually along the bottom of the chart.

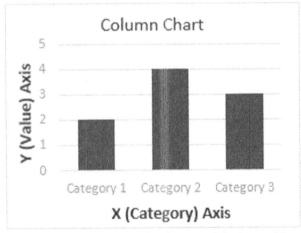

The X and Y axes of (vertical) column and (horizontal) bar charts.

No X Axis: Pie and Donut Charts

Pie and Donut charts have no X axis, but still plot using categories. All I will say about Pie and Donut charts here is don't use too many of them, and keep them simple. Don't plot more than a handful of points (segments, wedges) in each, and don't plot more than one series in a Donut chart. You can read more about this in Jon Acampora's "Why the Love / Hate for Pie Charts?" on page 69.

Chart Formatting

Formatting should be kept simple. Use simple 2D chart styles (avoid 3D charts). Don't use shadows, bevels, and other effects, and use gradients and fill patterns sparingly.

Pie and Donut charts require each point to be colored separately, but you should not vary colors by point in most charts. The chart below left shows an excessive use of color, while the chart below right shows an appropriate use of colors to highlight a single point.

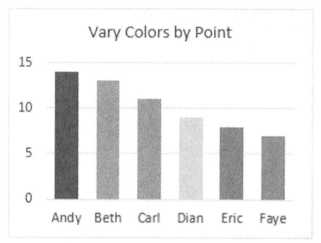
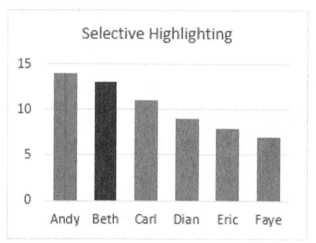

Excessive use of color (left) compared with more appropriate highlighting (right).

Labels applied to data points can help identify your data more effectively than legends.

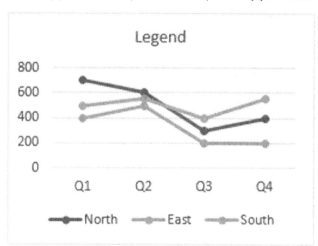
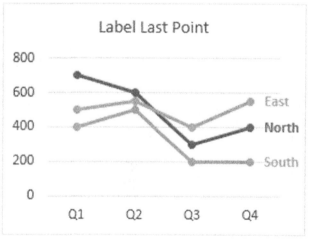

Replace legend (left) with data labels directly on plotted points (right).

Chart Tricks and Techniques

Here are a few examples that show how flexible and powerful Excel charts can be, when you know how they work. Don't forget the first trick from the Good Chart Data section: keep the top left cell(s) of the source data range blank, to help Excel parse your data into X and Y values and series names.

Bar Chart Upside Down (Format Axis)

When you create a bar chart, the vertical axis labels are in the wrong order, opposite to the way they appear in the worksheet. This is shown by the upper data and chart in the figure below. This chart layout makes sense, if you consider that the origin of the chart is its bottom left corner, and the first category is at the top of the worksheet list but closest to the origin.

But who cares if it makes sense, your chart looks wrong!

Don't worry, it's an easy fix. Select the vertical axis and press Ctrl + 1 to format it. Near the bottom, check the 'Categories in reverse order' box, then under Horizontal axis crosses, select 'At maximum category'. These steps are shown in the 'Format Axis' pane below and in the bottom chart in the screenshot.

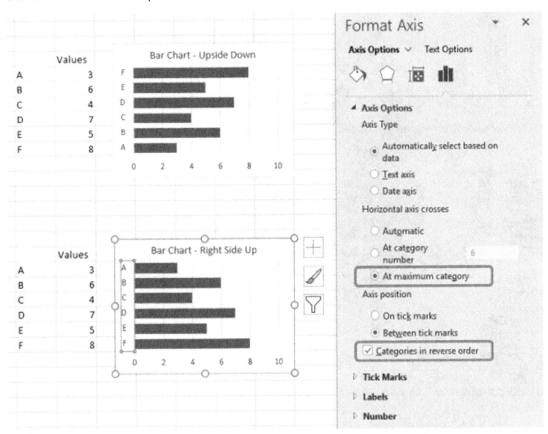

It's easy to fix an upside-down bar chart.

Label Sums on Stacked Columns (Hidden Series)

You have a stacked column chart, and the individual points (bars) are labeled, but you can't figure out how to label the totals above the bars. You probably even have calculated the totals, as in the data at the top of the figure below.

It's easy to add the totals to the original chart (top left chart below) with a hidden series. Extend the chart data to include the Total series (top right chart). Right-click the added series, choose 'Change series chart type' from the pop-up menu, select a Line Chart type (bottom left chart). A little formatting makes it look nice: format the labels so they are 'Above the points'; format the series so it uses no line and no markers; select the legend, then select the 'Total' legend entry, and press Delete.

Date	Alpha	Beta	Gamma	Total
A	0.3	0.5	0.6	1.4
B	0.5	0.7	0.8	2.0
C	0.4	0.6	0.7	1.7
D	0.6	0.8	0.9	2.3
E	0.5	0.7	0.8	2.0

It's easy to add totals to your stacked column chart.

See the image above in color. Scan here:

Target Range (Combination Stacked Column and Line Chart)

You've created a Line chart, and you want a subtle way to indicate the target range for this data on your chart. The data shown in the figure below includes the Actual values, as well as Min and Max for the target. The column labeled Target is the width of the target range, that is, Max minus Min.

Extend the source data of the original chart (top left chart below) so that it includes Min and Target (top right chart). Right-click one of the added series, choose 'Change series chart type' from the pop-up menu, select stacked column for both Min and Target (bottom left chart). Clean it up with some formatting: change 'Gap Width' of one of the column series to 0%; format the Min columns to use no fill color; format the Target series to use a light color with enough transparency so the gridlines show through.

Label	Actual	Min	Target	Max
A	0.1	0.15	0.3	0.45
B	0.3	0.15	0.3	0.45
C	0.2	0.15	0.3	0.45
D	0.4	0.15	0.3	0.45
E	0.3	0.15	0.3	0.45
F	0.5	0.15	0.3	0.45

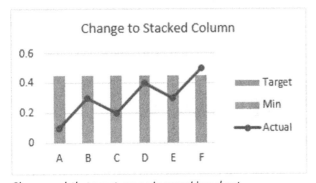

Show a subtle target range in your Line chart.

Conditional Formatting (Multiple Series with Formulas)

You can conditionally format a chart, not by actually formatting points according to conditions, but by adding series to the chart that highlight just those conditions. The figure below shows how.

In the data range we see Months as our categories across the top row and monthly values in the next row. These are average monthly temperatures in Brisbane, Australia, in °C. Then there are two rows, for Coolest and Warmest. Cell B3 contains the formula

```
=IF(B2=MIN($B$2:$M$2),B2,"")
```

And cell B4 contains the formula

```
=IF(B2=MAX($B$2:$M$2),B2,"")
```

Both formulas are filled across the range.

The top left column chart shows the monthly data using the top two rows, formatted in a medium gray. The top right chart shows the chart with Coolest and Warmest added, by extending the data by two more rows. Max is formatted with white fill and a thin dark gray border, and Max is formatted with dark gray fill. It's not yet clear what we're looking at.

The bottom left chart shows the chart with the series overlap set to 100%, so the Coolest and Warmest bars overlap the Actuals.

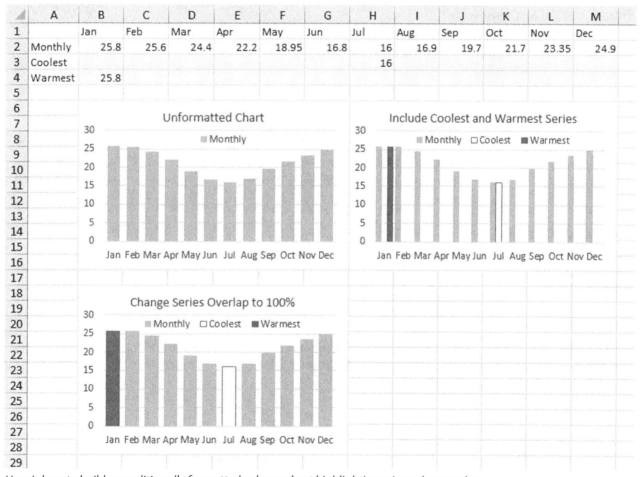

Here is how to build a conditionally formatted column chart highlighting min and max values.

Creating Charts for Presentations
By Dave Paradi

Introduction

Since presentations are becoming an increasingly important way to communicate financial and other numerical information, you need to become proficient at creating charts for use in presentations. Creating a default chart in Excel and copying it into PowerPoint is not good enough. This chapter will show you:

- how preparing a chart for use in presentations is different from use in a document.
- how to select a chart based on the message you want to communicate in the presentation.
- how to create the chart so it looks good in your presentation.
- different methods for copying an Excel chart into PowerPoint.
- ways to make the chart come alive in PowerPoint using animation techniques.

Charts for presentations are different compared to charts for reports

When you are preparing a chart in Excel for use in a presentation, there are a number of areas you need to be aware of that are different than when you prepare a chart for use in a report.

Time Spent Interpreting

When a reader encounters a chart in a report, they can take all the time they need in order to interpret the chart and its meaning. A chart in a presentation is displayed for perhaps only a few seconds so the viewer has to be able to quickly understand the message from the chart in a short period of time. Charts for presentations must be designed to be easily interpreted.

Number of Messages

Charts for reports can contain multiple messages because the reader can spend the required time to interpret each message. In a presentation, the chart should only contain one message since each slide should contain a single message. This may lead to multiple charts each on their own slide if you want to present multiple messages from the data.

Amount of Context

A chart in the middle of a report allows the reader to gain context from the text before and after the chart. In a presentation, the chart usually appears on a slide with little additional text, so the chart has to be very clear in communicating the message.

Animated vs. Static

In a report, the chart is static, and the reader must do the work to interpret each element of the chart. In a presentation, a chart can be built element by element using animation which allows a more complex chart to be explained by the presenter, so that the viewer understands it more easily.

Opportunity for Questions

If the reader of a report has questions about a chart, it is not easy to get the answer. In a presentation, the viewer can ask the presenter at the time the chart is displayed so any questions can get addressed right away.

Font Size

The text in a chart for a report is usually consistent with the font sizes used in the report because the reader is close to the page. A chart for a presentation needs to use much larger fonts so that the viewer, who is at a distance from the screen, can easily read the text.

Select the Chart Based on the Message You Want to Communicate

Many resources for selecting charts use an approach of considering the data or the relationships between the data elements. In a presentation, I think you should choose the chart based on the message you want to communicate.

Since the chart will play such an important role in helping the viewer understand your message, it is important that you are very clear on the message *before* you select the chart.

One way to become clear about your message is to write a headline that summarizes the point, similar to how newspapers write headlines for their articles. The headline should succinctly explain the importance of the message to the viewer. This engages the viewer and makes them want to look at the chart and hear your explanation. If you struggle to write a headline for a slide, you need to consider whether you actually have two messages and need two slides, or whether you don't really have an important message and should cut that slide from your presentation.

In my experience of analyzing thousands of tables and charts, I have concluded that there are six categories of messages that cover almost every situation business professionals will encounter when presenting numerical information:

- Trends
- Comparing Values to a Standard
- Comparing Values to Each Other
- Contribution of Segments
- Rank
- Portion of a Total

In the following sections, I will give some tips on how to identify if your message falls into each category and some example visuals that communicate that message succinctly.

Trends

In a message conveying a trend, it is the fluctuations in the values (usually over time) that are important, not the individual values. You are likely communicating a trend when you use words such as "increased", "decreased", "risen", "fallen", "declined", "growing", "growth rate", "changed over time", or "fluctuated" in the headline of the slide.

A line graph is the best chart to use to show a trend. It is easy for the viewer to see the trend and any changes during the time period. This is an example of the trend in the value of one dollar invested over a 10-year period.

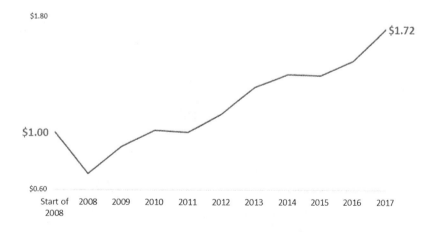

Example of a line chart showing a trend in a single data series.

When comparing trends in data series that are not measured in the same units, you can apply indexing, a concept from economics, to start all the series at the same value and you can then show the trends over time.

This example shows data series measured in number of companies, number of people, and dollars:

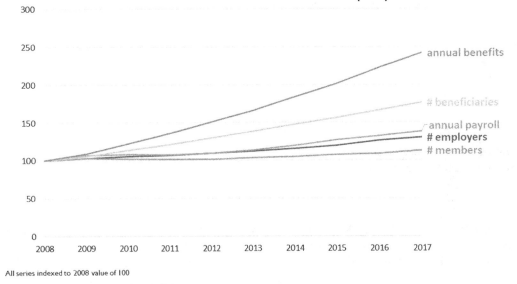

Benefits paid out and # of beneficiaries growing much faster than # of members or payroll

All series indexed to 2008 value of 100

Example of an index line chart showing trends in series measured in different units.

Comparing Values to a Standard

A standard can be a goal, average, or industry benchmark that you want to compare values to in order to show how the values met, exceeded, or failed to meet the standard.

This is an example of values compared to a goal that applies to all regions:

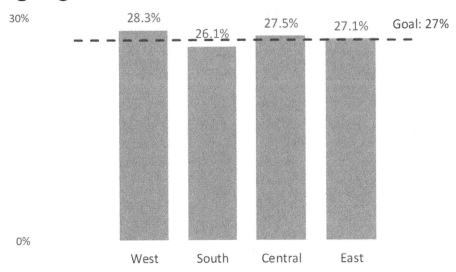

Only South region did not meet Margin goal in Q3

Example of a chart comparing values to a single standard.

This is an example of a forecast applying only to the latest time period because the forecast is updated each month.

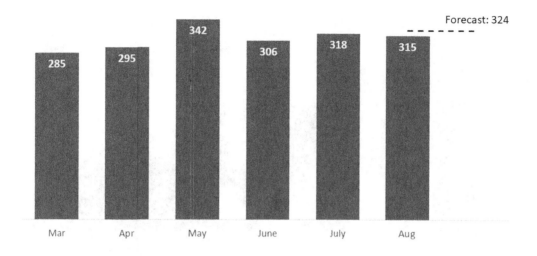

August sales did not meet revised forecast

Forecast: 324

Example of a chart comparing one value to a standard.

Comparing Values to Each Other

When you want the viewer to focus on the values in the data series, then your message is likely to fall into this category. Look for words in the headline such as "higher", "lower", "better", "worse", "above", "below", "difference", "more", or "less", that indicate a message of comparing values to each other.

This following example shows the difference between asset values in two years so the viewer can see which areas have the largest differences.

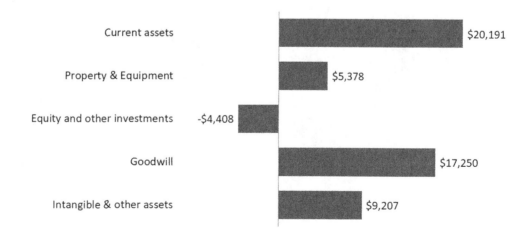

Asset increase mainly due to Current assets and Goodwill

Current assets — $20,191
Property & Equipment — $5,378
Equity and other investments — -$4,408
Goodwill — $17,250
Intangible & other assets — $9,207

Change in assets 2017 vs. 2016; all figures in millions

Example of a bar chart comparing values to each other.

This next example shows the comparison of performance against an industry benchmark in different time periods.

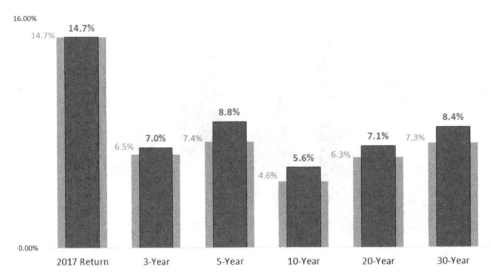

Total Fund returns consistently outperform benchmarks

Example of an overlapping column chart comparing values in two data series.

Contribution of Segments

A message in this category is focused on showing how the segments (could be sectors, areas, departments, months, quarters, regions, or items) contribute to an end result.

This example shows a net income walk to visualize the calculation of net income from revenue and expense areas.

Reducing COGS and SG&A are best ways to boost Net Income

Example of a chart showing the contribution of segments to a total value.

This example below shows a waterfall chart that illustrates the components of change between the original and current forecast amounts.

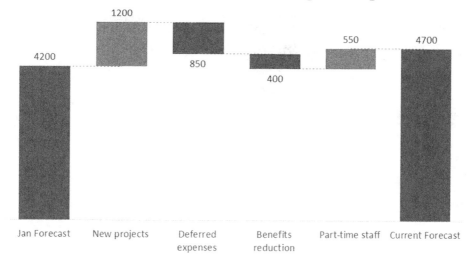

New projects & staff spend not offset by reductions in expenses resulting in higher forecast

Example of a waterfall chart showing the segments that explain the difference between the starting and ending values.

Rank

When the order of values matters so that the viewer may focus on the one or few values that are most important, you are explaining a message in this category. Words such as "most", "highest", "more than others", or "best" are often seen in the slide headline for a message in this category.

This example shows the two largest expense areas being the most important.

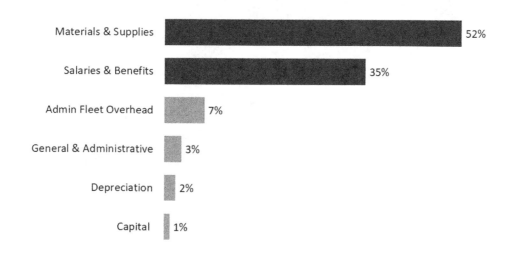

Materials & Supplies and Salaries & Benefits account for 87% of Fleet Maintenance expenditures

Example of a bar chart ranking values.

This next example shows the top sales locations and illustrates the use of an "All Others" category to consolidate the smaller values and make the message of the chart easier to understand.

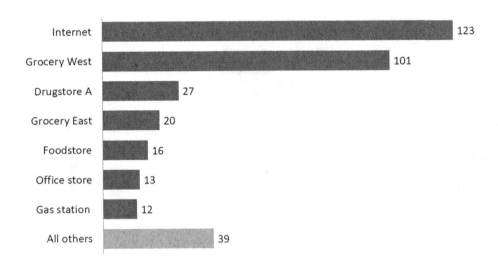

Sales locations Week 14

Location	Value
Internet	123
Grocery West	101
Drugstore A	27
Grocery East	20
Foodstore	16
Office store	13
Gas station	12
All others	39

Example of a bar chart ranking values with a category for all small values.

Portion of a Total

When your message is about the proportion or percentage of the total amount, you are communicating a message in this category.

This example uses a donut chart to show that almost all the investment expenses go to outside managers.

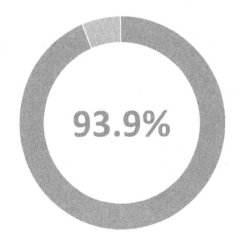

Almost 94% of investment fees & expenses are for outside money managers

93.9%

Example of a donut chart showing one portion compared to the total.

This final example uses a waffle or isotype visual to compare the percentage of international transactions to the percentage of fraud attempt transactions that come from international sources.

Example of waffle diagrams showing percentages.

Creating Charts for Presentations

When you are creating a chart for use in a PowerPoint presentation, you should be consistent with your organization's colors and clean up the default graphs so they are clear.

Creating Excel Charts that use a PowerPoint Color Theme

There is an efficient and effective way to make graphs in Excel match your organization's color scheme from the approved PowerPoint template: apply the theme from the PowerPoint template to the Excel file. Here's how you do this.

Step 1: Export the theme from the PowerPoint template

Open the current PowerPoint template you have downloaded from your organization's intranet branding or marketing page. On the Design tab in the ribbon, click on the button to expand the Themes section and click on Save Current Theme.

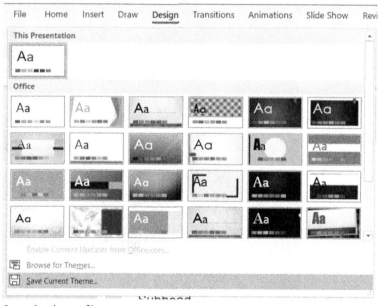

Save the theme file on your computer.

Step 2: Apply the saved theme to the Excel file

Open your Excel file. On the Page Layout tab of the ribbon, click on the triangle to expand the Themes button and click on Browse for Themes.

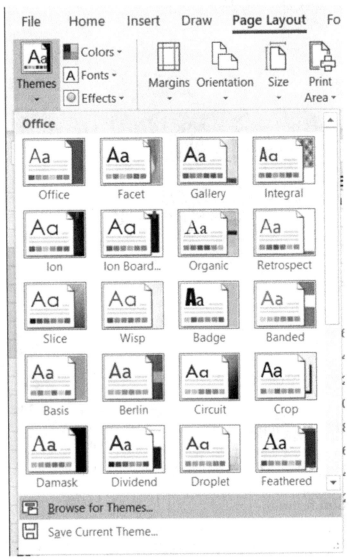

Browse for Themes.

Select the file you saved in step 1 (above) and click on the Open button to apply the theme to this Excel file.

Step 3: Create graphs in Excel

With the Excel file now using the colors from the organization's PowerPoint template, you can create the graphs you want knowing that they will be compliant with the PowerPoint template.

Cleaning up the Default Excel Charts

After you create a chart in Excel, there are some elements you will want to clean up in order to make the chart clearer for the viewer.

Replace the legend with direct labels

Research by Professor John Sweller shows that explanatory text built as part of the visual leads to better comprehension than a legend. Use data labels with the series name or category name instead of a legend so the text is placed near the data it is describing.

Remove the chart title

The default chart title on an Excel chart isn't necessary because the slide title will explain the key message.

Consider whether gridlines are necessary

Almost all default charts in Excel contain gridlines. There are only two situations with line charts where I think gridlines help the viewer:

- the slope of a line is so slight that the viewer needs a known horizontal line to compare it to.
- the trend of the line moves in one direction and then the other and the gridline helps the viewer see if the line returned to the previous value or not.

Consider whether axis labels are needed

If you use data labels on a column or bar chart, you likely don't need the measurement axis since it duplicates the information in the data labels. If you do need a minimalist axis, create one where only the minimum and maximum values are shown.

Use a large enough font size

The default font sizes for charts are too small for use in presentations. You will want to use an 18-point font or larger so that when the chart is in the presentation the viewers can read it easily.

Expert-level chart creation techniques

If you want to create advanced charts for presentations, there are four areas of expert-level techniques you can use.

Advanced Labelling

Move beyond the default data labels for data points in charts and you can start to use labels to add explanatory text and combine text with values. This saves a lot of time when updating a chart because the text updates along with the values. The labels in the examples of Comparing to a Standard above use these techniques to place the standard description and value as part of the graph that will update if the scale changes or the values change.

Invisible Elements

In order to position visible elements in a chart you may need to use invisible elements. These can be column segments, bar segments, or lines that are set to No Fill and No Color, so they do not appear on the chart. They are used to position other segments or data labels that are visible on the chart. In the Net Income example (above, in Contribution of Segments), the segments that 'float' in mid-air are actually supported by invisible segments below.

Combination / Multiple Charts

Excel allows you to use multiple charts in one chart. This allows you to combine different chart types to create the visual you want. The examples of Comparing Values to a Standard above use a column graph and a line graph to create the visual.

Multiple Data Series

By using multiple data series instead of a single data series, you can more easily format charts where different values have different meanings. If you want to format values that represent spending above budget different from the values that represent spending below budget, you can use two data series instead of one. The waterfall chart example above uses one data series for the values that represent an increase and a second series for the values that represent a decrease.

Copying Excel Charts into PowerPoint

Once you have created the chart in Excel, you need to copy it to PowerPoint in order to integrate with the other content in your presentation. There are different methods of copying an Excel chart into PowerPoint, each with their own advantages and disadvantages.

Copy as Picture

If you want to copy the chart as an image to your PowerPoint slide, select the chart in Excel and copy it. In PowerPoint, click on the triangle below the Paste button on the Home tab of the ribbon and click on Paste Special. Select the Picture (Enhanced Metafile) option and click OK. This pastes the chart in as a vector image which allows resizing without distortion or becoming fuzzy. The advantages of this method are that others cannot change your graph and the graph can be scaled without distortion. The disadvantages are that you can't make last minute changes before you present and you can't build the graph using the animation feature in PowerPoint.

Link to Data in Excel

If you want the data in the graph to be able to be updated from the source Excel sheet, you can copy the chart using the basic Paste (Ctrl + V). This creates a graph object on the PowerPoint slide that has the data linked to the cells in the Excel worksheet. All of the formatting can be done in PowerPoint and only the data is linked to Excel. The advantages are that you can format the graph in PowerPoint, you can animate it, and the data can be easily updated from the Excel worksheet in the future by clicking on the Refresh Data button. The disadvantages are that the data can't be changed if you don't have access to the original worksheet and any formatting done in PowerPoint is not reflected in the chart in Excel.

Embed Excel Data

In order to have the chart data in the PowerPoint file, you can use a method that embeds the data. When you are pasting into PowerPoint, click on the triangle below the Paste button on the Home tab of the ribbon and select the icon that says it will embed the workbook and use the formatting in PowerPoint. The advantages are that the chart can be formatted and animated in PowerPoint and the data can be changed at the last minute because it is part of the PowerPoint file. The disadvantages are that the data is not linked to the original source Excel file and the entire workbook (all cells on all sheets) is embedded, potentially exposing confidential information that may be in other cells or sheets in the workbook.

Link to Excel Chart

If you want the chart to be automatically updated from Excel, you must use the Paste Link method. When copying the chart into PowerPoint, click on the triangle below the Paste button on the Home tab of the ribbon and click on Paste Special. Click the Paste Link radio button on the left side of the dialog box and click OK. The chart is inserted as an Excel object. The advantage is that the chart data and formatting automatically update each time the PowerPoint file is opened. The disadvantages are that the update dialog box says it is a Security Warning which can be off-putting to some people, and the object is not a chart in PowerPoint so it can't be updated, formatted, or animated.

Create Chart in PowerPoint using Excel Data

There is no one method of copying an Excel chart into PowerPoint that will meet every need. You may want to consider creating the chart in PowerPoint itself. PowerPoint has the same chart features as Excel so it can create the same clear effective charts. When you create a chart in PowerPoint it starts with some sample data. You can just copy the data you want to use from the cells in Excel and then format the graph in PowerPoint. There are no links back to the data in the source Excel file, but it does give you all the chart and animation tools in PowerPoint.

Focusing the Viewer using Chart Animation in PowerPoint

One of the features in PowerPoint that you can use to help tell the story of a chart is the Animation feature.

Drawing Lines on a Chart

If you want to make it look like you are drawing each line in a line chart from left to right as you would on a piece of paper, use the Wipe entrance animation effect. Set the options so it builds by each data series and set the direction from left to right. Often you will want to increase the duration of the effect so the viewer will see the line being drawn on the slide.

Making Columns or Bars Grow

If you want to make columns or bars grow dramatically from the axis to their value, consider, consider the Wipe entrance animation effect. Set the direction so it grows correctly and increase the duration to at least one second or more so the viewer sees the column or bar grow in length.

Advanced Filter

by Roger Govier

In this book you have encountered the new FILTER and UNIQUE functions in "A Look to the Future – Dynamic Arrays" on page 45.

All these new Dynamic Array functions are fantastic and are great additions to the huge arsenal of tools that we have at our disposal within Excel.

But these are / will be only available in Office 365 versions of Excel, so many users will say "What about me?"

"I am using Excel 2013 or 2010 or an even earlier version of Excel, how can I achieve the same type of thing as FILTER?"

This article will show you how you can achieve something similar, with a function that has been within Excel for as long as I can remember but has not been used by many Excel users.

It is a fantastic function which I use all the time in so many ways, and it is extremely powerful and very fast. It can be invoked manually, or, with a few lines of VBA code, it can be made to operate automatically as you change any of your selection criteria, and I will cover the VBA element later in the article.

There are two sample files to accompany this chapter.

- Advanced Filter.xlsx which does not contain any VBA code
- Advanced Filter with VBA.xlsb which use VBA to automate Advanced Filter

Source Data

For my source data, I created some fictitious data of sales of mobile phones of differing manufacture and colours and sold by differing salespeople operating in 4 different regions. All the data uses dates within the calendar year 2017. There are 3,000 rows of data in my source (as in the example file included with this article).

The data can be in simple Lists or in Tables, but there are a couple of "gotcha's" you need to be aware of with Tables that I will cover later.

Even with simple lists, I prefer to use dynamic named ranges for the data rather than referring to cell ranges. In this case I have created some named ranges as follows.

My source data is on the sheet called Data List and is in cells B2:K3002. I have created a dynamic named range

```
drData ='Data List'!$B$2:INDEX('Data List'!$K:$K,COUNTA('Data List'!$B:$B)+1)
```

Tip: I always prefix my dynamic named ranges with "dr" and any fixed or static ranges with "sr". That way, I always know whether they are dynamic or fixed, but more importantly when building formulae with the function editor, when you type "dr" the autocomplete function will show a list of all names beginning with the letters dr

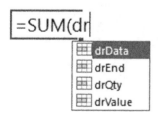

Autocomplete offers a list of names starting with dr.

So, here's what the data looks like

	Date	Name	Customer	Region	Product	Colour	Price	Qty	Value	Month
3	08 Jul 17	Paula	Siemens	West	One	Silver	378	8	3024	Jul
4	22 Jan 17	Sue	Jones & Partners	West	Huawei	Silver	163	6	978	Jan
5	09 Dec 17	Jack	BBC	East	iPhone	Yellow	411	7	2877	Dec
6	06 Oct 17	Kevin	Amazon	North	iPhone	Black	555	5	2775	Oct
7	20 Mar 17	Sue	Siemens	West	Blackberry	Yellow	162	3	486	Mar
8	26 Apr 17	Paula	BBC	West	iPhone	Yellow	310	8	2480	Apr
9	01 Aug 17	Lyn	Siemens	South	Huawei	Red	319	7	2233	Aug
10	20 Dec 17	Sue	BBC	West	Motorola	Silver	210	7	1470	Dec
11	05 Sep 17	Roger	Google	South	Blackberry	Blue	145	5	725	Sep
12	13 Feb 17	Barry	Company A	North	Samsung	White	441	1	441	Feb
13	04 Apr 17	Lyn	BT	South	iPhone	Black	290	8	2320	Apr

One row of headings followed by 3000 rows of data.

Setting the Filters

With Advanced Filter, you can either choose to filter that data in situ, or to extract the filtered data to another place. Personally, I always extract to another sheet. It is just as quick (blindingly fast even with huge datasets), and for summarising the data you then only need simple functions like, Sum, Count, Average etc.

So, on another sheet, you can set up the criteria you want to use for your filtering. You can copy all the column headings from your Source, or just some of them, or if you type them onto your extraction sheet, you must ensure that they are typed identically.

When you run Advanced Filter manually, you must always start on the sheet where your selection criteria are located. So, if you are wanting to extract to a separate sheet, that is where you would place your criteria and have your output and that would have to be the selected sheet when you invoke the Advanced Filter Function.

(the same restriction does not apply when you use VBA to run Advanced Filter)

With your criteria set up and selected choose Data > Filter > Advanced Filter and a dialogue box will appear like the following

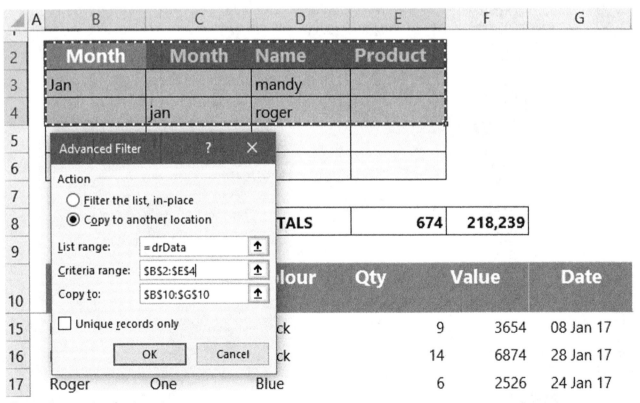

Choose Copy to Another Location.

Here, you can see I have selected the option to Copy to another location (the default is Filter in place). You then can fill in the locations for your

- **List Range** (Source data)
- **Criteria range**
- **Copy to location** (Destination range)

At the bottom of this dialogue, there is an optional check box for **Unique records only**.

I have left this blank (unchecked) here but will deal with this feature later in the chapter.

In the example, I have entered =drData as the List range, and as this has already been defined, Excel knows where to find this data.

As no sheet names have been included in the other ranges, Excel assumes they are on the current sheet, so the Criteria range has been set to B2:E4 and the Copy to (Destination) has been set to cells B10 to G10, where I had already typed the names of the columns I wanted in my output, and in the order that I wanted them.

So, in this case Advanced Filter will look at all of the data in my source (drData – 3000 rows of transactions) and will filter it according to the Criteria I have set within B2 to E4, and copy the transactions that match to cells B10:G10 and as many rows below as there are transactions that meet the selection.

If you give Advanced Filter a Copy to location of a single cell, e.g. B10, and you leave that cell totally Blank, then it will copy across all of the column headings from your source in exactly the same order as they appear in the source.

One of the excellent things about Advanced Filter though, is you can have as many or as few of the columns brought across form the source, AND they can be in whatever order you have typed them in your Copy to location. This is fantastic when you are dealing with large data sets which are 30 or more columns wide, but for your analysis you are only actually interested in the figures in a small number of columns.

Equally, I often don't bother to have the column heading of the Criteria I have set, as I don't want to see Region West all the way down my destination sheet. I trust Excel, that if I have asked to filter for Region West, then each of the transactions shown will have that Region and I don't need to waste my valuable screen estate on repeated data, which I am not going to process further.

Any column which has varied data, that I may wish to process further e.g. summarise with Totals, Averages etc. are the columns that I do want to see in my destination sheet, but I would prefer not to be distracted by superfluous data.

What do the Filter Criteria mean?

When criteria are placed in the same row, each criterion is And'ed with each of the others in that row.

When criteria are placed on different Rows, they are Or'ed

This would just be Month = Aug

	A	B
2		Month
3		Aug

Filter to August.

The filter below would be impossible, however, as you could not have the same transaction being Aug AND Sep, it can only be in one or the other so this filter would fail

	A	B	C
2		Month	Month
3		Aug	Sep

This won't work.

Repeating the criteria column a second time, and placing the second month in another row would work

	A	B	C
2		Month	Month
3		Aug	
4			Sep

Now we are saying Month Aug OR Month Sep

But equally, just having a single column for Month but putting the months on separate rows achieves the same thing: Month Aug OR Month Sep

	A	B
2		Month
3		Aug
4		Sep

Alternate method for August or September.

A	B	C	D	E
1				
2	**Month**	**Name**	**Product**	**Colour**
3	June	Roger	iPhone	Red

Find records that match all four of the criteria.

When the Criteria are all on the same row, they are all And'ed. So, the example above is for Month = June, AND Name = Roger AND Product = iPhone AND Colour = Red

Below would be Month Not Equal to June AND Customer = Any value AND Region is Not Equal to West AND Colour equals Red.

A	B	C	D	E
1				
2	**Month**	**Customer**	**Region**	**Colour**
3	<>June		<>West	Red

A blank in the Customer column essentially says "any Customer".

If the Criteria are on different rows, they are Or'ed. The following will give you Nokia sales in either August or September.

A	B	C
1		
2	**Month**	**Product**
3	Aug	Nokia
4	Sep	Nokia

August or September, but the product has to be Nokia.

This would be all transactions for Aug OR all Transactions for Sep regardless of Customer and Product OR all Transactions for Sainsbury OR all transactions for Blackberry regardless of which month.

A	B	C	D	E
1				
2	**Month**	**Month**	**Customer**	**Product**
3	Aug			
4		Sep		
5			Sainsbury	
6				Blackberry

Four criteria joined by Or.

As you can have as many columns for criteria as there are columns in your source, and they can be repeated where required and you can have as many rows for your criteria, you are able to build up very detailed sets of filters for extracting data from your source.

Final Report

Having extracted the data using Advanced Filter, the transactions can then be summarised to give Totals, Counts Averages etc., using very simple and fast functions like SUM(), COUNT() and AVERAGE().

Because there are no hidden rows on the destination sheet, only rows that meet the criteria that have been set, there is no need to use SUBTOTAL() or AGGREGATE() to obtain your summary data.

Equally, because Advanced Filter has set all of the criteria, there is no need to use SUMIFS() or SUMPRODUCT() to obtain the answer.

As I like to use Dynamic Named Ranges as mentioned earlier, I create some for my destination sheet so that I can use them in my summary formulae and they will automatically adjust according to the quantity of data that has been filtered.

In this example, and the included workbook, I used the following

drEnd	`=COUNTA('Extract List'!$B$10:$B$1000000)+9`
drQty	`='Extract List'!$E$11:INDEX('Extract List'!$E:$E,drEnd)`
drValue	`='Extract List'!$F$11:INDEX('Extract List'!$F:$F,drEnd)`

Then the formula in E8 `=SUM(drQty)` and in F8 `=SUM(drValue)`

	A	B	C	D	E	F	G
2		**Month**	**Month**	**Name**	**Product**		
3		Jan		mandy	iphone		
4			jan	roger	iphone		
5							
6							
7							
8				**TOTALS**		170	64,928	
9							
10		**Name**	**Product**	**Colour**	**Qty**	**Value**	**Date**
11		Mandy	iPhone	Silver	9	3564	24 Jan 17
12		Roger	iPhone	Black	9	3654	08 Jan 17
13		Roger	iPhone	White	17	5627	08 Jan 17
14		Roger	iPhone	Silver	19	6080	19 Jan 17
15		Roger	iPhone	Blue	20	8640	25 Jan 17
16		Roger	iPhone	Red	18	8208	11 Jan 17
17		Roger	iPhone	White	11	5544	25 Jan 17
18		Roger	iPhone	Yellow	21	8673	17 Jan 17
19		Roger	iPhone	Yellow	7	2807	13 Jan 17
20		Mandy	iPhone	Yellow	19	7011	21 Jan 17
21		Mandy	iPhone	White	20	5120	02 Jan 17

Summing the results of the filter.

Advanced Filter is extremely fast and extremely powerful (and in my opinion, as clever as some of the brand-new functions just being introduced) and it has always seemed a shame to me that is has not been widely used over all these years.

It is not just confined to single workbooks either. I recently had a situation where I needed to copy some 530,000 rows of data from one file to another. There were various reasons why I could not use Power Query (another fantastic function) to achieve this.

When I tried copying and pasting, Excel just "choked" on the amount of data and froze completely after a certain amount of time.

Eventually, I tried Advanced Filter, with a single criterion block of B2:B3, where B2 contained the same heading as the first column of the Block of data I wanted to copy, and B3 was left Blank – meaning I wanted all transactions. Advanced Filter brought across all 530,000 rows in a couple of seconds with no problem at all.

I guess this is because Copy and Paste does two things. First if copies everything to the Clipboard, and then it Pastes from the Clipboard to the destination. There are performance issues with the Clipboard and my guess is that this is what was causing Excel to choke. Advanced Filter is "always your friend"

Creating a UNIQUE list

One of the other clever new functions that was introduced with Dynamic Arrays, was the UNIQUE() function. This is superb and =UNIQUE(some range) will generate a an array of the unique items within that range. UNIQUE() can also be nested within other functions and all of this has been described in "A Look to the Future – Dynamic Arrays" on page 45.

Once again, "what about me?" if I am not using the latest Office 365 version which has these new functions. "how can I generate a Unique list?"

Once again, Advanced Filter is your friend. You will recall the Advanced Filter dialogue had an option check box for Unique records only. Well applying this to our data set with just Product as the column and leaving the criterion blank, and setting the Copy to location to being just a single cell called Product with the Unique records box checked (as below)

This produces an output of just the 7 unique products from the source of 3000 records.

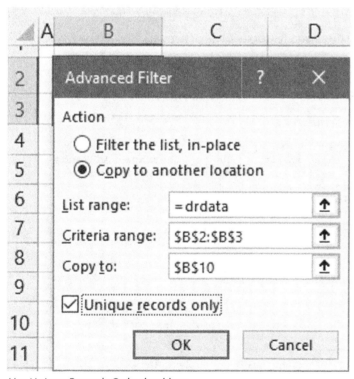

Use Unique Records Only checkbox.

Unique list in B11.

Similarly, if we had placed Name in cells B2 and B10 and run the Advanced Filter again, then we would generate a list of the 12 people whose name appears within the 3000 records.

Having generated our unique lists, they can be sorted alphabetically if required, and then used as the source for data validation for example.

Using Advanced Filter with Tables

You can use Advanced Filter with tables in the same way as with ordinary ranges or dynamic named ranges, and I include sample of this in the attached workbook. But there are some limitations.

I have the same set of source data in the file in a table called tbData, and the resultant extract table on the destination sheet is called tbDest.

(Again, I prefix all my table names with "tb" to make it easier to use them with autocomplete in the function editor).

I don't use a table to hold my criteria. Why not? Well because I often need to have a column heading repeated twice in the criteria range, e.g. to have Month twice in order to have Month = Jun Or Month = Jul, Tables will not permit a duplication of header name, it would call the second instance of Month, Month2. As Month2 is not the same as Month, then Advanced Filter would not function correctly.

If you are not repeating column headings in your criteria, then you can use a table to hold the criteria.

There are a couple of problems when using tables to hold the output from Advanced Filter, and for that reason I tend to always use a range (along with some dynamic names) even if I use a table as the source.

Because Advanced Filter was created well before Tables were introduced, it has no knowledge of Table structure and does not cause tables to resize when data is added or removed from then when Advanced Filter operates.

If the next time Advanced Filter is run, it brings through fewer rows than previously, then there will be blank rows in the destination table (which does not matter), but the Totals will still be correct.

However, if the Advanced Filter brings through more rows than were in the previous destination table, the extra rows will spill over below the table, and these will not be included within the totals UNLESS you first resize the destination table.

Also, if the destination table is completely empty (just headers with nothing in any row) then manually running Advanced Filter will give an error message saying "The extract range has a missing or illegal name".

Both problems can be overcome with VBA, as used in the example workbook, which resizes the destination table after the Advanced Filter has been run

Create the MAGIC of Advanced Filter Using VBA to Automate selection

It is very easy to automate Advanced Filter with relatively little VBA code.

```
Private Sub Worksheet_Change(ByVal Target As Range)
    Dim mySource As Range, myCrit As Range, myDest As Range, testrange As Range
    Application.EnableEvents = False ' switch off events to prevent second call
    Set myCrit = Range("B2").CurrentRegion ' adjust B2 to suit
    If Not Intersect(Target, myCrit) Is Nothing Then
        'changed cell is within Criteria range then continue
        Set mySource = [drData] ' adjust with your data source
        Set myDest = Range("B10:G10") ' adjust this to suit your destination
        Call FilterData(mySource, myCrit, myDest)
    End If
    Application.EnableEvents = True ' switch events back on
End Sub
```

First, you need to apply some Event code to the sheet which contains the Extract Criteria, to detect when there has been a change in any of the cells containing the criteria. If there has been any change, then the routine to run Advanced Filter should be called.

This Event code sits behind Sheet Extract List and is for dealing with cases not involving Tables

Application.EnableEvents= False switches off events once the code starts running until the end of the code when it is switched on again. This prevents unnecessary further running of code as any other data is written to the sheet.

myCrit = Range("B2").CurrentRegion calculates the range of cells that are contiguous with cell B2. With the example above, that would resolve to B2:E4 as there is data in rows 2:4 and there is data in columns B:E

If the cell that was active when return or tab is pressed (the Target cell) falls within that range, then the Function FilterData is called with the relevant data which defines what the Source data is, where the Criteria lie, and where the Destination should be, which are the three ranges required in the Advanced Filter dialogue as we saw earlier.

The Function FilterData has to be copied into an ordinary module in VBA, and the code would be

```
Function FilterData(mySource As Excel.Range, myCrit As Excel.Range,
    myDest As Excel.Range,
    Optional blnUnique As Boolean) As Boolean
    mySource.AdvancedFilter Action:=xlFilterCopy, _
        CriteriaRange:=myCrit, _
        CopyToRange:=myDest, _
        Unique:=False
End Function
```

So, with very few lines of VBA code, Advanced Filter can be automated and as the user changes any values within the Criteria area, so the data gets filtered very quickly. This is the way in which I prefer to use Advanced Filter, as you don't have to manually invoke advanced Filter every time you change any of the criteria.

Merely changing the value in any of the cells within the criteria range cause an immediate change in the result on my destination sheet reflecting just the rows of data which match the new criteria.

Where Tables are involved, as stated earlier, Excel will give an error if the Destination Table is totally empty (i.e. has no entries in any cells below the header row). Within VBA, it throws Error 1004 (which is the wrong error anyway) and the code would stop running. So there is an extra step in the procedure for the event code sitting behind the sheet Extract Tables to deal with this.

The code tests to see if the Destination table is empty, and if so then it writes a number 1 into the first cell of the table. It doesn't matter what is written there, it just ensures that the table is not empty, and the code will then run. Whatever has been entered there will be overwritten by any data which is extracted from the source by Advanced Filter.

```
Private Sub Worksheet_Change(ByVal Target As Range)
    Dim mySource As Range, myCrit As Range, myDest As Range
    Application.EnableEvents = False ' switch off events to prevent second call
    Set myCrit = Range("B2").CurrentRegion ' change B2 to suit
    If Not Intersect(Target, myCrit) Is Nothing Then
        ' channged cell is within Criteria range then continue
        Set mySource = Sheets("Data Table").ListObjects("tbData").Range
        Set myDest = Me.ListObjects("tbDest").HeaderRowRange
        ' because the Destination is a table, ensure that the table is not empty.
        ' If it is, populate first row before proceeding
        If Me.ListObjects("tbDest:).DataBodyRange Is Nothing Then ' table is empty
            Range("B11") = 1 ' write 1 to 1st cell of table to prevent it being empty
        End If
        Call FilterData(mySource, myCrit, myDest) ' carry out Advanced Filter
        Call ResizeTable ' Filtering to a Table: resize the table after filtering
    End If
    Application.EnableEvents = True ' switch events back on
End Sub
```

As mentioned earlier in the chapter, Advanced Filter will not cause the Table to automatically resize itself after the filter has taken place. Also, at the end of the routine, it calls another macro to resize the table.

If you ask VBA to find the last row used on a sheet which contains a Table, it will find the last row of a Table, regardless of whether there is any data at all within those rows. So essentially, the macro has to first convert the table to have just a single data row after the header. Then it can determine where the true last row exists. It then resizes the Table again, and this time sets its length so that it includes all of the rows of data that have been extracted with Advanced Filter.

I have noticed that on many occasions when running this ResizeTable code (which I use whenever I have written any data to a Table just to be sure I have the correct size), it sometimes changes the formatting in the first row of the table. For this reason, I have added two lines of code which copy the format from row 2 of the table and paste the formats to row 1.

```
Sub ResizeTable()
    Dim T As Variant, lr As Long, fc As Long, fr As Long
    Set T = ActiveSheet.ListObjects(1)
    If Not T Is Nothing Then T.Resize T.Range.Resize(2)
    fc = T.DataBodyRange.Column    ' first column of table
    fr = T.HeaderRowRange.Row
    lr = Cells(Rows.Count, fc).End(xlUp).Row - fr ' last row used in 1st col. of table
    T.Resize T.Range.Resize(lr + 1)
        ' sometimes row 1 gets formatted differently by this routine
        ' so copy row 2 format to row 1
    ActiveSheet.ListObjects(1).ListRows(2).Range.Copy
    ActiveSheet.ListObjects(1).ListRows(1).Range.PasteSpecial xlPasteFormats
End Sub
```

Power Query: Manipulate Your Data Like a Pro
by Frédéric le Guen

Whatever your job and the way you use Excel, one thing is common when you start an Excel workbook: you need to manipulate and manage your data source. This is where Power Query may help you.

Presentation of Power Query

Let's be honest, the name is not friendly. If you are not a little bit curious, you will miss this amazing tool. The best to present and to understand Power Query is to know its genesis.

Genesis of Power Query

In 2012, a new "beta" project was released by the Microsoft developers. The purpose of this tool was to simplify the way to collect and manage data. Its name was brilliant: **Data Explorer**.

In 2013, with the release of Office 2013, Data Explorer was still under development. However, other great tools had been added in the meantime, like Power Pivot, Power View, and Power Maps. To keep the same name strategy for the new tools of Excel 2013, the COM add-in Data Explorer was renamed **Power Query** (now that makes sense to me).

Then, for the release of Excel 2016 and Office 365, Power Query was directly added to the Data tab in the ribbon. It seemed that the name Power Query had been changed to **Get & Transform**. This didn't go down too well

Of course, as an Extract, Transform & Load (ETL) tool, **Get & Transform** is more understandable. However, when you want to do a research on the web, the keyword Power Query returns much more result than Get & Transform. A compromise appears to have been met. The tool is still in the 'Get & Transform' grouping of the Data tab, but when opened it now reveals the Power Query Editor. Clear!?

Note: even if the official name is Get and Transform, all the users still call it Power Query.

Where is Power Query on the Ribbon?

It depends on the version you have.

With Excel 2013, the only way to get Power Query is to download the add-in on the Microsoft website (https://www.microsoft.com/en-us/download/details.aspx?id=39379). When the add-in is installed, Power Query appears on its own tab:

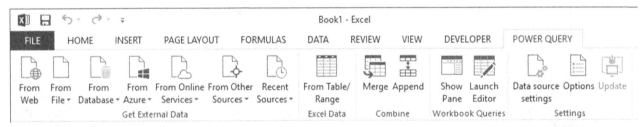

Power Query menu for Excel 2013.

With Excel 2016, Power Query is reachable directly from the Data tab:

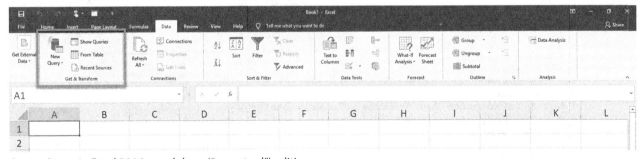

Power Query in Excel 2016 standalone ("perpetual") edition.

With Office 365 and Excel 2019, Power Query is still on the Data tab, but it has moved to first position, on the left. The former connectors under the earlier 'Get External Data' grouping have been removed because they are out of date.

Power Query in later Excel editions.

Note: The localization of Power Query means your version may not look as above, but the functionalities are the same.

Secure Your Source of Data

When you open a text file in a spreadsheet, Excel converts it to be readable. In that way, you are in edit mode regarding the source. If you do some manipulations on your file and you forget to save it with a new name, you will change your original file and that might not be a good thing!

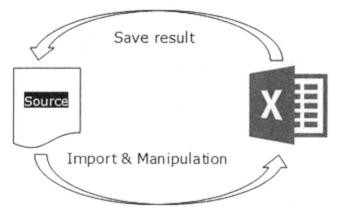

Making changes may affect the source.

With Power Query, the logic is different. The tool connects to your source (text file, Excel file, database, …) in read only mode. Then, in the Power Query interface, you can arrange your data as you require and finally, you may load your modification into a spreadsheet.

How Power Query differs when you edit it.

Connecting to Power Query

Let's see how Power Query can help us to import data. We have the following document and we want to import it into a worksheet:

```
Report: IV056R                    Tracking report - Details of the tracking point
  Date: 10/04/19                          Cur Plant: City of Tamaris

  | |XXXX    |Document          |Station      |Created Date |Created Time|Created by |Article ID    |Familly Doc.
  | |001     |B4F03511584900001 |C-BOUC3C01   |05.04.2019   |09:51:45    |8S7ED55    |BO0000192741  |BOX
  | |001     |                  |C-WKZ-USMSOR |04.04.2019   |17:18:27    |ST15793    |BO0000192741  |BOX
  | |001     |                  |C-WKZSVZAK   |05.04.2019   |07:22:32    |8S7FF59    |BO0000192741  |BOX
  | |001     |                  |D-C31P18     |05.04.2019   |10:05:47    |8S7ED55    |BO0000192741  |BOX
  | |001     |                  |D-CC01Q      |05.04.2019   |08:15:57    |8S7FF59    |BO0000192741  |BOX
  | |001     |                  |ZCO8SO-OUT-I |04.04.2019   |17:18:05    |ST15793    |PL0025540001  |BOX
  | |001     |                  |ZLR0200120   |02.04.2019   |19:25:03    |8S7F434    |PL0025540001  |BOX
  | |001     |B4F03511584910001 |C-WKZ-USMSOR |04.04.2019   |18:05:55    |ST15793    |BO0000192742  |
```

Sample data.

Analyse the File

At the first glance, the file looks easy to manipulate. However, when you look at it carefully, there are a lot of difficulties in this file, such as you might wish to:

- remove the first three columns.
- remove the first four rows of the file.
- make the fifth row the header of our final document.
- make the report more complex.
- merge the date and time, which are presently in two different columns.
- ensure the 'Document ID' contains data.
- add a special column: when the column 'Familly Doc.' *(sic)* contains 'BOX', we need to extract the last six digits of the 'Article ID'.

Connect to a CSV or Text File

To load a CSV or text file in Power Query, it's very easy. In Excel, go to the Data tab on the ribbon, select 'From Text/CSV' and then choose your file.

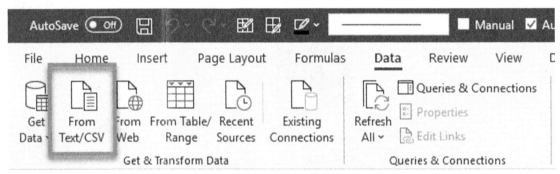

Selecting a Text / CSV file.

I am going to choose the file 'Example_PQ_1.txt'. Once I have located it, Power Query opens a dialog box, where we may click on 'Transform Data':

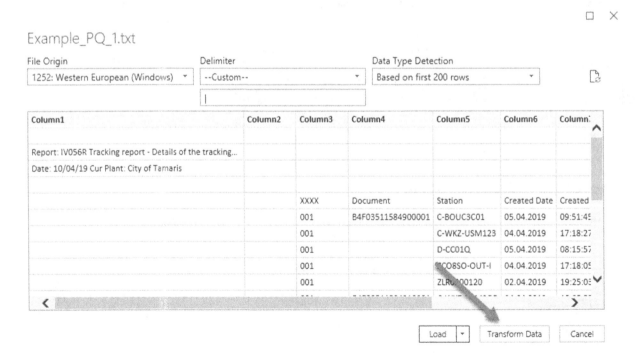

Selecting the file and choosing to transform the data.

The Power Query Interface

When your file is loaded, it opens on the following interface

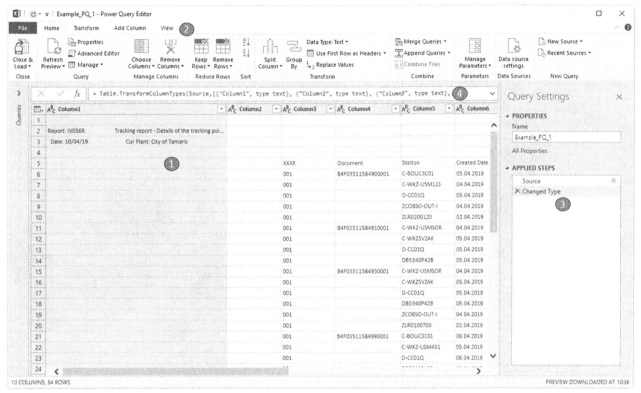

The Power Query Editor.

The grid (highlighted as item 1, above) looks exactly like Excel, but here you can't modify the contain of any cell; it's all read only.

To manipulate the data, you can find all the tools in the ribbon (item 2), just like in Excel. Each manipulation is recorded (see 'APPLIED STEPS', item 3), and you can follow the process of importation in this part of the screen.

You can then visualize the code generated by Power Query in the formula bar (item 4). By default, the formula bar is not displayed. To display the formula bar, simply go to the View tab and tick the checkbox.

One of the main reasons to use Power Query to connect to any source of data is the fact that you can load millions of records with little restriction, that being chiefly the memory of your computer. On the other hand, you are not in an Excel worksheet. That means, for example, you can't navigate to the end of your list easily.

Your First Manipulations with Power Query

It's time now to play with Power Query!

Step 1: Connection to the Source

We have seen on that it's very easy to connect Power Query to a source (e.g. CSV, Excel, text). More than that, in the case of a CSV / text files, Power Query has 'guessed' the delimiter between the columns.

You can display the detail of each step by clicking on the gear icon on each step in the 'APPLIED STEPS' section. For example, for the step 'Source', you can see all the arguments used for the import.

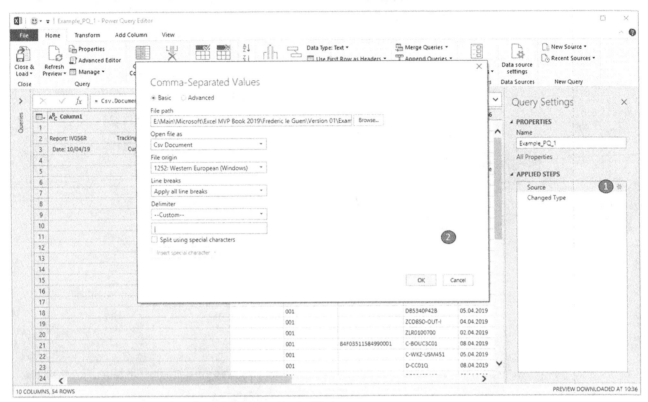

In the dialog box, you can see that the delimiter used is the "|" character.

Step 2: Changed Type

Did you see, another step has been added automatically? It's the step 'Changed Type'. Power Query can detect the type of data (e.g. date, decimal, text) for each column (field) of your import.

However, in our example, this step is not useful yet because the file is not clean. Let's add some cleaning (transformation) steps and we will apply another detection of the data type later.

To remove a step, you simply have to point your mouse cursor before a step's name to display the delete icon:

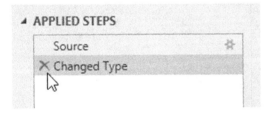

Deleting a step.

All you have to do is click on the red cross that appears. Steps can be deleted out of sequence – unlike in Excel – but be *very* careful if you do that.

Step 3: Remove the First Four Rows

To remove the first four rows, select the menu Home -> Remove Rows -> Remove Top Rows, ensuring you are in the final step of 'APPLIED STEPS' (and check this for all subsequent actions too).

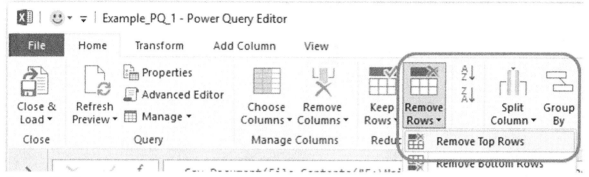

Remove Top Rows.

Choose the value four (4) in the resulting dialog box:

Deleting the top four rows.

Step 4: Remove the First Three Columns

Removing a column is very easy to do because the action is similar in a spreadsheet. To do this:

1. Select the first column (here, Column 1).
2. Hold down the Shift key.
3. Select the last column of your selection (here, Column 3).

This selects all the columns between the Columns 1 and 3 inclusive. Then, you may right-click on the *header* of one of the columns selected (you can use the 'Remove Columns' button on the Home tab too).

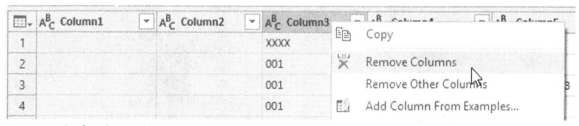

Removing the first three columns.

Step 5: Remove Spaces Before and After (Trim)

This step is not necessarily obvious, but when you import data, especially from a text file, there are often blank characters before or after the text strings. If you ignore unrequired blank characters, there is a risk that the data type will not be detected properly (e.g. dates, time, numbers).

With Power Query, you may easily remove all the *unnecessary* blanks of your cells (this is known as "trimming"):

1. Select your first column for trimming.
2. Press the Shift key.
3. Select the last column for trimming.
4. Right-click on the header.

5. Go to Transform -> Trim (again, this may be achieved by going to the 'Transform' tab, clicking on the 'Format' drop-down and selecting 'Trim).

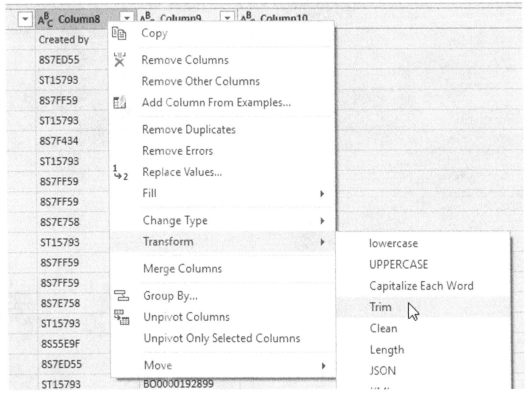

Trimming your data.

Step 6: Use the First Row as Headers

Quick summary so far: we have selected all the rows and columns that we wish to keep, and we have trimmed all the relevant cells. Now, we are going to indicate that the first row will be the header of our document. This is also known as promoting headers. To do this, simply click on the header icon and select the option 'Use First Row as Headers':

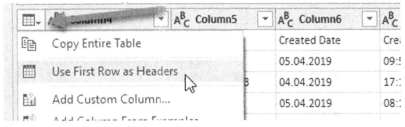

Use the first row as headers.

Remark about the data type

Once again, Power Query has added automatically a step to detect the data type, but this time we will keep it. Since we have removed all the extra blank spaces on a previous step, Power Query is now able to detect all the types of data for all your columns. However, you should always check this to be sure.

Changed Type step added automatically after promoting headers.

You easily visualize the type of data with the icon on the right of the header; a calendar for the date, a clock for the time, ABC for text, and so on. Also, at any time, you can request that Power Query detects your data type with the option Transform -> Detect Data Type.

Step 7: Fill the Empty Cells

Now it's time to see how Power Query can perform more complex tasks. The column Document has a lot of empty cells. We must make amends.

1. Select the Document column.
2. Right-click on the header of this column.
3. From the menu, select Fill -> Down.

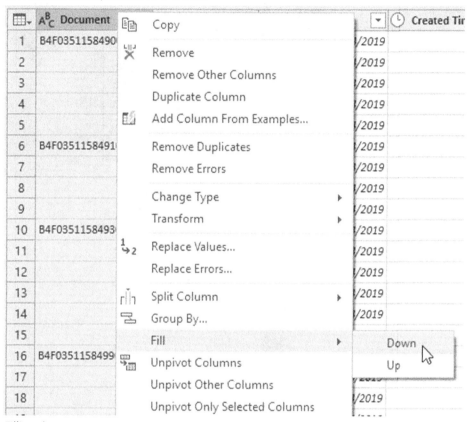

Filling down.

Unfortunately, this action will not fill the empty cells. Why? This is because the cells are technically not empty and only empty cells may be filled. For Power Query, an empty cell always has the indication *null*. However, in the Document column, none of the cells that look empty have this indication. Therefore, we must add a step where we replace nothing by null (it looks silly, but it works!). Having deleted this step:

1. Select the Document column.
2. Right-click on the header.
3. Select 'Replace Values'.

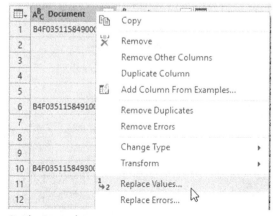

Replacing values.

In the dialog box, let the first text box remain empty and type "null" (in lower case – Power Query is often case sensitive) in the 'Replace With' box.

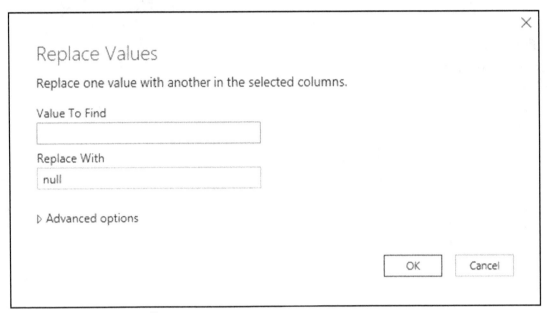

Replacing nothing with "null".

Now, the Document column is suitable for filling.

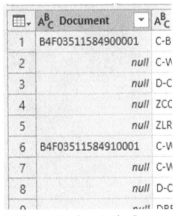

Nulls now in place in the Document column.

We can now fill down on all the empty cells:

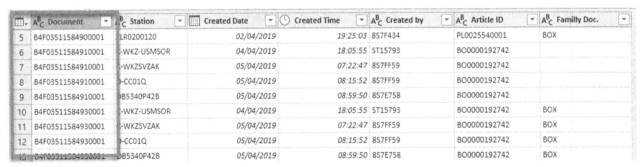

	Document	Station	Created Date	Created Time	Created by	Article ID	Familly Doc.
5	B4F03511584900001	LR0200120	02/04/2019	19:25:03	8S7F434	PL0025540001	BOX
6	B4F03511584910001	-WKZ-USMSOR	04/04/2019	18:05:55	ST15793	BO0000192742	
7	B4F03511584910001	-WKZSVZAK	05/04/2019	07:22:47	8S7FF59	BO0000192742	
8	B4F03511584910001	-CC01Q	05/04/2019	08:15:52	8S7FF59	BO0000192742	
9	B4F03511584910001	B5340P42B	05/04/2019	08:59:50	8S7E758	BO0000192742	
10	B4F03511584930001	-WKZ-USMSOR	04/04/2019	18:05:55	ST15793	BO0000192742	BOX
11	B4F03511584930001	-WKZSVZAK	05/04/2019	07:22:47	8S7FF59	BO0000192742	BOX
12	B4F03511584930001	-CC01Q	05/04/2019	08:15:52	8S7FF59	BO0000192742	BOX
13	B4F03511584930001	B5340P42B	05/04/2019	08:59:50	8S7E758	BO0000192742	BOX

Document column after filling down.

Note: This step is a little bit tricky because of the null cell but in reality, nothing is hard. I shall be trying my hand at neurosurgery next week.

Step 8: Merge Date and Time

We want to merge the columns 'Created Date' and 'Created Time'. However, because the data types for the two fields are different, this task is not so easy – but then again, it's not so difficult with Power Query!

1. Select the 'Created Date' column.

2. Press the Ctrl key.
3. Select the 'Created Time' column (the order of selection is very important, as columns will be joined in order).
4. Go to the Transform tab.
5. Open the Date menu.
6. Select 'Combine Date and Time'.

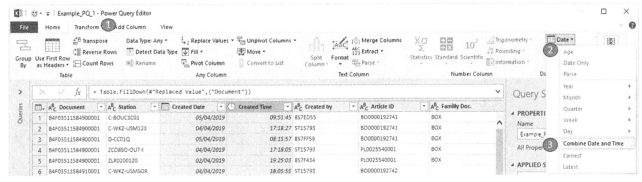

Combining data and time.

This creates the following Merged column, which replaces the two source fields:

	AᴮC Document	AᴮC Station	ABC 123 Merged	AᴮC Created by	AᴮC Article ID	AᴮC Family Doc.
1	B4F03511584900001	C-BOUC3C01	05/04/2019 09:51:45	8S7ED55	BO0000192741	BOX
2	B4F03511584900001	C-WKZ-USM123	04/04/2019 17:18:27	ST15793	BO0000192741	BOX
3	B4F03511584900001	D-CC01Q	05/04/2019 08:15:57	8S7FF59	BO0000192741	BOX
4	B4F03511584900001	ZCO8SO-OUT-I	04/04/2019 17:18:05	ST15793	PL0025540001	BOX
5	B4F03511584900001	ZLR0200120	02/04/2019 19:25:03	8S7F434	PL0025540001	BOX
6	B4F03511584910001	C-WKZ-USMSOR	04/04/2019 18:05:55	ST15793	BO0000192742	

Creating the Merged column.

In this step, we have replaced the 'Created Date' and 'Created Time' columns with the new column 'Merged'. You may perform a similar action with the 'Add Column' tab. In that case, the result is displayed in a new column and you keep your two original columns. 'Add Column' does exactly what it says on the tin.

Step 9: Add a Column with a Condition

As you can see, with Power Query, you can easily manipulate your data, but you can do so much more. You may also transform your data by creating conditional columns (columns created subject to a logical test, like an IF statement or conditional formatting in Excel).

You can also create a column by example. Strictly speaking, you can add 'Column From Examples'. This is magic! You write the result you expect, and Power Query understands your need and writes your result. Let me show you.

First, we want to extract the last six characters of the 'Article ID' column.

1. Select the 'Article ID' column.
2. Select the 'Add column' tab.
3. Then click on 'Column From Examples.'
4. However, ensure you choose 'From Selection'.

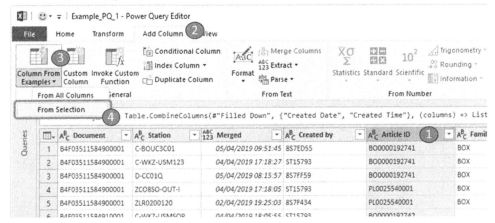

Adding Column From Examples From Selection.

This action adds a new column, but it's an input dynamic column where you type in what you want Power Query to return and the calculation engine tries to figure out what you are trying to do. Just as with genies, you get three wishes (attempts)!

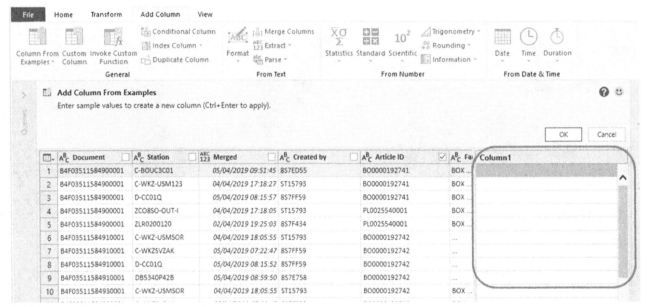

Add Column From Examples input column.

Thus, you write '192741' and immediately Power Query shows you the following result:

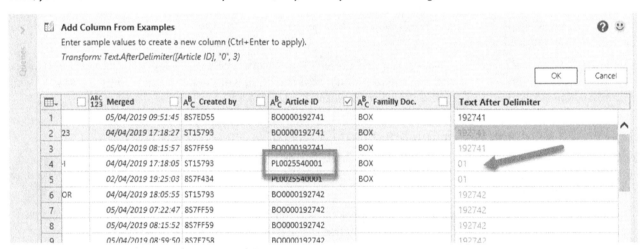

Power Query attempts to guess what you are doing.

As you can see, the whole column is populated but there are some mistakes. No problem! Just correct the wrong result with the result you want.

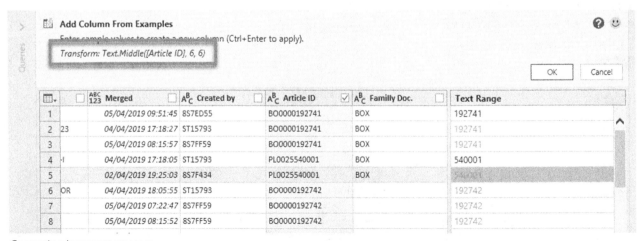

Correcting incorrect guesses.

Now we have what we want. The more you fill cells, the more you teach Power Query. Once you are satisfied, click on OK and you have a new column, 'Text Range'.

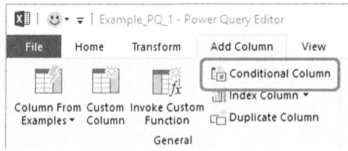

#	Document	Station	Merged	Created by	Article ID	Familly Doc.	Text Range
1	B4F03511584900001	C-BOUC3C01	05/04/2019 09:51:45	8S7ED55	BO0000192741	BOX	192741
2	B4F03511584900001	C-WKZ-USM123	04/04/2019 17:18:27	ST15793	BO0000192741	BOX	192741
3	B4F03511584900001	D-CC01Q	05/04/2019 08:15:57	8S7FF59	BO0000192741	BOX	192741
4	B4F03511584900001	ZCO8SO-OUT-I	04/04/2019 17:18:05	ST15793	PL0025540001	BOX	540001
5	B4F03511584900001	ZLR0200120	02/04/2019 19:25:03	8S7F434	PL0025540001	BOX	540001
6	B4F03511584910001	C-WKZ-USMSOR	04/04/2019 18:05:55	ST15793	BO0000192742		192742
7	B4F03511584910001	C-WKZSVZAK	05/04/2019 07:22:47	8S7FF59	BO0000192742		192742

Accepting the correct formula.

Now, we are going to use this result to create a conditional column. Eagle-eyed readers will note the 'Familly Doc.' column is misspelt. Don't worry for now. We will sort that out soon.

In the meantime, if the column 'Familly Doc.' contains the word 'BOX' then we wish Power Query to return the contents of the newly-created column, 'Text Range'.

You must be getting sick of me saying this, but again, it's very simple. Go to the 'Add Column' tab and select 'Conditional Column':

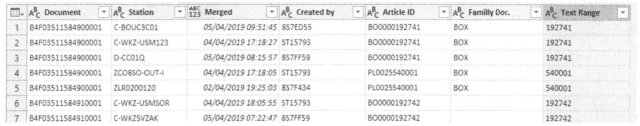

Location of 'Conditional Column'.

1. Create your condition by selecting the 'Familly Doc.' Column.
2. Ensure the 'Operator' is 'equals'.
3. Write the value to test (here 'BOX').
4. Click on the Output button.
5. Select the option 'Select a column'.

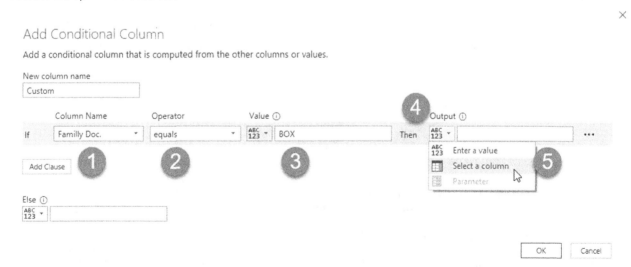

Using 'Conditional Column' is easy.

Finally, select 'Text Range', the column we have just created:

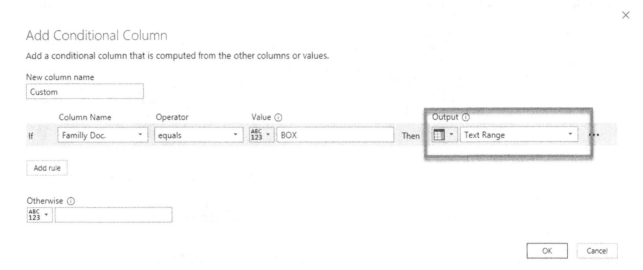

Selecting 'Text Range'.

Click on OK and a new column is added with our rule:

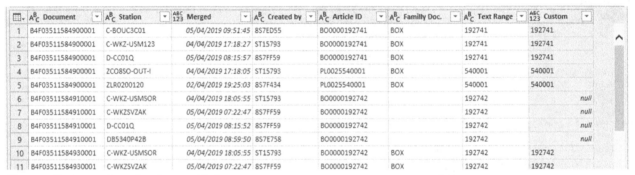

The new Custom column has been added.

Step 10: Remove and Renaming Columns

The column 'Text Range' has been created simply to generate the conditional column. We don't need to keep it.

> **Note**: That's the beauty of Power Query: you may remove temporary columns without breaking your result.

To do this:

- Go to the header of the 'Text Range' field.
- Right-click.
- Select 'Remove'.
- At the same time, we should really sort out that misspelt field:
- Go to the header of the 'Familly Doc.' field.
- Right-click.
- Select 'Rename…' and try something the English language might recognize instead.
- You may wish to consider renaming the 'Merged' column too.

Step 11: Load the result into Excel

We have finished all the transformations on our file, as far as this chapter is concerned. It's time to load the result into Excel.

- Go to the Home tab.
- Click on 'Close & Load'.

Close & Load.

This inserts the result into Excel:

	A	B	C	D	E	F
1	Document	Station	Date and Time	Created by	Article ID	Family Doc.
2	B4F03511584900001	C-BOUC3C01	05/04/2019 09:51	8S7ED55	BO0000192741	BOX
3	B4F03511584900001	C-WKZ-USM123	04/04/2019 17:18	ST15793	BO0000192741	BOX
4	B4F03511584900001	D-CC01Q	05/04/2019 08:15	8S7FF59	BO0000192741	BOX
5	B4F03511584900001	ZCO8SO-OUT-I	04/04/2019 17:18	ST15793	PL0025540001	BOX
6	B4F03511584900001	ZLR0200120	02/04/2019 19:25	8S7F434	PL0025540001	BOX
7	B4F03511584910001	C-WKZ-USMSOR	04/04/2019 18:05	ST15793	BO0000192742	
8	B4F03511584910001	C-WKZSVZAK	05/04/2019 07:22	8S7FF59	BO0000192742	
9	B4F03511584910001	D-CC01Q	05/04/2019 08:15	8S7FF59	BO0000192742	
10	B4F03511584910001	DB5340P42B	05/04/2019 08:59	8S7E758	BO0000192742	
11	B4F03511584930001	C-WKZ-USMSOR	04/04/2019 18:05	ST15793	BO0000192742	BOX
12	B4F03511584930001	C-WKZSVZAK	05/04/2019 07:22	8S7FF59	BO0000192742	BOX
13	B4F03511584930001	D-CC01Q	05/04/2019 08:15	8S7FF59	BO0000192742	BOX
14	B4F03511584930001	DB5340P42B	05/04/2019 08:59	8S7E758	BO0000192742	BOX

The output loads into Excel as a Table.

Note: If selecting 'Close & Load' for the first time, the result is always loaded inside a Table in Excel.

Conclusion

As you can see, with Power Query it's very easy to manipulate a file. In this chapter, I have shown you some of the manipulation you can do but there is so much more.

Be curious and try by yourself to test the other tools. It's safe because if one action doesn't return what you want, just remove it from the steps list.

If you want to discover more about Power Query, refer to these chapters.

- Ken Puls' "Combine All Files in a Folder" on page 132
- Mike Girvin's "Power Query M Code Approximate Match Lookup Formula" on page 145
- Tony de Jonker's "Financial Modelling" on page 188

Combine All Files in a Folder

by Ken Puls

A common problem that faces many users is the job of consolidating multiple files into a single file for use in reporting or analysis. In the classic world of Excel, this would involve the following steps:

- Collect each data source file.
- Open each file and transform the data into a consistent format.
- Copy the transformed data from the source file and paste it into the 'Master' file.
- Make sure the reports are all updated.

So what could possibly go wrong? Besides the amount of manual effort wasted in consolidating the data, this process exposes us to a variety of potential issues including:

- Rows getting missed when clearing the historical 'Master' file.
- Data not being transformed consistently in each source file (the more complicated the data transformation required, the more likely this could happen).
- Data rows getting missed during the copy.
- Someone pasting the copied data over one or more rows of the consolidated set.
- Reports pointing at last period's ranges don't get updated to refer to the current data range.

Tedious, manual and fraught with peril, no one should be doing this work manually today. Why? Because you have Power Query to make it easy and refreshable, eliminating every potential issue listed above.

Recipe Summary

Power Query provides you with the ability to import, clean up and append the data from all files in a folder very easily (for example, see Frédéric le Guen's "Power Query: Manipulate Your Data Like a Pro" on page 118). In addition, it follows a specific set of steps each and every time. This chapter will explain each of those steps in full detail with examples, but we also wanted to provide you with a quick reference guide so that you can return here later, and easily apply this to your own data. Rather than stuff it at the end of the chapter, we're throwing it right up front so you have the summary, as well as a quick road map of where this chapter will take you.

The recipe for combining all files in a folder is as follows:

Step 1 – Create a FilesList Query

- Connect to your data source using the appropriate Step 0 from this chapter.
- Filter to specific subfolders as required
- Rename the query to FilesList.
- Convert the Extension column to lowercase.
- Filter the Extension column to only the extension you need.
- Filter the Name column to exclude file names that begin with the ~ character.
- Load the Query as a Connection Only query.

Step 2 – Combine the Files

- Right click the FilesList query and choose Reference.
- Immediately rename the query from FilesList (2) to a more sensible name.
- Click the ⬇ (Combine Files) button.
- Choose the table, range, or worksheet you wish to retrieve.

Step 3 – Modify the Transform Sample Query

- Select the Sample Transform query.
- Perform data cleanup and reshaping as required.

Step 4 – Modify the Master Transform Query

- Return to the Master transform query.
- Remove and replace the Changed Type step if it errors.
- Perform any additional data cleanup and reshaping as required.
- (Re)define the data types for all columns.
- Load the query to your desired destination.

That's all there is to it, as you'll see if you follow along.

Example Files

To illustrate both the process and the benefits of Power Query's combine files experience, let's look at a real-world business problem.

You've been hired to work as an analyst at Data Monkey Inc., a manufacturing company with four divisions: East, West, North and South. They make 10 different products, which require different combinations of six different parts in order to assemble the finished products.

You've been tasked with creating a summary of the parts that they'll need to order to satisfy production for the next quarter. Specifically, you've been asked for a list that shows the data in this format:

	A	B	C
1	Part Nbr	Ship To	Units
2	Part 1	North	3,490
3	Part 1	South	16,861
4	Part 1	West	5,268
5	Part 1	East	7,883
6	Part 2	West	13,968
7	Part 2	North	13,234
8	Part 2	South	12,877
9	Part 2	East	25,119

Format required for data.

Your predecessor set up an Excel "template" file for the plant managers to work out the number of parts they need. That template contains two worksheets:

- The Matrix worksheet, which contains a parts matrix by product, formatted as a "proper" Excel Table.
- The 'Forecast' worksheet, which forecasts the total number of parts needed based on the production forecast.

The only problem? While the data is formatted to *look* like a proper Excel Table, it's just a pretty range, and not a Table at all.

While you would love to fix the template, the reality is that the files have already been submitted, and you don't have the time right now to re-architect it. You've decided that you'll just have to roll with it as is this quarter, and figure out how to work with data that is in the following format:

Production Forecast					
For the quarter ending Dec 31, 2019					
Units to Produce	1,896	1,396	1,143	1,756	6,191
Parts needed by product					
Part Nbr	Product A	Product B	Product C	Product D	Total
Part 1	-	-	-	5,268	5,268
Part 2	3,792	1,396	-	8,780	13,968
Part 3	3,792	6,980	-	5,268	16,040
Part 4	-	4,188	2,286	7,024	13,498
Part 5	3,792	6,980	5,715	1,756	18,243
Part 6	1,896	6,980	3,429	5,268	17,573
Total	13,272	26,524	11,430	33,364	84,590

Production Forecast example.

In addition, just to add another wrinkle, not every division produces the same products. The West division (shown above) only produces Products A-D. Further, while the East division produces Products A-F, the North only produces Products E-G and South produces Products H-J. This means that both the number and names of the columns to be combined are variable.

The final problem that you will be facing is that the system architect didn't include the division's name anywhere within the file contents. Instead, the managers save the workbook with their divisional name (North, South, East or

West), and email the workbook to you. You have decided to save each of these files into a folder on a network drive under the following file path:

```
H:\Production\Source Data\2019 Q4
```

Step 0:   Connecting to a Folder

There are three potential options when you want to consolidate files in a folder. You can combine files in one of:

- Local / Network folder
- SharePoint folder
- OneDrive for Business folder.

Note: Unfortunately, there is no connector to be able to connect to the web-based version of a OneDrive (personal) folder that is hosted in the cloud, although you can connect to a locally synced version on your computer by using the Local / Network folder option.

Step 0A: Connecting to a Local / Network Folder

Connecting to a local folder or subfolder with Power Query is fairly straight forward:

- Go to Data -> Get Data -> From File -> From Folder
- Browse to the folder you wish to use -> select it -> click OK

Note: Where possible, it's a good idea to connect to a UNC file path (Uniform Naming Convention, such as \\ Server\Volume\File), rather than a mapped network drive. While they both go to the same place, a solution that targets a UNC path is more portable than one targeting a mapped drive, as there is a chance that users will have mapped different drive letters to the same UNC path.

Caution: Files stored in folders synced to OneDrive or SharePoint return the web path upon opening. This can cause dynamically sourced file paths to fail upon update as Local / SharePoint connectors are different! To force a workbook to open ignore the web path, pause OneDrive syncing, then re-open the workbook:
    Right click OneDrive -> Pause Syncing -> 2 Hours.

Step 0B: Connecting to a SharePoint Folder

Connecting to a SharePoint folder is a bit trickier than connecting to a local or network folder. There are two reasons for this:

- You have to locate the correct URL to connect to
- No matter which folder you want, you MUST connect to the root of the SharePoint site, then filter and drill down to find the folder you want.

Determining the Path to Your SharePoint Folder

The easiest way to determine the path to a SharePoint folder is to open a web browser and navigate to that folder in SharePoint. Once done, the full URL will be shown in the address bar at the top of the page and the correction portion can be extracted.

The rule of thumb to do this is to look for the term "/Forms/" in the URL, then back up and take everything before the previous "/" character.

For example:

```
https://<SharePointDomain>/sites/orders/rockets/Forms/AllItems.aspx

<----------- connect to this --------->|<---- ignore all this ---->
```

Connecting to the SharePoint Folder

Once the URL is known, simply use the SharePoint connector to connect to the root of the folder:

- Go to Data -> Get Data -> From File -> From SharePoint Folder
- Enter the URL as determined above
- Log in when requested.

Note: If you are using an Office365 backed site, you'll need to log in with the Office365 authentication. If you're using an internal SharePoint install, you may need to use Windows credentials. If one doesn't work, try using your credentials using the other option.

Step 0C: Connecting to a OneDrive for Business Folder

Connecting to the cloud hosted OneDrive for Business folder has some similar setup and challenges to working with a SharePoint folder. This shouldn't be surprising, as OneDrive for Business is just a personal folder on SharePoint after all!

Like SharePoint connections, there are two issues:

- You have to locate the correct URL to connect to.
- No matter which folder you want, you MUST connect to the root of the OneDrive for Business (SharePoint) site, then filter and drill down to find the folder you want.

Note: If you prefer, you can always connect to the locally synced version of this folder using the steps from Step 0A.

Determining the Path to Your OneDrive for Business Folder

In order to work with a OneDrive for Business folder, you need to know both your organization's official Office 365 tenant name (which is usually different from your domain), as well as the correctly formatted version of your email address.

The easiest way to determine both of these items is again to just browse to your OneDrive from Business folder in your favorite web browser. The URL will be presented for you as follows:

```
https://<tenant>-my.sharepoint.com/personal/<email>
```

At this point, you'll be able to learn both your tenant name, as well as see how your email address gets manifested for SharePoint with all periods "." and "@" symbols replaced with underscores.

Assume, for example, that Joe's email is joe@datamonkey.com, and the datamonkey.com domain is registered to the diybi.onmicrosoft.com tenant. When navigating to his OneDrive for Business folder in a web browser, the URL for Joe's account would show as follows:

```
https://diybi-my.sharepoint.com/personal/joe_datamonkey_com
```

Note: When copying this URL, ensure that you stop immediately after the email address, ignoring any other characters that may be present.

Connecting to the OneDrive for Business Folder

Armed with the URL, connecting to a OneDrive for Business folder is done via the SharePoint connector:

- Go to Data -> Get Data -> From File -> From SharePoint Folder.
- Enter the URL as determined above.
- Log in when requested.

Note: If you are using an Office365 backed site, you'll need to log in with the Office365 authentication. If you're using an internal SharePoint install, you may need to use Windows credentials. If one doesn't work, try using your credentials using the other option.

Step 1: Creating a FilesList Query

Now that we know which connectors we have available to us and how to use them, it's time to make it all happen. The first step in the process is to create a query that talks to the folder which contains the files we wish to combine. As you do this, it is important to remember a couple of Power Query's nuances:

- When combining files, they must be of consistent file types and structure internally. While we can't easily tell what the internal structure of the files looks like, we can ensure that we don't experience errors when someone drops an mp3 or txt file in our folder of Excel files. Before you begin this process, we recommend that you **ALWAYS** filter to one type of file, even if – today – there is only one type of file present.
- Power Query is case sensitive. If you filter for ".xlsx" files, Power Query will eliminate ".XLSX" files from the list. For this reason, we want to future proof our solution in case someone in the company gets their caps lock key stuck in the "On" position. (We don't want to unknowingly miss critical files in future!).

Keeping this in mind, let's walk through the process of combining and cleaning the four divisional files to create the order summary we've been asked for.

Connecting to the Data Source

Following the recipe from the summary section at the beginning of the chapter, the first step in the process is to:

- Create a new query as per the appropriate Step 0.

In this case, we've stored all the files in the following location: H:\Production\2019 Q4\Source Data. This is a mapped network drive, so we'll follow the outline of Step 0A, namely:

- Go to Data -> Get Data -> From File -> From Folder -> Browse.
- Browse to H:\Production\Source Data --> select it -> click OK -> click OK.

This will launch the Power Query preview window, which shows that we have eight files in this folder. Why eight? Power Query lists all folders and subfolders, and we actually had both Q3 and Q4 folders here:

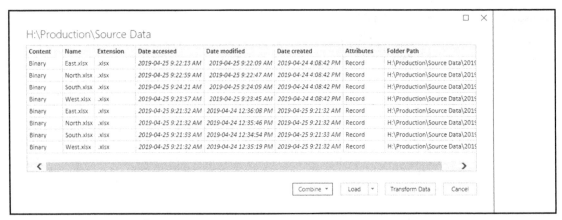

Power Query preview window.

Now, sadly, Microsoft has chosen a default button of "Combine", but don't click it! The reality is that 80% of data needs to be modified before it is useful, and this is certainly not an exception, as we need to get rid of those Q3 files...

- Click Transform Data.

> **Note:** The text on this button has been known to change as Microsoft tries to make it more enticing for users to click. The rule of thumb with Power Query dialogs is to always click the "button to the left of cancel" when prompted with a preview window.

You will now be launched into the Power Query editor where you will be looking at a detailed list of the files in the folder.

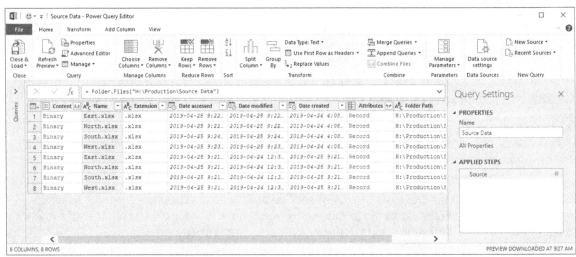

Detailed list of files in the folder.

> **Caution:** Don't worry if you don't see all the files in your folder. Power Query works with previews, so it's quite possible that the file you want to see may not fit in the preview!

Drilling into a Subfolder

Depending on the recipe you used for Step 0, you may now need to filter into a subfolder. This is easy to accomplish by simply filtering the 'Folder Path' column, but unfortunately, this column contains the entire file path to each folder, making it really hard to read and locate the one you want. To fix this, we recommend taking the following actions:

- Right click the Folder Path column header -> Replace Values.
- Replace the entire folder path you used (plus the trailing "\") in Step 0 with nothing.

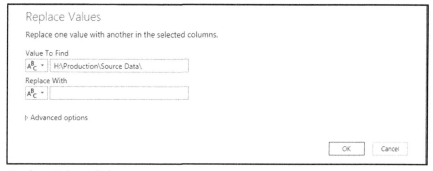

'Replace Values' dialog.

With the leading file path removed, we now have just our subfolders listed in the 'Folder Path' column, making it much easier to work with.

> **Tip**: If you didn't copy the file path, just click one of the entries in the 'Folder Path' column. This will bring up a preview window at the bottom of the screen where you can select the text and copy it for use in the 'Replace Values' dialog.

- Click the filter arrow on the Folder Path column -> un-check the '2019 Q3' folder

> **Tip**: If you need to drill down deeper into your folder structure, repeat the last 3 steps replacing the names of subfolders with nothing to drill in further

> **Warning**: If your folder contains any rows with errors, it will truncate the list, and there is nothing you can do to fix it. Should this happen, advise your IT department that you have a corrupt file in the SharePoint folder. In addition, please report the error to Microsoft using the Feedback feature so that they can issue a fix to deal with this problem.

Future-Proofing the FilesList

The next step is to make sure we add appropriate filters to safeguard against inconsistent data files. To do this:

- Right click the Extension column -> Transform -> lowercase.
- Click the filter arrow on the Extension column -> Filter -> Equals.
- Click Advanced.
- Configure the filter for 'Extension equals .xlsx and Name does not begin with ~' as shown below:

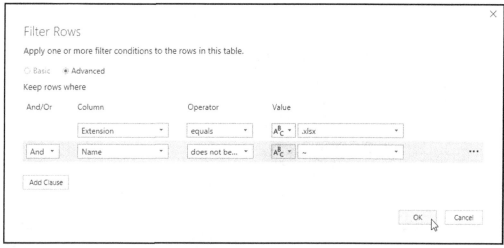

Filtering rows.

Oddly, it doesn't appear any different, but the good news is that we are now protected against file extensions that are not cased consistently, as well as file types that don't belong in our solution.

Finalizing the FilesList Query

The final step of creating the FilesList query is to:

- In the 'Query Settings' pane (on the right under Properties), change the query name to FilesList.
- Go to Home -> Close & Load -> Close & Load To...
- Change the load behavior to Connection Only.

Upon returning to Excel a 'Queries and Connections' pane pops up on the right side of the Excel window with your new query:

'Queries & Connections' pane.

> **Note**: Changing the load behavior to Connection Only allows Power Query to call this query from another query. It doesn't consume any processor or RAM until such time, so it won't bloat your file size or slow things down unnecessarily.

Step 2: Combining the Files

With the FilesList query created, we can now get set to combine all the workbook data into a single table for analysis.

Triggering the File Combination

To begin the file combination process:

- Go to the Queries & Connections pane -> right click the FilesList query -> Reference.
- Change the name of FilesList(2) to a new logical name: in this case 'Orders'.
  > **Caution**: Do not forget to rename this query before you move on to the next step. If you do, you'll end up with a bunch of queries that have misleading names!

- Click the ↓↓ (Combine Files) button at the top of the Content column.

You'll now be taken to a preview window which allows you to choose the sample file you'd like to start with:

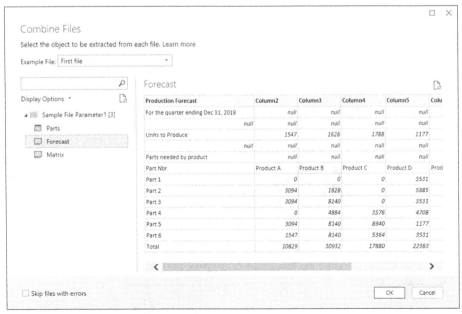

'Combine Files' dialog.

Unfortunately, due to the way Power Query interprets the FilesList query, you only have the option of using the first file in the list, even if there are more than one. The most important part of this window is the ability to choose the correct piece of data to collect from each file or workbook.

As you can see in the preview, there is a Parts table, as well as the Forecast and Matrix worksheets in this file. As mentioned previously, the system architect didn't set the Forecast up as a proper Table, so we'll just target the worksheet as shown above.

- Select the Forecast worksheet -> OK.

The Big Bang of Power Query

Once you click OK, Power Query will think for a bit, then suddenly explode with a bunch of new queries on the left-hand side of the window. This can be a bit intimidating at first, but it's entirely expected and – in fact – incredibly awesome. These queries give you a ton of power that you wouldn't have without them. But how do you know what to do with them?

The simple answer is that if it looks like a table (it has rows and columns) then it's safe for you to work with. If it doesn't, it isn't, so stay away from it. What does that mean? Let's take a look:

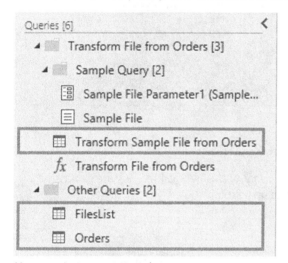

New queries are generated.

Notice the commonality between the three highlighted queries: they all have a table icon beside them. These are the three queries that are safe to play with, and the rest should just be ignored. What do they all do?

- FilesList simply generates the list of files that will be combined. You can select it and see the complete list of files you'll be working with.
- Transform Sample File from Orders is a single file from your list (the first file from the FilesList query). This query acts as a template for us to do transformations that will be applied to the rest of the files in the list.
- Orders is your Master query. This query applies the pattern defined in your sample transformation to each file, then appends those files into one big long list.
- The rest of the queries are simply helper pieces that are needed to get the job done and should be ignored.

Step 3: Modify the Transform Sample File

As it stands, Power Query has already helpfully combined all the files for us, but if you scroll up and down the display in the Orders query, you'll notice that the data of each worksheet has been appended. While the data sets have been put together in a single table, they contain every header row, and each of the pivoted tables is still shown in a stacked format. We need to clean that up.

Which Query Should You Modify?

One of the incredible benefits of the Combine Files functionality is the Transform Sample File query. This query allows us to perform our transformations as close to the data source as possible and allows us to modify data before it is appended. While it is entirely possible to unstack this data in the Orders query, it would be inefficient and complicated to do so. Using the Transform Sample File query it becomes easy, allowing us to focus on one specific file. The pattern we build there will then be applied to each file before they are appended.

Let's take a look at the data in our Transform Sample file:

- Select the Transform Sample File from Orders query (on the left).

The data should look as shown below:

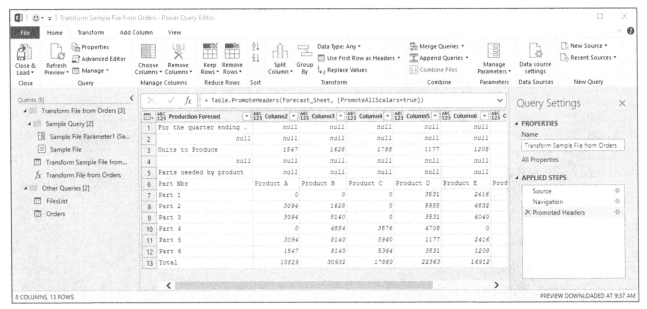

Data from Transform Sample file.

Unpivoting our Forecast File

When we look at the data, we can see that the first five rows don't add a lot of business value. They are simply the worksheet headers, and not of interest to us. Therefore, let's clean this up a little:

- Go to Home -> Remove Rows -> Remove Top Rows -> 5 -> OK.
- Go to Home -> Use First Row as Headers.
  Warning: Power Query is famous for adding data types to columns after certain operations, including promoting headers. While this can be helpful, it hard codes the column names. If we try to apply this pattern to a file without these columns, we'll get an error. For this reason, we need to remove the Changed Type step that is added to the query settings in the 'APPLIED STEPS' window.

- Go to the 'APPLIED STEPS' window (right side) -> click the X beside Changed Type.

We are now looking at our data table as shown here:

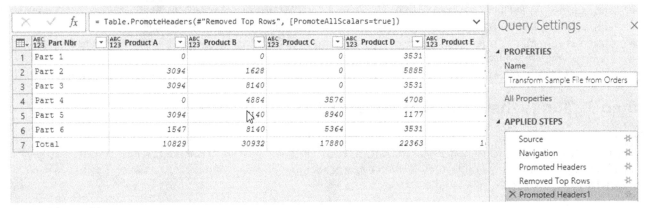

Revised data table.

This data set still contains some unnecessary data: totals and subtotals. In fact, we have both a Total row as well as a Total column. Let's get rid of them both, then unpivot the data:

- Click the filter arrow on the 'Part Nbr' column -> uncheck Total.
- Select the Total column -> press the DEL key.
- Right click the 'Part Nbr' column -> Unpivot Other Columns.

And BOOM!

⊞ ▾	ABC 123 Part Nbr	▾	A B C Attribute	▾	ABC 123 Value	▾
1	Part 1		Product A		0	
2	Part 1		Product B		0	
3	Part 1		Product C		0	
4	Part 1		Product D		3531	
5	Part 1		Product E		2416	
6	Part 1		Product F		1936	
7	Part 2		Product A		3094	

After unpivoting other columns.

Just like that, the data is unpivoted and almost ready for use. (Can you imagine having to do that manually? Yuck!)

● Double click the Attribute column's header -> change the name to Product.
● Double click the Value column's header -> change the name to Units.
● Filter the Units column -> uncheck 0.
● Click the ABC123 icon on the Part Nbr and Product columns -> set to Text.
● Click the ABC123 icon on the Units column -> set to Whole Number.

We've now completely transformed a single file into a beautifully unpivoted list which can be appended to the other files. Every action you've taken here has been recorded in the 'APPLIED STEPS' window, as well as rolled into the "Transform File from Orders" function, which can be applied to each of the files in the FilesList query before being appended in the Master query (Orders). How cool is that?

Step 4:   Modify the Master Transform

With the modifications of the Transform Sample File complete, we can now return to the Master transform (Orders) to do further processing on the combined results of all the files.

● Go to the Queries Pane on the left -> click on Orders.
Unfortunately, things often go horribly wrong at this point…

 Expression.Error: The column 'Production Forecast' of the table wasn't found.
Details:
    Production Forecast

We are presented with an 'Expression.Error'.

Dealing with Step Level Errors

This type of error is called a "Step Level" error. It occurs during one step of the query and must be dealt with before the query can continue to be processed. It's also VERY likely to occur if you make any modifications to your Transform Sample.

The cause of this error is that the 'Production Forecast' column of the table is no longer there (in fact, neither are Column1, Column2, etc.). Each of those columns was present when we originally combined the files, but when we modified the Transform Sample, we removed them by promoting a new row to headers, then unpivoting our data and renaming columns. The challenge? These names were hard coded when Power Query applied a Changed Type step in the Master query upon combing the data.

This issue is so common that it forms part of our file combination recipe:

● Go to the 'APPLIED STEPS' window -> click the X next to Changed Type step to remove it.
● Reset each of the data types by clicking the ABC123 at the top of each column and set:
  • Part Nbr -> Text.
  • Product -> Text.
  • Units -> Whole Number.

And at that point the data should look great again. But unlike the Transform Sample, which shows the contents of a single file only, you now have a table with all rows from each file combined into one long list.

The only problem? Which rows came from which division?

Preserving File Properties

If you think back to the original FilesList query, the managers all saved their forecasts using the name of their division. So how can we retain that information?

If you go to the 'APPLIED STEPS' window, you can select each of the steps and see how the query is progressing:

- Source: shows the results of the FilesList query before doing anything else.
- Filtered Hidden Files1: added during the Combine Files action, this remove hidden files from the list.
- Invoke Custom Function1: added during the Combine Files action, this step adds a new column that applies the steps to each file from our Transform Sample.
- Removed Other Columns1: removes all the columns except the Invoked Function.

It's this last step that removed the file names from the results. So, let's modify it:

- Go to 'APPLIED STEPS' window -> select Removed Other Columns1 -> click the gear icon.

This will bring up a list of all the original columns from the previous step.

- Check the box next to Name -> OK.
- Select the Changed Type step.

We have now preserved the file name as shown below:

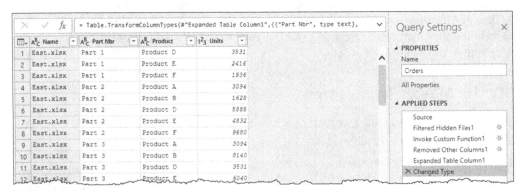

File name is now preserved.

As amazing as this is, the data isn't perfect, so let's clean it up a bit:

- Double click the header of the Name column -> change the name to 'Ship To'.
- Right click the 'Ship To' column -> Replace Values -> Replace '.xlsx' with nothing.

We are now ready to group the data by location and part number.

Performing Grouping in the Master Query

Grouping is quite easy in Power Query:

- Go to the Transform tab -> Group By.
- Click the Advanced button.
- Set up Group By levels for 'Part Nbr' first, and add a grouping for 'Ship To'.
- Configure a new column called Units which uses the SUM operation on the Units column.
- Click OK.
- Click the filter arrow on the 'Part Nbr' column -> Sort Ascending.

The final output will look exactly as we need it:

Part Nbr	Ship To	Units
1 Part 1	East	7883
2 Part 1	West	5268
3 Part 1	North	3490
4 Part 1	South	16861
5 Part 2	East	25119

Final output in Power Query Editor.

The only step left is to load the data to the worksheet:

- Go to Home -> Close & Load.

A new worksheet will be created with our finished output:

	A	B	C
1	Part Nbr ▼	Ship To ▼	Units ▼
2	Part 1	North	3,490
3	Part 1	South	16,861
4	Part 1	West	5,268
5	Part 1	East	7,883
6	Part 2	West	13,968
7	Part 2	North	13,234
8	Part 2	South	12,877
9	Part 2	East	25,119

Finished output.

Updating the Solution

Despite the fact that Power Query makes combining the files easier than the old manual methods, the real value is in the ability to update this in future when the data changes.

When an Updated Source File is Received

Dealing with an updated source file is ridiculously easy. When we get an updated file, we simply need to save it over the old one, then go to Data -> Refresh All, and the report will be updated.

When a New Division is Added

Catering for a new division is also deadly simple. Assuming we get a new division called 'Europe', we can use the same file template that the other divisions are using. We just save the new division under the name 'Europe.xlsx' into the same folder, then go to Data -> Refresh All in Excel. It's just that easy.

Updating the File Path for the Next Quarter

When we created this solution, we targeted the 2019 Q4 subfolder. Obviously, the next quarter's data will live in a different path. So how do we update this?

This does take a little bit of work, but it's not hard:

- Go to the Data tab -> Queries & Connections.
- Go to the Queries and Connections pane (on the right) -> right click FilePath -> Edit.
- Select the Filtered Rows step -> click the gear icon.
- Change the selection to use the subfolder you want -> OK.
- Go to Home -> Close & Load.

At this point the data will update to include all files in the newly selected subfolder.

Updating the File Path to a New Drive Letter

When discussing network folder paths, every file path ultimately maps back to what is called a UNC path. As explained previously, this path is unique in the network and presents in a format as follows:

```
\\ServerName\ShareName\Folder\SubFolder\
```

To make life easier for the end user, however, your IT department "maps" these UNC paths to drive letters. In the case of this example, we had a folder that was mapped to the H:\ drive, and from there we were able to build our solution against H:\Production\Source Data.

So far so good. As new files are added to the H:\Production\Source Data\ folder, you'll be able to just open the Excel workbook, go to Data -> Refresh All, and all the new files will be pulled in. It's a thing of beauty!

But then things go horribly wrong. Your colleague opens the solution, attempts to refresh and received an error:

DataSource.NotFound: File or Folder: We couldn't find the folder 'H:\Production\Source Data*'.

Details:

    H:\Production\Source Data

DataSource.NotFound error.

The challenge here is that your colleague's drive path has been mapped the network share to the J:\ drive, not the H:\ drive, so Power Query can't find it.

> **Note**: If the original path was set to the UNC path, there wouldn't have been an issue, as this path name doesn't change. It's only causing problems since the path is mapped inconsistently between the 2 devices.

So how do you fix it? You'll need to repoint the file path in Power Query. To do this:

- Go to the Data tab -> Queries & Connections.
- Right click the FilesList query in the Queries & Connections pane -> Edit.

You now have two options:

Option 1:   Modify the Source Step of the FilesList Query

To update the source step in this way:

- Select the Source step of the FilesList query.
- Click the gear icon -> Browse.
- Browse to and select the correct file path -> OK.
- Click OK to close the file path dialog.

At this point the file path will be updated, and the changes will flow through the Power Query chain. Simply click 'Close & Load' to apply them.

Option 2:   Use the Data Source Settings Button

The other option you have is to perform the following actions

- Go to Home -> Data Source Settings.
- Select the file path you wish to update -> Change Source -> Browse.
- Browse to and select the correct file path -> OK -> OK.
- Click Close to close the Data Source Settings dialog.

> **Note**: If you have not created a separate FilesList query, Option 1 will potentially cause an error. This is because the file path gets hard coded into the Sample Parameter query as well as the query used to combine the files. While this error can be avoided by using the Data Source Settings dialog, we recommend creating the FilesList query separately as it future proofs against a user causing themselves an error when they try to change a path using Option 1.

Changing the Sample File

While we advocate using the FilesList query in order to guard against errors when changing a file path, the injection of this query does cause us one problem; it removes our ability to choose which file to use as a sample, forcing us to always use the first one from the FilesList query. So how do we change that file to use a different one?

The answer is surprisingly easy: edit the FilesList query and sort it so that the file you want to use as your sample is at the top. It sounds super simple, but sometimes it can be a bit more complicated than you'd like, so here's some strategies to help:

- To create a sort, just click the drop-down arrow at the top of a column. This will give you the option to sort in Ascending or Descending order.
- Unlike Excel's default sorting, Power Query allows you to layer multiple sorts on top of each other, sorting successively within the previous results. To do this, sort one column, then just immediately sort by another.
- If you don't like your sort order, just select the step in the 'APPLIED STEPS' window and click the X to make it go away.
- You have multiple columns that can be used in your sorts, from File Names to file paths to dates and times created.
- If you can't find any other way to sort, consider going to Add Column -> Conditional Column in order to add a column that returns a value of 1 for the file you want, and 0 for everything else. You could then sort that record to the top to get it as the first file in your list.

Power Query M Code Approximate Match Lookup Formula
by Mike Girvin

The goal of this chapter is to learn how to write a Power Query M Code formula to perform an approximate match lookup. Although in an Excel Worksheet we have function like VLOOKUP to perform approximate match lookups, the equivalent single function does not exist in Power Query. To follow along with the examples in this article, open the Excel Workbook file named "MikeGirvinPowerQueryApproximateMatchLookup".

Initial Data Setup & Goal:

As seen in the picture below on the Excel Worksheet named "Tables", there is a transaction Excel Table named "Transactions", a lookup Excel Table named "Discount", and both Excel Tables have been imported into the Power Query Editor as Connection Only and renamed as "TransactionQuery" and "DiscountQuery", respectively (query names in the Queries & Connections Pane on the right).

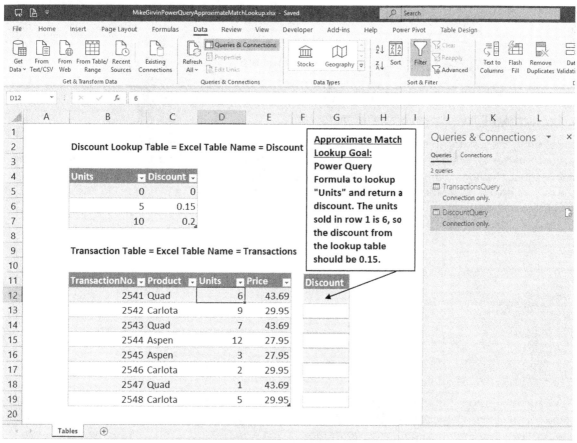

Two Excel Tables have been imported into the Power Query Editor.

To edit our queries in the Power Query Editor, double click one of the queries in the Queries & Connections Pane. The two queries can be seen in the Queries Pane on the left. The picture below shows that the "DiscountQuery" has been selected on the left and the Applied Steps for this query can be seen in the Applied Steps list in the Queries Setting Pane on the right.

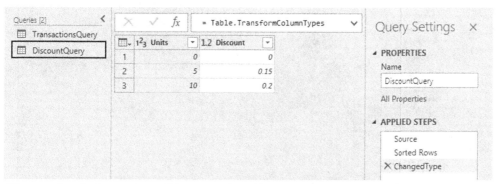

After opening the Power Query Editor, we select the DiscountQuery on the left.

Because we are going to use the lookup table in each row of the transaction table, we want to buffer the lookup table to improve the lookup formula performance. When we buffer a table, the query is allowed to pull the lookup table data, store it as a static table, and reuse it in each row of the transaction table, rather than having to call the data in each row of the transaction table as a separate and fresh query. The six steps for buffering the lookup table can be seen in the picture below. The formula used is Table.Buffer(ChangedType) and the Applied Step should be named "BufferedLookupTable". This last step is the output for the "DiscountQuery" and therefore when we use the query in a later formula, we will be using the buffered table.

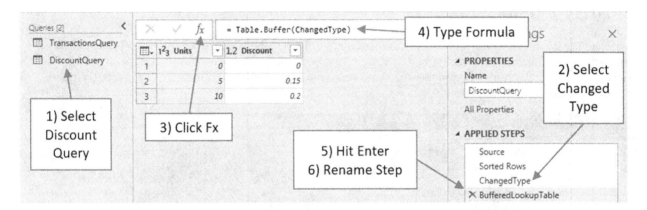

The Table.Buffer Function will buffer the table for better performance.

Next we want to bring the lookup table into each row of the transaction table. To accomplish this, we select the "TransactionQuery" in the left Queries Pane, then select the "ChangedType" Applied Step in the Query Settings Pane on the right, then go to the Add Column Ribbon Tab, then in the General group, click the Custom Column button. As seen in the picture below, create the new column, "Discount" and the custom column formula for the buffered lookup table: =DiscountQuery.

Custom Column

Add a column that is computed from the other columns.

New column name

Discount

Custom column formula ⓘ

= DiscountQuery

The buffered lookup table query name is our formula for the Custom Column.

After you click OK in the Custom Column dialog box, the buffered lookup table appears in each row in the transaction table's Discount column. Rename the Applied Step to "ApproximateLookup". To see the lookup table in row two of the transaction table, carefully click to the right of the word "Table" in the row 2 Discount column cell. You can then see the lookup table in the lower part of the Power Query Editor window (if you mistakenly click on the word "Table" you will create a new Applied Step that adds the full table as a new step and you will have to delete the step).

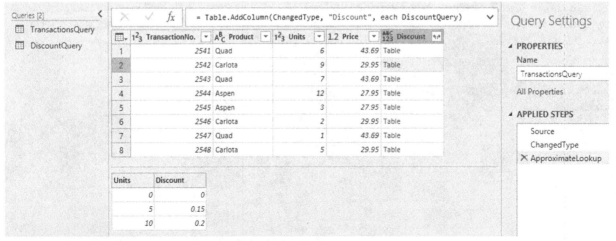

The Discount column has the full lookup table in each row.

Taking a closer look at the Table.AddColumn function in the picture below we see three arguments. The first argument holds the table that will receive the new column. The second argument is the name of the new column. The third argument requires a formula, or Custom Function. By default, the "each" keyword is used in this argument to allow the formula to be copied down the column, make a calculation in each row, and if needed, to access values for each row in the table listed in the first argument. The keyword "each" is shorthand for an explicit Custom Function with defined variables. At this point in the formula, the "each" works because we are not using back-to-back Custom Functions, but later in our formula, we will have to replace this occurrence of the "each" keyword with a Custom Function.

```
= Table.AddColumn(ChangedType, "Discount", each DiscountQuery)
```

Table.AddColumn uses the "each" keyword as a shorthand for a Custom Function.

To help understand what the formula will be required to do in our next step, we can think of the table in each row of the Discount column as the "Inside Table" and the transaction table as the "Outside Table", as seen in the below picture:

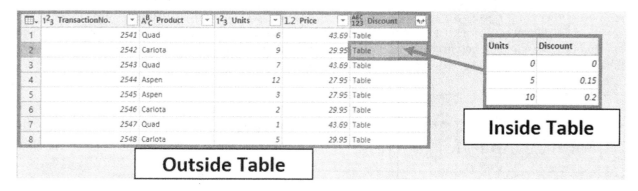

The transaction table is the Outside Table and the lookup table is the Inside Table.

The next step we need to take, is to filter the lookup table (Inside Table) in each row in the Discount column so that the lookup table contains only the records where the units are less than or equal to the units sold from the transaction table row (Outside Table), as seen in the below picture.

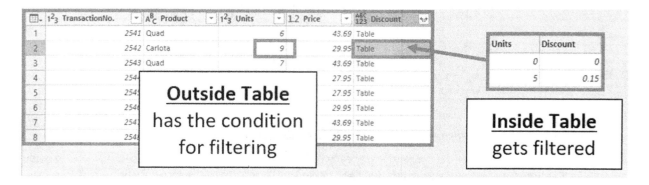

Condition from the Outside Table needs to filter the Inside Table.

The complication we will run into when we build a formula to filter the Inside Table, is that we need to use the Table.SelectRows function inside the Table.AddColumn function and because both functions use the "each" keyword to make the iterating row-by-row calculations, it would be impossible for the two functions to simultaneously access columns in both the Inside Table and Outside Table unless we deliberately avoid the "each" keyword by switch to an explicitly defined Custom Function. Before we fully look at the meaning and mechanics of the formula to filter our Inside Table, we will create the formula by clicking in the formula bar and editing the formula so that it becomes: = Table.AddColumn(ChangedType, "Discount", (OT) => Table.SelectRows(DiscountQuery, (IT) => IT[Units] <= OT[Units])). The formula and the results, including the filtered table in row 2, can be seen in the picture below:

Table.SelectRows function inside 3rd argument of the Table.AddColumn function.

But why the strange syntax "(OT) =>"? In the picture below we can see that the OT is the name of the variable, the parentheses house the variable and the "=>" is the Go To Operator, which means that everything after the Go To Operator defines how we use the variable. The official definition of a Custom Function in Power Query is: "user defines the arguments and creates a mapping of the arguments for the function so it can deliver a value", and although there are many different uses for Custom Functions, we are creating a Custom Function so that we can access columns from the Outside Table and from the Inside Table simultaneously. Without these Custom Functions, we would not have a way to distinguish the Outside Table or Inside Table columns.

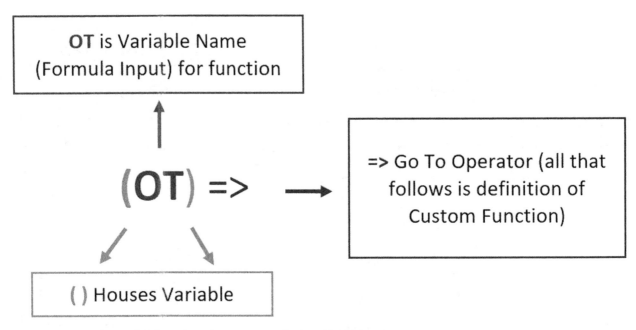

Custom Function that will define when we can access the Outside Table columns.

The complete formula that we need to correctly filter each row of the lookup table can be seen in the picture below. The Table.AddColumn function uses the syntax "(OT) =>" rather than "each" for its Custom Function. The Table.SelectRows function uses the syntax "(IT) =>" rather than "each" for its Custom Function. As an important note, we could have chosen a different variable name, for example x and y rather than OT and IT because the names of the variable are entirely a personal choice. The Variables OT and IT can now be used in front of a column name like [Units] to instruct the formula to pull the column from either the Outside Table or Inside Table, respectively. Further, the Table.SelectRows functions contains two arguments: the first argument is the table to be filtered, and the second argument contains the condition for filtering.

OT is variable we use to access columns in first argument of Table.AddColumn function, the ChangedType table.

↑

= Table.AddColumn(ChangedType, "Discount", (OT) =>
Table.SelectRows(**DiscountQuery**, (IT) => IT[Units] <= OT[Units]))

↓

IT is variable we use to access columns in first argument of Table.AddColumn function, the **DiscountQuery** table.

OT variable to access Outside Table, and IT variable to access Inside Table.

Still looking at the above picture, if it is true that our logical test calculation for filtering the lookup table is: IT[Units] <= OT[Units] , the question arises: "How does the formula know how to get a value from each row in the OT[Units] column, but take the entire column for the IT[Units] column"? The answer comes from the fact that the OT variable is working in the third argument of the Table.AddColumn function which makes a row-by-row calculation and pulls out the row element for each row in the transaction table, but the IT variable is working in the second argument of the Table.SelectRows function which is programmed to use the entire column from the lookup table.

The next step in our formula requires that we pull out the column of discount values from the filtered lookup table. In M Code when we want to extract or lookup an entire column from a table and deliver a list of values, we use the Field Access Operator, which is open and close square brackets with the correct field name inside the square brackets places directly after the full table. In general terms, we use this syntax to extract a list of values from a table: TableName[ColumnName]. The picture below illustrates this fully.

M Code Syntax to extract column to create list of values:

TableName**[ColumnName]** = Extracted List

Table.SelectRows(DiscountQuery, (IT) => IT[Units] <= OT[Units])**[Discount]** = List of Discounts from Filtered Table

| Table | Column |

Which allows us to extract column from table and create list of values:

Full Table

Units	Discount
0	0
5	0.15

→

Extracted List

List
0
0.15

M Code syntax to extract a list of values from a table: TableName[ColumnName].

Editing our formula in the Formula Bar, we add the formula element [Discount] after the result of the Table. SelectRows function, to accomplish our goal of extracting the list of discount values from each filtered table, as seen below.

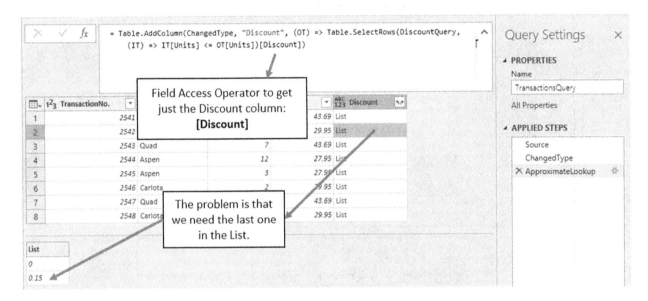

We use Field Access Operator to extract list of discounts for each row.

Because we need the last discount in each list of discounts for each row, we can now place the formula element that created the list of values into the Power Query function: List.Last, as seen in the picture below.

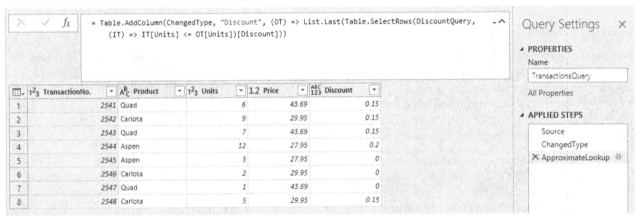

Our final formula for performing an approximate match lookup.

In conclusion, although we do not have a single built-in function in Power Query to perform an approximate match lookup, with a little M Code and a couple of Custom Functions, we can accomplish the goal of doing approximate match lookup.

The Power Behind the Boringest Sentence in Excel

by Bill Jelen

The lowliest sentence in Excel arrived in Excel 2013 at the bottom of the Create PivotTable dialog: 'Add This Data to the Data Model'.

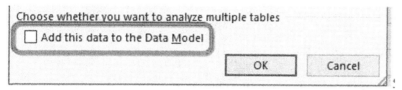

Choose this box when creating your PivotTable.

I do 35 Excel seminars a year, and you won't believe the wide variety of questions that can be solved with the answer of choosing the box next to the sentence, 'Add This Data to the Data Model':

- How can I get the totals at the bottom of a filtered PivotTable to show the grand total of all records, since the 'Included Filtered Items in Subtotals' has been greyed out since January 30, 2007?
- How can I report text in the values area of a PivotTable?
- How can I count the number of distinct customers in a PivotTable?
- How can I report medians in a PivotTable?
- How can I convert my PivotTable to a series of formulas that I can cut and paste into a nicely formatted dashboard report?
- How can I use one set of slicers to control data coming from two different tables?
- How can I include data from Sheet1 and Sheet2 in a single PivotTable?

Part 1 - Unlocking Features Reserved for OLAP PivotTables

When you have data in an Excel worksheet and create a PivotTable using Insert -> PivotTable, you are creating a PivotCache PivotTable. There are a handful of useful features that are not available in PivotCache PivotTables. By choosing the box to 'Add This Data to the Data Model' ("ATDTTDM" from here on out), you have accidentally created an external data store. This allows Data Model PivotTables to be super-fast. Even better, the side benefit is that you unlock all of those features that are not available for PivotCache PivotTables.

Include Filtered Items in Totals

The Subtotals drop-down menu on the Design tab for a PivotTable offers an item called 'Included Filtered Items in Totals'. Imagine you've filtered a PivotTable to show the top three products and you would like the grand total at the bottom of the PivotTable to include all products. This setting would allow it, except the setting has been greyed out since January 30, 2007.

By choosing the ATDTTDM box, you can filter to the top three and have the grand total include all products. Notice the asterisk next to the Grand Total in D7.

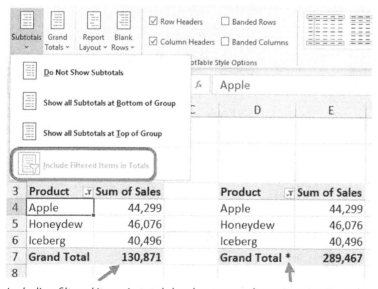

	Product	Sum of Sales		Product	Sum of Sales
3	Product 🔽	Sum of Sales		Product 🔽	Sum of Sales
4	Apple	44,299		Apple	44,299
5	Honeydew	46,076		Honeydew	46,076
6	Iceberg	40,496		Iceberg	40,496
7	Grand Total	130,871		Grand Total *	289,467
8					

Including filtered items in totals has been greyed out since 2007 – unless your PivotTable uses the data model.

By the way, to find the 'Top 3' filter, use the Product drop-down in either A3 or D3 and choose Value Filters, Top 10…. In the 'Top 10 Filter (Product)' dialog, choose Top and then the number three (3).

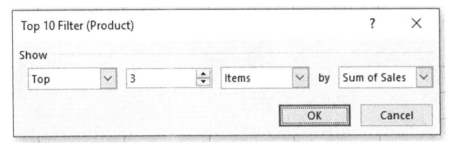

Although called Top 10, it can be any number, Top or Bottom, and Items, Percent, or Total - a very flexible filtering tool.

Reporting a Distinct Count

Based on the PivotTable below, you can see there are three customers in the Communications sector, two in Energy, and four in Financial.

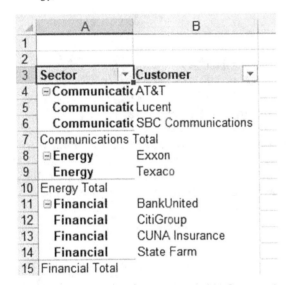

You can see there are three customers in Communications.

However, if you drag Customer to the Values area, the resulting PivotCache PivotTable shows numbers that are completely wrong. The heading says 'Count of Customer' but it is really telling you the number of orders found in each Sector.

Sector	Count of Customer
Communications	48
Energy	70
Financial	84
Healthcare	4

But a regular PivotTable reports 48 customers in communications.

If you re-create this PivotTable and choose ATDTTDM, you can change the calculation to Distinct Count. Double-click the 'Count of Customer' heading and choose the secret 'Distinct Count' option.

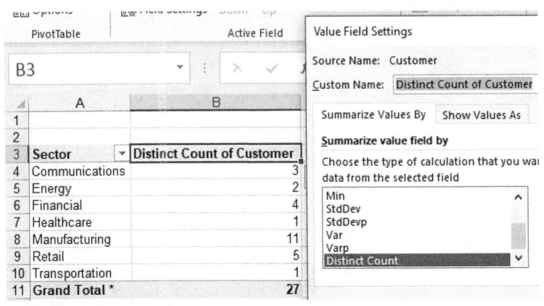

The Data Model offers a new calculation option – Distinct Count.

Converting a PivotTable to Formulas

PivotTables are powerful ways to summarize data, but they never look great. Even if you customize the PivotTable style, it will still look like a PivotTable. If you create the PivotTable based on the data model, you can quickly convert the entire PivotTable to formulas that can be cut and pasted into a nicer-looking report.

Consider this PivotTable:

	A	B	C
3	**Product** ▾	**Sales Rep** ▾	**Sum of Qty**
4	⊟ **Apple**	Bob	6768
5	**Apple**	Kevin	4840
6	**Apple**	Roger	13848
7	⊟ **Banana**	Bob	7540
8	**Banana**	Kevin	7183
9	**Banana**	Roger	14983
10	⊟ **Cherry**	Bob	8115
11	**Cherry**	Kevin	3785
12	**Cherry**	Roger	13940
13	**Grand Total**		**81002**

A typical PivotTable.

On the PivotTable Analyze tab, open the OLAP Tools and choose 'Convert to Formulas'.

Convert to Formulas is greyed-out in regular PivotTables.

The result: a series of formula using CUBEMEMBER and CUBEVALUE functions. You can cut and paste into a report that does not look like a PivotTable.

=CUBEVALUE("ThisWorkbookDataModel",$F5,C$3)

	E	F	G	H	I
	Apple				
		Bob	6768		
		Kevin	4840		
		Roger	13848		

After converting to formulas, you can reposition the report into new cells.

Part 2 – Unlocking a New Formula Language

Calculated fields and calculated items in regular PivotTables are difficult to use. They work some of the time, but not all of the time. The Data Model supports a new type of calculated field called a **measure**. It uses a formula language called DAX – which stands for Data Analysis eXpressions. It is possible to do calculations with DAX that are not possible in regular PivotTables.

Reporting Median in a PivotTable

A normal PivotTable offers 11 calculations: Sum, Count, Average, Max, Min, Product, Count Numbers, StdDev, StdDevP, Var, and VarP. Every once in a while, at my Power Excel seminars, someone will ask how to create a Median in a PivotTable. It is not an option in regular PivotTables. But since DAX includes a function for MEDIAN, it is easy when you check the box for 'Add This Data to the Data Model'.

Starting in Excel 2016, you can add a measure by right-clicking the table name in the 'PivotTable Fields' list and choosing 'Add Measure…'.

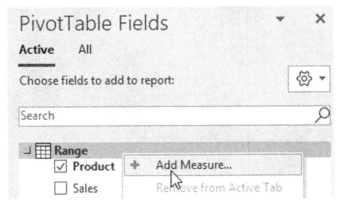

Before Excel 2016, you needed the Power Pivot add-in to create measures.

In the Measure dialog box, type a measure name such as Median Revenue. In the Formula, type

=Median(

and choose a field from the AutoComplete list.

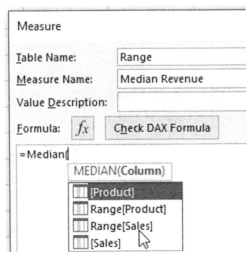

Build a DAX formula.

When you click OK, the new measure is not automatically added to the PivotTable. You have to choose the new measure from the 'PivotTable Fields' list.

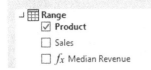

Any measures appear in the Fields list with an italic fx.

One small bonus feature of measures versus calculated fields: you can specify a number format for the measure using the settings in the bottom of the Measure dialog box.

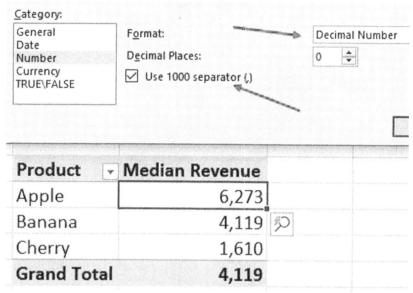

Medians in PivotTables were previously impossible.

Reporting Text in the Values Area of a PivotTable

Typically, the Values area of a PivotTable shows numbers. But, a new CONCATENATEX function added to DAX now allows you to report text in the Values area of a PivotTable.

Consider the data set shown here. You would like a report showing the original versus revised codes from column E. But – instead of numbers, column E contains text.

◢	A	B	C	D	E
1	Region	Market	Rep	Version	Code
2	East	NYC	Andy	Original	Guava
3	East	NYC	Andy	Revised	Lime
4	Central	ORD	Barb	Original	Guava
5	Central	ORD	Barb	Revised	Melon

You want to report the codes from column E in the PivotTable values.

Build a PivotTable using the data model. Add fields to the Rows and Columns areas.

> **Caution:** The Grand Total cell in this PivotTable can get unusually large very quickly, as it concatenates every unique text entry in column E. Before creating the measure, you should right-click the Grand Total heading for both the Grand Total row and the Grand Total Column and choose Remove Grand Total. If you accidentally allow the grand total cell to hold more than 32,767 characters, the PivotTable will stop responding.

Once you have the PivotTable built, right-click the table name in the PivotTable Fields panel and choose 'Add Measure.'

In the current example, the table is called Range and the field is called Code. The formula to use is

=CONCATENATEX(VALUES(Range[Code]),Range[Code]," ")

By wrapping the first argument in the VALUES function, it ensures that nothing will repeat in any cell of the PivotTable. For example, instead of "Lime, Lime, Cherry, Cherry, Guava, Banana", you will see "Lime, Cherry, Guava, Banana".

Region		Market	Rep	Version Original	Revised
⊟ Central		⊟ MSP	Ed		
Central		MSP	Kelly		
Central		MSP Total			

Measure	
Table Name:	Range
Measure Name:	Codes
Value Description:	
Formula: *fx* Check DAX Formula	

`=CONCATENATEX(VALUES(Range[Code]),Range[Code],", ")`

Build a formula to concatenate the unique list of codes.

Add the new field to the PivotTable and you will have text where the values usually appear.

Codes				Version	
Region		**Market**	**Rep**	**Original**	**Revised**
⊟ **Central**		⊟ **MSP**	Ed	Cherry	Guava
Central		MSP	Kelly	Lime	Lime
Central		**MSP Total**		**Lime, Cherry**	**Guava, Lime**
Central		⊟ ORD	Barb	Guava	Melon
Central		ORD	Hank	Banana	Banana
Central		**ORD Total**		**Guava, Banana**	**Melon, Banana**
⊟ **East**		⊟ **ATL**	Gary	Fig	Fig

The concatenated text values appear in the values area of the PivotTable.

Once the concatenated text measure has been added, you can rearrange the PivotTable and the field continues to calculate.

Codes		Version	
Region	**Market**	**Original**	**Revised**
⊟ **Central**	MSP	Lime, Cherry	Guava, Lime
Central	ORD	Guava, Banana	Melon, Banana
Central Total		**Guava, Lime, Cherry, Banana**	**Guava, Lime, Melon, Banana**
⊟ **East**	ATL	Fig, Cherry	Fig, Orange
East	NYC	Guava	Lime
East	PHL	Lime, Fig	Lime, Fig
East Total		**Guava, Lime, Fig, Cherry**	**Lime, Fig, Orange**
⊟ **West**	LAX	Apple, Elderberry	Lime, Fig
West	SFO	Honeydew, Elderberry	Honeydew, Iceberg
West Total		**Apple, Honeydew, Elderberry**	**Lime, Fig, Honeydew, Iceberg**

Even the original West Total is able to eliminate duplicate Elderberry from LAX and SFO.

Part 3 – Reporting from Multiple Tables

VLOOKUP (and now XLOOKUP!) is one of my favorite functions in Excel because it allows you to join two tables to-gether like you might do in Microsoft Access. You might need to use VLOOKUP less often because the Data Model allows you to create relationships between tables in Excel.

Joining Two Tables Together

This example uses two data sets. The main data table contains invoices from two years. There are fields for product, date, customer, quantity, revenue, and so on. A lookup table maps each customer to an industry sector. You would like one PivotTable to report total revenue by sector. Normally, you would break out a VLOOKUP to bring the sector information back into the main table. But VLOOKUP is slow and imagine if you had a million records of data – the whole workbook would slow down as you wait for one million VLOOKUP formulas to finish calculating.

Instead, you can create a relationship using the data model. For this example, each of the ranges in Excel have to be converted to a table using Ctrl + T or Home -> Format as Table. Select one cell in the first table and press Ctrl + T. Make sure that the 'My Data Has Headers' box is checked in the 'Create Table' dialog box. Repeat for the lookup table.

Initially, Excel will name these Tables as Table1 and Table2. You should rename each Table now, before creating the PivotTable. Select one cell in the table and go to the 'Table Tools' tab in the ribbon. The first item in the ribbon is the table name. Click there and type a useful name, such as 'Data' and 'Sectors'.

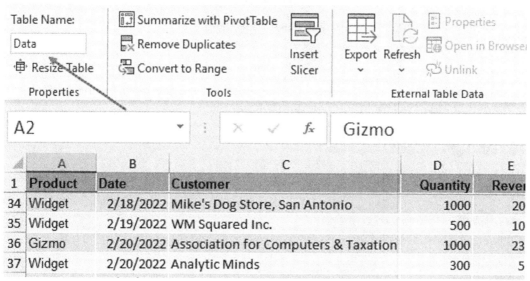

Name the first table as 'Data'.

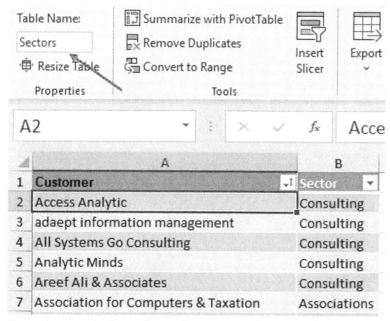

Name the second table as 'Sectors'.

Once you have two tables created, go to the Data tab in the ribbon and click Relationships.

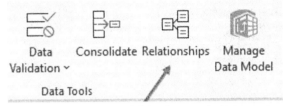

The Relationships icon debuted in Excel 2016.

Building a relationship is simple: The Data table has a Customer field that is related to the Sector table's Customer field.

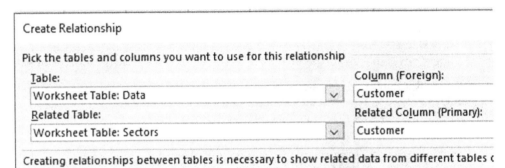

Create Relationship

Pick the tables and columns you want to use for this relationship

Table: Column (Foreign):

Worksheet Table: Data   Customer

Related Table: Related Column (Primary):

Worksheet Table: Sectors   Customer

Creating relationships between tables is necessary to show related data from different tables

Choose the table and field names for the relationship.

By defining two tables using Ctrl + T and then creating a relationship, you have created a Data Model in the workbook. Since the data model already exists, you can start your PivotTable from a blank worksheet. In the 'Create PivotTable' dialog box, the default source will be 'Use this workbook's Data Model'.

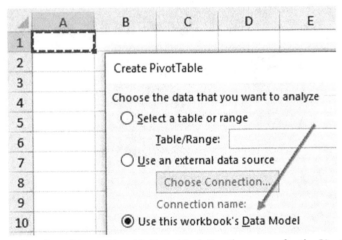

Create PivotTable

Choose the data that you want to analyze

○ Select a table or range

   Table/Range:

○ Use an external data source

   Choose Connection...

   Connection name:

● Use this workbook's Data Model

Select 'Use this workbook's Data Model' as the source for the PivotTable.

Check out the 'PivotTable Fields' pane shown below: both Tables are available to be used in the PivotTable.

PivotTable Fields

Active   **All**

Choose fields to add to report:

Search

> 🔳 Data

> 🔳 Sectors

The PivotTable Fields pane lists all of the Tables in the workbook.

Expand each Table by clicking the Table name in the 'PivotTable Fields' list. Choose Revenue from the Data table and Sector from the Sectors table. The result: a PivotTable reporting from both Tables – without creating any VLOOKUP formulas.

	A	B	
1	Sector ▼	Sum of Revenue	
2	Applications	482074	
3	Associations	418988	
4	Consulting	2904312	
5	Retail	570426	
6	Services	877055	
7	Training	935397	
8	Utilities	519560	
9	Grand Total *	6707812	
10			

Data
- ☐ Product
- ☐ Date
- ☐ Customer
- ☐ Quantity
- ☑ **Revenue**
- ☐ Profit

Sectors
- ☐ Customer
- ☑ **Sector**

This PivotTable is reporting from two different Tables.

This functionality brings the power of Access or SQL Server into Excel. While this first debuted in Excel 2010 using the Power Pivot add-in, changes in Excel 2013 and then Excel 2016 have allowed you to easily create the PivotTable, even if your company is not paying the extra $2 a month for Power Pivot.

Sharing Slicers from Two Data Sets

Slicers are a great way to filter PivotTables. While one slicer can control many PivotTables that originated from the same data set, how can you have one slicer control PivotTables that come from two different data sets?

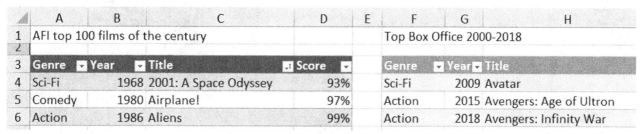

	A	B	C	D	E	F	G	H
1	AFI top 100 films of the century					Top Box Office 2000-2018		
2								
3	Genre ▼	Year ▼	Title	Score ▼		Genre ▼	Year ▼	Title
4	Sci-Fi	1968	2001: A Space Odyssey	93%		Sci-Fi	2009	Avatar
5	Comedy	1980	Airplane!	97%		Action	2015	Avengers: Age of Ultron
6	Action	1986	Aliens	99%		Action	2018	Avengers: Infinity War

Can one Genre slicer control PivotTables from both data sets?

While many try to solve this with convoluted VBA, the Data Model provides an easier way. Copy the Genres from both tables into a new table and remove duplicates.

K	L	M
Genres from Either List		
Genre ▼		
Action		
Adventure		
Animated		
Comedy		
Drama		
Horror		
Sci-Fi		
Westerns		

Build a super-set of genres from either list.

Make all three data sets into tables. Define a relationship from each of the original two tables to the new Genre table.

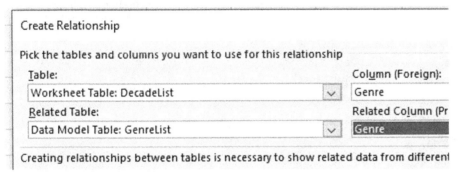

This is the first of two relationships.

Think of the Genre table sitting in the middle between the other two tables. This is a view from the 'Diagram View' inside the 'Manage Data Model' feature.

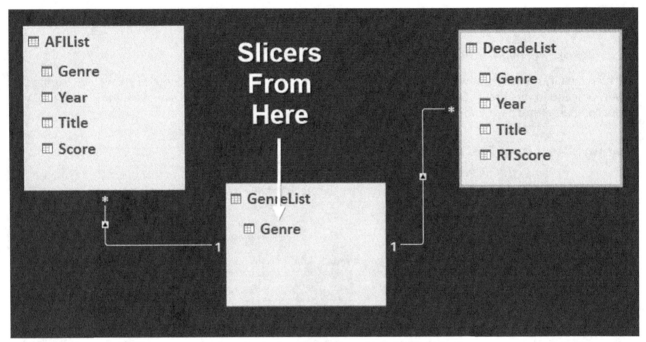

While DecadeList and AFIList cannot communicate directly, the GenreList joins them both.

From the Insert tab, choose Slicer. In the 'Existing Connections' dialog, choose the 'Data Model' tab and then 'This Workbook Data Model'.

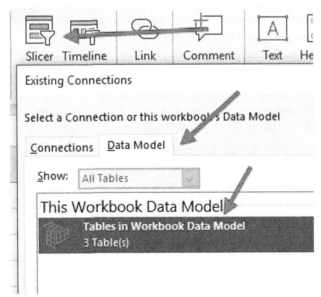

Build the slicer from the data model.

When inserting the slicer, choose Genre from the GenreList table, not from either of the original two tables.

Once you have the slicer, select the slicer. A Slicer tab appears in the ribbon. Choose 'Report Connections'. Hook the slicer up to all of your PivotTables.

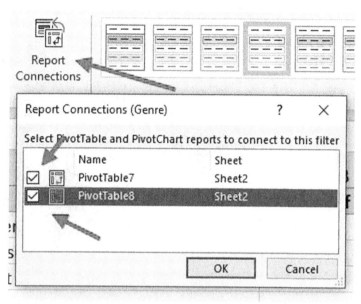

Connect the slicer to the PivotTables.

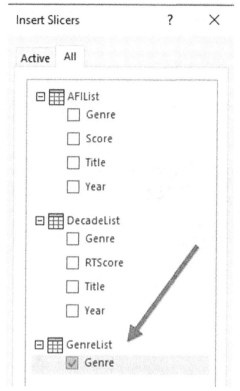

Always build the slicer from the tiny GenreList.

The result: one slicer that will control PivotTables made from different data sets.

	A	B	C	D
1	**Title**	**Average of Score**		
2	The Adventures of Robin Hood	100%		
3	The Treasure of the Sierra Madre	100%		
4	Aliens	99%		
5	King Kong	98%		
6	Mad Max 2	98%		
7	Raiders of the Lost Ark	95%		
8	Casino Royale	94%		
9	**Grand Total**	**98%**		
10				
11				
12	**Title**	**Average of RTScore**		
13	Black Panther	97%		
14	The Lord of the Rings: The Two Towers	95%		
15	The Dark Knight	94%		
16	Wonder Woman	93%		
17	Spider-Man 2	93%		
18	Iron Man	93%		
19	The Lord of the Rings: The Return of the King	93%		
20	**Grand Total ***	**79%**		
21				

By using the Data Model, you can filter multiple PivotTables without VBA.

And Finally…Should All PivotTables use the Data Model?

With all of the power unleashed by basing your PivotTables on a data model, why wouldn't you base all future PivotTables on the data model?

When Power Pivot and the Data Model debuted as an add-in for Excel 2010, there were a dozen limitations why you would not want to do this. However, today, in 2019, there is one oddity that remains: months and weekdays will not automatically sort into the correct sequence when you use the data model.

We take it for granted, but when a regular PivotTable reports January, February, March, and so on, it is happening because regular PivotTables support using Custom Lists. In contrast, the Data Model will present data in alphabetical sequence, leading to alphabetical sequence of April, August, December, or Friday, Monday, Saturday and so on.

3	Average of Sales	Weekday			
4	**Month**	**Friday**	**Monday**	**Saturday**	**Sun**
5	April	5,166	3,330	7,162	
6	August	6,200	3,532	6,560	
7	December	10,942	6,900	12,994	

By default, months appear alphabetically.

One ugly solution requires 16 clicks for every PivotTable:

- Open the Weekday drop-down menu in B3.
- Choose 'More Sort Options'.
- Click 'Ascending by Weekday'.
- Click 'More Options….'
- Uncheck 'Sort automatically every time the report is updated'.
- Open the drop-down menu for First Key Sort Order. Choose 'Sunday, Monday, Tuesday, ….'
- Click OK to close 'More Sort Options (Weekday)'.
- Click OK to close 'Sort Options'.
- Repeat similar steps to sort Months.

3	Average of Sales	Weekday			
4	**Month**	**Sunday**	**Monday**	**Tuesday**	
5	January				
6	February				
7	March				
8	April				
9	May				

More Sort Options (Month)   ?   ✕

AutoSort

☐ Sort automatically every time the report is updated

First key sort order

January, February, March, April, May, June, July, Augus ⌄

Sorting requires a bunch of extra clicks.

You have to decide if the sorting is a deal-breaker for you. If you want all future PivotTables to start as a Data Model PivotTable, go to File -> Options -> Data, and choose the box to 'Prefer the Data Model when Creating PivotTables, QueryTables and Data Connections'.

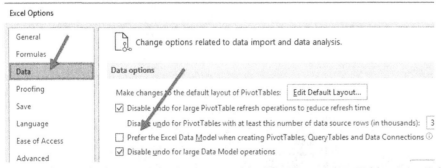

How to choose the box to 'Prefer the Data Model when Creating PivotTables, QueryTables and Data Connections'.

Understanding Context in Power Pivot
by Henk Vlootman

What is Context?

"Context" has several different definitions. This depends upon the, er, context – and within a context, there can be multiple sub-contexts. Let me explain.

The first definition of context is the results context:

- **Results context** is the environment in which the results of a calculation are displayed. This context can be one-dimensional or multi-dimensional.

But context can also be found in every table:

- **The table context** consists of two elements: the column and the row context.

The last definition of context is the one that is created by filtering:

- **Filtering context** refers to the way calculations are filtered.

So, let's dive in a bit more into these contexts.

The Results Context

In classic Excel, this context is straightforward and one-dimensional. If you have the formula

=A1*B1

in cell C1, the result is always the same, unless you change the input in one of the source cells. Excel basically recalculates the formula when the content in the source cells has been changed.

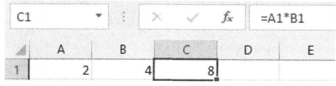

One-dimensional results context in "classic" Excel.

Things become different if you use an Excel PivotTable. If you create a PivotTable with no filtering, the results will also produce a one-dimensional context:

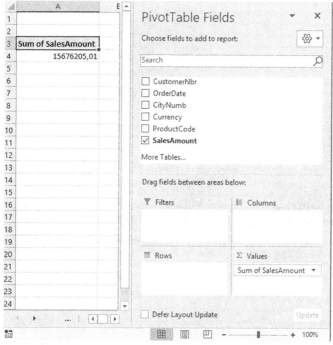

One-dimensional results context in an Excel PivotTable.

Here, the results start to change if you add fields into the Filters, Columns and / or Rows sections of the 'PivotTable Fields' pane, as pictured above.

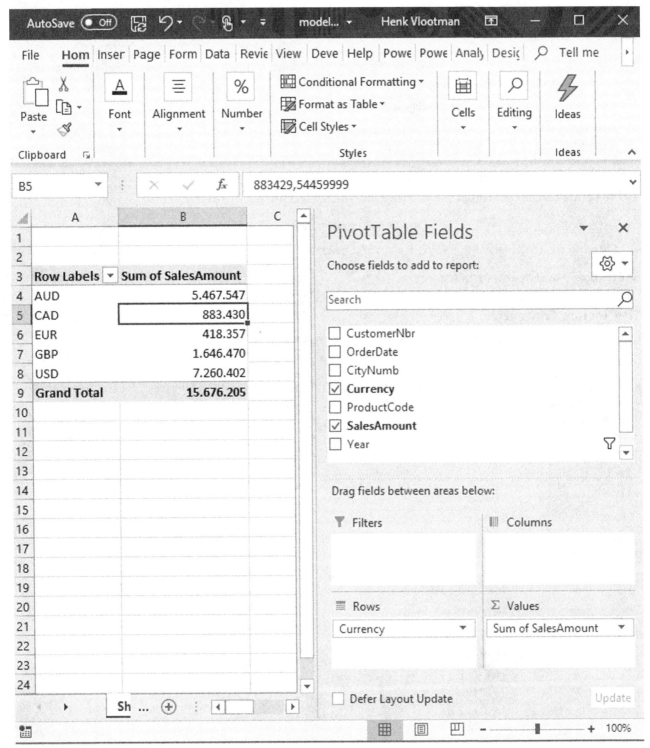

Multi-dimensional context in an Excel PivotTable.

As you can see above, the PivotTable filters the calculation (which totals the same in the last row as seen in the previous image) to the categories uniquely placed in the rows of the PivotTable. If you hide the total row (assuming the active cell is in the PivotTable, go to the Design tab on the ribbon, then click on the 'Grand Totals' dropdown to select 'Off for Rows and Columns') you will lose the visual reference to the total.

If you add more information, for instance a slicer for the year (see below), by right-clicking on the field in the 'PivotTable Fields' pane and select the option 'Add as Slicer', you can get another context in your visualization.

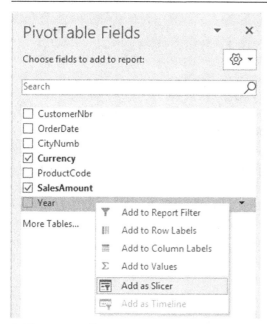

Adding a year slicer.

If you select the year 2015, the results will be filtered by currency in the rows in the PivotTable *and* by the year 2015. By now the total, as shown below, is not the same as the original one-dimensional calculation.

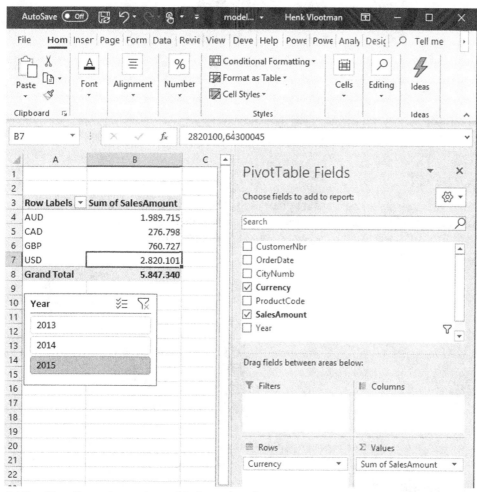

Adding filter dimension to the multi-dimensional context.

Be aware that a slicer works in the same way as adding a field in the section filters in the PivotTable. There is a difference in adding a field in the row or column context and adding the same field in the filter context.

> **Note**: Using fields in the row or column sections of a PivotTable will divide the values over the filter criteria. This is called the **selection context**. In this process no loss of value(s) will occur. Using a filter means loss of values in rows that don't meet the filter criteria. This is called the **filter context**.

Table Context

In Power Pivot and Power Query, data is stored in tables. You can also create a Table in Excel by using the Table function (from the Insert tab on the ribbon, select Table from the Tables section).

An Excel range can therefore be turned into a Table. The definition of a range is a set of contiguous cells surrounded by blank cells. To find the edges of a range, just position the active cell somewhere in the range and press Ctrl + * (this will select all cells in the range). Excel modelling works best when ranges are "respected". Data that needs to be together should never be separated by columns or rows and data that has no relation with each other should be separated by at least a column or a row.

If you add an Excel data range into Power Query or Power Pivot, Excel will transform that range into a Table, based on the above definition of a range.

Note: Typically, in an Excel range or Table, the top row is a header row. Excel will not treat this row as data if identified as such, but as a description of the underlying data that lives in that column.

This best shown if you use a filter on a range, as shown here:

In a filter, the header of the range is not part of the data.

The header is very important and should always be part of a range or Table. The header is also called a field (name) in a PivotTable. The description used is vital for understanding the nature of the data in that column. The header also impacts upon the nature of the columns. We will explain this when we talk about the row and column context.

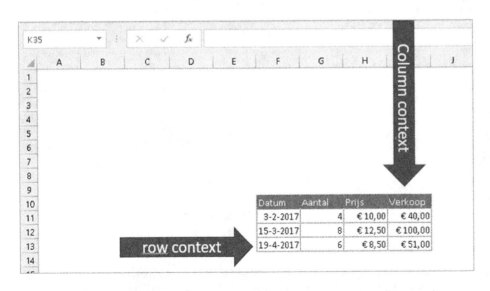

Row and column context in a table.

Note: If you want to understand the **table context**, you need to consider the row and column context. This is true of every table from every source you use to import data.

Column Context Within a Table

Note: The column context is the data that is available in a single column.

Rubbish	
Text	<- Text
3	<- Number
4	<- Number
7	<- Calculation
1-feb	<- Date

An unwanted column context in Excel.

In Excel, the column context can be blurry. That is because Excel is cell based and does not have the structured referencing prevalent in a Table. In the image above, you see a column context that will prove awkward for Power Pivot. Therefore, it is not recommended to create such a context in Excel.

Why is this a problem? Well, columns rely on the data type. The data type needs to be consistent over that column. If a column has different data types, errors may occur in calculations. Since the concept of Power Pivot is based on columns and tables, an "in-between calculation" in as shown above can prove problematic.

Row Context within a Table

Note: The row context is the relation across one row in a table (a record of data, so to speak).

K	L	M	N
OrderDate	Currency	ProductCode	SalesAmount
29-6-2013	CAD	BK-R93R-62	3578,27

The row context.

If you look at the image above, you can read the row context: on 29 June 2013, product code BK-R93R-62 was sold for ($) 3,578.27 (using European number formatting). The row context tells the story of a record. It is very important to keep the row context intact. In Excel, it is possible to sort just one column in a range. Excel will issue a warning, because this action will destroy the row context. At all times, you should avoid this behavior.

The row context is even more important in Power Pivot, since relationships are heavily bound to this principle.

Power Pivot Relationships Between Tables

Power Pivot adds another dimension that is unknown to Excel. In Excel, the source for a PivotTable is a range or a Table. In Power Pivot, you may select more ranges or Tables, but Power Pivot is used to create relationships between the data tables.

Basically, relationships work with specific columns, named key columns. Those columns are bound by the relationship. Often, these key columns are based on numbers.

To let a relationship work you need to have two different types of tables: dimension (filtering) tables and fact tables. You normally – but not always – create a relationship between these types of tables.

The Fact Table

Note: The Fact Table contains, as the words said, the facts of said data.

	CustomerNbr		OrderDate	CityNumb	Currency	ProductCode	SalesAmount	Add Column
1		11245	29-6-2015 00:...	132	USD	WB-H098	4,99	
2		16313	29-6-2015 00:...	160	USD	WB-H098	4,99	
3		12390	30-6-2015 00:...	140	USD	WB-H098	4,99	
4		21440	30-6-2015 00:...	336	USD	WB-H098	4,99	

A fact table.

These facts are stored in rows within a table and are called rows or records. These are mostly the results of transactions detailed elsewhere. Think of any type of data: sales records, bookkeeping records, product records, and lots of other type of transactions.

In our example, we have a column named 'CustomerNbr'. In that column, there are no visible names but just a whole number. That is not an error, it is deliberate. Numbers can often be a large table's best friend. It has to do with speed of your model.

Within a fact table there can be specific columns (key columns) that are designed to work with the dimension tables. The column named 'CustomerNbr' is an example of such column. Since it contains numbers, it would be inappropriate to use this column in a summary report: nobody knows who is behind a number. That question will be answered later.

The numbers in the key column can appear multiple times: for example, you can sell goods to one customer multiple times. Each row in that fact table in the customer column will have the same number.

Best Practice in Power Pivot is to have as few columns as possible in fact tables. Power Pivot is optimized for rows. Therefore, more rows and less columns will make your model quicker.

The Dimension Table

Note: Dimension tables are the lookup tables of your database.

Customer...	CityNmb	Customer type	CustomerName	TradeType	Add Column
1	11170	612	Direct Customer	Carol Howard	Not Applica...	
2	11187	612	Direct Customer	Jennifer Cooper	Not Applica...	
3	11205	612	Direct Customer	Abby Fernandez	Not Applica...	
4	11224	612	Direct Customer	Tiffany Li	Not Applica...	
5	11254	612	Direct Customer	Johnathan Vance	Not Applica...	
6	11255	612	Direct Customer	Colin Lin	Not Applica...	

A dimension table.

Just as fact tables are essentially facts stored in rows in a table, dimension tables return the detail that's missing that is required time and time again. In a dimension table, you will also find key columns. These need to contain the same type of information as the related fact tables. Therefore, in the dimension table called 'Customer', there must be a column of numbers which represents the 'CustomerNbr' equivalent of the previous fact table.

There is one major difference though. If we are essentially going to be looking up data, the data in this key column needs to be unique (e.g. I cannot look up a customer number and see that it belongs to two unrelated customers). That makes sense. If you look at the dimension table that belongs to customer fact table, it distinguishes the row context for every single customer. There are other columns that contain information about this customer, such as name, address etc. The row context of this table will describe each client. Using a number as the key column makes it easier to make that record unique. For instance, if you take the last name instead, you might have two or more customers named Jones. If you live in Wales, that might be *the entire dataset...*

Relations Between Tables

As said previously, relationships are typically made between fact tables and dimension tables. This link needs to be made between the two key columns. You make relationships in the 'Diagram View' window of Power Pivot. You simply drag one of the key columns to the other key column and drop it there. Power Pivot will make the relationship for you.

So now you have a relationship, the question becomes, what does it do? Well, you can see the relationship as an extension of the row context in the fact table with the row context of the dimension table. Another way of looking at a relationship is how you should do this in Excel. In Excel, you can only use one range, so you would use a VLOOKUP function to extend the range with the values from another pre-defined range. We do this all the time.

But relationships are much more than a lookup function. Since multiple fact tables can be bound by one dimension table for example, all those row contexts would be bound to that dimension table. This means you are able to do so much more.

However, before we take a serious look at context, we need to know more about the different kinds of calculations, and how these calculations refer to context.

Calculations in Power Pivot

In Excel, you can have calculations with operators, such as + or - etc. In Power Pivot you can use operators, based upon the calculation of complete columns in a table (the fields). These calculations are performed most frequently in aggregation. In Power Pivot, we are most likely to use DAX calculations. There are a lot of DAX functions. They range from simple SUM functions to very complex DAX (filter) functions. You need to keep in mind that calculations in DAX are always dynamic. That means that the results depend on the context in which the calculation is positioned.

If you want to categorize functions and DAX in Excel and Power Pivot, it falls into just two categories: calculated columns (or row-in-column calculations) and measures (or aggregation) calculations. Just two? Yes, just two.

Calculated Columns

Note: a **calculated column** makes a calculation in a new column in the range of a table. The result is shown as one value for each row in the table.

A Calculated Column in Power Pivot

We previously mentioned the VLOOKUP function. Its counterpart in DAX is called LOOKUPVALUE. There is a significant difference in using this function in an Excel range and the use of the DAX equivalent in Power Pivot.

This difference is created by the different ways Excel and Power Pivot work. Since Excel is cell based, you need to create the function for each row in the range. Excel has a very handy way to work with it by using the fill handle to copy the formula into adjacent cells. However, if your range contains 50,000 rows, you need to create the 50,000 calculations.

In Power Pivot, both table and column based, just one calculation is required. Even if the table is expanded by the Refresh function, the values in added rows will automatically be calculated.

In Power Pivot, it's Best Practice not to use a calculated column. With the import into Power Pivot, the data will be compressed, which will very much contribute to the speed of the model. A calculated column is made after this importation and that will not be compressed. In a fact table (with a lot of rows and data), calculated columns can seriously slow down your model.

Measures or Aggregate Calculations

Note: in Power Pivot, an aggregate calculation is called a **measure**. Excel doesn't have a name for it. Typically, the result of this calculation will be just one value.

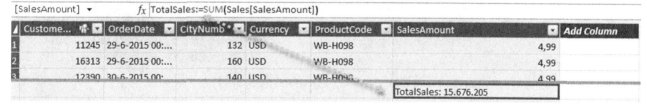

A Measure

Aggregate calculations are by default not part of a table or range. In Power Pivot, the measure is separated in the section beneath the table. In Excel, it is common practice to place a SUM function (by using the AutoSum function) directly under the range. If you want to make it clear and avoid potential double counts, you should consider having at least one empty row and / or column between the range and the aggregate calculation.

There is a huge different in how Excel's PivotTables and Power Pivot tables act. The Excel PivotTable creates aggregates for you. You simply drag the header in the Σ Values section of the pane. If Excel thinks this represents a column with numbers, it will use the SUM aggregation, otherwise the pivot table will use a COUNT aggregation (assuming the data type is text). In total, you can use 11 different kinds of aggregations. For many years, this was thought to be enough.

The Σ Values in a Power Pivot PivotTable can be used the same way. If you drag a column with numbers into the PivotTable, it will automatically create a DAX summation. However, in this way, you are not using the full potential of Power Pivot.

You can drag *every* DAX aggregate into the Σ value field. Yes: every DAX measure may be used by the PivotTable. If you make a measure like this one

```
TotalYtD = TOTALYTD([TotalSales],Date[Date])
```

and you drag this measure into the PivotTable, your year-to-date total sales (which this is calculating) will be computed and filtered directly and dynamically. All the incredible, rich world of DAX is at your feet.

The Different Contexts in DAX Calculations

If you start to work with DAX, you need to know in which context the DAX lives. Therefore, let's look at the behavior of calculations in PivotTables.

Query Context

Note: **query context** is the combination of selection context and filter context in the PivotTable that determine a measure's result.

The difference between Excel and Power Pivot PivotTables stems from the relationships. If you filter a dimension table, the relationship by default propagates the selection context to rows in the fact table. Since this number of rows can be more than one (1), Power Pivot cannot directly reference a column. Measures, which respond with one single value, are the key to success.

There are two different ways a filter context influences the columns in a table. The filter on a column can either be directly or indirectly filtered. This subtle difference can change the context of your aggregation.

ProductNr	Category	Product
101	Furniture	Desk
102	Furniture	Office chair
103	Furniture	Conference table
104	Furniture	Drawer
105	Furniture	Conference chair
106	Furniture	Coat rack
107	Furniture	Desk lamp

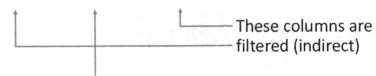

These columns are filtered (indirect)

There is a filter on this column (direct)

The difference between direct and indirect filtering.

Special DAX Calculations to Determine the Context

Power Pivot has four DAX calculations that let you know in which way your PivotTable is filtered:

- ISFILTERED
- ISCROSSFILTERED
- HASONEFILTER
- HASONEVALUE.

The next image shows the relation between these four DAX calculations. Most of the time, you may use these DAX functions in conjunction with the IF DAX function, thus controlling the context of the PivotTable.

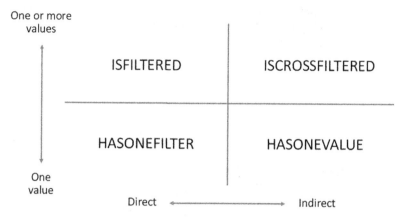

Direct and indirect filtering.

The DAX CALCULATE Function

Filtering doesn't exist exclusively in a PivotTable. There are special DAX calculations for filtering. The most commonly used is the DAX function CALCULATE. The syntax of this DAX function is:

```
CALCULATE (<expression>, [filter1], [filter2], ...)
```

Let's see how CALCULATE works. Consider the following DAX:

```
SalesWest = CALCULATE([TotalSales], Customer[Region]="West")
```

This DAX does the following:

- it creates a filter context.
- then it removes existing filters from tables or columns that are referenced in the filter argument: Customer[Region].
- next it adds a new filter: **Customer[Region]="West"**.
- finally, it will calculate the results of the measure **[TotalSales]** in the new filter context.

Let's dive a little deeper into this with another example. Look at the following DAX:

```
Number sold all products (naive) = CALCULATE([Number Sold],
    ALL('Product'[Product]))
```

Now look at the results (below). There is a selection context on the Product field and a filter context on the category. The DAX CALCULATE function only removes the filter on Product[Product]. The resulting context contains all rows for product category 'Furniture':

Category
☐ Accessories
☐ Equipment
■ Furniture
☐ Kitchen tools
☐ Office supplies
☐ Paper products

Product	Number sold all products (naive)
Coat rack	1.180.908
Conference chair	1.180.908
Conference table	1.180.908
Desk	1.180.908
Desk lamp	1.180.908
Drawer	1.180.908
Office chair	1.180.908
Total	**1.180.908**

An example of the DAX CALCULATE function at work.

In this picture, because the initial filter context is based on Category, this filter has carried through unchanged by the CALCULATE function. The resulting numbers are from the application of two filters – one filter context from the Slicer, and one query filter from the CALCULATE function.

Now look at the next graphic. Instead of filtering items by Category, the Slicer is based on Product, with the same furniture items being selected. In this figure, the same DAX is used. The difference is the filter context. What has happened here? The CALCULATE function removes the filter on Product[Product]. The resulting context contains the rows for all products.

Product	
☐ Archiving box	
☐ Bank envelope	
☐ Batteries	
☐ Bucket	
☐ Calculator	
☑ Coat rack	
☐ Coffee can	
☐ Coffee machine	
☐ Computer bag	

Product	Number sold all products (naive)
Coat rack	20.129.846
Conference chair	20.129.846
Conference table	20.129.846
Desk	20.129.846
Desk lamp	20.129.846
Drawer	20.129.846
Office chair	20.129.846
Total	**20.129.846**

Another example of the DAX CALCULATE function.

Caution: Keep in mind that the number of filter arguments in CALCULATE can be zero. In that case, the current context is replaced by a filter context! Consequently, DAX functions may behave differently. When you use a measure as part of a DAX calculation without filter arguments, the calculation is implicitly applied. That means the measure is always evaluated within a given filter context.

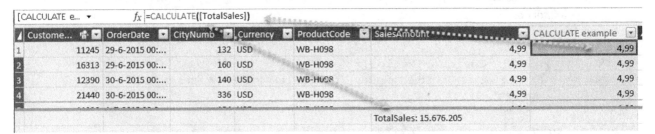

CALCULATE DAX in filter mode.

Using a measure in a calculated column returns the total amount of the measure. If you wrap the DAX formula in a CALCULATE function, each row will be filtered and the same amount in the row context will be retrieved.

Context in Table Functions

As well as DAX calculations that aggregate on columns, there are also DAX calculations that work on a table. You recognize those DAX functions by the X on the end of the name. Look at the following formula:

```
TotalSales = SUMX(Sale, Sale[UnitPrice] * Sale[Sale[number])
```

The complexity of this DAX formula comes from the mixture of context. The SUMX, if used in a measure, creates a Query context, while the last argument (UnitPrice multiplied by Number) performs a row context calculation between the two columns.

Be aware that the second argument, the table, can also be made by a table expression:

```
TotalSales above 10 = SUMX(

FILTER(Sale,Sale[number]>10),

Sale[UnitPrice]*Sale[Sale[number])
```

You can even stack filters in a table function:

```
Number of products above 300 = MAXX(

FILTER(Product,Product[ProductNr] > 300),

Countrows(Product))
```

As you see in this DAX, a filter is placed in the table argument, that creates a virtual table which only contains the rows with a ProductNumber large than 300 and the DAX COUNTROWS refers to a table. Since this DAX contains only one answer, the MAXX DAX serves as what is known as a **container**.

Since a container contains only one, non-filtering value — the numbers of rows of the filtered table —, the result of this double table context filter DAX expression is one-dimensional.

Knowing Context Means Mastering Your Calculations

Knowing the behavior of row, query and filter contexts, and more importantly, the differences between them, is the key to success. You then need to think in terms of context, not in terms of queries. That leads to the conclusion that with proper understanding of context you will become a real "power Power Pivot user".

Thinking Through the Modelling of a Seating Chart
by Oz du Soleil

Introduction

This chapter is more of a thought process than a nuts and bolts how-to. Therefore, rather than start with a finished product and explain it, this will start with the need and slowly build toward the result and address new challenges as they show up.

So, the goal is not to build the seating chart. The goal is to dig into the things that aren't in an Excel cell; the things that are in the developer's head. Things like:

- How can I work smarter during development?
- How can I test scenarios?
- What alerts will be good for the user?
- What are my options and why did I pick the one I picked?

The World of the Event Planner

Event planners are fascinating to me and that's why we're focusing on a seating chart. Event planners have lots of data to manage to ensure a fun event. They handle:

- Their client's budget
- Venue sizes, availability, amenities and requirements
- Number of guests
- Deadlines
- Decorations
- Food: enough but not too much
- Dietary requirements
- Alcohol: yes or no
- Liquor licensing and insurance
- Tables, chairs, linens and centerpieces
- Entertainment: DJs, comedians, live bands
- Photographer / videographer

One area of fascination is that there are standard calculations for things we wouldn't expect. For example:

- You rent 15% more napkins than the number of attendees.
- For a cocktail party, you need 10 square feet per attendee whereas, a dance party can have as little as five square feet per attendee.

My Curiosity

As an Excel developer and someone who works with data, I realize there's a lot of messiness that's unique to each expertise. Reality gets in the way and makes a simple calculation complicated.

So, I asked an event planner, "do you ever have to deal with people who insist they will not sit at the same table with some specific person?".

He shook his head and sighed, "That's ALWAYS a headache. HUGE HEADACHE!"

Along with the seating requests, he's told the details of all the family history that lead up to why Mars doesn't like Vince, and what happened between Larry and Helga.

Our Scenario and What We Want to Model

Let's imagine we've got 100 people and we've decided to go with 8-tops (tables that seat eight people). Now

```
100 ÷ 8 = 12.5
```

On this basis, we need 12.5 tables. But we can't rent half a table and it wouldn't make sense to have 12 8-tops and a single 4-top. The solution is: 12 8-tops and 4 of those tables will have to seat 9 people. REALITY STRIKES! On top of that:

- The phone rings and it's Larry saying that he will not sit with his ex-wife, Helga and her new husband, Bernard.
- Of course, Bernard and Helga need to sit together.

- An email comes in: Connie wants to sit with her co-worker Vince and Vince's daughter, Elva.
- Another email: Denise, Angie and Mars want to sit with Larry but refuse to sit with Vince.

Suddenly there's more than a need to have enough chairs for every backside. So, here's the real challenge:

- A seat for everyone
  - Assign everyone to tables.
  - Satisfy the various seating requests to accommodate the friends, families and foes.

NOTE: There are a lot of online seating charts to help with this. However, these charts will create a floor plan with the 12 tables and slots for names around each table. They don't deal with these rules.

How do we figure this out in Excel?

Thinking This Through

I talked with my friend Jordan Goldmeier, about this problem. He grimaced and remarked that this is a heavy statistical challenge that you only take on if the stakes are high enough.

Jordan explained that we're looking for a permutation of those 100 people that will meet all requirements. How many possible permutations would we have to sift through?

How many possible permutations are we looking at? If we had 100 seats and started populating them with our 100 people, then 100 could sit in the first seat, 99 in the second, 98 in the third, and so on, until we're down to one person and the last chair. The total number of permutations would be 100 x 99 x 98 x ... x 3 x 2 x 1. This is known as the factorial of 100, or 100! or =FACT(100). It is equal to:

93,326,215,443,944,152,681,699,238,856,266,700,490,715,968,264,381,621,468,592,963,895,217,599,993,229,915,608, 941,463,976,156,518,286,253,697,920,827,223,758,251,185,210,916,864,000,000,000,000,000,000,000,000

or

9.33×10^{157}

Ordering is important and it's exactly why this is so difficult. This is the difference between a combination and a permutation. With a combination, order is not important. If you have a combination lock, you've been mis-sold (it's a permutation lock!) – if the combination to open it were 1-2-3-4, then 3-1-4-2 and 3-4-1-2 would also open it. That's not what we are considering here. We're talking permutations here.

The image below is a tiny representation of what Jordan was describing. This represents three tables, 10 people (A thru J) and eight possible permutations (P1 thru P8) of how the 10 people can be seated. Based on the rules, P7 is the only permutation that fits the rules.

		P1	P2	P3	P4	P5	P6	P7	P8
		A	F	E	B	D	A	C	J
Table 1		B	D	C	J	H	C	F	I
		C	I	H	G	A	F	G	H
		D	C	F	D	I	B	J	G
Table 2		E	H	J	I	G	I	A	F
		F	B	B	E	E	H	E	E
		G	J	I	F	F	G	I	D
		H	G	A	H	J	E	H	C
Table 3		I	A	D	C	B	D	D	B
		J	E	G	A	C	J	B	A

RULES
- C cannot sit wth J
- A and E must sit together
- E cannot sit with H

Example representation of the larger problem.

This problem is much more manageable. The number of permutations is a mere 10!, which is a paltry 3,628,800 possibilities.

Here are a few of our options for getting 100 people seated at 12 tables vis-à-vis their seating requests:

- Generate every possible permutation and find one that fits the seating rules. However, remember what Jordan said, you only do this if the stakes are high enough. These stakes are not high enough.
- We could generate, say, 20 permutations and hope that one of them satisfies all requirements. In other words: hope to get lucky.
- We could start adding names to a chart and rearrange the names around until we get it right. This could take a long time, it'd be tedious, and we'd probably still get something wrong.

The options range from purely automated to purely manual. Our solution is going to be a blend of purely automated and purely manual. This decision is key to building a model: **if you can't get something purely automated, can you develop something that will alleviate a significant amount of the workload?**

Building the Model: Starting Small

One thing I always suggest: **build a small model that represents enough of the data and scenarios to get the tool functioning**.

If we were to try building this tool with all 100 people, that would be a lot of unnecessary and distracting scrolling around and flipping between worksheets. We need to get something working and we can scale it out and make it pretty later.

In other words: Get the concepts down before diving in and solving the full problem.

Thus, we're not going to build this model with 100 people (first names, last names, email addresses, phone numbers, RSVP status, etc.) and 12 tables. This chapter will focus on building a model with

- 36 first names
- six tables
- six seats at each table

In anticipation of having to type a lot, we're going to simplify things by adding an ID column. The IDs will be easier to type, re-type, switch around and test. By using IDs this also mean that at some point in the development we'll need a piece that converts each number to a name, e.g. 26 would convert to Brent.

Now we need a set of seating rules for testing, and a way to model the seating arrangement. The rules are shown in the image on the next page in the sections: MUST NOT SIT TOGETHER and MUST SIT TOGETHER. The seating assignments on the worksheet in cells K1:R8.

We see that Heather, Phillip and Cyrril (7, 6, 18) must not sit together, and Lucienne and Johann must sit together (1, 8).

GUESTS	ID
Lucienne	1
Mitsuru	2
Terry	3
Stephanie	4
Mitzy	5
Philip	6
Heather	7
Johann	8
Paulo	9
Skip	10
P. J.	11
Ardis	12
Josheen	13
Rhonda	14
Gail	15
Jeremy	16
Raoul	17
Cyrril	18
Pam	19
Tina	20
Lois	21
Ben	22
Dave	23
Angie	24
Julie	25
Brent	26
Paul	27
Athena	28
Kristopher	29
Elise	30
Francisco	31
Michael	32
Ivan	33
Piper	34
Omar	35
Sunny	36

List of guests (numbered).

	A	B	C		D	E	F	G	H	I	J	K	L	M	N	O	P	Q	R	S
1	GUESTS	ID	Assigned												Tables, by ID					
2	Lucienne	1	CHECK												A	B	C	D	E	F	
3	Mitsuru	2	CHECK											1							
4	Terry	3	CHECK											2							
5	Stephanie	4	CHECK											3							
6	Mitzy	5	CHECK										Seats	4							
7	Philip	6	CHECK											5							
8	Heather	7	CHECK											6							
9	Johann	8	CHECK																		
10	Paulo	9	CHECK						MUST NOT SIT TOGETHER												
11	Skip	10	CHECK					7	6	18											
12	P. J.	11	CHECK					34	15	4											
13	Ardis	12	CHECK					24	11	14											
14	Josheen	13	CHECK					3	6												
15	Rhonda	14	CHECK																		
16	Gail	15	CHECK					MUST SIT TOGETHER													
17	Jeremy	16	CHECK					1	11	5											
18	Raoul	17	CHECK					17	26	18											
19	Cyrril	18	CHECK					1	8												
20	Pam	19	CHECK					24	16	4											
21	Tina	20	CHECK					28	10												
22	Lois	21	CHECK					31	22												
23	Ben	22	CHECK					2	12												

Seating assignments set-up.

The next step is to randomly input some seating assignments. Notice in the image below, person 15 is entered twice—at tables C and D in seat 1:

Tables, by ID						
Seats	A	B	C	D	E	F
1	5	11	15	15	33	7
2	6	8	36	18	29	17
3	19	22	28	1	20	30
4	10	35	23	9	26	2
5	31	34	12	13	32	3
6	14	4	27	21	16	24

Random seating assignments.

Entering 15 twice is deliberate because now we're anticipating the types of problems that can come up in the use of the model. It would be a perfectly human error to enter an ID twice. Since an ID can be entered twice, what is the other problem that's caused by this? Answer: It's not easy to see which ID is left out.

This adds new requirements to the final product:

- Identify duplicated IDs—people with more than one seat.
- A mechanism for identifying unassigned IDs—people who haven't been assigned a seat.

Note: As developers we have to think beyond the primary functionality. We're now thinking about how easy the application may be used and adopted as a valued tool.

To resolve the issue of "one backside, multiple chairs" we use conditional formatting to highlight duplicate values.

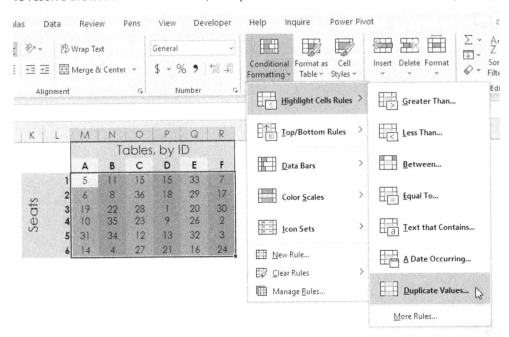

Conditional formatting is used to highlight duplicate values.

The image below shows the option of yellow fill and regular font for duplicate values:

Tables, by ID					
A	**B**	**C**	**D**	**E**	**F**
5	11	15	15	33	7
6	8	36	18	29	17
19	22	28	1	20	30
10	35	23	9	26	2
31	34	12	13	32	3
14	4	27	21	16	24

Duplicate values are now highlighted.

Next! How do we know who's missing a seat?

In the list of guests and IDs, we add an 'Assigned' column and use COUNTIF to count how many times an ID is in the seating assignments section. If an ID is represented one time, perfect! The cell remains blank. If an ID is represented zero (0), or two (2) or more times, the cell will show CHECK:

```
=IF(COUNTIF($M$3:$R$8,[@ID])=1,"","CHECK")
```

LEFT   ✕   ✓   *fx*   =IF(COUNTIF($M$3:$R$8,[@ID])=1,"","CHECK")

	A	B	C	D	K	L	M	N	O	P	Q	R	S
1	**GUESTS**	**ID**	**Assigned**				Tables, by ID						
2	Lucienne	1	"CHECK")				**A**	**B**	**C**	**D**	**E**	**F**	
3	Mitsuru	2					5	11	15	15	33	7	
4	Terry	3					6	8	36	18	29	17	
5	Stephanie	4					19	22	28	1	20	30	
6	Mitzy	5					10	35	23	9	26	2	
7	Philip	6					31	34	12	13	32	3	
8	Heather	7					14	4	27	21	16	24	
9	Johann	8											

Using the 'Assigned' column.

Now it's clear: Gail (15) has two seats and Julie (25) is unassigned:

	A	B	C
1	**GUESTS**	**ID**	**Assigned**
2	Lucienne	1	
3	Mitsuru	2	
4	Terry	3	
5	Stephanie	4	
6	Mitzy	5	
7	Philip	6	
8	Heather	7	
9	Johann	8	
10	Paulo	9	
11	Skip	10	
12	P. J.	11	
13	Ardis	12	
14	Josheen	13	
15	Rhonda	14	
16	Gail	15	CHECK
17	Jeremy	16	
18	Raoul	17	
19	Cyrril	18	
20	Pam	19	
21	Tina	20	
22	Lois	21	
23	Ben	22	
24	Dave	23	
25	Angie	24	
26	Julie	25	CHECK
27	Brent	26	

Results stand out in the 'Assigned' column.

Change the entry of '15' in Seat 1, Table D to '25', and the yellow cell highlighting will go away.

Managing the Seating Rules

Who Must Not Sit Together?

This was tricky to figure out. How can we know if 7, 6 and / or 8 are at the same table? One solution is to count and get a sum. For example:

If 7, 6 or 8 are at Table 1, count how many of them are at the table. If the sum is greater than one, we're setting ourselves up for an un-fun event.

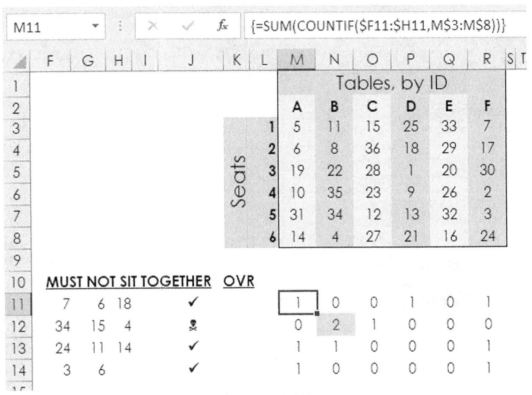

Table used to assess who must not sit together.

Below is the formula in cell M11. It's an array formula that must be completed with Ctrl + Shift + Enter. (For those who have the Dynamic Arrays – see Liam Bastick's "A Look to the Future – Dynamic Arrays" on page 45 – and the new Excel calculation engine, Ctrl + Shift + Enter is not necessary.)

```
{=SUM(COUNTIF($F11:$H11,M$3:M$8))}
```

The formula says: count the number of times 7, 6 or 8 show up on Table A and then sum. The result is 1 because only one person, number 6, is at the table. However, for the second rule, at Table B there's a 2 because 34 and 4 are both assigned to this table.

Also, notice that conditional formatting has been used to highlight that 2. This is another feature in the model to ensure that the user sees that something is wrong.

In the image below, an alert is added to tell us if a rule is okay or not:

	F	G	H	I	J	K	L	M	N	O	P	Q	R	S	T	U	V
		V11				f_x	=IF(MAX(M11:R11)<2,"ok","fix")										
10	**MUST NOT SIT TOGETHER**					**OVR**											
11	7	6	18		✓			1	0	0	1	0	1				ok
12	34	15	4		☠			0	2	1	1	0	0				fix
13	24	11	14		✓			1	1	0	0	0	1				ok
14	3	6			✓			1	0	0	0	0	1				ok

Alert has been added.

The formula in V11 is:

```
=IF(MAX(M11:R11)<2,"ok","fix")
```

If the MAX number in the row is less than two (2), we're fine. The formula would show "ok", otherwise "fix." Finally. In the image below, we use the Wingdings font to show a checkmark if a rule is met or a skull-and-crossbones if a rule is broken.

```
=IF(V11="ok","ü","N")
```

| | J11 | ▼ | : | × | ✓ | fx | | =IF(V11="ok","ü","N") | | | | | | |

◢	F	G	H	I	J	K	L	M	N	O	P	Q	R	S T U	V
10	MUST NOT SIT TOGETHER				OVR										
11	7	6	18		✓			1	0	0	1	0	1		ok
12	34	15	4		☠			0	2	1	1	0	0		fix
13	24	11	14		✓			1	1	0	0	0	1		ok
14	3	6			✓			1	0	0	0	0	1		ok

Using Wingdings to make the messages clearer.

Who MUST sit together?

Note: In this section, the seating assignments have been modified so that we have a mix of satisfied and violated rules for testing.

As in the 'Who Must Not Sit Together' section, the range M17:R23 is using SUM and COUNTIF in an array formula to count the number of IDs at each table based on the rules.

Cell M18 results in zero (0) because not one of the IDs 17, 26 or 18 is assigned to Table A.

◢	F	G	H	I	J	K	L	M	N	O	P	Q	R	S T U	V
1										Tables, by ID					
2								A	B	C	D	E	F		
3							1	5	11	15	25	33	7		
4							2	28	9	36	18	29	17		
5							3	19	22	6	1	20	30		
6				Seats			4	10	35	23	8	26	2		
7							5	31	34	12	13	32	3		
8							6	14	4	27	21	16	24		
9															
16	MUST SIT TOGETHER				OVR										
17	1	11	5		☠			1	1	0	1	0	0		3 fix
18	17	26	18		☠			0	0	0	1	1	1		3 fix
19	1	8			✓			0	0	0	2	0	0		2 ok
20	24	16	4		☠			0	1	0	0	1	1		3 fix
21	28	10			✓			2	0	0	0	0	0		2 ok
22	31	22			☠			1	1	0	0	0	0		2 fix
23	2	12			☠			0	0	1	0	0	1		2 fix

Must Sit Together computations.

The image below shows that COUNTA is used for counting how many IDs are in the rule:

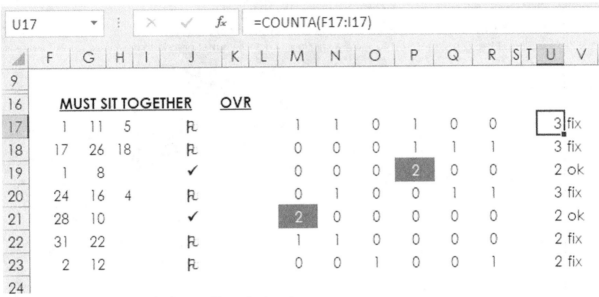

COUNTA is used for counting how many IDs are in the rule.

The next image shows a more complex formula. What's important here is that the formula is used to compare the MAX number in the row against the number of IDs in the rule and result in either "fix" or "ok". Here is the formula in V17:

```
{=IF(K17="x","ok",IF(MAX(M17:R17)<COUNTA(F17:H17),"fix","ok"))}
```

In row 17, there are three people who must sit together: 1, 11 and 15. However, at each of the tables the maximum is one (1). For this rule to be satisfied, we need a 3 at one of the tables. Hence, in column V the result is "fix" and in column J the error is reinforced with a flag.

In row 19, IDs 1 and 8 are two people who are assigned to table D. The max in the row is two (2) — highlighted using conditional formatting — and column V shows "ok" so there's a checkmark in column J.

F	G	H	I	J	K	L	M	N	O	P	Q	R	S	T	U	V	W	X
9																		
16	MUST SIT TOGETHER			OVR														
17	1	11	5	🚩			1	1	0	1	0	0			3	fix		
18	17	26	18	🚩			0	0	0	1	1	1			3	fix		
19	1	8		✓			0	0	0	2	0	0			2	ok		
20	24	16	4	🚩			0	1	0	0	1	1			3	fix		
21	28	10		✓			2	0	0	0	0	0			2	ok		
22	31	22		🚩			1	1	0	0	0	0			2	fix		
23	2	12		🚩			0	0	1	0	0	1			2	fix		

Cell reference: V17 — `=IF(K17="x","ok",IF(MAX(M17:R17)<COUNTA(F17:H17),"fix","ok"))`

Flagging what works and what does not.

Adding an Override

What if we have requests that are impossible to satisfy or a request that we know will be ok if it's not satisfied? Here are a couple of examples:

- **Impossible to satisfy:** five rules that, if met, would require 14 people to sit at a table designed for eight people.
- **Not crucial:** three people who'd like to sit together but they're good friends with everyone at the party. Therefore, if seating them together is conflicting with crucial requests, we can override their request, and everyone will still be happy.

That's how the override works in column K:

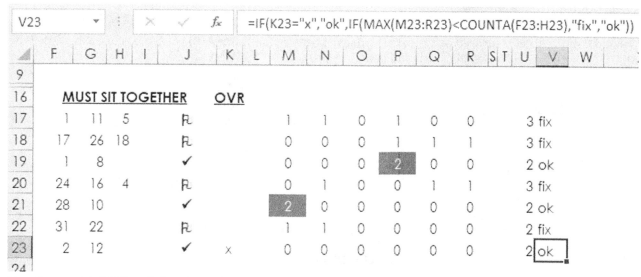

How the override 'OVR' works in column K.

With an x in K23, the formula in V23 uses an IF statement to ignore the comparison of the MAX and COUNTA results. In the image below, the Wingdings checkmark is populated by an IF statement that's checking for "ok" in column V, even though person 12 is at Table C and person 2 is at Table F.

	F	G	H	I	J	K	L	M	N	O	P	Q	R	S	T	U	V
9																	
16	**MUST SIT TOGETHER**					OVR											
17	1	11	5		℞			1	1	0	1	0	0				3 fix
18	17	26	18		℞			0	0	0	1	1	1				3 fix
19	1	8			✓			0	0	0	2	0	0				2 ok
20	24	16	4		℞			0	1	0	0	1	1				3 fix
21	28	10			✓			2	0	0	0	0	0				2 ok
22	31	22			℞			1	1	0	0	0	0				2 fix
23	2	12			✓	x		0	0	0	0	0	0				2 ok
24																	

Formula bar: J23 =IF(V23="ok","ü","O")

Override column in action.

Let's Make This Thing Work!

Let's look at how an event planner would use this tool. Starting with the assignments empty… it's beautiful!

Column C shows "CHECK" for everyone because no one has been assigned a seat. The rules are accurate because the MUST NOT SIT TOGETHER rules aren't being violated and the MUST SIT TOGETHER rules are all unsatisfied.

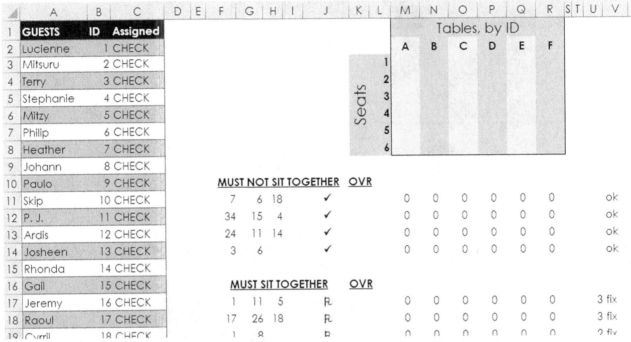

Starting with the assignments empty.

The manual part of this tool will be the assignment of seats one at a time while referring to the rules. The image below shows all of the seating requests have been satisfied and column C shows us all of the people who still need to be assigned seats.

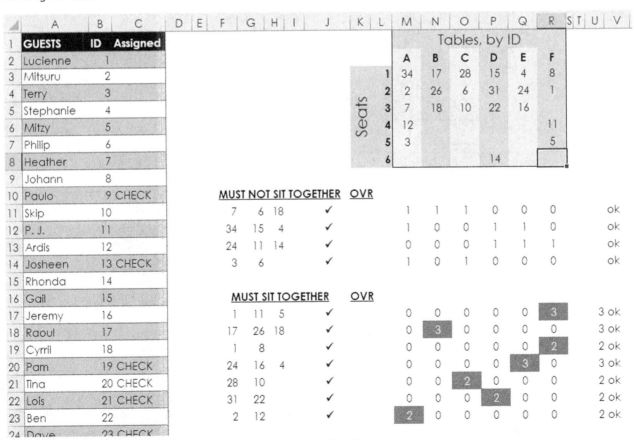

Assigning seats one at a time to make it work with the rules in place first.

We keep going – and here we are! Everyone has a seat. No alerts are showing. We're ready to have a good time!

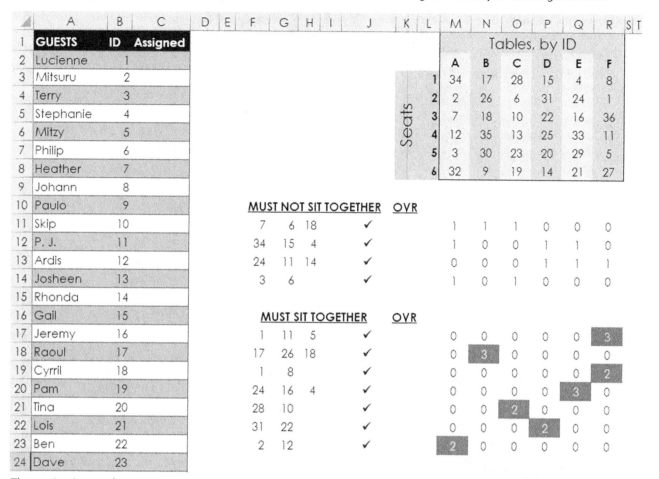

The seating is complete.

Final Touches

Converting the IDs to Names

In range X2:AC8, we can see the names associated with the IDs. This uses INDEX to look in the corresponding cell in Tables, by ID range, to grab the ID and retrieve the name from the guests list. Thus, 3 in M7 is the third person in the guest list and Terry is populated in cell X7 and assigned to Table A. The formula in cell X7 is

```
=INDEX(Table1[[GUESTS]:[GUESTS]],M7)
```

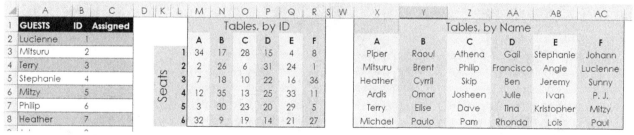

Providing the names.

Seating Chart Visual: One of Few Good Uses for a Donut Chart

On a new worksheet named Seating Chart, in range U8:Z13, these values are simply being retrieved from the Tables, by Name range, on the Seating Assignments worksheet. The list of ones (1s) in column AA are required because we need values to make the donut chart:

    ='Seating Assignments'!AA3

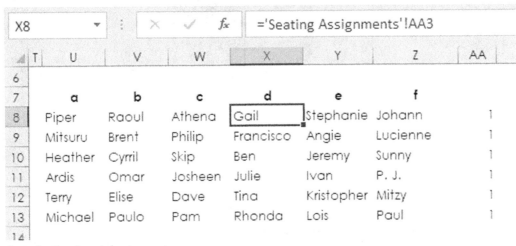

Data for the donut chart.

The image below shows all six tables and assignments represented as donut charts. The chart for Table D is selected and you can see that the chart is generated from the list of names in the column 'd'.

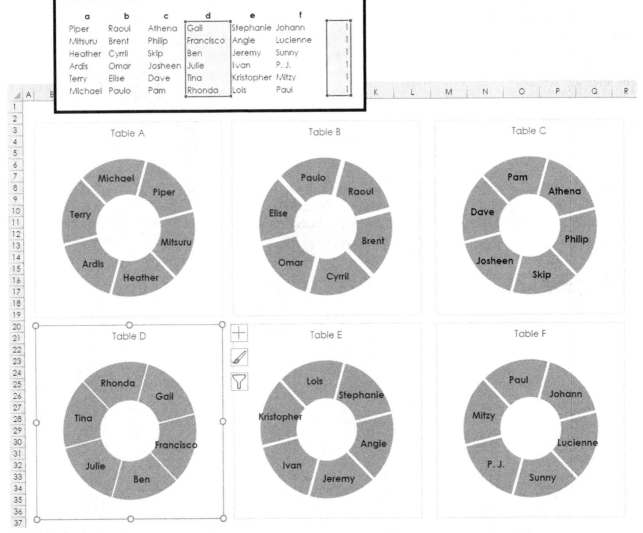

Set of donut charts.

a	b	c	d	e	f	
Piper	Raoul	Athena	Gail	Stephanie	Johann	1
Mitsuru	Brent	Philip	Francisco	Angie	Lucienne	1
Heather	Cyrril	Skip	Ben	Jeremy	Sunny	1
Ardis	Omar	Josheen	Julie	Ivan	P. J.	1
Terry	Elise	Dave	Tina	Kristopher	Mitzy	1
Michael	Paulo	Pam	Rhonda	Lois	Paul	1

The 1's on the right are used as the data for each of the donut charts.

Now What?

If you'd like, you can download the workbook and modify it to solve the original challenge of 100 people and 12 tables.

Hopefully, you appreciated this journey through the thought process of building a model. When the idea for this book came up, I thought about various how-to topics. However, I've noticed that there isn't enough of the thinking process presented as part of teaching. Even when I studied bass guitar, instructors would show me what to play and they never explained the *why* or detailed *how* they made decisions when they had multiple options.

Being exposed to the thought process behind a finished project can be more empowering than simply showing the final inner-workings. They give us a way to recover when things fall apart, and they give us a starting point when we're starting from nothing.

Financial Modelling
by Tony de Jonker

Introduction

Excel is used by many finance professionals such as accountants, controllers and analysts to prepare a diversity of financial reports. Such reports include the Balance Sheet, the Profit & Loss Statement and the Cash Flow Forecast. They must be reported in a specific prescribed fashion as dictated by management and / or by law which prevent the use of PivotTables as a report layout.

Data is normally stored in an Enterprise Resource Planning (ERP) system (a book-keeping system, say) to record the historical details. Descriptions such as "budget" and "forecast" are future-oriented data and are usually administered at an aggregated level. Typically, the budget is set at the beginning of the year and will remain the same during the year, while forecast numbers may be adapted on a monthly basis. The time horizon should be dynamic, e.g. we may compare months, weeks or days. The data presented usually show actuals (history) and budget / forecast (future).

To capture all these features in an all-encompassing Excel model would be quite mind boggling if you do not have a structure and follow the laws of effective modelling. In traditional financial modelling literature, you'll see how to set up a Balance Sheet, Profit & Loss statement and the Cash Flow Statement. However, they are often geared towards professionals working for banks and do not show how to deal with big data as it appears in real business life. Neither does it show how to create a dynamic Cash Flow forecast based on the direct method.

Most models I have seen are prepared without any of the new "Power" tools in Excel, such as Power Query and Power Pivot, although it would make sense to use these tools in conjunction with traditional financial modelling because it will save you a lot of time in preparing the reports and you'll gain a better insight in the numbers.

In this article, I will show you the challenges that I have encountered in my practice when developing financial models for clients. Among these challenges are:

- How to report detailed actuals against aggregated budget / forecast.
- How to create a dynamic timeline.
- How to consolidate data from different entities.
- How to apply the power tools in financial models.

Reporting Actuals versus Budget / Forecast

Actual numbers are stored in an ERP system such as SAP or Microsoft Dynamics. On a monthly basis you would download the Trial Balance to Excel, which might have the following layout:

- Column A: Account number
- Column B: Account description
- Column C: Date
- Column D: Amount

	A	B	C	D
1	Acc No	Account Description	Date	Amount
2	8001	Turnover Europe	Dec-17	€ -
3	8001	Turnover Europe	Jan-18	€ -11.347,00
4	8001	Turnover Europe	Feb-18	€ -9.892,00
5	8001	Turnover Europe	Mar-18	€ -10.566,00
6	8001	Turnover Europe	Apr-18	€ -11.727,00
7	8001	Turnover Europe	May-18	€ -11.785,00
8	8001	Turnover Europe	Jun-18	€ -9.517,00
9	8001	Turnover Europe	Jul-18	€ -8.464,00
10	8001	Turnover Europe	Aug-18	€ -11.259,00
11	8001	Turnover Europe	Sep-18	€ -11.934,00
12	8001	Turnover Europe	Oct-18	€ -10.737,00
13	8001	Turnover Europe	Nov-18	€ -11.172,00
14	8001	Turnover Europe	Dec-18	€ -10.315,00
15	8002	Turnover USA	Dec-17	€ -
16	8002	Turnover USA	Jan-18	€ -8.020,00
17	8002	Turnover USA	Feb-18	€ -11.591,00
18	8002	Turnover USA	Mar-18	€ -8.590,00
19	8002	Turnover USA	Apr-18	€ -10.627,00

Example Trial Balance layout.

As you can see, the numbers are stored at an account level. The budget numbers are usually maintained (manually) in Excel spreadsheets by account group and months running horizontally. This is what we call a cross-table and might have the following layout: Column A: level. Columns B through M: Jan-19, Feb-19, …, Dec-19.

Level	Jan-18	Feb-18	Mar-18	Apr-18	May-18	Jun-18
Turnover	€ 17.132	€ 32.933	€ 29.270	€ 20.873	€ 27.694	€ 38.829
Cost of Sales	€ 16.696	€ 15.811	€ 18.029	€ 16.433	€ 18.815	€ 18.318
Personnel	€ 2.479	€ 3.522	€ 2.478	€ 3.911	€ 2.232	€ 2.191
Travel	€ 557	€ 589	€ 649	€ 579	€ 797	€ 879
Communication	€ 332	€ 867	€ 664	€ 938	€ 921	€ 521
Marketing	€ 659	€ 390	€ 216	€ 864	€ 917	€ 351
Occupancy	€ 925	€ 564	€ 691	€ 902	€ 629	€ 760
General & Admin	€ 506	€ 882	€ 203	€ 922	€ 328	€ 881
Financial Costs	€ 698	€ 946	€ 622	€ 345	€ 503	€ 795
Depreciation	€ 1.881	€ 1.839	€ 1.774	€ 1.348	€ 1.803	€ 1.692
Taxes	€ 1.204	€ 2.204	€ 2.360	€ 1.441	€ 1.397	€ 2.179

Example of a cross-table.

The budget / forecast is stored in a cross-table style to keep the data entry simple for the user.

A database style entry would make it difficult for the user to compare numbers throughout the periods. Expenses and revenues are entered as positive numbers. However, in the Trial Balance, revenues are usually entered as credit amount, i.e. represented as negative numbers.

To merge Budget / Forecast and Actuals, we must find a link between the account number in the Actuals and Account Group in Budget / Forecast. You will find this important piece of information in the Chart of Accounts, which might have the following layout:

- Column A: Account number
- Column B: Account description
- Column C: Type
- Column D: Level
- Column E: Sign.

Acc No	Account Description	Type	Level	Sign
8001	Turnover Europe	PL	Turnover	-1
8002	Turnover USA	PL	Turnover	-1
8003	Turnover Asia	PL	Turnover	-1
8004	Turnover Africa	PL	Turnover	-1
7001	Cost of Sales Europe	PL	Cost of Sales	1
7002	Cost of Sales USA	PL	Cost of Sales	1
7003	Cost of Sales Asia	PL	Cost of Sales	1
7004	Cost of Sales Africa	PL	Cost of Sales	1
4000	Accounting Fees	PL	General & Admin	1
4010	Advertising & Marketing	PL	Marketing	1
4020	Bank Charges	PL	Financial Costs	1
4030	Cleaning Expenses	PL	Occupancy	1
4040	Computer Expenses	PL	General & Admin	1
4050	Consumables	PL	General & Admin	1
4060	Electricity & Water	PL	Occupancy	1
4070	Entertainment	PL	Travel	1
4080	Equipment Hire	PL	Occupancy	1
4090	Insurance	PL	General & Admin	1
4100	Legal Fees	PL	General & Admin	1
4110	Motor Vehicle Expenses	PL	Travel	1
4120	Postage	PL	General & Admin	1

Example Chart of Accounts.

The common denominator between Actuals and Budget is the field 'Level', after we have linked account number in Actuals to the appropriate level.

We have one file containing three separate sheets for Actuals, Budget and Chart of Accounts. All the sheets have been converted to Tables via the option on the ribbon, Insert -> Table. The Tables have been assigned appropriate names, such as DataActual, DataBudget and DataCOA.

It would be quite a struggle to merge Budget and Actuals in a traditional way, i.e. without using any of the modern Excel Power Tools. Power Query is here to your rescue: on the ribbon, you'll find the feature now under Data -> Get & Transform.

Steps to Merge Actuals and Budget

The first step is to make sure that the data is stored as an Excel Table. You get an Excel Table when you choose from the ribbon Insert -> Table, while having the cursor placed in the Table. The next step is figuring out which transformation steps you must take. In this example, we will perform the following steps:

- Load all tables into Power Query.
- Revert as connection only.
- Actuals.
  - Add account group or level by merging with Chart of Accounts.
  - Convert amount.
  - Delete account number.
  - Add type 'Actuals'.
- Budget.
  - Unpivot months.
  - Add type 'Budget'.
- Stack Budget and Actuals.

If you want to follow along, the step-by-step approach is as follows.

To begin, we need to load all the Tables into Power Query. To do so, go to the sheet where your Actuals reside. Select from the ribbon, Data -> Get & Transform Data -> From Table / Range.

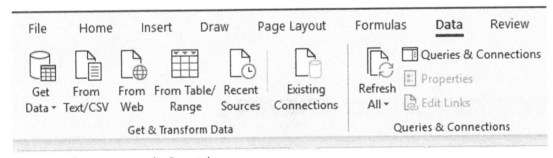

Get & Transform group on the Data tab.

You will now be presented with the Power Query Editor:

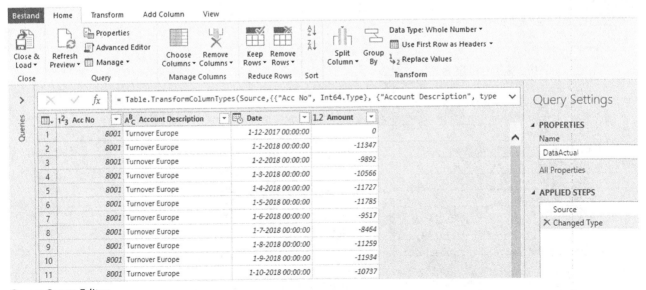

Power Query Editor.

Select from the ribbon, Home -> Close and Load -> Close and Load To -> Import Data dialog -> Only Create Connection -> OK.

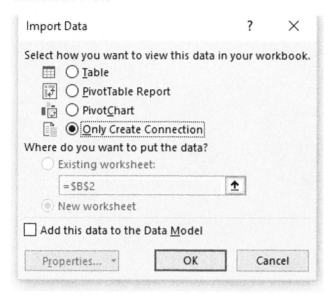

Import Data dialog to Only Create Connection.

On the right-hand side, the 'Queries & Connections' pane will be opened, and you'll see the first query **DataActual** appearing:

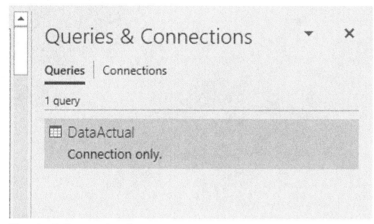

'Queries & Connections' pane.

Now go to the other sheets and do the same, thereby loading the Tables for Budget and Chart of Accounts.

Return to the Query of DataActual by double-clicking on the DataActual Query in the 'Queries & Connections' pane. Select from the ribbon, Home -> Combine -> Merge Queries. In the dialog box you will see DataActual appearing. Now, consider the second Table DataCOA and select the matching columns in both tables, i.e. the account number (Acc No) and click on OK.

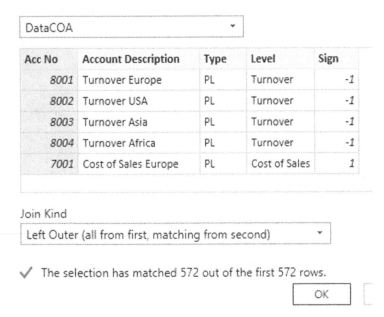

Merge

Select a table and matching columns to create a merged table.

DataActual

Acc No	Account Description	Date	Amount
8001	Turnover Europe	1-12-2017 00:00:00	0
8001	Turnover Europe	1-1-2018 00:00:00	-11347
8001	Turnover Europe	1-2-2018 00:00:00	-9892
8001	Turnover Europe	1-3-2018 00:00:00	-10566
8001	Turnover Europe	1-4-2018 00:00:00	-11727

DataCOA ▾

Acc No	Account Description	Type	Level	Sign
8001	Turnover Europe	PL	Turnover	-1
8002	Turnover USA	PL	Turnover	-1
8003	Turnover Asia	PL	Turnover	-1
8004	Turnover Africa	PL	Turnover	-1
7001	Cost of Sales Europe	PL	Cost of Sales	1

Join Kind

Left Outer (all from first, matching from second)   ▾

✓ The selection has matched 572 out of the first 572 rows.

OK

Merging Tables example.

An additional column called DataCOA has been added. Click on the double arrow and deselect all items. Select the fields Level and Sign and click on OK.

Field with the double arrow in the top right-hand corner.

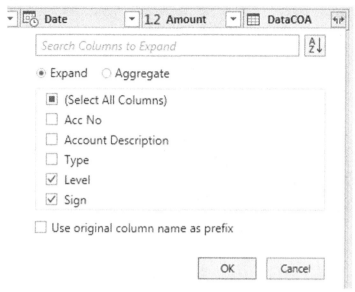

Expanding the Table for selected fields.

Delete columns Account number and Account Description:

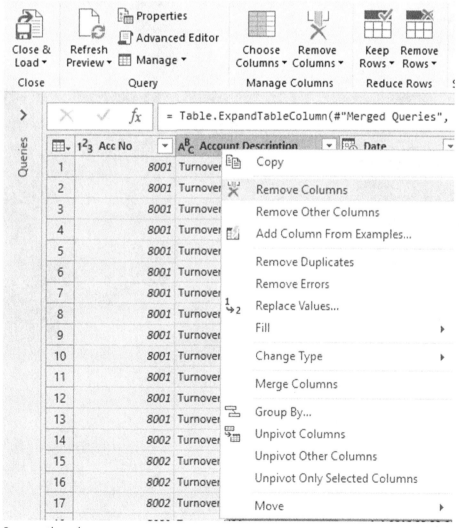

Remove the columns.

We need to multiply the sign by the amount. You can do so by inserting a new column. From the ribbon, choose Add Column -> General -> Custom Column. Type the new column name 'Amt', insert [Amount], type *, insert [Sign] and click OK. Make sure that no syntax errors have been detected.

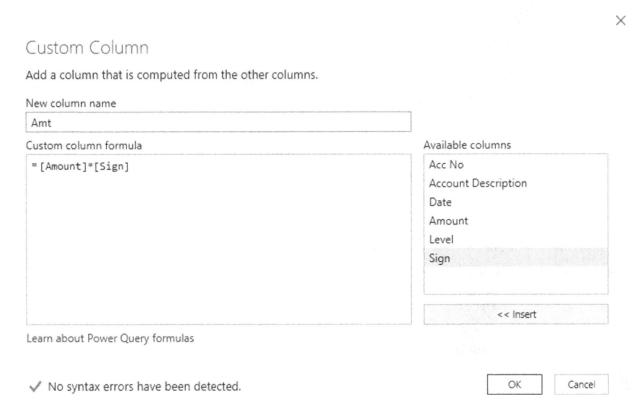

Custom Column dialog box.

Change header Amt into Amount and change format to 1.2 Decimal number.

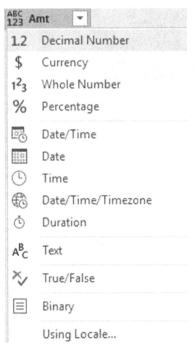

Changing to Decimal Number.

Delete columns **Amount** and **Sign** and change format of column **Date** from Date / Time into Date.

Insert Custom Column to denote the data type: Add Column -> General ->Custom Column. Type new column name: Type, insert "Actual" and click on OK. Change format into ABC (text).

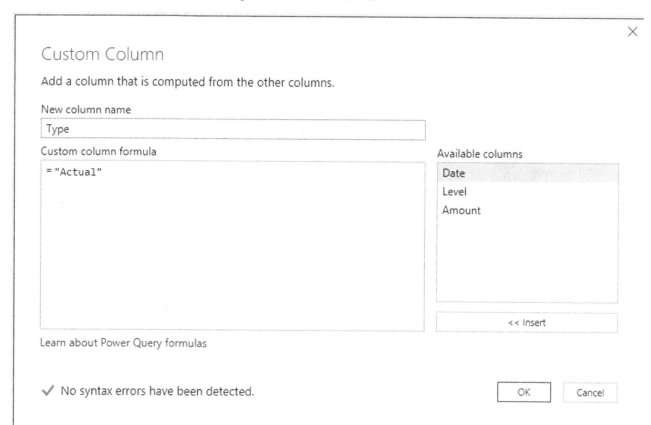

Creating a Custom Column.

Rearrange the columns so the order becomes: Type, Level, Date and Amount. You can rearrange by dragging the column heading left or right.

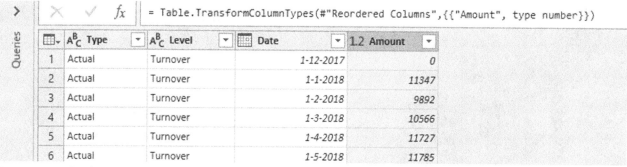

Rearranging the data.

Next is the transformation of DataBudget, so select the Query DataBudget. Select column Level and choose from the ribbon, Transform -> Any Column -> Unpivot Columns -> Unpivot Other Columns.

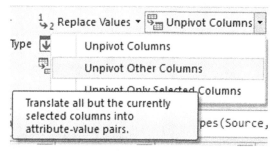

Unpivoting other columns.

The result after the unpivot looks like this:

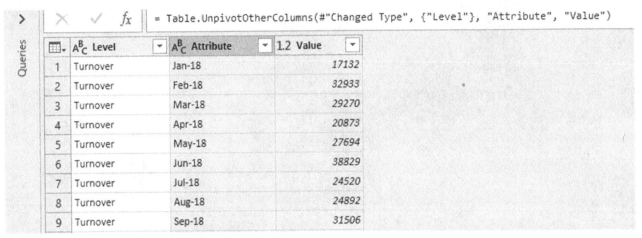

Result after the unpivot has happened.

Change the header 'Attribute' to 'Date' (and hence change the date type into Date as well as Value to Amount).

Insert Custom Column to cater for the Data Type: Add Column -> General -> Custom Column. Type the new column name: Type, insert "Budget" and click on OK. Change the data type to ABC (text).

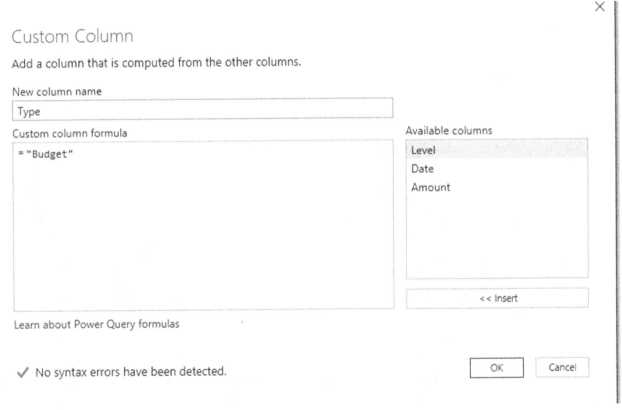

Adding a Custom Column.

Rearrange the columns so the order becomes Type, Level, Data and Amount. The result should look like this:

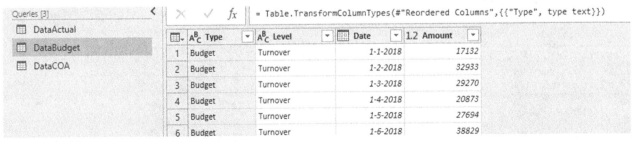

Reordered table.

The last transformation step is stacking the data. Select Home -> Combine -> Append Queries -> Append Queries as New -> Two Tables -> Primary Table: DataActual ->Table to Append -> DataBudget and click OK.

Append dialog.

Change Append Query name to Consolidated and Close and Load -> Close and Load To -> Import Data: Only Create Connection -> OK.

Creating a PivotTable

Based on the consolidated query, you can make a PivotTable, showing Actual versus Budget. Choose Insert -> PivotTable -> Use an external source -> Choose Connection.

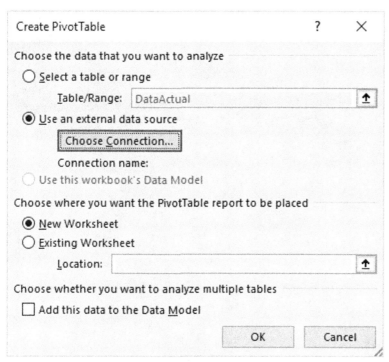

Create PivotTable dialog.

Select 'Query – Consolidated' and click on OK.

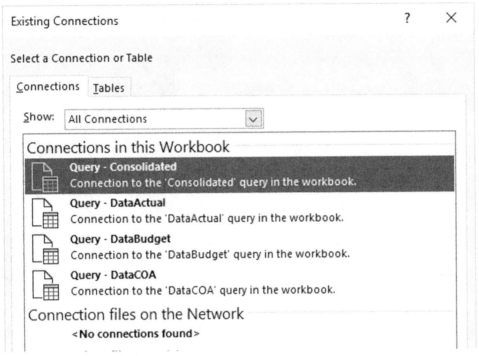

Existing Connections dialog.

Click OK again to close the dialog box. When you create the PivotTable, it's recommended to leave out the grand totals, since you do not want to add Actual to Budget. With the cursor on the PivotTable, select from the ribbon, PivotTable Tools -> Design -> Layout -> Grand Totals -> On for Columns Only.

Sum of Amount	Type	
Level	Actual	Budget
Cash	749.376	
Communication	3.765	8.371
Cost of Sales	302.335	209.515
Current Assets	767.064	
Current Liabilities	238.184	
Depreciation	22.160	21.034
Equity	652.075	
Financial Costs	9.285	7.361
Fixed Assets	1.262.260	
General & Admin	22.136	7.731
Long Term Debt	1.708.260	
Marketing	16.375	8.046
Occupancy	21.325	7.481
Personnel	36.091	31.922
Taxes	12.278	21.397
Travel	1.725	7.087
Turnover	476.125	326.636
Grand Total	6.300.820	656.581

Example PivotTable.

You can add a timeline to your PivotTable. Select from the ribbon, PivotTable Tools -> Analyze -> Filter -> Insert Timeline.

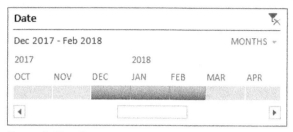

Example Timeline.

To calculate the difference between Actual and Budget, place your cursor on any of the dark red highlighted cells in the PivotTable:

Sum of Amount Type		
Level	Actual	Budget
Cash	156.124	
Communication	628	1.199
Cost of Sales	51.575	32.507
Current Assets	167.762	
Current Liabilities	50.358	
Depreciation	3.340	3.720
Equity	150.375	
Financial Costs	1.587	1.644
Fixed Assets	294.990	
General & Admin	1.256	1.388
Long Term Debt	406.683	
Marketing	1.250	1.049
Occupancy	2.956	1.489
Personnel	5.713	6.001
Taxes	3.509	3.408
Travel	0	1.146
Turnover	80.000	50.065
Grand Total	**1.378.106**	**103.616**

Highlighted PivotTable.

Select from the ribbon, PivotTable Tools -> Analyze -> Calculations -> Fields, Items & Sets -> Calculated Item. Type 'Difference' as the name.

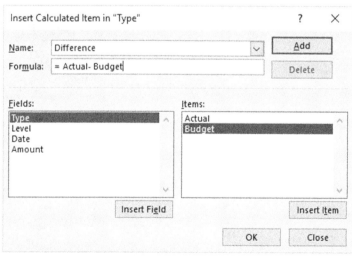

Inserting calculated item.

Select under Fields: Type. Click in the formula box. Select Actual under Items, click Insert Item, type minus, select Budget, click Insert Item and click OK.

The PivotTable should look as follows now:

Sum of Amount Level	Type ▾ Actual	Budget	Difference
Cash	156.124		156.124
Communication	628	1.199	-572
Cost of Sales	51.575	32.507	19.068
Current Assets	167.762		167.762
Current Liabilities	50.358		50.358
Depreciation	3.340	3.720	-380
Equity	150.375		150.375
Financial Costs	1.587	1.644	-57
Fixed Assets	294.990		294.990
General & Admin	1.256	1.388	-132
Long Term Debt	406.683		406.683
Marketing	1.250	1.049	201
Occupancy	2.956	1.489	1.467
Personnel	5.713	6.001	-289
Taxes	3.509	3.408	101
Travel	0	1.146	-1.146
Turnover	80.000	50.065	29.935
Grand Total	**1.378.106**	**103.616**	**1.274.490**

Revised PivotTable.

Creating a Dynamic Timeline

When you want to compare numbers for a certain Timeline in a custom report, you must cater for flexibility since you may want to view the numbers for other time buckets as well. To do so, you should start with an anchor cell displaying the start date. You could enter this manually or select via a data validation feature. The following periods can be calculated through a dynamic formula.

Displaying the Following Months

Our table looks as follows:

◢	A	B	C	D	E	F
1	Expense type	May-19	Jun-19	Jul-19	Aug-19	Sep-19
2	Rent	798	662	287	526	696
3	Car	912	148	657	642	179
4	Office	778	419	541	612	222

Example table.

To create a dynamic timeline from C1 towards the right, you need to mark the range, for example C1 to N1 and type the following formula:

=DATE(YEAR(B1, MONTH(B1)+1,1)

and press Ctrl + Enter.

Display the Following Weeks

The table layout is as follows:

	A	B	C	D	E	F	G
1	Week	18					
2							
3	Expense type	29-Apr-19	06-May-19	13-May-19	20-May-19	27-May-19	03-Jun-19
4	Rent	209	591	132	767	619	470
5	Car	589	670	786	486	640	252
6	Office	882	575	417	450	800	880

Another example table.

You can enter the week number. The start week of the chosen week is calculated in cell B3:

=DATE(YEAR(TODAY()),1,-2)-WEEKDAY(DATE(YEAR(TODAY()),1,3))+B1*7

To calculate the following weeks, highlight the range, i.e. C1 to G1 and type the following formula: **= B3+7** and press Ctrl + Enter.

Therefore, by changing the week number in cell B1, the entire timeline will change accordingly.

Consolidating Data

A very time-consuming job for financials is the consolidation of several uniform files, such as budgets and actuals. Just imagine doing a copy / paste for more than 100 files. You can write a VBA batch macro if you know how to do that or use Power Query. This was described previously in "Combine All Files in a Folder" on page 132. The following steps represent a simpler use of the feature.

To start, you must store all these files in a separate directory.

Let's suppose that the file has one sheet called data containing data in a Table format:

	A	B	C
1	date	product	amount
2	30-Mar-18	audio	€ 7.223
3	22-Sep-18	audio	€ 8.917
4	10-Jan-18	audio	€ 3.802
5	27-Nov-17	video	€ 5.240
6	20-Aug-17	computer	€ 7.666
7	30-Dec-17	audio	€ 3.740
8	31-Mar-17	audio	€ 7.150
9	10-Dec-17	video	€ 4.584
10	29-Aug-18	other	€ 4.453
11	18-Dec-18	audio	€ 5.007
12	13-Jun-18	other	€ 8.402
13	20-Sep-18	other	€ 8.084
14	15-Oct-17	audio	€ 6.576
15	17-Dec-17	video	€ 3.235
16	02-Dec-17	other	€ 7.127
17	29-Dec-18	video	€ 1.740

Sample data in a Table.

The table name is called DataBudget. All other files must have the same layout and same table name. They are stored in one directory:

> BudgetFiles

☐ Naam ⌃	Gewijzigd op	Type	Grootte
☑ Amsterdam.xlsx	8-5-2019 16:31	Microsoft Excel-w...	21 kB
London.xlsx	8-5-2019 16:32	Microsoft Excel-w...	21 kB
New York.xlsx	8-5-2019 16:32	Microsoft Excel-w...	21 kB
Paris.xlsx	8-5-2019 16:33	Microsoft Excel-w...	21 kB

Data stored in one directory.

Follow these steps to consolidate the data with Power Query.

Start with a new sheet and select from the ribbon, Data -> Get & Transform Data -> Get Data -> From File -> From Folder.

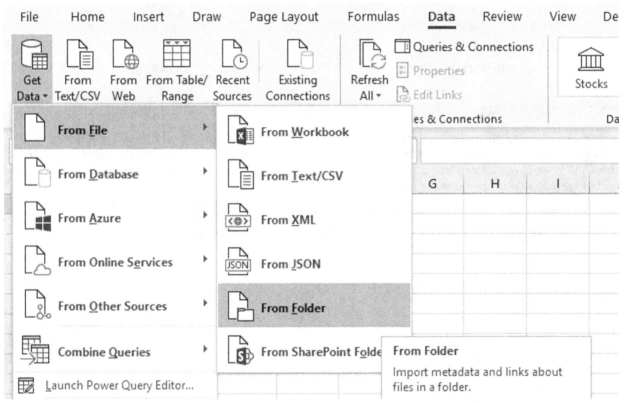

Get data From Folder.

Browse to the desired folder and click OK.

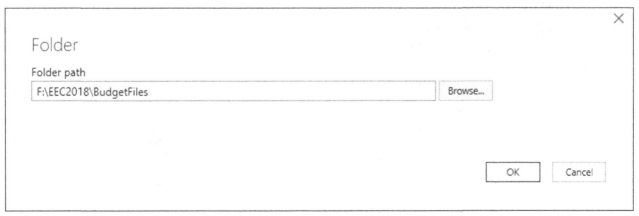

Selecting the folder.

In the next dialog box, you will see all files in the chosen directory.

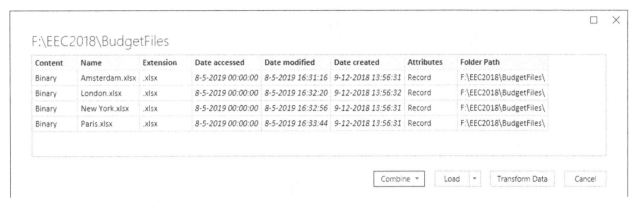

List of files in the chosen directory.

Click on the selection of the Combine button and you will be presented with the following options:

- Combine & Edit
- Combine & Load
- Combine & Load To...

List of Combine options

Warning: Typically, selecting Combine at this stage is a disaster waiting to happen. It is usually best to edit imported data first before electing to combine.

Choose 'Combine & Load' and select DataBudget.

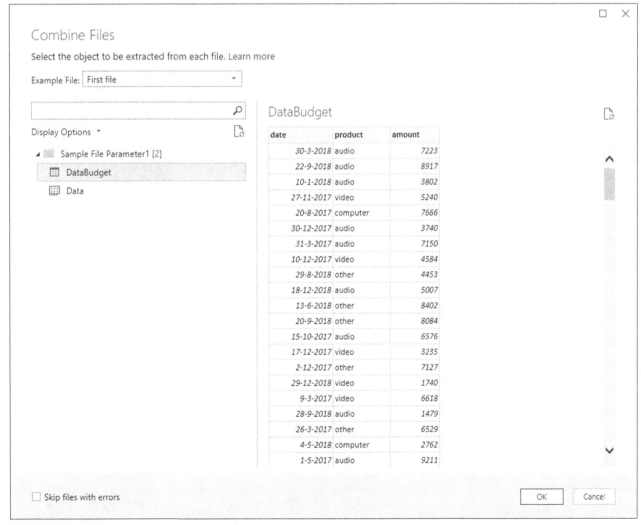

Combine Files dialog.

Click OK to load all the data. This may take several seconds. You will see the result appearing as a separate Table.

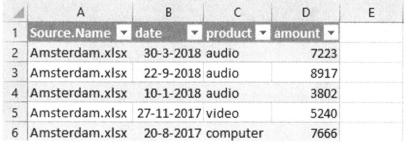

Combined Table.

When you click on the filter of Source.Name, you will see all the files:

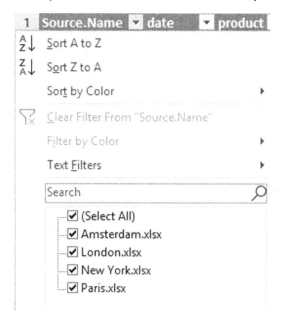

On the 'Queries & Connections' pane, you will see the transformation steps that Power Query has performed.

'Queries & Connections' pane once more.

In addition, you can se how many records are loaded. When you hover with your mouse above BudgetFiles you can see the last time the file has been refreshed.

BudgetFiles ✕

Source.Name	date	product	amount
Amsterdam.xlsx	30-3-2018	audio	7223
Amsterdam.xlsx	22-9-2018	audio	8917
Amsterdam.xlsx	10-1-2018	audio	3802
Amsterdam.xlsx	27-11-2017	video	5240
Amsterdam.xlsx	20-8-2017	computer	7666
Amsterdam.xlsx	30-12-2017	audio	3740
Amsterdam.xlsx	31-3-2017	audio	7150
Amsterdam.xlsx	10-12-2017	video	4584
Amsterdam.xlsx	29-8-2018	other	4453

Columns [4]

Source.Name, date, product, amount

Last refreshed

18:18

Load status

Loaded to worksheet

Data Sources [1]

f:\eec2018\budgetfiles

VIEW IN WORKSHEET	EDIT	•••	DELETE

BudgetFiles details.

Adding New Files

When you add a new file to the directory, you can refresh the data using one of the following three options:

- From the ribbon, select Data -> Queries & Connections -> Refresh All
- Right-click on the table and select Refresh
- In the 'Queries & Connections' pane, click on the Refresh icon (found on the last line next to BudgetFile):

Refresh icon for adding new files.

Creative Excel Model Development
by Hervé Thiriez

In my mind, the potential of Excel for creative and efficient modelling – in any domain – knows almost no limits. It is just up to you! I am using the term "creative" for several reasons:

- When I analyze the needs of a customer, I do not ask him what kind of Excel model he needs. If I did that, he would be limited in his imagination by his personal level of Excel expertise. What I ask him to describe to me is the model he dreams of, taking no account of what he knows or does not know about Excel.
- I always try to make my models as flexible as possible. Most of my charts are flexible (they automatically adapt to how much data has been entered), they have pull-down menus, dynamic titles (titles which include dynamic information), checkboxes, scroll bars, etc.
- Many of my consulting models include "movies". It is in fact quite easy to use Excel to make movies, as I show in the last section of this chapter.

The father of Excel, Multiplan, did not have a chart engine. When you wanted to create a chart, you had to export the data to an independent graphing software. However, in my book "Les secrets de Multiplan", published in 1986, I had a 20-page chapter showing how to create charts within Multiplan.

In Excel, most users are familiar with the Filter command in the Data tab of the ribbon. Well, this feature did not exist 20 years ago. However, in the bimonthly 24-page Excel newsletter (La lettre d'Excel) which I created in 1990 and published until 2005, I showed a macro that did exactly what the Filter command would do years later.

The two preceding examples illustrate how creativity may be applied to spreadsheets.

How I Became Involved with Spreadsheets

From 1963 onwards, I specialized in Applied Mathematics. At the time, I programmed in the Fortran language, with assembly language routines when speed was required. In 1969, I received a Ph.D. at MIT and became an Associate Professor.

My Ph.D. thesis, about airline crew scheduling, was very practical and American Airlines paid $10,000 to obtain my program. I was also contacted by NASA, for whom I then developed a model for the optimization of their budget allocations for the activities planned over the next 20 years.

In 1979, I bought one of the first Apple IIs sold in France, straight from London with an American keyboard and documentation. It came with VisiCalc, the first spreadsheet ever, the grandfather of Excel.

I was immediately convinced that both the microcomputer and the spreadsheet were major innovations. I then wrote the first book in French on VisiCalc and created the first Apple journal in France, Pom's, more than a year before Apple France was founded.

I have since developed all my models with spreadsheets (VisiCalc, Multiplan, Javelin and Excel).

To this day, I developed more than 1,000 models for more than 100 businesses in more than 10 countries.

A Chart which Replaces Many Charts

One day, I met a manager from Aéroports de Paris (AdP) at the Roissy airport who had a major problem with an Excel file analyzing the pedestrian traffic at different locations in the airport throughout the day. The file was 50MB in size and, when you opened it, there was a 50% chance of it crashing Excel. Simply saving the file took minutes.

This file had a good number of sheets, each of which contained several charts.

My solution was to eliminate all the charts on all the sheets and to add a chart sheet with only a single chart. The trick was that the chart used pull-down menus and other gimmicks allowing the user to select the day of the week, the terminal, and so on.

The title of the chart is a pull-down menu with eight possibilities. Then, going down on the left, you choose the day of the week (seven options), the type of chart (two options, independent or cumulative values), the satellite (eight options), opened banks (three options each). This single chart allows you to create 8,064 different charts (8 ** 7 * 2 * 8 * 3 * 3).

As a result, after I had also added some new features to this model, I scaled it down from 50MB to less than 10MB and all its problems disappeared.

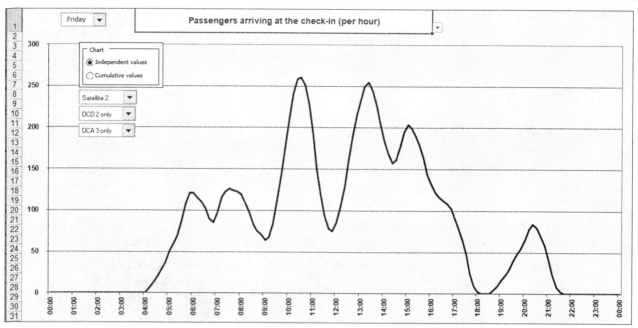

Pedestrian flow at the Roissy airport.

We will see below how it is possible – and not so difficult in fact! – to create a chart which replaces many charts based on data of different sizes located on a variety of sheets. In our example, we will create in a unique position a chart representing four charts using sets of data coming from two different sheets.

Present Multiple Graphs Through a Single Chart

We take a simple example with the data for four series, three on one sheet and one on another sheet. The technique we will use for charting all four series on a single chart is applicable to any number of series present on any number of sheets. With this technique, you could represent the 8,064 different charts of the Roissy example.

The following screenshot shows the three series located on the first sheet and, as an insert on the right, the series located on the second sheet.

	A	B	C	D	E	F	G	H	I	J	K	L	M	N		O	P
1	Product 1	Sales		Product_2	2010	2011	2012	2013	2014	2015	2016	2017	2018	2019		Product 3	Sales
2	Jan-18	1,000 €		Sales	2,000 €	2,071 €	2,338 €	2,772 €	2,867 €	3,732 €	4,730 €	5,240 €	4,793 €	2,650 €	1	Jan-17	3000
3	Feb-18	1,147 €													2	Feb-17	3247
4	Mar-18	1,001 €													3	Mar-17	3364
5	Apr-18	824 €		Product 4											4	Apr-17	3841
6	May-18	1,002 €		Jun-18	3,000 €										5	May-17	4094
7	Jun-18	926 €		Jul-18	3,232 €										6	Jun-17	4320
8	Jul-18	1,003 €		Aug-18	3,423 €										7	Jul-17	4623
9	Aug-18	1,049 €		Sep-18	3,265 €										8	Aug-17	4267
10	Sep-18	1,004 €		Oct-18	3,340 €										9	Sep-17	3510
11	Oct-18	1,314 €		Nov-18	3,806 €										10	Oct-17	3048
12	Nov-18	1,005 €		Dec-18	3,686 €										11	Nov-17	3248
13	Dec-18	1,056 €		Jan-19	3,327 €										12	Dec-17	3211
14	Jan-19	1,006 €		Feb-19	3,906 €										13	Jan-18	2814
15	Feb-19	906 €		Mar-19	3,211 €										14	Feb-18	2775
16	Mar-19	1,007 €		Apr-19	3,588 €										15	Mar-18	2852
17	Apr-19	1,180 €		May-19	3,835 €										16	Apr-18	2393
18	May-19	1,008 €													17	May-18	2207
19															18	Jun-18	2590
20															19	Jul-18	2258
21															20	Aug-18	1814
22															21	Sep-18	1814
23															22	Oct-18	1579
24															23	Nov-18	1364
															24	Dec-18	1231
															25	Jan-19	1405
															26	Feb-19	1469
															27	Mar-19	1645
															28	Apr-19	1633
															29	May-19	1901
															30		

Example data.

The screenshot below now shows the top of the chart sheet, which is located right after the other two worksheets. The A1:D5 block lists the data related to each series: Name, X and Y coordinates, and type of unit used, € or 0 (integer number).

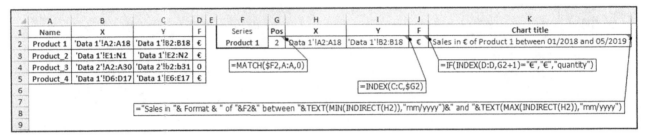

Top of the chart sheet.

In cell F2, there is a data validation list defined by $A$2:$A$5, so the user can see a pull-down menu with the list of chart names. A comment has been added to show the formulas used in the cells G2, I2, J2 and K2.

> **Note:** The entries in B2:B5 start with two single quotes. The first one is to indicate there is text and the second one to begin the text which shows on the screen. In order to obtain this result easily in B2, I typed "=" and then selected the appropriate area on the worksheet and finally replaced the "=" sign by a second single quote.

Creation of the Chart

In order to create the chart, the fastest and easiest solution is to first define the names for the X and the Y series:

My_X	=INDIRECT(Chart!$H$2)
My_Y	=INDIRECT(Chart!$I$2)

Naming the series.

and then to select any of the four data sets and create a chart for it. If you select the first series, you then obtain this formula for the chart:

```
=SERIES(,,'Data 1'!$A$2:$A$18,'Data 1'!$B$2:$B$18,1)
```

The trick is to click after the first "!" and then replace "$A$2:$A$18" with "My_X" and after the second "!" and replace $B$2:$B$18 with My_Y. Do you see how it works immediately and you now have the chart you wanted according to the pull-down menu in cell G2 of the Chart sheet?

Also, you may observe that in the **SERIES()** formula for the chart, both occurrences of 'Data 1' have been replaced by the name of the current Excel file. How so?

Well, this can be explained. Earlier, we had the $A$2:$A$18 and the $B$2:$B$18 addresses which were both references within the 'Data 1' sheet. We replaced these addresses with names, but names are not properties of a sheet, they are properties of a file. This is why the file name automatically replaced the sheet name with the file name in the **SERIES()** formula!

A Dynamic Title for the Chart

In cell K2, I entered a formula for the chart title. You are not allowed to type a formula like this for the title of a chart, but you can select a chart title and then enter in the formula bar the formula **=K2**. This is how you create a "dynamic title"!

Dynamic titles are very interesting: they do not limit themselves to being fixed text; they can add information relative to the series being shown on the chart. This is what we have here with the title showing additional information such as the nature of the data (quantities or euros) and the initial and final dates of the series.

Insert the Pull-Down Menu in the Chart

If you look at the initial graph of this chapter, the Roissy model, you will notice that the pull-down menu is inside the chart, not located in a separate cell. This is because I used another solution here. I used the Developer tab on the ribbon and the Insert command in order to insert a combo box linked to the A2:A5 range and putting the result in cell G2. This is a second way to solve the problem: it is a little more complex, but user-friendly as it allows you to put the combo box inside the chart.

The Charts

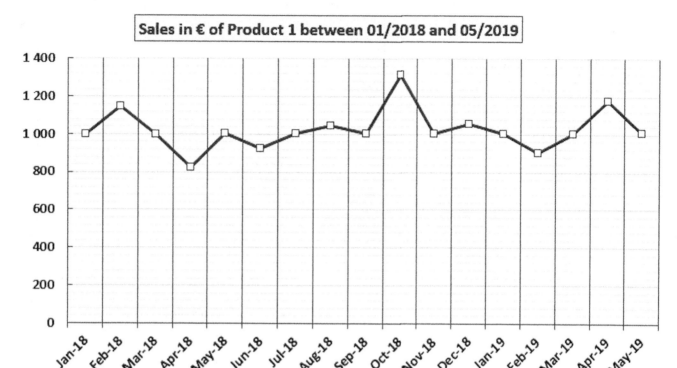

One of several example charts.

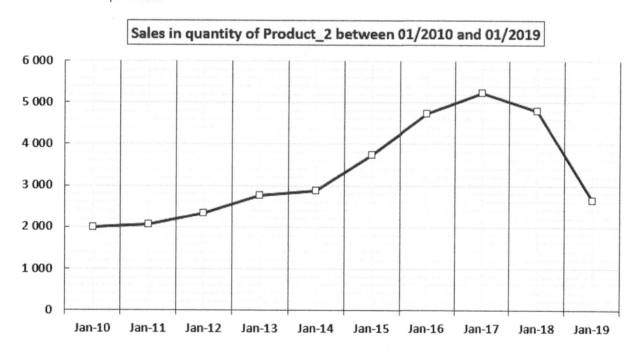

Another example chart.

The screens above and below show the charts obtained for the four series. We observe that the only chart which does not represent the values shown in the screen copy with the data is the Product_3 chart. This is because I used random values for this precise series so that the user could see in real time how the chart changes every time the F9 key is pressed.

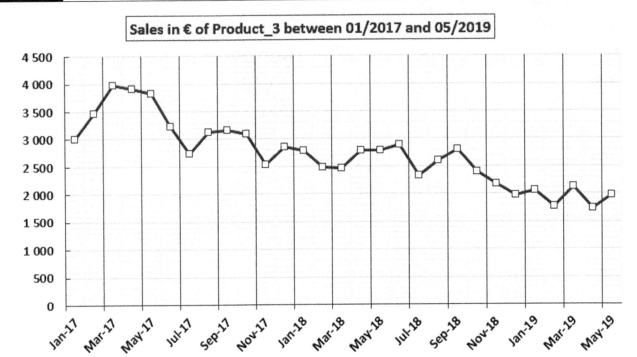

And yet another.

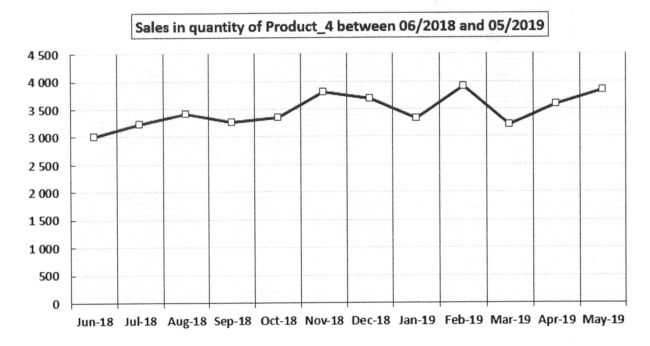

And the final one…

Selection of an Image Amongst Many

There are situations where you would like to select a subject from a pull-down list and immediately show a photograph or a drawing of the selection. It could be the picture of a person in a department (or any other group of people), a presentation of an object your company sells, or whatever else.

To illustrate this feature, I created a model where we select an animal and then obtain a picture of this animal on the screen. Here is what we obtain when we consecutively select any of our four possible animals:

Four images to choose from.

In order to achieve this result easily, there are four consecutive steps you need to go through:

- Select each image you pasted onto this sheet and give it the name of the animal.
- In column E, create a list of the names of the animals (or people or objects).
- Create a data validation list in cell C1, defined by a list: **=$E$1:$E$4** in this case.
- Attach the following macro to the sheet:

```
Private Sub Worksheet_Change(ByVal Target As Range)
    If Target.Address = "$C$1" Then
        Me.Pictures.Visible = False
        Me.Pictures(ActiveCell.Value).Visible = True
    End If
End Sub
```

It is just as simple as that.

If we wanted to add a little flexibility, all we would have to do would be to replace the **=$E$1:$E$4** validation list address with a flexible name – using the **OFFSET()** function – which would automatically adapt to integrate any new item entered below cell E4.

So here is what our final model looks like:

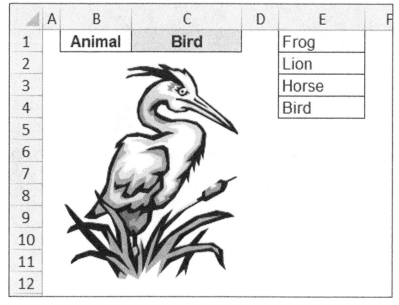

Final model.

A Dynamic Chart Range

In many business models, data is entered on a monthly basis. Therefore, it is highly practical if the chart could adapt automatically when data is entered for a new month (or week, for a weekly model), integrating the new data immediately.

There are at least two ways to achieve this result: with the `OFFSET()` function – a solution which works with all versions of Excel! – or by using Tables, which were introduced with Excel 2007.

A Solution with OFFSET()

Consider the chart example below. There are 10 values in the chart and we want to make the chart dynamic, i.e. automatically integrate any new data entered below cells A11:B11. If you select the chart and look at the formula bar, you see:

```
=SERIES(,Dynamic!$A$2:$A$11,Dynamic!$B$2:$B$11,1)
```

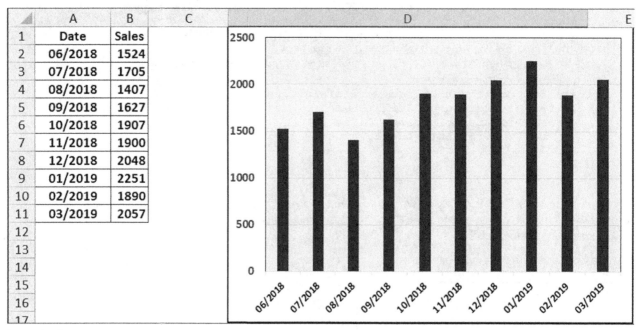

Example chart.

Now, let's create two names (Ctrl + F3):

`Dyn_X =Dynamic!$A$2:OFFSET(Dynamic!$A$2,,,COUNT(Dynamic!$A:$A))`

`Dyn_Y =OFFSET(Dyn_X,0,1)`

Now, all you have to do is to edit the `SERIES()` formula and replace `$A$2:$A$11` with `Dyn_X` and `$B$2:$B$11` with `Dyn_Y` and confirm the formula. You will immediately observe in the formula bar that the sheet name has been replaced with the file name. If you add data in cells A12:B12, you will see that the chart automatically integrates this new row of data.

A Problem with the SERIES Formula

At one time, I had a customer who wanted me to transform more than 25 charts in the same model with this approach. I then discovered that Excel refused to validate the modified formula in some cases. It turned out that it only happened when the names began with "C" or "R".

There must have been a collision somewhere in the programming of Excel with the use of "C" or "R" for "column" and "row". Even in the French version where "row" is "ligne", it is the "R" which generates a problem, not the "L"!

Strangely enough, I discovered that the problem could be solved by using names which did not start with "C" or "R". The modified `SERIES()` formula was then accepted by Excel. After that, you could modify these names into names starting with "C" or "R" and the problem was solved!

A Solution with a Table

The other way to solve the problem, without the OFFSET() solution, is to create a table with the A1:B11 range. The formula for the chart is: =SERIES(Dynamic!$G$1,Dynamic!$F$2:$F$11,Dynamic!$G$2:$G$11,1)

You do not have to do anything else. With this Table solution, there is nothing to change in the SERIES() formula. Any addition in cells F12:G12 is automatically integrated in the chart.

What you may find a little more difficult, however, is to customize this chart to look exactly like the preceding chart. A simple copy format and paste format from one chart to the other does not work.

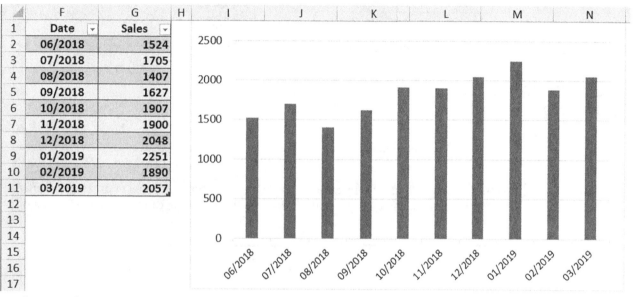

Similar example.

A Dynamic Drop-Down Menu

Sometimes, you need to define a cell using a data validated list which picks up its elements from a list which may have one of the two following problems:

- the list you need to propose is not sorted in alphabetical order.
- the list you need to propose is very long and is not practical for the user.

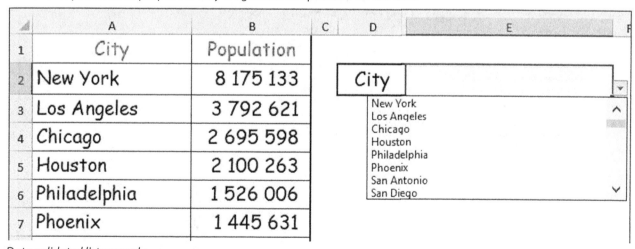

Data validated list example.

A very nice way to solve this problem is to let the user enter some characters in the cell and then limit the list to only the items in the list which include these characters. In the above example, we use a list of the 120 largest cities in the US.

As we can see in the screenshot (above), if we define the list of cities as the input to the validation list, we get the complete list where it might be difficult to locate the city we need to select. Our objective is to limit the search to only the cities which include a given series of characters.

In the example below, we entered "el" in cell E2 and then opened the list drop-down. As you may observe, only the cities including "el" in their name are now selected:

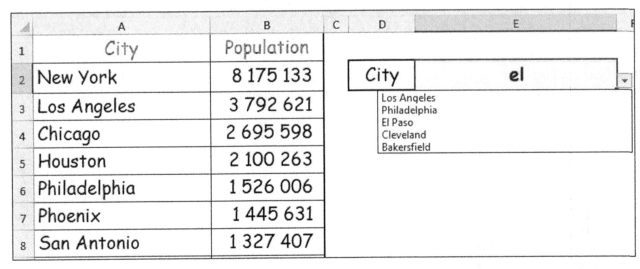

Filtered list.

What is really nice is that there are two standard wildcards in Excel, "?" for one single character and "*" for potentially more than one. For a string of characters of any length, both work perfectly well, as we can see with the following screen copies:

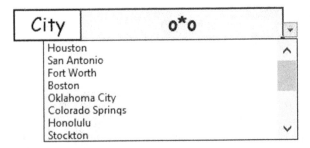
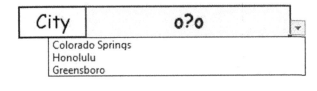

Examples of filtered lists.

In order to achieve our objective, we need to create two columns on the right. In column G, we use a formula which adds one (1) when the characters we are looking for are found in the cell in the same row in column A. In the following screen, we see that G3 is equal to 1 and G6 is equal to 2. This is because we find Los Angeles in row 3 and Philadelphia in row 6 of column A.

The formula in column H retrieves the name of the city which is in the row of the first 1 in G:G, of the first 2 in G:G,…

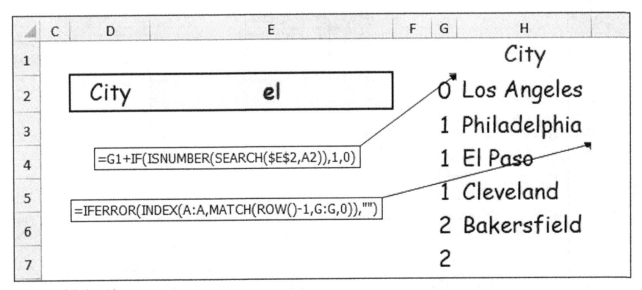

Example of "helper" list.

The drop-down menu in E2 above has two modifications compared to a standard drop-down menu with a list. The name of the list is "City". It is a *dynamic* name, defined as:

```
=City!$H$2:OFFSET(City!$H$1,MAX(City!$G:$G),0)
```

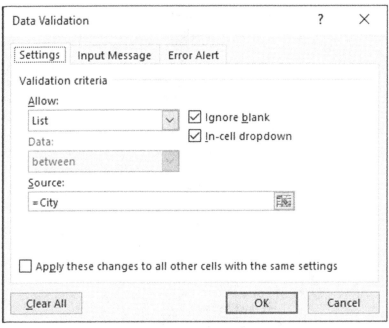

Dynamic name.

The second modification is that we need to allow the user to enter characters which are not the name of a valid city. This is achieved by unchecking the checkbox of the third validation tab, in order to avoid the error message which normally shows when what you type is not a valid city name:

Data validation changes.

All you have to do now is hide columns G and H (since the user does not need to see them) in order to prevent the current formulas from being changed by accident.

Car Traffic Simulation Without Circular References

The engineers in my consulting company once asked me if I could help them simulate car traffic for one of their customers. The following chart represents how they had divided the road network into segments.

They installed traffic counters (number of cars and average speed) analyzing the traffic on each segment for every minute of the day. There was one Excel file for each day with 1,441 rows each (24*60+1), and two columns for each segment.

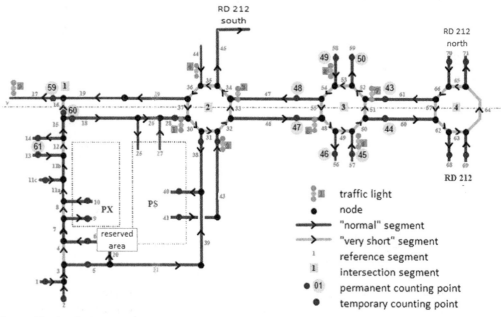

Car traffic simulation graphic.

Each file had a label identifying whether it was a normal day, a beginning of a weekend, an end of a weekend, a beginning of a holiday, a holiday period, an end of a holiday, and so on. I was given half of the files so I could build my model. The customer kept the other half so he could test my model once it was finished.

I started by modelling the traffic on a normal day until I could get a good fit between the traffic I predicted and what the counters had registered. I then started to enrich my model until it also provided a good fit between my predictions and the observations for each of the other types of days.

When all of this was finished, the customer checked my model with the Excel files he had kept for himself and confirmed that the traffic predictions of the model were satisfactory.

Three months later, our customer told us that the model, which I had billed at €50,000, had already been paid back. They had envisioned replacing a roundabout by a traffic light in order to solve a traffic problem, and my model had proved that the problem would then have reappeared several hundred meters further, at another location instead.

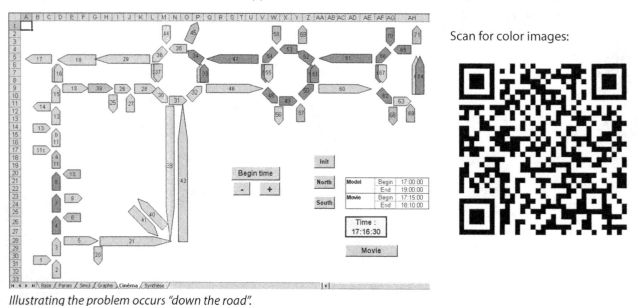

Scan for color images:

Illustrating the problem occurs "down the road".

A major problem with a traffic model like this is that it naturally includes circular references. At each roundabout, in the higher part of the model, e.g. for blocks 30 through 37, each segment feeds the other segments of the loop, but is also fed by them: how did we solve this problem?

Well, if you look at the upper part of the model in the image above, you will observe that segments 16, 33, 37, 55, 51, 67 and 64 have been duplicated. This is because I wrote a macro which, at each iteration, transfers the traffic from the duplicate to its next segment, and from the segment itself to its duplicate. Thanks to this trick, all the circular references in the model disappeared!

How to Make Movies with Excel

During my career, I developed several consulting models with movies. This is a creative way of modelling with Excel which opens many opportunities. You can see below how to make a movie with Excel.

Let's create a small model. In cells A1:A500, we have consecutive dates. In B1, copied down to B500, we have the formula

$$=SIN(PI()*(ROW()-1)/22.5)*(1-COS(PI()*(ROW()-1)/17)).$$

In D1, copied down to D100, we have the formula

$$=INDEX(B:B,\$C\$2+ROW()-1).$$

In C1, we have the formula $=INDEX(A:A,C2)$.

When we enter a number in C2, we indicate at which position the series in column D will begin.

The following screenshot shows the chart with the 500 values of column B:

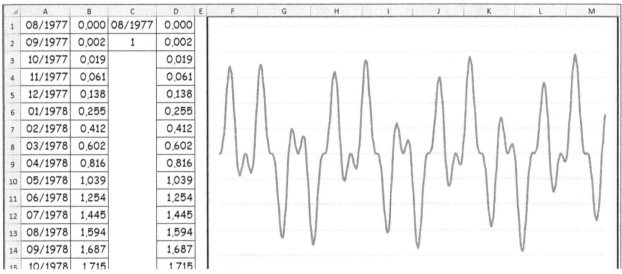

The 500 values in column B.

To make the movie, we replace the preceding chart, which showed all 500 points, with the chart below which represents the 100 points in column D starting with the position in C2. Below, you see the result of this model, during the movie, when the C2 cell has respectively values of 8 and 23 during the movie…

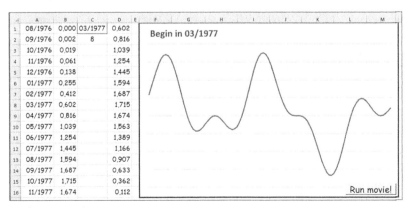

Replacement chart.

As you can see, it is very easy to create a movie with Excel. I have used this technique to simulate cars in traffic, bags on conveyor belts, pedestrians walking around, plane arrivals, an X-ray machine checking bags, toll booths, etc.

In my movie models, there are usually two scroll bars. The first one allows me to see the picture at any selected time in the time interval covered by the simulation. The second one is used to modify the speed of the movie.

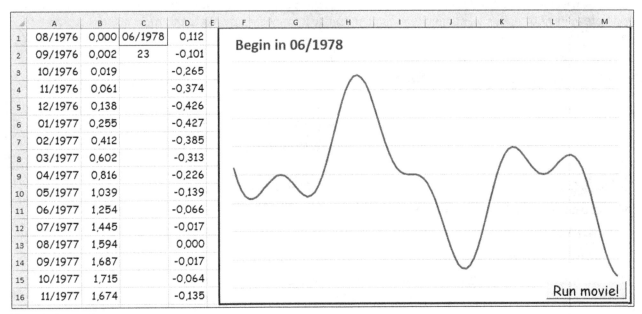

The movie continues…

Here is the macro I used in order to increment the value in cell C2:

```
Sub Movie()
    Dim I as Integer
    For I = 1 To 400
        Range("C2") = I
        DoEvents: DoEvents
    Next I
End Sub
```

In practice, I found that the speed of the movie could vary quite a lot between a powerful computer and a weaker one, and that it also depended on what other software was active. This is why I often add the following code before the "**Next I**" instruction:

```
For j = 1 To 50
    x = x + 12 ^ 2
Next j
```

And, in order to be even more flexible, I usually replace 50 with **Range("C3").value**, where C3 is the result of a scroll bar. That allows me to modify the speed of the macro by using the scroll bar in order to modify cell C3.

I hope this chapter has convinced you of Excel's richness and infinite potential. Now it's up to you!

An Introduction to Simulation in Excel
by Ian Huitson

What is Simulation?

According to Wikipedia, *"…A simulation is an approximate imitation of the operation of a process or system; the act of simulating first requires a model is developed. This model is a well-defined description of the simulated subject, and represents its key characteristics, such as its behavior, functions and abstract or physical properties."*

So, effectively every Excel model is a simulation. Let me be clear: every financial model, every production tracking or estimating model, every bank reconciliation spreadsheet, indeed every Excel model.

In this chapter, we are going to look at two types of models to demonstrate different simulation techniques:

- The first example evaluates the value of π (**Pi**) using the relationship between the area of a circle and the area of a square and a few thousand random numbers.
- The second looks at how to add stochastic (**Monte Carlo**) simulations to your existing models.

Simulating Pi

There are many, many ways to calculate the value of Pi. One method to estimate the value of Pi (3.141592…) is by using what is known as a **Monte Carlo method**. This is a generic term used to recognize a broad class of computational algorithms that rely on repeated random sampling.

In the example shown below, we have a circle of radius 1.0 (units), enclosed by a 2 × 2 square. The area of the circle is $\pi r^2 = \pi \times 1^2 = \pi$, whereas the area of the square is 2 x 2 = 4.

If we divide the area of the circle by the area of the square, we get $\pi/4$. That is, the ratio of the area of the circle to the area of the square is $\pi/4$.

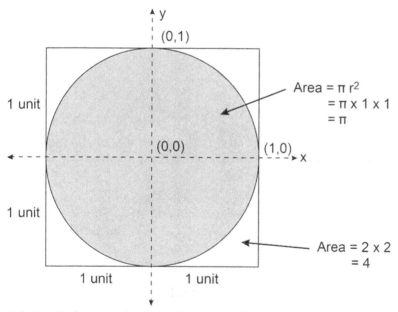

Relationship between the circle of radius 1 and the 2 x 2 square.

We can use this relationship to estimate the value of Pi by choosing thousands of random number pairs for the x and y values, in a process that is similar to throwing thousands of darts at a dartboard, sitting inside a square frame. We then count the number of points inside the circle as a ratio to the total number of points:

area of circle : area of square = π : 4 = **no. of points in circle : no. of points in square.**

Rearranging, we see that Pi = 4 x number of points in circle / total number of points.

The fraction Pi/4 applies equally to a quarter of a circle and a square from (0,0) to (1,1) which simplifies the math in an Excel model.

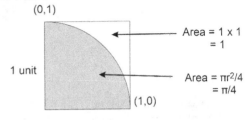

(0,1)

Area = 1 x 1
= 1

1 unit

Area = πr²/4
= π/4

(1,0)

1 unit

Inspecting one-quarter of the square.

area of quarter of a circle : area of quarter of a square = π : 4 = no. of points in quarter of a circle : no. of points in quarter of a square.

Again rearranging, we see that Pi = 4 x number of points in quarter of a circle / total number of points in quarter of a square.

To model this in Excel, we need to simply generate a large table of random number pairs and determine if the pair is inside the unit circle and then total them up. To do that, we generate a large number of uniformly distributed random points and plot them on the graph. You can refer to the file: **Pi Estimator.xlsx**.

Copy the two RAND functions down 100,000 rows:

Point No	X Value	Y Value	Radius
1	=RAND()	=RAND()	=N(SQRT(C3^2+D3^2)<=1)
2	0.255793	0.326485	1
3	0.549688	0.464662	1
4	0.576815	0.706528	1
5	0.219301	0.497184	1
6	0.041592	0.174254	1
7	0.275314	0.860886	1
8	0.986072	0.456747	0
9	0.758729	0.487268	1
10	0.477935	0.369063	1

Generating a large number of uniformly distributed random points.

These points can be in any position within the square, i.e. between (0,0) and (1,1). The Excel RAND function returns values >=0 and <1 using a uniform distribution (i.e. all values equally likely to occur), hence you can see why using a quarter circle is preferred.

To calculate whether a point is within the circle, we need simply to determine its distance from the origin (0,0). This is done using Pythagoras' theorem to calculate the distance of the point from the origin = SQRT($x^2 + y^2$). If the value is less than or equal to 1, it is within the circle; otherwise, it is outside the circle. We can check this and set it to 1 inside or 0 outside by using:

`=N(SQRT(C3^2+D3^2)<=1)`

If the points fall within the circle, they are colored blue; otherwise, they are colored red.

We keep track of the total number of points, together with the number of points that are inside the circle. If we divide the number of points within the circle by the total number of points, we get a value that approximates the ratio of the areas we calculated above, and by multiplying this value by 4, we get an estimate for Pi.

We can then tabulate these results for a varying number of iterations. This is done using a COUNTIF function and counting the specified number of rows. The data can also be shown graphically as well as cumulatively:

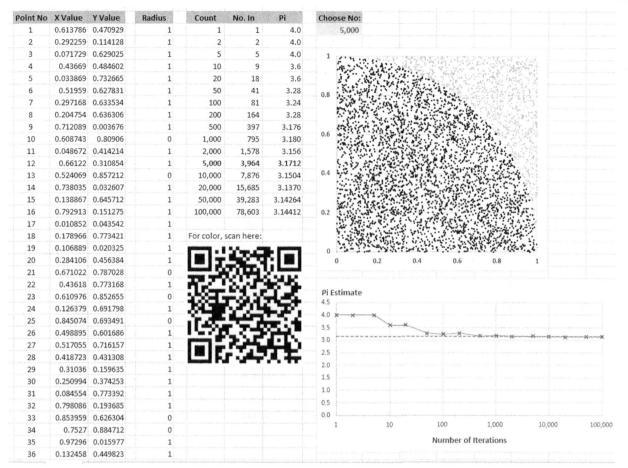

Point No	X Value	Y Value		Radius		Count	No. In	Pi		Choose No:
1	0.613786	0.470929		1		1	1	4.0		5,000
2	0.292259	0.114128		1		2	2	4.0		
3	0.071729	0.629025		1		5	5	4.0		
4	0.43669	0.484602		1		10	9	3.6		
5	0.033869	0.732665		1		20	18	3.6		
6	0.51959	0.627831		1		50	41	3.28		
7	0.297168	0.633534		1		100	81	3.24		
8	0.204754	0.636306		1		200	164	3.28		
9	0.712089	0.003676		1		500	397	3.176		
10	0.608743	0.80906		0		1,000	795	3.180		
11	0.048672	0.414214		1		2,000	1,578	3.156		
12	0.66122	0.310854		1		5,000	3,964	3.1712		
13	0.524069	0.857212		0		10,000	7,876	3.1504		
14	0.738035	0.032607		1		20,000	15,685	3.1370		
15	0.138867	0.645712		1		50,000	39,283	3.14264		
16	0.792913	0.151275		1		100,000	78,603	3.14412		
17	0.010852	0.043542		1						
18	0.178966	0.773421		1		For color, scan here:				
19	0.106889	0.020325		1						
20	0.284106	0.456384		1						
21	0.671022	0.787028		0						
22	0.43618	0.773168		1						
23	0.610976	0.852655		0						
24	0.126379	0.691798		1						
25	0.845074	0.693491		0						
26	0.498895	0.601686		1						
27	0.517055	0.716157		1						
28	0.418723	0.431308		1						
29	0.31036	0.159635		1						
30	0.250994	0.374253		1						
31	0.084554	0.773392		1						
32	0.798086	0.193685		1						
33	0.853959	0.626304		0						
34	0.7527	0.884712		0						
35	0.97296	0.015977		1						
36	0.132458	0.449823		1						

Visualizing the data.

When we only have a small number of points, the estimation is not very accurate, but when we have hundreds or thousands of points, we get much closer to the actual value – to within two decimal places of accuracy. You may change the **Choose No.** input in the sample file and see what difference it makes.

This example demonstrates how we can simulate a solution using an Excel Model. In the next example, we look at how to vary inputs to a model and monitor the results.

Monte Carlo Simulation

As explained earlier, Monte Carlo Simulation is a technique used to understand the impact of risk or uncertainty in financial, project management, cost or many other models.

Monte Carlo Simulation allows the user to quantify the risk or uncertainty of a model's outputs achieving a result and allows the user to use distributions in the input variables of a model instead of fixed values.

Let's start by looking at a simple model first.

A Simple Addition Model

Our model will add two numbers together. We do this so that we may clearly see what is going on mathematically and understand it, before applying the techniques to more complex models.

Consider

```
Answer = x + y.
```

If x equals 100 and y equals 10, then Answer would be 110. However, if the y value may vary between two (2) and 18 then our model will have an Answer that varies between 100 + 2 = 102 to 100 + 18 = 118.

We have two concepts we need to understand:

- what is the probability of the input y having these values?
- what is the distribution of the input variable y?

By this stage, the concept of a probability is "probably" well understood, but what about a "distribution"?

Distributions

Distributions describe the probability that an input variable has a certain value. There are a large number of different distributions available to us as modelers. Some common distributions include the uniform distribution (described earlier), the Normal distribution and the Exponential distribution.

- **Uniform:** All values have an even or near even chance of selection; think of rolling a single die where each number has a one in six chance of occuring.
- **Normal:** Bell shaped around a mean, sometimes referred to as the Gaussian distribution.
- **Exponential:** Low or high values have a much higher probability than other values.
- **Triangular**, etc.

One of the most common distributions is the Normal Distribution, which we shall use for our example, where

Answer = x + y

becomes

    Answer = 100 + Value selected from Normal distribution

where this value will typically lie between two (2) and 18.

On average, after selecting many different values, this should tend towards

    Average = 100 + Normal distribution average

Since a Normal distribution is defined by its mean and its standard deviation, we may derive it as follows.

In particular, the mean is the average value of the distribution, so here it would be 10.

The standard deviation is a measurement of the spread of the values around the mean. For the Normal distribution, this means 99.8% of the time, the values would lie within three (3) standard deviations of the mean as pictured:

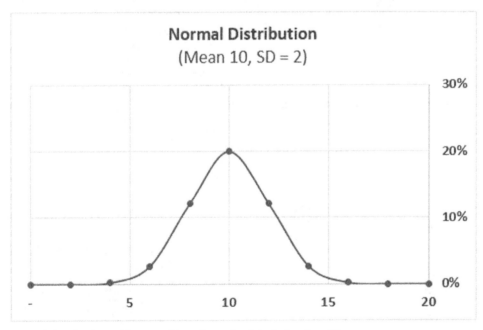

Normal distribution with mean 10 and standard deviation two (2).

We can see that the curve extends from two (2) to 18, and that it has a mean of 10.

So how do we use it?

The Normal distribution has a property that allows us to use a random number to select which value to use. It is the area under the Normal distribution that is of interest. It is of interest as the cumulative area below the curve is always equal to one (1) in any probability distribution. This means that the cumulative probability of getting any possible result is always 1 (100%).

This cumulative probability proves very useful when constructing simulations.

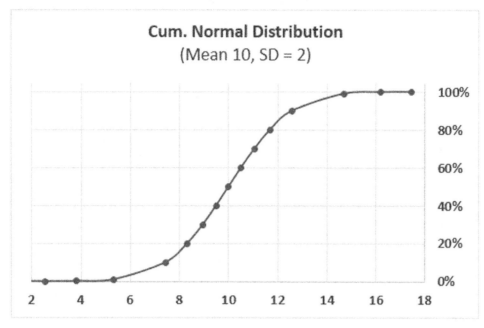

Cumulative Normal distribution.

The shape of the curve reflects the distribution of the original data. However, it is the property of the cumulative Normal distribution curve that is of interest to us is, in that the curve extends on the y Axis from 0 to 1. This allows us to use the Excel worksheet function, RAND, to choose a value and we can then back calculate the x value that is the value that generates the random value using the identity

$$P(\text{value} \le x) = y$$

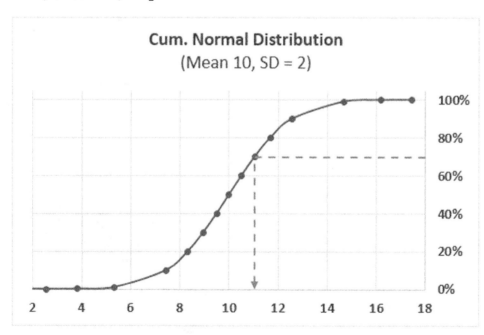

How to derive x given the random value y.

For example, in the above chart, we may select a value of 70% and see that an x value of 11.05 corresponds to 70%. In other words, 70% of the y values in our model are less than 11.05.

The good news is that Excel has functions that allow us to do this in our models:

- The NORM.INV function allows us to return the x value that a probability has based on a known mean and standard deviation.
- If you have an older version of Excel (prior to Excel 2010), you will need to use the NORMINV function instead.

To see this let's set up a table:

Probability	x Value
0.001%	1.47
0.01%	2.56
0.10%	3.82
1.0%	5.35
10%	7.44
20%	8.32
30%	8.95
40%	9.49
50%	10.00
60%	10.51
70%	11.05
80%	11.68
90%	12.56
99.0%	14.65
99.90%	16.18
99.99%	17.44
100.00%	#NUM!

Example table.

The observant will notice that neither two (2) nor 18 are at the extremes. Normal distributions have infinite tails (at both ends), so values below two (2) are possible (hence 1.47 in the table). The *#NUM!* occurs by design when the probability is 1 (this is because the distribution continues forever and does not end, and infinity is too large a number for the table!)

The left column is simply a list of probabilities from very low 0.001% to just under 1 (99.99%). The x values are derived from the formula

=NORM.INV(Probability, Mean, SD)

We know the mean is 10 and we are using a standard deviation of two (2), so you can use the formula

=NORM.INV(Probability, 10, 2)

We can see that our model has modelled the distribution for y from 2 to 18 with a mean of 10. This is shown below similar to our previous chart:

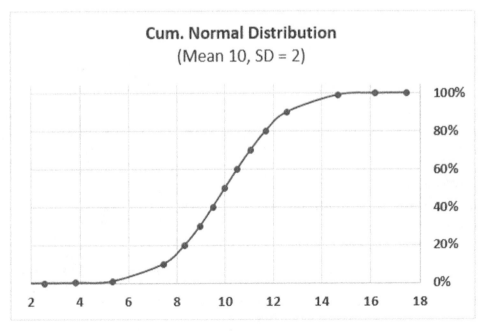

Cumulative Normal distribution, as required.

To use this in our model, we can simply replace the probability with a random number. In Excel, we may use the RAND function, which returns values >=0 and <1 uniformly. Therefore, our formula

```
=NORM.INV(Probability, Mean, SD)
```

becomes

```
=NORM.INV(RAND(), Mean, SD)
```

In our model we now use

```
=100 + NORM.INV(RAND(), Mean, SD)
```

(Technically, if Rand generates a value of precisely zero, this would cause a problem, but in practice, this extreme occurrence is tolerable for the purposes of this chapter and is ignored.)

This will return a random number between 102 and 118; you can press function key F9 a few times to watch it change. Rather than just run this a few times, though, what we now need to do is run our model hundreds or thousands of times and make note of all the results. We can do that manually, but better is to utilize the power of Excel and the Data Table functionality to perform the work for us.

To do this, let's set up a model in Excel. You can open the Addition Model.xlsx, or simply follow along below.

Firstly, set up the 'Mean' and 'Standard Deviation' parameters in cells C6 and C7. Then, I will apply a range name to these cells to simplify their later use ('Mean' and 'SD' respectively). Next, we will set up the Addition model:

- Cell C11 contains a text string to remind us what our model is: '=100 + y'.
- In cell C12, enter: `=NORM.INV(RAND(),Mean, SD)`.
- In cell C13, enter: `=100 + C12`.
- Then name cells C12 **y_Value** and cell C13 **Result**.

The model should look similar to that shown below:

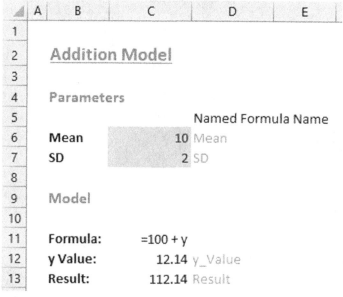

Addition Model construction.

Now we add a Data Table section to the model, where we may record the results of multiple trials simultaneously. We will first set up an area for the Data Table. You can follow along in the Data Table group in the sample workbook.

- Start with a column of numbers from 1 through to 10,000 in cells C68:C10067 (if using the same ranges as me – we will be including a Model Analysis section in the blank rows later).
- Next, add two Labels for the y_Value and Result.
- Below those labels, add formulas that return the y_Value and Result from the cells, with D67:`=y_Value` and E67:`=Result`.

I prefer to shade and outline the Data Table area, so that the area is clearly distinguishable:

Running the Model

Next, we need to use the Data Table to run the 10,000 iterations of our model.

To do this, select the Range C67:E10067 and go to Data -> What-If Analysis -> Data Table menu on the ribbon:

Note: The following image was too wide for this book. The What-If icon is usually farther to the right.

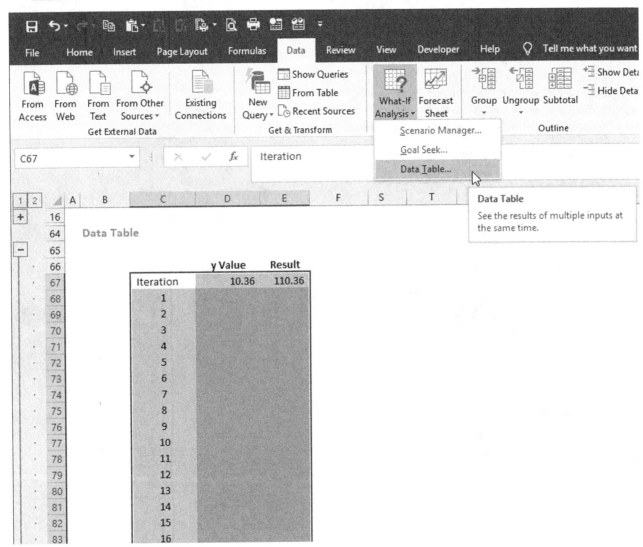

Accessing the Data Table feature in Excel.

Complete the dialog leaving the row input cell field blank and put any cell reference (i.e. it is simply a dummy value) in the column input cell field. You must ensure that this reference is a blank cell and not connected to the model. Select OK.

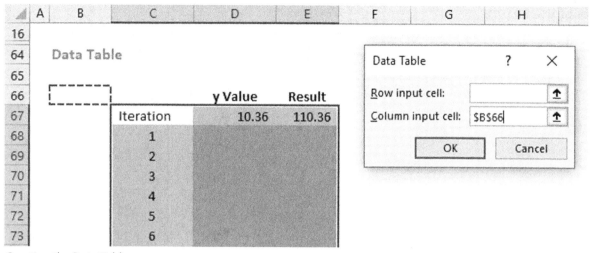

Creating the Data Table.

The model will now be calculated 10,000 times. For each calculation the y_Value and Result are stored in the cells adjacent to the Iteration (run) number. You should note that by placing the column input cell in a blank cell the Iteration number is effectively not used.

What happens here is that each value in the Input Column C68:C10067 is taken in turn and placed into the blank cell B66. The model is recalculated which triggers the y_Value to be recalculated based on a new random number and a new Result is generated. The y_Value and Result are then transferred back to the adjacent cells in the Data Table. However, because B66 doesn't form part of the model, it has no impact on the calculations. We are simply using the Data Table functionality to step through the iterations without using any VBA Code.

The final data table will appear like the table below, but with different numbers due to the Random function used in the model:

	A	B	C	D	E
16					
64		Data Table			
65					
66				y Value	Result
67			Iteration	8.36	108.36
68			1	11.29	111.29
69			2	11.96	111.96
70			3	10.53	110.53
71			4	13.05	113.05
72			5	9.09	109.09
73			6	12.55	112.55
74			7	7.19	107.19
75			8	7.50	107.50
76			9	9.32	109.32
77			10	8.81	108.81

Generating results.

Analysis of the Results

Now that we have calculated the model 10,000 times and have a table of results, we can analyze the results and see what they mean. The easiest way to analyze this data is graphically. You can follow along in the Model Analysis grouping in the sample workbook.

Firstly, we need to set up a table of the minimum, maximum and bucket size:

Model Analysis

Min	102.35
Max	117.73
Bucket Size	1.00

Model Analysis.

The Min, cell D17, is the Minimum of the Results range

=MIN(E68:E10067).

The Max, cell D18, is the Maximum of the Results range

=MAX(E68:E10067).

The Bucket Size is a manually entered value, which is typically about 1/20th of the Max – Min value, so in the above example, one (1) is appropriate. Now, we set up a table:

- C21: Label, 'Bucket Mid'
- C22: =MROUND(D17,0.5)-D19/2
- C23: =C22+$D$19
- D21: Label, 'Count'
- D22: =IFERROR(COUNTIFS($E$68:$E$10067,">"&(C22-$D$19/2),$E$68:$E$10067,
  "<="&(C22+$D$19/2)),0)
- E21: 'Frequency'
- E22: =D22/10000
- F21: 'Cum. Freq'
- F22: =SUM($E$22:E22)

Copy these bottom cells down several rows as shown in the diagram below.

We can now add a scatter chart using the 'Bucket Mid' as the x axis and 'Frequency' as the Y Axis

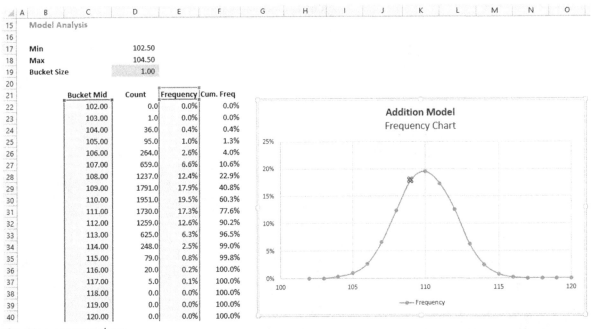

Creating a scatter chart.

We can now see the results of the Addition Model. As expected, the mean or average value is 110. However, we can now see that the results vary between about 103 and 117. This is caused by the randomly selected values according to our y_Value input distribution:

```
=NORM.INV(RAND(), Mean, SD)
```

We can get so much more from this chart. Let's add a cumulative frequency line to the chart.

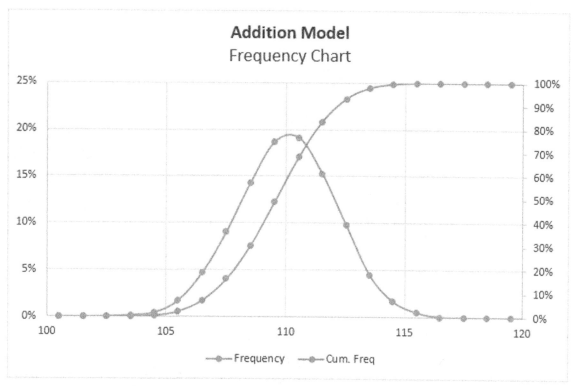

Frequency chart with cumulative frequency line.

The grey line in the chart above is the cumulative frequency line. As this shows the cumulative frequency, we may use that to answer a lot of questions. For instance, if we want to know the Answer value either 20% of values are below or 80% above, we could easily derive these values.

I have also added a line to allow us to visually show what is going on with the values to answer the question above:

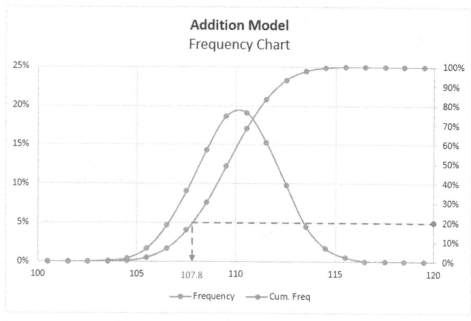

Frequency chart identifying the Answer value for p(value ≤ X) = 20%.

We can see that 20% of the values are below 107.8, that is 20% of the y_Values are below 7.8. This also means that 80% of the y_Values are above 7.8.

If we want to know what the probability of getting an answer of 112 or more, we do a similar, but "reverse", calculation:

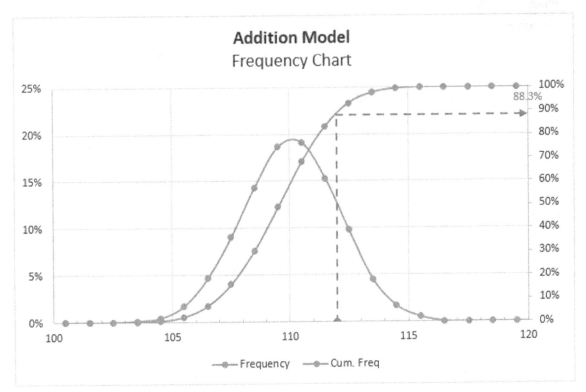

Frequency chart may identify the probability of getting a value of 112 or more.

Starting at 112 on the x axis we head up until we hit the cumulative frequency chart. Then, we traverse horizontally to the secondary vertical axis. This shows that 88.3% of the Results are less than or equal to 112, which means that 11.7% of the results are better than 112.

> **Note**: It is important to remember that cumulative frequency curves always show the probability of obtaining a result less than or equal to a given value.

You can generate these results manually or you can set up some formulas to calculate the results for you. The formulas for these calculations are shown in the sample file.

This was a simple exercise of adding two numbers together, one was fixed and the second was from a distribution. In real life things are never so simple. In the following example, we will look at a simplified cashflow model for the development of a proposed mining operation. We will model several inputs using several normal distributions and then review the results.

Mining Cashflow Model

To demonstrate how this can be applied to a cashflow model, I have developed and supplied a very simplistic Mining Cashflow Model. You can follow along using the Mining Model.xlsx file.

The model is based around the development of a gold mine. It consists of one year of construction, five years of production and one year of decommissioning. All costs are in Australian Dollars except for the Gold Price which is in U$. A U$ / A$ exchange is also assumed.

The numbers are totally fictitious and are for demonstration purposes only. The model calculates gold production, costs and revenues and a few simple financial measurements from the derived cashflows.

| | | 2020 | 2021 | 2022 | 2023 | 2024 | 2025 | 2026 | Total |

Mining Cashflow Model

Assumptions

			Named Formula Names	Base/Mean	Standard Deviation
Simulated Model	TRUE				
Gold Price	1,407	U$	Gold_Price	1,300	100
Exchange Rate	0.74	U$/A$	Exchange_Rate	0.74	0.08
Yearly production	1,000,000	t	Yearly_production		
Grade	4.00	g/t Au	Grade	4.0	0.2
Plant Recovery	93.1%	Au Recovery	Plant_Recovery	94.0%	1%
Operating Costs	949	A$/Oz	Operating_Costs	1,000	100
Capital Cost	249	A$M	Capital_Cost	250	10
Capital recovery	4.6%		Capital_recovery	5%	0.25%

Calculations

Date		2020	2021	2022	2023	2024	2025	2026	Total
Exchange Rate	U$/A$	0.78	0.82	0.81	0.74	0.63	0.78	0.56	
Processing	tpa		1,000,000	1,000,000	1,000,000	1,000,000	1,000,000		5,000,000
Grade	g/t Au		3.97	3.96	3.77	3.78	3.82		3.86
Gold Recovered	Oz Au		118,963	118,540	112,821	113,221	114,418		577,963
Construction	A$M	-248.7							-248.7
Capital Recovery	A$M							11.5	11.5
Revenue	A$M	0.0	205.0	205.9	215.1	252.4	206.4	0.0	1,084.9
Operating costs	A$M	0.0	-112.9	-112.5	-107.1	-107.5	-108.6	0.0	-548.6
Cash Flow	A$M	-248.7	92.1	93.4	108.0	144.9	97.8	11.5	299.1
Cum. Cash Flow	A$M	-248.7	-156.6	-63.2	44.8	189.8	287.6	299.1	

Financial Summary

Cum. Cashflow	A$M	299.1	Cum_Cashflow
Net Present value	A$M	159.5	Net_Present_value
Internal Rate of Return	%	31.1%	Internal_Rate_of_Return

Example of a Mining Cashflow Model.

The model uses a base set of assumptions (known as "Base Case"), but the model also has the ability to use several distributions for key variables. The mean and standard deviations applicable to these variables are shown to the right of the Named Formula Names column displayed above.

The Grade and Exchange Rate values have a distribution applied on a year by year basis in the Calculations section. Therefore, the model will see different mined grades and exchange rates every year, replicating what actually happens in a real mine. We can see that in the screenshot the base model currently has an NPV of A$159.5m and internal rate of return (IRR) of 31.1%.

Changing the Simulated Model input Cell (D6) to TRUE enables the model to operate as a Monte Carlo simulations model.

Please examine the input cells highlighted in the model. For example, the Gold Price formula is shown below:

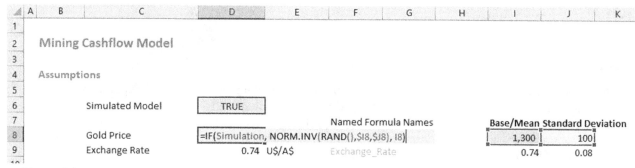

Mining Cashflow Model

Assumptions

			Named Formula Names	Base/Mean	Standard Deviation
Simulated Model	TRUE				
Gold Price	=IF(Simulation, NORM.INV(RAND(),$I8,$J8), I8)			1,300	100
Exchange Rate	0.74	U$/A$	Exchange_Rate	0.74	0.08

Gold Price formula.

The formula

```
=IF(Simulation, NORM.INV(RAND(),$I8,$J8),$I8)
```

is similar to before (the IF calculation checks to see whether 'Simulation' (cell D6) is TRUE before running the simulations). If so, this computes the frequency of the various NPV results after 10,000 iterations of the model.

We can see that the NPVs average is A$100m, but now we can also see that at worst the NPV will be negative at about -A$250m. It's not all bad news though: the model also shows there is upside with an NPV of potentially A$600m+.

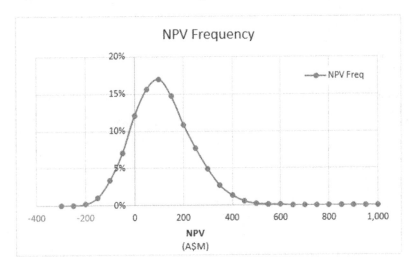

NPV frequency chart for the gold mine.

Once again, we may use the cumulative frequency curve to better analyze these results. To understand what the probability of the project having a Positive NPV, say, we use the chart similar to before.

In the chart below, start at NPV = 0 and go up and across from the cumulative frequency line until you hit the secondary y axis. This shows that there is a 12.7% probability that the proposed mine will not make a positive NPV, and a 87.3% probability the mine will be NPV positive.

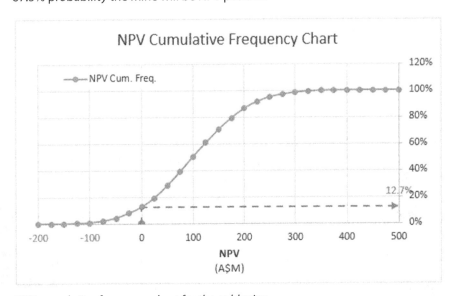

NPV cumulative frequency chart for the gold mine.

Summary

This has been a quick introduction to Simulation in Excel. It has been designed to whet your appetite as to what is available and what can be achieved by simply using Excel. The distributions used above have been used for simplicity's sake and in real life, you should spend the time and effort to understand the key drivers of a model and then analyze the actual distributions of the inputs accordingly. Excel can easily model most distributions including skewed and bi-modal "Camel Humps" distributions relatively easily.

As with all computer models, garbage in equals garbage out, and this is particularly relevant when applying these techniques. The user must be very careful in the use of real and meaningful statistics in your models.

Staying out of Trouble
by Jan Karel Pieterse

Introduction

Excel is a powerful modelling tool and spreadsheet models can be everything from a simple shopping list up to and including very sophisticated financial models containing lots of complex formulas, formatting and oftentimes even VBA code to automate processes.

It is no exception for a model to have a lifespan of several years. This is often because the model calculations (hopefully) have been validated and proven correct, which is a good reason to re-use them "as is".

Given that a model may be decades old, this will also mean the model may have an editing history of decades and has survived various versions of Excel. Sometimes this causes Excel to show error messages when you use the file. What errors do I mean? To get started, let me show you the dreaded "Too many different cell formats" error message, which used to surface a lot on ancient Excel files in the past:

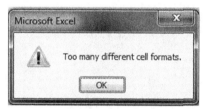

The "Too many different cell formats" error message.

Luckily Microsoft has raised the limits on how many of these "cell formats" a file can contain, so this error has become rare.

In this chapter I will discuss some of the issues I have encountered in my consulting projects in the past 15 years or so. I will advise on strategies to avoid the problems to begin with and in the reference material, I will point you to some tools to get them out of your way should you encounter an issue.

Range Names

You can find the examples used in this chapter from https://mrx.cl/mvpfiles in the file called Names tester.xlsm.

Intricate spreadsheet models often use range names (see "Relative Named Ranges – When Named Ranges Go Walkabout" on page 26). Range names are one of the many areas for strong opinions on whether you should use them in your model. There is no single truth here I'm afraid, so I advise you to use them wisely, for example, for these purposes or situations:

- When a value is used throughout your model, such as the reporting year or the download path of an important source
- When your model has VBA code, and the VBA code addresses areas on your spreadsheet (which is often the case). Avoid hard-coded cell references in VBA like the plague and use range names instead.
- To point to list sources for Data Validation (although if you are using a recent version of Excel, consider using Format as Table.)
- To create dynamic references you cannot otherwise achieve, for example if you are using 12 month moving averages.

While being extremely useful and versatile, range names also come at a cost. They are not directly visible and hence easily overlooked when hunting for problems. Moreover, range names may also cause unexpected and annoying behavior.

Let's take a look at a sample file (afternamestest.xls) I've been using (together with Charles Williams) while working on Name Manager. Clicking the Formulas, Name Manager button (or pressing Ctrl + F3) on this file shows:

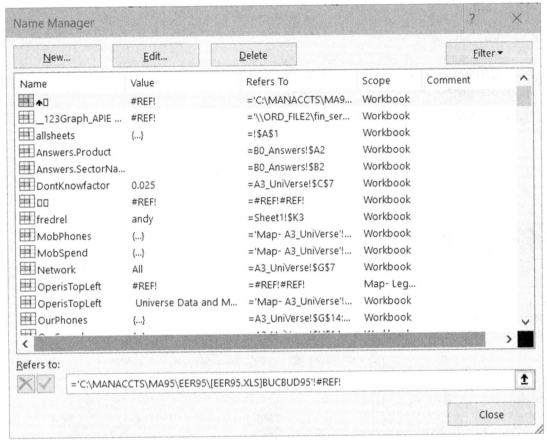

Name Manager showing some Range Name problems.

The very first two names in this list include three problems:

- Their name is odd
- The name yields to an error (see the Value column)
- The 'Refers To' detail contains an external reference.

Moreover, if you try to delete the first name listed using VBA: **ThisWorkbook.Names(1).Delete** you can't, the delete command causes a runtime error.

Let's discuss some frequent problems with Range Names and how they are caused.

Hidden Names

There are several add-ins out there that add range names to the workbooks they operate on: FactSet is one of them, Capital IQ is another. The range names are used to store all sorts of meta information in the workbook, so the add-ins may do their work. Unfortunately, not many of these add-ins appear to clean up after themselves.

Mostly, these range names have identical prefixes (Capital IQ uses a prefix of "IQ_") and very often they do not point to any cells, but rather contain constants which are frequently hidden.

Such hidden range names containing constants are mostly harmless to your file, other than making its footprint larger. They can be deleted safely (unless you use one of those add-ins). Since they are hidden, you need some VBA to unhide them before you can delete them from Name Manager:

```
Sub ShowAllNames()
 Dim oNm As Name
 For Each oNm In ActiveWorkbook.Names
  If oNm.Visible = False Then oNm.Visible = True
 Next
End Sub
```

Duplicated Names

Range names come in two flavors:

- Workbook scope (default)
  You can create a workbook scoped range name in various ways, the simplest being by clicking in the (New) Name box, typing the name and pressing Enter. The examples below were created using the sample file 'Names Tester.xlsm'. The 'New Name' dialog (below), which you can open from the New button on Name Manager's window or from the Define Name button on the Formulas tab, shows you how you create a workbook-scoped name:

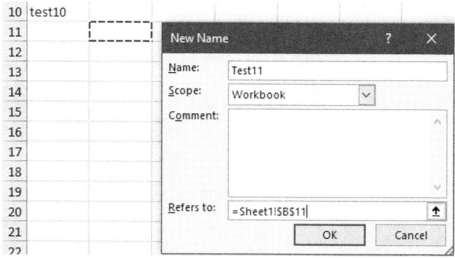

Defining a workbook-scoped name.

- Worksheet scope
  You can also define a name local to a worksheet:

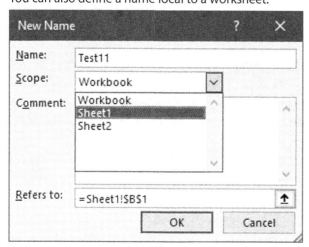

Defining a worksheet-scoped name.

This is done by choosing any of the worksheets available in your workbook by using the Scope drop-down list.

Unfortunately, Excel allows you to define both workbook-scoped names and worksheet-scoped names with the same name. Even worse, Excel sometimes causes that to happen without your consent. Take the sample file again and create a copy of Sheet1 by control-dragging the sheet tab and letting it go. You should end up with something like this:

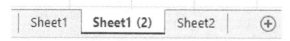

Copied worksheet in example file.

Name Manager will look like this:

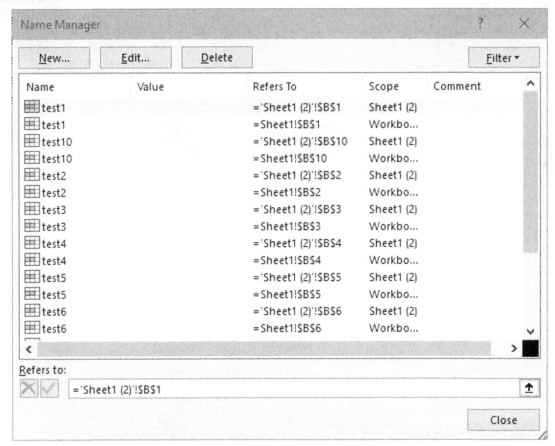

Name Manager after copying a worksheet in example file.

Warning: Copying worksheets in models is a relatively frequent operation and you can imagine what kind of mess you may get into if your model is using a lot of range names.

One of the main issues with these duplicated workbook-level and worksheet-level range names is that it becomes quite confusing which version of a range name has been used by your formula. This will depend on the location (mostly worksheet) containing the formula.

Duplicate Range names behave oddly too. Suppose you copied Sheet1 as I showed you earlier in this chapter. If you created a formula in a cell on Sheet2, pointing to cell B1 on worksheet 'Sheet1 (2)', the formula would look like this:

```
='Sheet1 (2)'!test1
```

This is the formula syntax to point to a worksheet-level name called test1 on worksheet 'Sheet1 (2)'. While this is ugly and confusing, we can make this even worse. Delete worksheet 'Sheet1 (2)'. Look what happens to the formula. Rather than an expected *#REF!* error, the formula changes to:

```
='Names tester.xlsm'!test1
```

This is the syntax to point to the Workbook-level name in Sheet1. Since there was both a worksheet-level name and a workbook level name, Excel decided to replace the reference in the formula to the workbook-level name when I deleted the worksheet, even though the workbook-level name points to a cell on a completely different worksheet.

Conclusion: I strongly advise you to make sure your model does not contain duplicated range names. In my view, there is only one exception to this rule: if all duplicated range names are worksheet-level range names.

Luckily, deleting a worksheet with worksheet-level names will normally also delete those names.

There is no panacea as to how to resolve duplicated range names, it requires good knowledge and understanding of the spreadsheet model to make the correct decision as to which range names should be kept and which should be deleted.

Names with #REF! Errors

It isn't hard to understand where *#REF!* names originate from (oxymoron intended). Simply delete any range to which a name points (or which is used in its formula), and its 'Refers To' formula will raise *#REF!* errors. A name can also have an error which looks like two concatenated *#REF!* errors:

=#REF!#REF!

#REF! errors often are caused by deleting a worksheet from the workbook. You would expect deleting a worksheet would delete the names pointing to the sheet as well, but Excel does not do that for so-called workbook-scoped names. Try this for yourself: open the example 'Names Tester.xlsm' file and delete Sheet1, then check Name Manager.

Names with External References

Creating a range name pointing to another file is simple enough. Simply take the Names Tester file again and copy Sheet2 to a new workbook. Right-click the Sheet2 tab and choose 'Move or Copy…' and choose these settings:

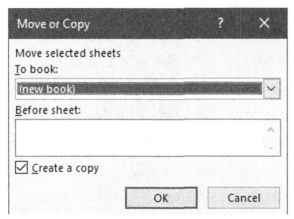

Copying a worksheet to another workbook to create range names pointing to an external file.

If you open Name Manager, you'll see the new workbook now contains one name, which points back to the original Names Tester file:

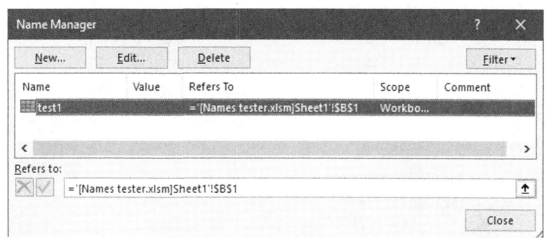

A range name with an external reference.

You could have avoided the external range name by copying both worksheets Sheet1 and Sheet2 to the new workbook.

Styles

Excel offers an option called cell styles. If you build complex workbooks, styles are a very good way to structure your formatting and your work. But that is an entirely different subject. Styles cause problems too. Have a look at the workbook called Many Styles.xlsm.

If you click on the Styles drop-down of the Home tab of the ribbon, this is what you will see:

Custom

JournalTe...	_%(SignOnly)	_%(SignSpac...	_Comma	_Currency	_Currency_Li...
_Currency_M...	_Currency_M...	_Currency_S...	_Currency_S...	_Currency_T...	_CurrencySp...
_Euro	**_Hea...**	**_Hea...**	**_Hea...**	**_Hea...**	**_Hea...**
_Highlight	_Multiple	_MultipleSpace	**_SubHe...**	**_SubHe...**	**_SubHe...**
_SubHe...	**_SubHe...**	_Table	_Table_Model ...	_Table_Model ...	_Table_Sheet6
_Table_Sheet...	_TableHead	_TableHead...	_TableHead...	_TableHead...	_TableHead...
_TableRow...	_TableRow...	_TableRow...	_TableRow...	_TableRow...	_TableSupe...
_TableSupe...	_TableSupe...	_TableSupe...	_TableSupe...	=C:\WINDO...	=C:\WINNT3...
•W_laroux	20% - Accent...	20% - Accent...	20% - Accent...	20% - Accent...	20% - Accent...
20% - Accent...	20% - Accent...	20% - Accent...	20% - Accent...	20% - Accent...	20% - Accent...
20% - Accent...	20% - Accent...	20% - Accent...	20% - Accent...	20% - Accent...	20% - Accent...
20% - Accent...	20% - Accent...	20% - Accent...	20% - Accent...	20% - Accent...	20% - Accent...
20% - Accent...	20% - Accent...	20% - Accent...	20% - Accent...	20% - Accent...	20% - Accent...
20% - Accent...	20% - Accent...	20% - Accent...	20% - Accent...	20% - Accent...	20% - Accent...
20% - Accent...	20% - Accent...	20% - Accent...	20% - Accent...	20% - Accent...	20% - Accent...
20% - Accent...	20% - Accent...	20% - Accent...	20% - Accent...	20% - Accent...	20% - Accent...
20% - Accent...	20% - Accent...	20% - Accent...	20% - Accent...	20% - Accent...	20% - Accent...
20% - Accent...	20% - Accent...	20% - Accent...	20% - Accent...	20% - Accent...	20% - Accent...
20% - Accent...	20% - Accent...	20% - Accent...	20% - Accent...	20% - Accent...	20% - Accent...
20% - Accent...	20% - Accent...	20% - Accent...	20% - Accent...	20% - Accent...	20% - Accent...
20% - Accent...	20% - Accent...	20% - Accent...	20% - Accent...	20% - Accent...	20% - Accent...
20% - Accent...	20% - Accent...	20% - Accent...	20% - Accent...	20% - Accent...	20% - Accent...

New Cell Style...

Merge Styles...

The Cell Styles gallery displaying many custom cell styles.

There are many styles in this workbook, so many in fact that Excel fails to display all of them in the Styles gallery. It takes a little bit of VBA (included with the aforementioned workbook) to discover how many there really are:

```
Sub HowManyStyles()
 MsgBox ActiveWorkbook.Styles.Count
End Sub
```

The code yields a message box displaying the total number of styles: a mere 39,819.

So how did these 39,819 styles end up here? The answer is simple, really: by copying cells (and or worksheets) from other files. As soon as there is any difference in formatting between a style in the source workbook and a style in the target workbook (into which the worksheets or cells are inserted or pasted), this style is added to the target workbook and a number is appended to the name of the style. Let's try to reproduce this behavior. Here are the steps:

- Open and a new, blank workbook
- Open Style tester.xlsx (available from the downloads for this book).
- Right-click Sheet1 and choose 'Move or Copy…'
- From the 'To Book' drop-down of the 'Move or Copy' dialog, select the blank workbook you created above
- Check the 'Create a copy' option and click OK.

Now open the Styles gallery. Note the new custom style named 'Input 2':

A new custom style 'Input 2' was added to the workbook.

Warning: If you have too many custom Styles, you may risk ending up with a workbook which Excel refuses to open.

Fortunately, there are add-ins which enable you to delete unused cell styles and you may wish to consider these.

Any time you copy a worksheet to another workbook, make sure you check the Styles gallery. Even better, check the gallery before you copy and when you activate the worksheet you wish to copy. If it contains as many styles as the file from the screenshot we saw earlier, beware!

VBA

This chapter is not about VBA best practices, if you are looking for that let me refer to Matthieu Guindon's "An Overview of Modern VBA Best Practices" on page 260

This part is about how a VBA project might run into trouble. Some of the problems I describe here are reproduced in the accompanying file 'VBA Tester.xlsm'.

I'll illustrate a couple of issues I have encountered over the past years and where there's a fix, I've included this as well.

Catastrophic Failure

Below is a screenshot of an error I received on a customer file very recently. I opened the file and was welcomed by

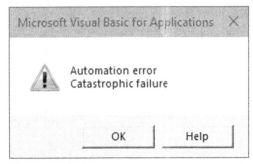

Much dreaded error caused by a problem with a workbook's VBA project.

As a consequence, none of the VBA procedures worked anymore. Any call to a routine resulted in the above message. Clicking OK left the editor in debug mode with no other option than to click the reset button on the VBA Editor toolbar.

In some cases (I had this problem multiple times with the same project!), the VBA project explorer would show multiple copies of modules and worksheet modules for that VBA project, even though they weren't copied in there by me.

The only way I found I was able to get out of this situation was by saving the file as a .xlsx file (thus removing the entire VBA project) and subsequently importing all modules from an older (backup) copy of the file back into the .xlsx file.

After a lot of trial and error, I discovered the likely cause of the issue: the project contained several VBA User Defined Functions and I was debugging one of them when I decided to press save. After doing so, opening the saved file would yield that error.

Ghost VBA Projects

Normally, the Project Explorer of the VBA editor displays VBA projects of all open workbooks and Excel add-ins. However, sometimes it displays a stray workbook which has already been closed.

You can mimic this behavior using the buttons on Sheet1 of the VBA tester.xlsm demo file. The root cause of this problem is sloppy programming. Here is the code from the sample workbook:

```
Option Explicit
Dim mBook As Workbook
Sub OpenAndCloseWorkbook()
 Set mBook = Workbooks.Add
 mBook.Close
End Sub
```

The problem is with the mBook object variable which has been declared at the top of the module. This variable is a so-called module-level variable. In effect, it means that if the variable gets a pointer to an object assigned to it, it remains assigned. This may cause the VBA editor to hold onto the object itself and therefore the editor keeps showing the VBA project (and all of its content!). You can even edit that VBA project and I don't think I need to explain why that is a very bad idea.

Here's a screenshot of the Project Explorer after clicking that first button:

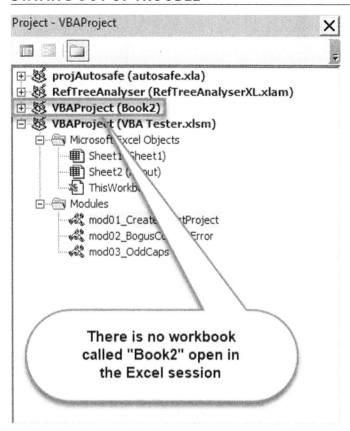

The project explorer displaying a VBA project of an already-closed Excel file.
To prove there is no such file, click back to Excel, click on the View tab and open the 'Switch Windows' drop-down:

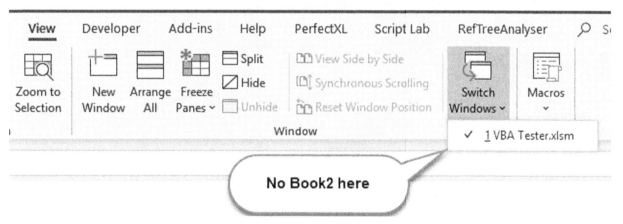

There really is no Book2 open in Excel!
Running the routine below removes the VBA project from the Project Explorer:

```
Sub ReallyCloseThatBook()
  Set mBook = Nothing
End Sub
```

This little routine removes the pointer to the Book2 object from memory, forcing the VBA editor to release the object and clear it, hence removing it from the list too.

It has frequently happened in the past that COM add-ins (these are add-ins written in .NET) do not properly release pointers to Excel files, causing this behavior. Power Pivot has exhibited this behavior in the past, but it has now been fixed. The key action to take in a .NET COM add-in is to meticulously release pointers to Excel objects when they are no longer needed and to make sure the garbage collector really does get rid of them as soon as you can.

Bogus Compile Errors

Sometimes a file yields compile errors on functions which normally do not cause a problem at all. For example, consider the Left function in this code:

A bogus compile error in a VBA project.

The root cause for silly compile errors is usually a missing reference. Indeed, if I open the References dialog from the VBA editor, I see one marked as "Missing":

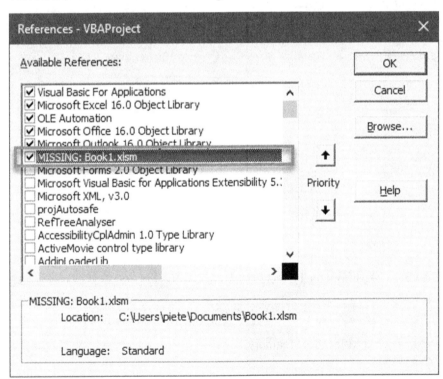

A missing reference in the VBA project.

I caused this problem myself by adding a reference to a VBA project of an Excel workbook 'Book1.xlsm'. I then saved the file, closed Excel and removed Book1.xlsm before opening the 'VBA Tester.xlsm' file once more.

Problems like this one often occur when you add references to other Office applications using a newer version of Office than your users may have. For example, if your code refers to the Outlook 16 library and your user uses Outlook 14 (Outlook 2010), your user will get this compile error.

To avoid problems like this one, make sure you use late binding when you are writing code for an environment with mixed Office versions.

Note: 'Late binding' is a runtime process of looking up a declaration, by name, that corresponds to a uniquely specified type. It does not involve type checking during compilation, when referencing libraries, including an object, is not required.

I find it also beneficial to avoid using external libraries where possible.

Editing Debris

The VBA Editor does a poor job of cleaning up after itself. When you write code, meta information is stored within your VBA project to which you have no access. To illustrate, open a blank workbook, insert a module into the VBA project and write a single line like this:

```
Dim ACTIVESHEET as Object
```

Now press Enter at the end of the line, remove that line and start coding. Write this little routine, make sure you type activesheet in lower case characters. You'll see the VBA editor update the word activesheet to all capitals as soon as you leave that line of code, it becomes:

```
Sub OddCapitalisation()

 MsgBox ACTIVESHEET.Name

End Sub
```

So the VBA editor now thinks it needs to capitalize ActiveSheet everywhere!

There might be several ways to fix this issue, one of them is by exporting and subsequently deleting all modules from the file and after that importing the deleted modules. There are several VBA tools which allow doing this automatically too.

Since the object modules belonging to worksheets and the ThisWorkbook module cannot be removed, I find it beneficial to make sure those modules contain as little code as possible. These modules cannot be cleaned using the method shown above. The only way to clean those Excel Object modules is by completely removing the VBA project and importing all code from a back-up copy.

Links

This part has two accompanying files: 'Links Tester.xlsx' and 'Links Tester Source.xlsx'.

Spreadsheet users often create links to other Excel workbooks. For instance, this may occur when they have a workbook to create invoices and they want to extract information from a master workbook containing customer information. These are links you may find in the Data-> Edit links tab. It is this kind of link that causes this dialog to open when you open a file with such a link:

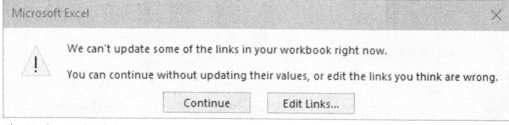

The 'Update Links' dialog.

Unfortunately, there are some issues with this dialog and with links in general:

- Users tend not to understand the message and click 'Continue' without giving it a second thought
- Links may be very hard to locate
- Novice users do not understand the concept of links.

I have undertaken several consulting projects in the past which involved analyzing a corporate network share for Excel files. Here are some statistics I obtained from those projects:

- Between 10% and 20% of all Excel files contain one or more links to other files
- About 80% of those files with links contain at least one broken link (a link is considered broken when the source file cannot be found).

An Anecdote

I once sat next to someone from the finance department of a bank who was about to update the monthly financial report. He opened the report file and the link warning message popped up. He pressed the 'Continue' button immediately. I asked him why he chose to click that button and his remarkable reply was that he was instructed to do so by his predecessor, telling him he didn't know what caused the message, but everything would be perfectly all right when doing so. He had also been told that his predecessor had tried to fix the issue by clicking the 'Break link' button on the 'Edit Links' dialog:

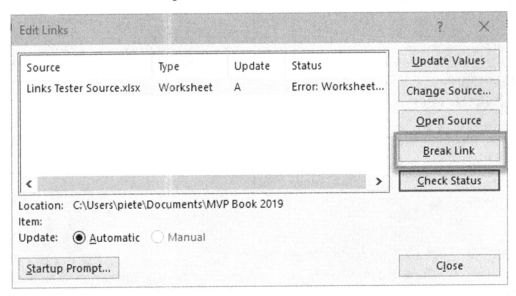

The 'Edit Links' dialog and the dangerous 'Break Link' button.
I analyzed the file and discovered the root cause of the link. More importantly, I also discovered the effect caused by pressing "Break Link". One of the charts in the file no longer pointed to any cells but had become static (it only had hard-coded values). The chart was on a dashboard and had been static for over a year.

> **Warning**: Never ever press that Break Link button, unless you are positive that that is truly the correct thing to do.

Before doing anything else, find out what items of your workbook contain links. The sample file 'Links tester.xlsx' contains two examples of links, one of which is hidden.

Links may be hidden in many places, including:

- Conditional formatting formulas
- Data Validation rules
- Chart elements like data labels and (axes) titles
- Buttons and other forms controls
- Range names
- Pivot tables
- Column formulas hidden in empty tables (this is demonstrated in the sample file).

Conclusion

I have shown you a number of areas which might cause your Excel model to go haywire. These are all mostly problems which come to existence due to very basic and expected actions like copying and pasting information from other sources. After reading this chapter, you will at least know what to look out for when you are editing an important spreadsheet model and you spot erratic behavior. More importantly, you now know when to "handle with care". Below, I've also tried to point you to possible fixes for the issues and to point you to software that may help you to trouble-shoot or even repair the file. I wish you a problem-free spreadsheet modelling future.

Get the Workbooks / Other Useful Links

The workbooks for this chapter (from https://mrx.cl/mvpfiles) contain the examples covered and useful links.

Make Your Own VBA Worksheet Functions

by Charles Williams

When none of Excel's native Functions do what you want, you can write your own Worksheet Functions (User Defined Function or UDF for short) using VBA. This chapter shows you simple step-by-step techniques that you may use to write efficient UDFs like a professional.

A Simple Averaging Function

Suppose you want to write a function that calculates the average of the absolute values from a range of cells while excluding from the average anything that is not a number or is less than a certain number, tolerance. Let's call the function **AverageTol**. To do this,

- Start Excel.
- Alt + F11 gets you to the Visual Basic Editor (VBE).
- Insert –> Module.

> **Note:** VBA Worksheet Functions MUST be in a standard module, not in a worksheet or other class module.

Then, enter the following VBA Code:

```
Function AverageTol(theRange, dTol)
    For Each Thing In theRange
        If IsNumeric(Thing) Then
            If Abs(Thing) > dTol Then
                AverageTol = AverageTol + Abs(Thing)
                lCount = lCount + 1
            End If
        End If
    Next Thing
    AverageTol = AverageTol / lCount
End Function
```

The function loops through every cell in the range and, if the absolute value of the cell is a number greater than the tolerance, adds it to the total and increments a count. Finally, it divides the total by the count and returns the result.

Now, go back to the Excel worksheet, enter some data in cells A1:A10 and in B1 enter

=AverageTol(A1:A10,5)

That was pretty easy and works well for 10 cells. However, if you have a lot of data, say 32,000 cells, then 15 formulas using this UDF takes 2.3 seconds to calculate on my laptop.

One major reason this is so slow is that I used all the defaults: I was lazy and did not declare any of the variables, so they all defaulted to Variants. That's **SLOW** … but I can easily improve it: here is version **A** of **AverageTol**:

```
Function AverageTolA(theRange As Range, dTol As Double)
    Dim oCell As Range
    Dim lCount As Long
    For Each oCell In theRange
        If IsNumeric(oCell) Then
            If Abs(oCell) > dTol Then
                AverageTolA = AverageTolA + Abs(oCell)
                lCount = lCount + 1
            End If
        End If
    Next oCell
    AverageTolA = AverageTolA / lCount
End Function
```

This is the same function but with each variable declared as a sensible Type. This is good programming practice and considerably faster. 15 formulas using this UDF on 32,000 cells now calculates in 1.8 seconds, that's 27% faster but still **SLOW**.

Transfer Data in One Large Block

One reason it is slow is that there is a large overhead each time a VBA program transfers data from an Excel cell to a VBA variable. This function does that lots of times (three times 32,000). If you transfer the data in one large block you can avoid much of this overhead:

```
Function AverageTolC(theRange As Range, dTol As Double)
    Dim vArr As Variant, v As Variant
    Dim lCount As Long
    On Error GoTo FuncFail
    vArr = theRange  ' Get Range into a variant array
    For Each v In vArr
        If IsNumeric(v) Then
            If Abs(v) > dTol Then
                AverageTolC = AverageTolC + Abs(v)
                lCount = lCount + 1
            End If
        End If
    Next v
    AverageTolC = AverageTolC / lCount
    Exit Function
FuncFail:
    AverageTolC = CVErr(xlErrNA) ' Return #N/A
End Function
```

The statement **vArr = theRange** takes the values from all the cells in the Range and transfers it to a two-dimensional Array of Variants. Then, the UDF loops on each element of the Variant array. I also added an error handling trap that makes the UDF return *#N/A* if any unexpected error occurs. Now, the 15 formulas calculate in 0.14 seconds: that is 13 times faster.

Use .Value2 rather than .Value

But we have not finished yet! Another speedup trick is to replace

vArr = theRange with **vArr = theRange.Value2**

That reduces the calculation time from 142 milliseconds (thousandths of a second) to 78 milliseconds. Using .Value2 rather than the default property (.Value) makes Excel do less processing.

We can also make another small speedup by using Doubles rather than Variants wherever possible and only using Abs() once:

```
Public Function AverageTolE( _
    theRange As Range, dTol As Double) As Variant
    Dim vArr As Variant, v as Variant
    Dim d As Double, r As Double
    Dim lCount As Long
    On Error GoTo FuncFail
    vArr = theRange.Value2
    On Error GoTo Skip ' skip non-numerics
    For Each v In vArr
        d = Abs(CDbl(v))    ' Double: faster than Variant
        If d > dTol Then
            r = r + d
            lCount = lCount + 1
        End If
Skip:
    Next v
    AverageTolE = r / lCount
    Exit Function
FuncFail:
    AverageTolE = CVErr(xlErrNA)
End Function
```

Now the calculation time has come down to 56 milliseconds. So, a series of small changes has improved the calculation speed of this simple UDF from 2.3 seconds to 0.056 seconds – that's 42 times faster!

Using Native Excel Functions in your UDF

Sometimes it is a great idea to call native Excel functions from your own VBA functions. Here's an example.

Linear interpolation is a commonly used technique for finding missing values or calculating a value that lies between the values given in a table. Suppose you have a table of values like this and you want to find the flow rate for a level of 66.25:

Level	Flow1	Flow2
64.00	0.10	2.59
64.50	0.77	3.18
65.00	2.19	3.73
65.50	4.02	4.28
66.00	6.19	6.88
66.50	8.64	12.04
67.00	11.36	13.85
67.50	13.45	14.84
68.00	15.00	16.37
68.50	16.41	21.12
69.00	17.71	21.68

Flow rates versus water level

Assuming the value is on a straight line between the flow for 66.0 and the flow for 66.5, you can calculate the answer like this:

$$6.19+(8.64-6.19)*(66.25-66.0)/(66.5-66.0)=7.415$$

Writing the function in the same way as the **AverageToIE** example gives:

```
Function VINTERPOLATEA(Lookup_Value as Variant, _
    Table_Array as Range, Col_Num as long)
    Dim vArr As Variant
    Dim j As Long
    vArr = Table_Array.Value2     ' get values
    ' find first value greater than lookup value
    For j = lBound(vArr) To UBound(vArr)
        If vArr(j, 1) > Lookup_Value Then
            Exit For
        End If
    Next j
    ' Interpolate
    VINTERPOLATEA = (vArr(j - 1, Col_Num) + _
        (vArr(j, Col_Num) - vArr(j - 1, Col_Num)) * _
        (Lookup_Value - vArr(j - 1, 1)) / (vArr(j, 1) - vArr(j - 1, 1)))
End Function
```

This is reasonably efficient: 20 formulas interpolating on a table 10,000 rows long takes 323 milliseconds.

But of course, we can do better!

When you look at this UDF you can see that the actual calculation only uses two rows of data, but to get those two rows it has to:

- Import 10,000 rows by three columns of data into an array.
- Perform a linear search on the first column.

This sounds suspiciously like a LOOKUP or MATCH.

So, let's try using Excel's MATCH function instead: you can call MATCH from inside your VBA UDF using Application. WorksheetFunction.MATCH. Since the data is sorted, we can use approximate MATCH. Once we have got the row number from MATCH, we can get the two rows we are interested in, using Resize and Offset.

The new UDF looks like this (I am ignoring error handling for the sake of simplicity):

```
Function VINTERPOLATEB(Lookup_Value As Variant, Table_Array As Range,
    Col_Num As Long)
    Dim jRow As Long
    Dim rng As Range
    Dim vArr As Variant
    ' create range for column 1 of input
    Set rng = Table_Array.Columns(1)
    ' lookup Row number using MATCH
    ' Approx Match finds row for the largest value < the lookup value
    jRow = Application.WorksheetFunction.Match(Lookup_Value, rng, 1)

    ' get 2 rows of data
    vArr = Table_Array.Resize(2).Offset(jRow - 1, 0).Value2
    ' Interpolate
    VINTERPOLATEB = (vArr(1, Col_Num) + _
        (vArr(2, Col_Num) - vArr(1, Col_Num)) * _
        (Lookup_Value - vArr(1, 1)) / (vArr(2, 1) - vArr(1, 1)))
End Function
```

This UDF takes 2 milliseconds on the test data – that's 160 times faster!

One reason it is so much faster is because it never brings the data across from Excel to VBA – it just brings across a small range object which is just a pointer to the table, and then passes this small range object back to the Excel MATCH.

The other reason is that it exploits the fast binary search algorithm built into MATCH's approximate match on sorted data.

> **Note**: there are two ways of calling Excel Functions such as MATCH from VBA: `Application.Match` and `Application.WorksheetFunction.Match`. The differences are mostly in error handling (for instance when no match is found for the exact match option):
> `Application.Match` returns a Variant containing an error, which allows the use of IsError: `If IsError(Application.Match …)`
> `Application.WorksheetFunction.Match` raises a VBA error which requires an `On Error` handler.

Returning an Array from your UDF

With the introduction of Dynamic Arrays in Office 365 (see "A Look to the Future – Dynamic Arrays" on page 45), returning an array of results from your UDF becomes the normal way of doing things, and array UDFs can also be very efficient. So here is an example: VSTACK, a UDF that stacks ranges on top of one another. The ranges can have different numbers of rows and columns and can be on different worksheets.

VSTACK introduces several new UDF techniques:

- Optional missing parameters.
- A variable number of parameters.
- Getting the range of cells that the UDF was called from.
- Dynamically resizing an array.
- Returning an array from a Worksheet UDF.

Normally, when Excel performs this kind of array operation the missing data caused by stacking ranges with different numbers of columns is shown by #N/A. This UDF has an optional parameter that you can use to replace the #N/A with zero or blank so that when you call the UDF from within an aggregating function like SUM it still works.

In Dynamic Array Excel, the UDF will dynamically spill its results to the neighboring cells. However, in Excel 2013, you must select enough cells to contain all the output data and enter the UDF using Control + Shift + Enter to create a multi-cell array formula.

```vba
Public Function VStack(Pad As Variant, _
    ParamArray Stacks() As Variant) As Variant
' Stack ranges vertically, padding missing data with Pad
' All items to be stacked must be Ranges
'
    Dim nRowsOut As Long
    Dim nColsOut As Long
    Dim jParam As Long
    Dim oRng As Range
    Dim varThisStack As Variant ' 2-D array of values from a range
    Dim j As Long
    Dim k As Long
    Dim jRow As Long
    On Error GoTo FuncFail
    If IsMissing(Pad) Then Pad = CVErr(xlErrNA) ' default pad is #N/A
    If UBound(Stacks) - LBound(Stacks) + 1 = 0 Then
        GoTo FuncFail ' no parameters
    End If
    ' find aggregate output dimensions of items to be stacked
    For jParam = LBound(Stacks) To UBound(Stacks)
        If Not IsObject(Stacks(jParam)) Then GoTo FuncFail
        Set oRng = Stacks(jParam)
        nRowsOut = nRowsOut + oRng.Rows.Count
        If oRng.Columns.Count > nColsOut Then
            nColsOut = oRng.Columns.Count
        End If
    Next jParam
    ' if CSE entered calling range is larger use that
    If Application.Caller.Rows.Count > nRowsOut Then
        nRowsOut = Application.Caller.Rows.Count
    End If
    If Application.Caller.Columns.Count > nColsOut Then
        nColsOut = Application.Caller.Columns.Count
    End If
    ' resize the output array
    Dim VarOut() As Variant  ' the array to be returned by VStack
    ReDim VarOut(1 To nRowsOut, 1 To nColsOut) As Variant
    ' copy each range in turn into the output array
    For jParam = LBound(Stacks) To UBound(Stacks)
        varThisStack = Stacks(jParam).Value2
        For j = LBound(varThisStack) To UBound(varThisStack)
            jRow = jRow + 1
            For k = 1 To nColsOut
                If k <= UBound(varThisStack, 2) Then
                    VarOut(jRow, k) = varThisStack(j, k)
                Else
                    VarOut(jRow, k) = Pad ' pad out extra columns
                End If
            Next k
        Next j
    Next jParam
'
    ' pad out extra rows in the caller range
    If jRow < nRowsOut Then
        For j = jRow + 1 To nRowsOut
            For k = 1 To nColsOut
                VarOut(j, k) = Pad
            Next k
        Next j
    End If
    VStack = VarOut  ' return the array
    Exit Function
FuncFail:
    VStack = CVErr(xlErrValue) ' return #Value! on error
End Function
```

	A	B	C	D	E	F	G	H	I	J	K
1	1	A1		100	b100	c100					
2	2	A2		101	b101	c101		{=VSTACK(0,A1:B10,D1:F5)}			
3	3	A3		102	b102	c102		1	A1	0	0
4	4	A4		103	b103	c103		2	A2	0	0
5	5	A5		104	b104	c104		3	A3	0	0
6	6	A6						4	A4	0	0
7	7	A7						5	A5	0	0
8	8	A8						6	A6	0	0
9	9	A9						7	A7	0	0
10	10	A10						8	A8	0	0
11								9	A9	0	0
12								10	A10	0	0
13								100	b100	c100	0
14								101	b101	c101	0
15								102	b102	c102	0
16								103	b103	c103	0
17								104	b104	c104	0
18								0	0	0	0
19								0	0	0	0

VSTACK stacking 2 ranges and padding with zeros in Excel 2013.

	A	B	C	D	E	F	G	H	I	J
1	1	A1		100	b100	c100				
2	2	A2		101	b101	c101		=VSTACK(0,A1:B10,D1:F5)		
3	3	A3		102	b102	c102		1	A1	0
4	4	A4		103	b103	c103		2	A2	0
5	5	A5		104	b104	c104		3	A3	0
6	6	A6						4	A4	0
7	7	A7						5	A5	0
8	8	A8						6	A6	0
9	9	A9						7	A7	0
10	10	A10						8	A8	0
11								9	A9	0
12								10	A10	0
13								100	b100	c100
14								101	b101	c101
15								102	b102	c102
16								103	b103	c103
17								104	b104	c104

In Dynamic Array Excel, just enter the Function in H3 and it will spill. Column K and rows 18:19 will not be used, but the UDF still must be able to pad out missing cells caused by the different number of columns.

Handling Missing Parameters

In VSTACK you can omit the Pad parameter (but you still need the comma separator): VSTACK(,A1:A10,D1:F5)

You can detect this in the VBA by using **IsMissing** and supply a default value.

```
If IsMissing(Pad) Then Pad = CVErr(xlErrNA) ' default pad is #N/A
```

Variable Number of Parameters

We don't know in advance how many ranges the user will want to stack, so the VBA code must handle a variable number of parameters. You can handle this with the ParamArray argument. ParamArray must be the last argument and must be defined as an array of Variants.

```
ParamArray Stacks() As Variant
```

A Variant can hold anything, and in VSTACK we want each element of the variant array to hold a Range object.

Note: the VBA must handle the error that occurs when the user enters a parameter (such as a number or an array) that is not a range.

The first task in VSTACK is to loop through each of the ranges to find the maximum number of columns used and to add up the total number of rows used.

```
' find aggregate output dimensions of items to be stacked
For jParam = LBound(Stacks) To UBound(Stacks)
    If Not IsObject(Stacks(jParam)) Then GoTo FuncFail
    Set oRng = Stacks(jParam)
    nRowsOut = nRowsOut + oRng.Rows.Count
    If oRng.Columns.Count > nColsOut Then
        nColsOut = oRng.Columns.Count
    End If
Next jParam
```

Getting the Range of Cells the UDF was Called From

In my Excel 2013 VSTACK example, the UDF has been array-entered into more cells than are currently needed to hold the stacked arrays. To avoid the #N/A for the extra cells VSTACK must find out how many extra columns and rows are needed (of course, in Dynamic Array Excel, you would not need to do this).

Application.Caller returns the range of cells that the UDF was called from.

```
' if CSE entered calling range is larger use that
If Application.Caller.Rows.Count > nRowsOut Then
    nRowsOut = Application.Caller.Rows.Count
End If
If Application.Caller.Columns.Count > nColsOut Then
    nColsOut = Application.Caller.Columns.Count
End If
```

Dynamically Resizing a VBA Array

Now we know how large the output array is, we can create an empty array to match, by first defining the array without any dimensions and then using ReDim to resize it.

```
' resize the output array
Dim VarOut() As Variant  ' the array to be returned by VStack
ReDim VarOut(1 To nRowsOut, 1 To nColsOut) As Variant
```

Filling and Returning the Output Array

Filling the output array is just a matter of looping through the Stacks ParamArray again, getting the values for each Range into a 2-D variant array and copying the elements of the array into the output array. Of course, VSTACK must also check if a Pad element needs to be inserted into the Output Array.

Finally, the output array is returned by assigning it to the VSTACK function.

```
VStack = VarOut  ' return the array
```

Note: the VSTACK function itself must be defined as a variant but does not need to be defined as an array of variants because a single variant variable can hold an array.

```
Public Function VStack(…) As Variant
```

Note: You may have noticed that the VBA name of the function is VStack but in the Excel formula it is VSTACK. Excel uses the capitalization that was used in the very first formula that used the function, and stubbornly resists attempts to change it afterwards.

Array Functions can be Faster

Replacing a number of non-array UDFs with one array UDF that reads ranges of data and returns an array of results can be very efficient. The reasons for this performance gain are:

- The input data is read once into a large array rather than many times into a small array.
- The overhead time to call a UDF is only incurred once rather than many times.

For example, using this technique on the AverageTol UDF (see AverageTolM in the AvTol.xlsm workbook) reduces the time from 83 milliseconds to 32 milliseconds.

Parameter Data Types: Double, Range and Variant

It is not always obvious which data type you should use for your UDF parameters.

Double and Other Simple Data Types

If you know that a parameter must always be a Double or a String or a Boolean, then it makes sense to declare the parameter as that data type. Excel will try to convert the data type of whatever is supplied in the function call.

Note: If the conversion fails the UDF just silently returns *#VALUE!*

Range

When the parameter must be a Range because your code will use Range methods such as Resize, Offset or Intersect, then use the Range type. However, if Excel cannot convert the supplied parameter to a Range (for example, a number, or a calculated range will fail) then the UDF will silently return *#VALUE!*

Variant

There is a lot to recommend defining your parameters as Variant. It is by far the most flexible type and allows parameters to be supplied as numbers or Ranges or calculated arrays or array literals or …

However, this flexibility means that your UDF needs to determine the type and dimensions of whatever that has been wrapped in the Variant and handle it appropriately. If all you want is the values, then a simple technique is to assign the Variant to itself:

```
varParam = varParam
```

If a range was supplied, this will convert it to values. All you then need to do is to determine if the result is a single scalar value, a two-dimensional array or a one-dimensional array.

Use TypeOf or TypeName() to determine the type of a Variant:

```
If TypeOf theVariant is Range then
If TypeName (theVariant) = "Range" then
```

Do not use VarType(theVariant): it is slow because it performs an expensive under-the-covers coerce of a Range to an array of values and then just throws the values away!

Here is an example subroutine that determines the dimensions of a Variant:

```vba
Sub VarDims(var As Variant, nRows As Long, nCols As Long)
'
    ' get the dimensions of the variant
    Dim oRng As Range
    On Error GoTo Fail
    nRows = 0
    nCols = 0
    If TypeOf var Is Range Then
        Set oRng = var              ''' 2D
        nRows = oRng.Rows.Count
        nCols = oRng.Columns.Count
    Else
        If IsArray(var) Then
            On Error Resume Next
            nCols = UBound(var, 2)
            On Error GoTo Fail
            If nCols = 0 Then
                nCols = UBound(var) - LBound(var) + 1
                nRows = -1             ''' 1D
            Else
                nRows = UBound(var) - LBound(var) + 1 ''' 2D
                nCols = UBound(var, 2) - LBound(var, 2) + 1
            End If
        Else
            nRows = -1             ''' scalar
            nCols = -1
        End If
    End If
Fail:
End Sub
```

Using these techniques, I modified the VSTACK UDF (in the StackRows.xlsm example workbook) to handle ranges, calculated expressions, arrays and scalar parameters:

⬛	A	B	C	D	E	F	G
1	95	18	59				
2	20	42	36				
3	20	22	28				
4	79	35	95				
5	52	11	96				
6							
7	Mixed parameter types: Ranges, calculated expressions,arrays, scalars.						
8							
9	=vstack2(0,A1:C5,Sheet3!A1:E1*1000,{42,43;44,45},999)						
10	95	18	59	0	0		
11	20	42	36	0	0		
12	20	22	28	0	0		
13	79	35	95	0	0		
14	52	11	96	0	0		
15	95000	50000	81000	78000	46000		
16	42	43	0	0	0		
17	44	45	0	0	0		
18	999	0	0	0	0		

The VSTACK2 UDF handling mixed parameter types and Excel 2016 Dynamic Arrays.

Function Dependencies, Volatility and Recalculation

Excel's smart recalculation engine calculates faster because it only recalculates the formulas that need to be calculated. These formulas are the ones that are dependent on changed cells or contain volatile functions.

Warning: Excel only calculates your UDFs when one of their parameters refers to a changed or volatile cell. This means that your UDF will not recalculate properly when it references other cells from within the body of the UDF.

For example, here are four UDFs:

```vba
Option Explicit
Public Function Depends1() As Variant
'
    ' no parameters
    Dim vArr As Variant
    Dim j As Long
    vArr = Worksheets("Sheet1").Range("A1:A4").Value2
    For j = LBound(vArr) To UBound(vArr)
        Depends1 = Depends1 + vArr(j, 1)
    Next j
End Function
Public Function Depends2(SingleCell As Range) As Variant
'
    ' single cell but resized
    Dim vArr As Variant
    Dim j As Long
    Dim oRng As Range
    Set oRng = SingleCell.Resize(4, 1)
    vArr = oRng.Value2
    For j = LBound(vArr) To UBound(vArr)
        Depends2 = Depends2 + vArr(j, 1)
    Next j
End Function
Public Function Depends3() As Variant
'
    ' volatile no parameters
    Dim vArr As Variant
    Dim j As Long
    Application.Volatile
    vArr = Worksheets("Sheet1").Range("A1:A4").Value2
    For j = LBound(vArr) To UBound(vArr)
        Depends3 = Depends3 + vArr(j, 1)
    Next j
End Function
Public Function Depends4(theRange As Range) As Variant
'
    ' no references to cells outside the input parameter
    Dim vArr As Variant
    Dim j As Long
    vArr = theRange.Value2
    For j = LBound(vArr) To UBound(vArr)
        Depends4 = Depends4 + vArr(j, 1)
    Next j
End Function
```

All the functions just add four numbers together. The first time the functions are entered everything looks good: they all give the correct answer.

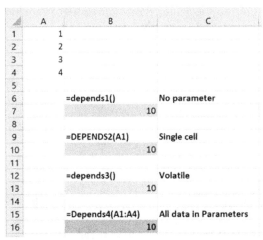

The four Depends functions correctly adding the numbers in A1:A4.

However, when you change cell A4 to 10 Depends1 and Depends2 do not recalculate and show the wrong answer.

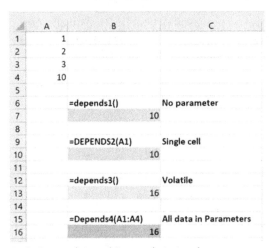

Only Depends3 and Depends4 give the correct answer.

Depends1 has no parameters and refers directly to A1:A4 from inside the UDF. Depends2 has a parameter, A1, but inside the UDF uses Resize to indirectly refer to A1:A4. Excel relies on tracking the dependencies using the parameters of these UDFs, and so does not know that they have a dependency on cell A4.

Making your UDF Volatile

Depends3 has ignored dependency tracking because it has been made Volatile by adding Application.Volatile. Volatile functions are recalculated at every recalculation regardless of dependency changes.

> **Caution**: Creating too many Volatile functions can slow your workbook speed to a crawl!

Sometimes (but rarely), it makes sense to make your UDF volatile. For example, a few of Excel's native functions are volatile either because they need to be refreshed at each recalculation (e.g. NOW(), DATE(), RAND()), or because they refer to cells that are not directly referenced in their parameters (OFFSET() and INDIRECT()).

Unexpected UDF Behaviors

- UDFs do not always behave the way you might expect. Here are some of the more frequently encountered "Gotcha's".

UDFs cannot Change Things in the Workbook

- UDFs are only allowed to return values to their parent calling cells. They cannot change other cells, alter the selection, change formatting or application settings (there are a few esoteric exceptions to this rule). If you need to do this, you probably should be using a VBA Sub called either from Event code or from a command button.

Handling Full Column References in a UDF

Many native Excel functions handle full column references in a sensible way, by only working with the real data in the column rather than all 1,048,576 cells. However, with a VBA UDF you must add special purpose code to subset the full column reference to the intersection with the used range of the parent sheet containing the full column reference.

For example, if the full column parameter is defined as

theRange as Range:

```
' allow for full column references:
' reset full column to intersect of input and used range
Set oRng = Intersect(theRange, theRange.Parent.UsedRange)
```

The AvTol.xlsm workbook contains two examples of this technique in AverageTolF and AverageTolM.

UDFs not Calculated when Formatting Changed

- Because Excel does not trigger a recalculation when the format (for example, the color) of a cell changes, it is hard to write a UDF to count the colors in a range of cells. The closest you can get is to make the UDF volatile so that it will count the colors at the next recalculation. However, if the only thing you do is change formatting, then no recalculation occurs and the UDF does not update.

Function Wizard Calculates UDF Multiple Times

- When you enter a UDF using Excel's Function Wizard, it tries to show you the result of your UDF as you enter the parameters. This means that your UDF will be calculated at least once for each parameter entered, which can be a serious problem with long-running UDFs. Your UDF can detect that it is being called from the Function Wizard using this VBA example:

```
If Not Application.CommandBars("Standard").Controls(1).Enabled Then
MsgBox "In the Function Wizard"
Exit Function
End If
```

UDF Calculated More than Once per Recalculation

In a complicated spreadsheet, Excel must work out what sequence to use when calculating the formulas in order to ensure that every formula gets the correct answer. Sometimes, this process means that Excel will try to calculate your UDF before one of the UDF parameters has been calculated (it may be further down the sheet or on another worksheet).

When this happens to your UDF:

- Any Variant or Range parameters will be Empty.
- The UDF will be calculated and then placed further down the dependency chain to be recalculated again later.
- To properly resolve this your UDF should test Variant and Range parameters using IsEmpty(), handle any resulting errors, and exit the function gracefully (particularly if it is a slow-to-calculate UDF).

UDF Unexpectedly Returning #Value!

It can be frustrating trying to work out why your UDF is unexpectedly returning *#Value!*

The first thing to try is to add a breakpoint to your VBA code (select a line of code and press F9), re-enter the formula containing the UDF and step through the code line by line using F8. If the code encounters an error condition it will stop executing and the UDF will return *#Value!* In this case you should either fix the error or add an appropriate On Error handler.

But sometimes Excel will return *#Value!* without even executing your UDF. Often this is because Excel cannot convert the value given as a parameter to the defined type of the parameter. For instance, a numeric value was given but the parameter is defined as a Range.

Many VBA UDF Calls in a Workbook Makes Calculation Slow

If you have hundreds or thousands of formulas in a workbook that call UDFs then calculation may be slowed down significantly by the "VBE Refresh Bug". This is because every time a VBA UDF is calculated the title bar in the Visual Basic Editor gets refreshed to show "Running". This is very slow, but you can minimize or eliminate the slowdown by:

- Minimizing the VBE window
- Closing the VBE Window (better)
- Never opening the VBE Window in this session of Excel (even better).

The best solution is to switch to Manual Calculation and trap the calculations using OnKey for F9, Shift + F9, Ctrl + Alt + F9 and Shift + Ctrl + Alt + F9, then call the calculation from VBA using Application.Calculate etc. This completely avoids the multiple refreshes.

Building a Function Library Addin

So far, all the VBA UDFs have been contained in the workbook that will use them. If other people will use your UDFs, or the UDFs will be used in more than one workbook you probably should create a centrally shared Function Library Addin (known as an "XLAM") so that there is a single maintainable version of your UDFs rather than multiple copies scattered across many workbooks.

Creating the XLAM

You can create the addin by saving a workbook containing the VBA UDF code as an XLAM (use File -> Save As and choose XLAM as the workbook type).

Note: Excel tries hard to put the Addin in AppData -> Roaming -> Microsoft -> Addins but you probably want to put it in a network share folder or another folder of your choice.

Note: When you open the XLAM workbook in Excel it becomes a hidden workbook and none of its worksheets are visible.

To make the UDFs available to other workbooks the XLAM must be open. You can make Excel always open it at startup by using File -> Options -> Addins -> Manage Excel Addins -> Go-> Browse to the location of the Addin, select and click OK until you get back to Excel.

Note: If offered the option of copying the Addin to the Addins Folder my advice is to say "No".

Adding Function Wizard and Intellisense Descriptions and Help

You can make it easier for others to use your UDFs by adding descriptions and help text for the UDF and for its parameters to show up in the Function Wizard dialog or when entering the UDF directly in a cell.

Registering your UDFs with the Function Wizard is done using Application.MacroOptions:

```
Sub RegFuncs_Macro()
'
   ' Register the Function for the Function Wizard Dialog
   Dim vArgDescription As Variant
   ''' cannot use MacroOptions directly from an Addin
   Application.ScreenUpdating = False
   ThisWorkbook.IsAddin = False
   vArgDescription = Array("The Range to be averaged", _
     "Exclusion Tolerance")
   Application.MacroOptions _
      Macro:="AverageTolG", _
      Description:="Calculates the average of a range" & _
      " for absolute values of numbers greater than Tolerance", _
      Category:=3, _
   HelpFile:="http://www.decisionModels.com/Func_Library.htm", _
   ArgumentDescriptions:=vArgDescription
   ThisWorkbook.IsAddin = True
   Application.ScreenUpdating = True
End Sub
```

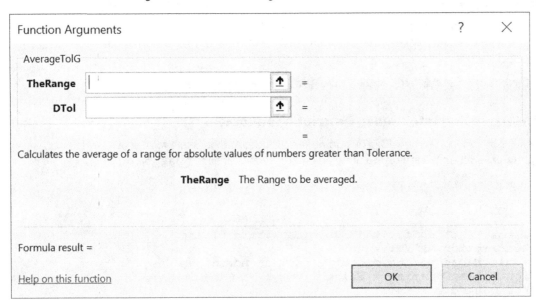

The Function Wizard Dialog for a UDF that is not registered.

Function Arguments

AverageTolG

TheRange [   ] ↑ =

DTol [   ] ↑ =

=

Calculates the average of a range for absolute values of numbers greater than Tolerance.

TheRange   The Range to be averaged.

Formula result =

Help on this function   OK   Cancel

The Function Wizard Dialog for a registered UDF, showing argument and function descriptions.

Adding Intellisense requires using Govert van Drimmelen's Intellisense XLL: see

https://github.com/Excel-DNA/IntelliSense

To see an example Function Library addin with both Function Wizard and Intellisense descriptions and help for two UDFs: AverageTolG and vStack3:

- Copy the FunctionLibrary.xlam, ExcelDNA.IntelliSense.xll and ExcelDNA.IntelliSense64.xll to a folder.
- Open the FunctionLibrary.xlam.
- Open a new workbook and start entering =AverageTolH(which has no Intellisense, and then =AverageTolG(

Entering a UDF without Intellisense.

=AverageTolG(

> AverageTolG(**theRange**, dTol)
> Intellisense: Calculates the average of a range for absolute values of numbers greater than Tolerance
> ***theRange:*** *The Range to be Averaged*

Entering a UDF with Intellisense, showing function and arguments descriptions.

The _Intellisense_ worksheet in the XLAM contains the descriptions used by the Intellisense XLL. The WorkBook Open in the XLAM contains this code to register the UDFs and load the Intellisense Xll.

```
Private Sub Workbook_Open()
   ' register UDFs for the Function Wizard
   RegFuncs_Macro
   '
   ' load the Intellisense XLL
  #If Win64 Then
      Application.RegisterXLL ThisWorkbook.Path & _
         "\ExcelDna.IntelliSense64.xll"
  #Else
      Application.RegisterXLL ThisWorkbook.Path & _
      "\ExcelDna.IntelliSense.xll"
  #End If
End Sub
```

Conclusion

It is easy to extend the power of Excel by writing your own worksheet functions using VBA. This chapter has shown you some simple techniques you can use to make your UDFs calculate fast and look professional.

An Overview of Modern VBA Best Practices

by Mathieu Guindon

VBA as a language might not have evolved much in the past 20 years, but the rest of the programming landscape did... *a lot*. Today Microsoft Excel runs not only on a Windows desktop, but also in any browser, or even on your smartphone; cross-platform Office extensibility is here with Office-JS, but the single-document nature of Office Online is currently preventing many useful automation scenarios... and that is why VBA is still an irreplaceable asset. For decades it *got the job done*, and massive amounts of VBA code was written... with programming guidelines from two decades ago alas, back when VB6 was all the rage and *Systems Hungarian* notation was considered legible. The 90's were wild, kids.

There's a reason VBA is crowning the top of the 2019 edition of the "Most Dreaded Languages" list in the annual *Stack Overflow Developer Survey*: most VBA code is *legacy code*, and reading legacy code is painful and exhausting. For many, legacy code is simply "old code I didn't write". Others think of legacy code as any line of code that ever gets deployed to production. Michael Feathers described it as, essentially, "code without tests". Code that *cannot* be tested without first *refactoring it in major ways*. Put it this way: you inherit someone's VBA project tomorrow. What are the odds that you'll be looking at clean, well-abstracted code that comes with a complete suite of unit tests covering every possible edge case and documenting the behavior of every function? Ok, no unit tests... let's just go with clean and well-abstracted code? Yeah.

Part of the problem is that if you search online for "VBA best practices", you will find articles about using `Option Explicit`, avoiding `Variant` variables and global state, and then a ton of misleading or wrong information about putting an error handler in every procedure; more misinformation about what early binding is, often presented as a one-size-fits-all solution to all binding issues. Every second self-respecting blog about "VBA best practices" includes a semi-comprehensive table filled with prefixes and suffixes that are supposed to make your code "easier to read and understand" by avoiding vowels and making things as utterly unpronounceable as possible... *consistently*. And then one site says `sFoo`, another says it's `strFoo`, a third one says it's `pstrFoo` because it's a parameter, but it would be `pm_sFoo` – wait no, `pm_strFoo` if it were a public field, but `g_strFoo` if it were a global variable.

Simple and consistent, right?

Meanwhile the official .NET design guidelines are clearly *elsewhere* – here's a handful of them:

- **DO** favor readability over brevity.
- **DO** use semantically interesting names rather than language-specific keywords for type names. For example, `GetLength` is a better name than `GetInt`.
- **DO NOT** use Hungarian notation.
- **DO NOT** use underscores [, hyphens, or any other nonalphanumeric characters].
- **DO NOT** use abbreviations or contractions as part of identifier names.

Quite the cultural clash! Truth is, the number of valid, good reasons to *not* adopt these rather *sane* naming conventions in modern VBA code... is zero.

But clean code isn't about naming and prefixes. In 1998, you didn't *refactor* a lengthy procedure in VBA / VB6. Instead you added an enormous screen-height comment block that explained everything there *was* to know about that procedure... back when it was first written, 17 revisions earlier (with each individual revision painstakingly summarized in more comments). Variables were all declared at or near the top of the procedure, again to make it *cleaner*: "I know where my variables are"! A claim I promptly answer with "well, *I don't*": All I know is that the declarations are never in sight, whenever I'd need to see them. Scrolling through a screen-height wall of declarations at the top of every procedure was common practice back then. The cognitive load of wading through what after a few years grew into a thousand-liner nightmare of intricate intertwined logic and execution sub-paths, while remembering the meaning of all these funny identifiers from scrolling up there earlier... I don't know about you, but I'm tired of this.

VBA deserves a better reputation. This isn't about dreading the "most dreaded language" status in 2020 and onward: it's about writing code that's more *modern*, for our own future selves' sake.

VBA is well overdue for revamped programming guidelines, better aligned with the general direction of today's software design guidance. I'm not saying that you *must* cover every single edge case with a bajillion unit tests, but should you choose to go ahead and write *a* unit test to cover that bug you're trying to fix, you will quickly find that in order to be able to do that you need to completely change how you *think* about code… and when you start to think about code in terms of individually testable, decoupled components that form a *unit* and its *dependencies*, you start architecting your solutions differently. Some common *design patterns* eventually emerge, and before we know it, we have a generation of VBA developers writing code that's objectively just as good as any well-written code in any other language.

But before we go over *writing* modern VBA code, let's stop a moment and think about how modern VBA code should *read*.

What Do We Want in "Good Code"?

We want explicit code that *says what it does, and does what it says*. VBA has a lot of features what make *writing* code "faster": Bang notation (**foo!bar**) and implicit *default members*, implicit type conversions, implicit **ByRef** modifiers, implicit **Public** access modifiers, even implicit variables if you really like living on the edge. Using these language features arguably make *writing* code easier, only, at the expense of explicitness: the code is "readable", but only if you know every implicit default in the language like the palm of your hand… and you shouldn't have to.

We want to read code like we read a good book: top to bottom, some kind of coherent story, consistently indented and formatted across all modules. We want to see explicit member calls and access modifiers, **ByVal** parameters, explicit variable declarations.

Good code validates its inputs and makes as few assumptions as possible: **Range.Find** can return **Nothing**, **Range.Value** can be a **Variant / Error**; **Range.Cells(0, 0)** is out of bounds and **Row** or **Column** can't be negative, etc.

Good code is *early-bound* as much as possible, so anything that yields a **Variant** or an **Object** is ideally cast to a compile-time known type by simply assigning to a local variable. That way, member calls against that object are compiler-validated. You get *IntelliSense* / autocompletion, and *Parameter QuickInfo* as you type them, and if you make a typo the compiler will tell you.

Good code declares its variables (one declaration per statement), and each variable has a single meaning and purpose. If you find yourself reusing a variable for a different purpose, take a moment to consider how many things this procedure is responsible for; tempted to append a digit to a variable's name? Consider using an array or a **Collection** instead: don't encode a *subscript / index* into an identifier if you can avoid it. Form controls should be named, as well as any worksheet **Shape** that's used in code or associated to a macro: if it has a purpose, it should have a name that tells us about it. **CommandButton14** means nothing; **DeleteLeftAxisButton** says so much more.

I like to think good code begins with good names. The only problem is, naming is *hard*.

Naming Things

Phil Karlton famously said: *"There are only two hard things in Computer Science: cache invalidation and naming things"* – and the story doesn't say whether he had a case-insensitive language in mind when he said it, but he was right anyway: good naming is critically important.

Now, if you've been using some elaborate Hungarian Notation prefixing scheme for many years and have grown weirdly fond of it, I won't hold it against you… but let's just *try* and step out of the comfort zone a bit.

In no particular order, I find that good identifiers in VBA…

- Don't encode a data type in some lowercase prefix or suffix, and avoid underscores.
- Never end with a digit, and are at a bare minimum 3 characters long.
- Use **PascalCase** for module and procedure names.
- Use **camelCase** for instance / module state and locals. I use it for parameters too (they're locals!), but the members in a lot of type libraries have **PascalCase** parameters, so… at your discretion!
- Spell complete words that read naturally and convey meaning and purpose.
- Use nouns for modules and properties, verbs for procedures.
- Avoid *shadowing* identifiers that already exist in the *global namespace*. It's ok to reuse a name that is already "taken" as a member name, such as **Value**: global namespace is more like **Excel.Application**, or **VBA.Interaction.MsgBox**: identifiers that are in-scope and already refer to something very specific.

- Bad names:
```
Dim oRange As Range
Dim lStrSql As String
Dim il As Long ' noticed this is not a lowercase L?
Dim o1, o2, o3 As Long ' everyone knows only o3 is a Long?
```
- Good names:
```
Dim controller As GameController
Public Function Play(ByVal enemyGrid As PlayerGrid) As IGridCoord
```

What makes naming challenging, is the part about names needing to convey *meaning and purpose*. For a variable that's meant to hold a function's return value, I like to use **result**. For loop variables, I like to use **currentFoo**, where **Foo** is whatever I'm iterating, for example **currentRow** or **currentSheet**.

In class modules, the private backing fields for public properties have historically been named **m_PropertyName**, and the corresponding properties **PropertyName**. Proponents of Hungarian notation say this **m_** prefix helps with *IntelliSense*, and they have a point: knowing at a glance that you're looking at an instance field *is* useful, and the prefix *does* make autocomplete (Ctrl + Space) work nicely for that purpose. I have been using a different approach for several years and haven't looked back since: I declare a **Private Type** struct in the class module, and name each of its members *exactly* as per the property it's backing. Often, the only private field we need in a class module is a single variable declared with that user-defined type:

```
Private Type TSomething
 Foo As Long
 Bar As String
End Type
Private this As TSomething

Public Property Get Foo() As Long
 Foo = this.Foo
End Property
Public Property Let Foo(ByVal value As Long)
 this.Foo = value
 this.Bar = Format(this.Foo, "Currency")
End Property

Public Property Get Bar() As String
 Bar = this.Bar
End Property
```

Now you get actual *IntelliSense*, not just autocompletion. As a bonus the debugger's *locals* toolwindow will now cleanly regroup all private instance data under an expandable **this** struct node, whereas with a prefixing approach you get a much more cluttered list.

Note: The **T** prefix is shamelessly Hungarian: just like abstract interface class names traditionally begin with an **I**, my private struct types names begin with a **T**. It's harmless though: I could just as well have opted to name it **InstanceState** in every class, but **TClassName** works for me.

Properties that only expose a **Get** *accessor* procedure are read-only (or "get-only"); the code that is using them can therefore not *assign* to it – and if you accidentally do, the compiler will confusingly complain about an "object required":

```
Dim item As Something
Set item = New Something
item.Bar = "cannot assign, Bar property is get-only"
```

This confusing compiler error is giving us a peek into how VBA sees things: this assignment is perfectly legal at compile-time if the **Bar** property returns an object that has a *default property* with a **Let** accessor that can be implicitly invoked to accept that assignment – if there isn't, error 450 is raised *at run-time*. Twisted and confusing? Absolutely, and this is why *default properties* and *implicit member calls* should generally be avoided!

Property Let procedures always have at least one parameter: I like use the name **value** *every single time* (in **Property Set** procedures as well), and thanks to case insensitivity this turns **Range.Value** into **Range.value**, but in my opinion that's a small price to pay for beautifully consistent *right-hand side* argument names - although **RHS** would be equally good: its value is provided by the *right-hand side* expression of a **Let** *statement* (explicit or implicit – the **Let** keyword is obsolete / redundant). A **Property Let** procedure is invoked when such a statement has that property on the *left-hand side* of the assignment operator (**=**):

```
Dim item As Something
Set item = New Something
item.Foo = 42 'implicit Let statement
Let item.Foo = 42 'explicit Let statement (obsolete)
```

In this example, The **Property Let Foo** procedure receives the value **42** through the **value** / RHS parameter.

> **Note**: the RHS (caller provided) parameter of a **Property Let** or **Property Set** procedure is always passed by value (**ByVal**), regardless of whether **ByVal** or **ByRef** is specified. This is potentially confusing, because in VBA if a modifier isn't specified, a parameter is always implicitly passed **ByRef**. For this reason, the **Let** / **Set** accessor procedures' RHS parameter should always have an explicit **ByVal** modifier.

I always use the name **this** to refer to the private instance state variable of a class. Other names might be better or more descriptive, but I find **this** is a good compromise between meaningful and concise. Do not confuse it with the **Me** reserved name – per language specifications (section 5.3.1.5 "Parameter Lists"), the static (compile-time) semantics of **Me** are as follows:

*Each procedure that is a method has an implicit **ByVal** parameter called the "current object" that corresponds to the target object of an invocation of the method. The current object acts as an anonymous local variable with procedure extent and whose declared type is the class name of the class module containing the method declaration. For the duration of an activation of the method the data value of the current object variable is target object of the procedure invocation that created that activation. The current object is accessed using the **Me** keyword within the **\<procedure-body\>** of the method but [its reference] cannot be assigned to or otherwise modified.*

In other words when you do this:

```
Dim item As Something
Set item = New Something
item.DoSomething
```

Under the hood, the VBA runtime is invoking the **DoSomething** method of the **item** object through its **Something** interface, and that can be pictured essentially like this:

```
Something.DoSomething item
```

The **DoSomething** method looks like this in our code at compile-time:

```
Public Sub DoSomething()
 'do stuff
End Sub
```

But what the VBA compiler is seeing is closer to something like this:

```
Public Sub DoSomething(ByVal Me As Something)
 'do stuff
End Sub
```

That's why the members of **Me** are always the members accessible from the class' *public* interface: the **Me** reference is provided from *outside* the object, so encapsulated / private instance data cannot be accessed through it. In contrast, the role of the module-level **this** variable is to formalize the *internal* state of the class.

Abstraction Levels

Regardless of whether you're reading a small macro or a full-blown object-oriented application project, if the code is written at the right *abstraction level*, it will read like a charm: the entry points have a very high level of abstraction and give a vague, bird's eye view of what's going on. As you drill down into the parts of interest, the abstraction level follows along – getting more and more detailed the deeper you follow the procedure calls, until you're in small, specialized procedures and functions that do very simple things, but at a very low abstraction level: that's where you want to see the gory details of every worksheet interaction happen. A good way to visualize this is to break down the problem you're trying to solve into a sequence of steps:

```
Public Sub MakeInstantCoffee()
 BoilWater
 AddCoffee
 AddHotWater
End Sub
```

At a glance, we know everything about the big picture, and by simply reading the invoked method names, we know this procedure likely does what it says.

You want the abstraction level of any given procedure to be consistent: the gains of one very high-level procedure call are destroyed if that call is followed by 20 lines of low-level instructions. A procedure that is written at *one* given abstraction level, will feel "exactly right", and despite how hard *naming things* is, should be relatively easy to name accurately with a descriptive, meaningful identifier.

```
Public Sub MakeInstantCoffee()
 BoilWater
 AddCoffee
 Dim sugars As Long
 sugars = InputBox("How Many Sugars?")
 AddSugar sugars
 AddHotWater
End Sub
```

Something isn't right: **InputBox** is popping a UI and returning user input... it's an *implementation detail* that belongs to another, lower level of abstraction. Perhaps like this:

```
Private Sub AddCoffee()
 Dim blend As String
 blend = PickBlend
 AddBlend blend
 Dim additives As String
 additives = PickAdditives
 AddAdditives additives
End Sub
```

Now something else isn't right: the procedure is doing too many things. It claims to add coffee, but it can very well add cocoa and chocolate chunks on top of a generous portion of whipped cream – clearly that's well beyond the responsibility of a procedure named "add coffee". This is undoubtedly a better design decision:

```
Public Sub MakeInstantCoffee()
 BoilWater
 AddCoffee
 AddHotWater
 AddOtherIngredients
End Sub
Private Sub AddCoffee()
 Dim blend As String
 blend = PickBlend
 AddBlend blend
End Sub
Private Sub AddOtherIngredients() 'TODO find a better name?
 Dim additives As String 'TODO argh! naming is hard!
 additives = PickAdditives
 AddAdditives additives
End Sub
```

We haven't seen the rest of the module, but we can *guess* it's going to include **PickBlend** and **PickAdditives** functions that might prompt the user for what coffee blend they want, and how many sugars, how much milk, or cream, or *Bailey's* is going to be dunked in. The prompt might be a simple **InputBox**, or it might be a fancy **UserForm**, or the inputs might be read from a worksheet: at this abstraction level, we couldn't care less.

Every standard module should be structured similarly, with the public, high-level member(s) at the top, and the related private, lower-level procedures underneath, perhaps in calling order. That way, reading the few lines of the public procedure is enough to grasp a summary of everything that's going on in that macro module. And when you want to dig deeper into such or such general aspect, you navigate down the call graph and find yourself at a lower abstraction level: each procedure call gets the abstraction closer to the *boundaries* of your code, the *seams* between your code and the Excel object model, or between your code and the file system.

In class modules, if you're like me you like having the public members regrouped by procedure kind (**Property** / **Function** / **Sub**) near the top, followed by the lower-abstraction private members, then the private event handlers and interface implementations.

Tip: You can get the VBE to automatically sort (alphabetically) event handlers and interface implementations, by selecting providers (left) and members (right) from the code pane dropdowns. When you select a member from the right-hand dropdown, the IDE automatically creates the method stub for that member, with the correct signature.

What matters isn't the guidelines being followed, it's how consistently they're applied across the project as a whole: if every code file reads like it was written by a different person, it's… distracting.

Commenting

Inconsistent abstraction levels are distracting, for many reasons. One of the chief reasons for this, is that it encourages the sprouting of all kinds of flow-interrupting comments, that usually have one of two effects on the reader:

- Stops to read a useless comment.
- Consistently skips over this useless comment; reader is trained to skip *all* comments.

Good code that's written at the correct abstraction level usually needs very little commenting: the reader might need to know *why* we're doing something, but *what* we're doing should be accurately conveyed by the code itself, using meaningful and descriptive identifiers.

Banner Comments

Of all types of distracting comments, *banner comments* that state the obvious have to be the most obnoxious:

```
' =======================================================
' ******************* VARIABLES *******************
' =======================================================
```

Please don't do this. Not to yourself, not to your successors. First, we know they're variables. **Good, useful comments say why, not what**. Besides if you have enough variables to justify that large a banner, take a step back and reconsider whether that procedure is doing one thing, at the right abstraction level.

Banner comments *can* be useful, especially in class modules that implement multiple interfaces. But unless they have something helpful to say, they're not really necessary. I wrote these a few months ago:

```
':GameSheet event handlers
':Messages sent from the view
':**************************
```

And a few dozen lines later:

```
':IGridViewCommands
':Messages sent from the controller
':********************************
```

…and I regret writing them. But that was before **Rubberduck** had a **@ModuleDescription** annotation:

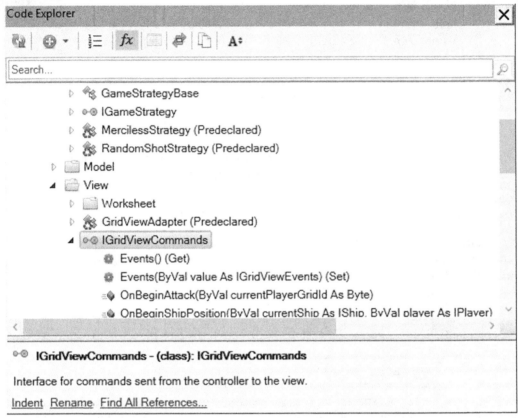

When the IDE tells you what you're looking at, do you still need noisy comments?

The most harmful banner comments are located inside procedure scopes: every single time, they indicate loud & clear that the procedure is doing too many things for its own good, and needs to be broken down into smaller, better abstracted procedures. For example, you might have a procedure that, at one point, needs to prompt the user for a file name:

```
'******************* Prompt for file name *******************
Dim filePath As String
filePath = Application.GetOpenFileName
If filePath = vbNullString Then Exit Sub
Dim book As Workbook
Set book = Application.Workbooks.Open(filePath)
```

Several things are wrong with this. First, not only we *prompt for a file name*, we're also opening it. We're gracefully handling the case where the user might have cancelled out of the prompt, but what if the user picked a file that Excel can't open? By abstracting this functionality into its own function, we get to replace all this boilerplate code by something much simpler and more expressive:

```
Dim book As Workbook
If Not GetWorkbookFromNetwork(book) Then Exit Sub
```

If the rest of the procedure is at that abstraction level, there's no need for any banner comments that say "the following chunk of code does XYZ", because *the code* is now speaking for itself: we don't need to know every detail of *how* we got that **Workbook**. We only need to know *whether* we have a usable **Workbook** object to work with, and this means we need not be bothered with any error-handling concerns: the lower-abstraction function is expected to return **False** if anything goes wrong.

Redundant Comments

I remember back in college, we were taught to "comment everything". Essentially every line of code needed an explanatory comment. In retrospect I believe this misguided requirement might have been for the teacher to assess whether we actually understood what was happening in the code… but in real-world code, this type of comment has no place:

```
Foo = Foo + 1 'increment Foo
```

You never need to write a comment that restates in plain words what the code already says; I've said this before, but *let the code say what, and let the comments explain why*. A more insidious type of redundant comment is the kind that, at a glance, *looks* like it might be helpful.

```
If foo Or bar Then
  '...50 lines of code...
End If ' foo Or bar
```

The problem with such comments, is that they are lipstick on a pig: if the **End If** is 50 lines underneath the corresponding condition expression, you might not necessarily remember what the condition was for that block – so instead of forcing the maintainer to scroll back up, you'd think copying the conditional expression in a comment near the **End If** token is useful. Except, it's not: what this comment is saying, is *whoever reads this, please break this massive block into smaller, more specialized procedures!* – because *that* is what the real solution is: refactoring the code to increase its abstraction level by extracting smaller procedures is going to naturally bring that **End If** token into the same screen as the conditional expression, reduce the cognitive load by moving a bunch of local variables to other scopes, and make debugging simpler by making errors occur in places that have fewer reasons to fail than they would in a larger procedure. Another problem with code-in-comments, is that it now makes *two* places to remember to edit if the condition ever needs to change.

Avoid adding a comment when increasing the abstraction level would do the same: pulling an expression into a new local variable, or extracting a series of instructions into their own procedure, both make much better alternatives to commenting about what's happening – especially if the new variable or procedure has a meaningful, descriptive name:

```
If Sheet1.Range("F" & currentRow).Value = Year(Date) Then
```

By introducing an aptly-named variable, the condition could be simplified, and the *intent* of the code becomes clearer, without any comments being added:

```
Dim isCurrentYear As Boolean
isCurrentYear = Sheet1.Range("F" & currentRow).Value = Year(Date)
If isCurrentYear Then
```

Every time you comment on the *what*, you *double the maintenance work* – because whenever the code needs to change, the comment needs to follow. Otherwise you end up with distracting comments that say one thing, and confusing code that says something else.

Common Mistakes

VBA is filled with "beginner traps" – shortcuts that look useful but inevitably come back to haunt you when you least expect it, like when you're presenting your work in front of its future users, and yet everything seemed to run perfectly fine the day before. There are many ways to write code that makes assumptions, without even realizing.

Unqualified Worksheet References

The difference between a keyword and a built-in function isn't always obvious, and to me it's among the reasons many people believe "Excel VBA" is a *flavor* of VBA, and "Word VBA" is another: if you think that way, member calls like **Range**, **Columns**, or **Rows** might feel very much like language-level keywords that magically know in what context to operate against… except, they're not. Only a **Worksheet** has a **Range**, **Columns**, **Rows**, or **Cells**: whenever you invoke these members unqualified inside anything other than a worksheet module, you are working against the hidden **[_Global]** interface.

When you're in a worksheet's code-behind module, an unqualified **Range** call refers to *that worksheet*'s **Range** property, the implicit object qualifier being **Me**. But in any other module type, an unqualified **Range** call refers to *whatever worksheet happens to currently be the* **ActiveSheet**… and that can quickly turn against you, because it hides assumptions and dependencies: things turn sour when, inevitably, one day the assumed active sheet isn't active:

```
With Sheet1
  .Range(Cells(1, 1), Cells(i, 1)).Value = 42
End With
```

Tip: Any worksheet that exists in **ThisWorkbook** at compile-time has no reason to ever need to be dereferenced from the **Sheets** (or better, **Worksheets**) collection:

```
Dim summarySheet As Worksheet
Set summarySheet = ThisWorkbook.Worksheets("Summary")
```

Instead, find and activate that sheet module in the Project Explorer (Ctrl + R), and then give its (Name) property a meaningful, **PascalCase** identifier – like **SummarySheet**; instantly, this identifier is now referring to a free, global-scope object that you can access everywhere in your code (although, you will want to restrict what modules you allow to directly consume global objects).

The above snippet means well; the **Range** member call is explicitly qualified by a **Sheet1** object variable, but parameterized with unqualified **Cells** invocations. Because **Cells** returns a **Range**, and because any **Range** object belongs to the **Worksheet** it lives in (you can access that sheet through the **Range.Parent** property), what's going to happen is that the code will look like it works just fine – as long as **Sheet1** is the **ActiveSheet**. That might be the expected case, but the code shouldn't be making that assumption. If **Sheet1** isn't active, the unqualified **Cells** calls might be pulling a **Range** from **Sheet2** or **Sheet3**, and that **Sheet1.Range** call will throw error 1004.

If you find code invoking **Range**, **Cells**, **Columns**, **Rows**, or **Names** without a qualifying object, consider making it an explicit member call against **ActiveSheet**. If that looks suspiciously wrong, use an appropriate **Worksheet** object qualifier.

These can be easy to miss in a legacy code base. Fortunately, Rubberduck can help you find them all – locating implicit **ActiveSheet** and **ActiveWorkbook** references being one of the many ways its static code analysis tool can identify potential bugs before you even run it.

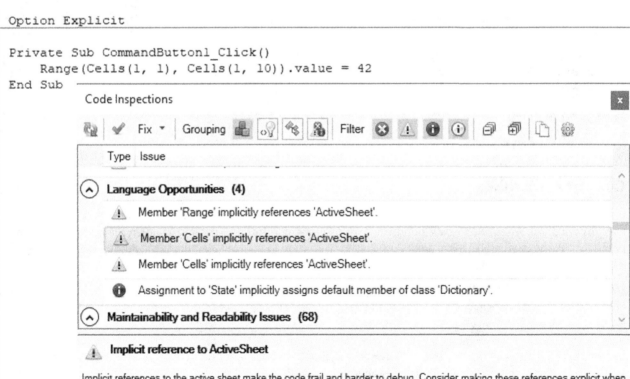

Rubberduck inspections can identify implicit references to ActiveSheet and ActiveWorkbook, warning you about places in your code where assumptions are making things more frail than they need to be.

I can't even begin skim the surface of everything Rubberduck can do, and I'm not saying this because I manage the project – this VBIDE add-in works in VB6, VBA6, and VBA7 (both 32 and 64 bits), in every host. Find the project on GitHub, give it a star if you like, and read the "user documentation" section of the wiki (and then help improve it and keep it up to date once you're familiar with it!), and you will want to regularly keep your install up-to-date, since the project has always been extremely active and constantly improving.

With over 80 code inspections, and well over 200 more ideas waiting to be implemented, Rubberduck's static code analysis covers a wide range of aspects. More importantly, it is able to analyze VBA code well beyond simple grammatical analysis: it's the difference between a tool that can warn if you assign to an undeclared variable or if **Option Explicit** is missing, and one that can warn you if that **Range** member call is resolving to some hidden **Global** object, explain that the code is implicitly referring to **ActiveSheet**, and then recommend qualifying it explicitly with a local **Worksheet** object variable. Rubberduck is a rather heavyweight IDE complement – perhaps similar to how JetBrains' ReSharper (R#) is a rather heavyweight plug-in for Visual Studio. But the breadth of the features offered makes it well worth the toll taken on overall performance. ReSharper taught me LINQ, and I wasn't the first nor the last; I hope someday, someone says Rubberduck inspections taught them something they didn't know about VBA, or that they located an edge-case bug they never knew was in there.

Among the most interesting and challenging (but completely possible) ideas the Rubberduck project entertains, we find inspections for code path analysis evaluating error paths and error handling in general… and this brings us to another common mistake: bad error handling.

Entangled Error Handling

Error handling is easy to get wrong in VBA: we're dealing with global run-time error state whose behavior isn't always obvious. To make things even more complicated than they already are, the IDE has settings to "break on all errors", "break on unhandled errors", and others – let's get these out of the way immediately: you want to **break on unhandled errors** all the time. Breaking on all errors is useful for debugging when an error is raised but your error-handling code is swallowing it, but confusing / surprising nonetheless if you find execution breaking on what should be a handled error, or even ignored by **On Error Resume Next**.

The ideal error handling, is no handling at all: if you know a certain input is invalid for a certain function, validate the input before you pass it to that function, and use regular flow control statements (**If…Else…End If**) to determine the execution paths. For example, we know that the **Range.Find** method returns **Nothing** when it doesn't find what it's looking for – and a member call against an object reference that's **Nothing**, will always throw run-time error 91. Instead of handling error 91 (specifically or not), we can capture the function's result in a local object (**Range**) variable, and verify whether the reference **Is Nothing**:

```
Dim result As range
Set result = Sheet1.Range("A:A").Find("needle", …)
If Not result Is Nothing Then
    …
End If
```

But error handling can't always be avoided with input validation and flow control: when you connect an **ADODB.Connection** to a remote server, you can't assume that the server is reachable, online, or authorizes a connection given the provided credentials, or that the connection succeeds in a timely fashion; when you **Open** a file **For Output**, you can't assume that the user running the code has write access to the file in question, or that the network path provided is accessible, or that another user or process isn't currently locking that file. Once an ADODB connection successfully opens, nothing guarantees an **ADODB.Command** against that connection will succeed as well, even if nothing is wrong with your VBA code.

Error handling is inevitable at the seams of a system. When writing a macro, your entry point is generally a parameterless procedure attached to some button or **Shape**: that procedure should have an **On Error** statement that catches any error that might have bubbled up from lower-abstraction procedures, and present them in a user-friendly manner. Popping **Err.Number** and **Err.Description** at the user is generally rather confusing… and useless – all the user needs to know in such situations is probably something along the lines of "something bad happened", and whether or not they can do anything about it, including to "please try again later".

Another instance where error handling is obligatory, is whenever global **Application** state is toggled: **Application.Calculation**, **EnableEvents**, and **ScreenUpdating** in particular. You might have read somewhere that disabling these will "make your VBA code run faster" (no, it doesn't make your code magically efficient: it simply cuts the *other code* that might otherwise run between two statements), so you've learned to toggle these off at the start of a macro, and back on at the end of it. But what if an error occurs – for any reason – and the calculation mode remains **xlCalculationManual**? This state affects the entire host application, not just your workbook, so you can effectively break other macros that assume automatic calculations by failing to handle an error in another completely unrelated macro in another workbook.

Errors should systematically be handled whenever you modify the state of any of these **Application** properties in a procedure:

- Calculation
- Cursor
- DisplayAlerts
- EnableEvents
- ScreenUpdating
- StatusBar

I like to call the default execution path of a procedure, the "happy path". This execution path typically ends with an explicit **Exit Sub** statement. The "error path" begins underneath that, and ensures the "clean-up" code is executed whether there's an error or not:

```
Public Sub DoSomething()
  On Error GoTo CleanFail
  Application.Calculation = xlCalculationManual
  ...
CleanExit:
  Application.Calculation = xlCalculationAutomatic
  Exit Sub
CleanFail:
   'handle error here
  Resume CleanExit
End Sub
```

Of course, it's not perfect. VBA error handling has many traps & pitfalls. But one that bites everyone at least once, is forgetting to clear the error state, and then attempting to redirect error handling *while inside* the error-handling subroutine (meaning, jumping out of the subroutine with a **GoTo** statement) – and you can't do that, since there's only ever a single run-time error that you can handle at once: any error that is raised when the VBA runtime is already in an error state, is *de facto* unhandled and will halt execution immediately.

Spare yourself the headaches: whatever you do, make sure the code in an error-handling subroutine can only ever execute in an error state; **If Err.Number <> 0** is a poor substitute for **Exit Sub**, that doesn't convey or enforce a separation of "happy" and "error" execution paths half as cleanly as an error handler that simply *cannot run* unless you're in an error state (run-time error 20 "Resume without error" is only waiting for you to make that mistake).

You may also have read that **Select Case Err.Number** might be a good idea: there's definitely something convenient about being able to handle different errors differently, however there's nothing sexy about half a screen's height (or more!) or error-handling code. It distracts from and obscures the *intent* of the code, and is a glaring sign that you're looking at a procedure that has too many responsibilities and does too many things, for it has too many reasons to fail. Indeed, a procedure that prompts for some text file's path, opens that file, reads it line by line, parses each line and writes the content into a 2D array, then closes the file, dumps the array onto a new worksheet in a new workbook, then makes that **Range** into a **ListObject** (table) and sorts by record date and filters out records prior to last week, ...is doing too many things, and has way too many reasons to fail.

With "traditional" procedural VBA code, that *is* one procedure – and the error-handling subroutine consists of a five-branch **If**...**ElseIf**...**ElseIf**...**ElseIf** block or, if you're lucky, a **Select**...**Case** block with as many **Case** statements, each handling a different error and **Resume**-ing to a different line label after showing a **MsgBox** with a custom, well-meaning, user-friendly error message.

I know I write a lot about OOP in VBA, but procedural code isn't inherently evil at all – and for a problem such as the above (ignoring that we're reinventing the "text import" feature... it's just an example), a procedural approach is perfectly fine and appropriate. The problem isn't with the procedural approach, it's with the lack of *abstraction* uselessly complicating error handling.

Contrast the monolith-procedure with a small function whose only responsibility is to return a path/filename to open and tell the caller whether the user cancelled the "browse" dialog:

```
Private Function PromptForFilePath(ByRef outPath As String) As Boolean
 Dim dialogResult As Variant
 dialogResult = Application.GetOpenFileName
 If VarType(dialogResult) = vbBoolean Then Exit Function
 outPath = CStr(dialogResult)
 PromptForFilePath = True
End Function
```

…then another function that takes a path and returns a **Workbook** object:

```
Private Function TryOpenWorkbookFile(ByVal path As String, ByRef outWorkbook
As Workbook) as Boolean
 On Error Resume Next
 Set outWorkbook = Application.Workbooks.Open(path)
 On Error GoTo 0
 TryOpenWorkbookFile = Not outWorkbook Is Nothing
End Function
```

What happened here? **On Error Resume Next**? Isn't that the embodiment of evil itself? In a monolithic proce-dure that does 12 different things, it absolutely is. Scoped to a single statement in its own separate procedure, it's a much better alternative than a full-blown error-handling subroutine: the function's sole purpose is to open a given file and return the workbook object for it – if anything goes wrong, regardless of the reason, we don't have a work-book to return. The calling code knows what to do when that happens: it's not the job of *this function* to know what to do with that information, and the calling code is in a much better position to handle it. By returning **False** in case of a failure in this function, the caller can pop a message box to tell the user the selected file couldn't be opened:

```
Dim path As String
If Not PromptForFilePath(path) Then Exit Sub

Dim book As Workbook
If TryOpenWorkbookFile(path, book) Then
 '…
Else
 MsgBox "Could not open file '" & path & "'."
End If
```

It's still completely procedural code, but now it's easier to follow and doesn't need any convoluted error handling… simply because extracting logic into smaller procedures has turned error handling into simple control flow logic – and that is how error handling is disentangled.

Unintended Late Binding

The term "late binding" refers to the VBA runtime resolving a member call against an object. It does this by querying **IUnknown** given a **Variant**, or **IDispatch** for an **Object**. These COM interface lookup mechanisms then get in-volved and either fail or succeed at finding the member and passing the provided arguments to it. **Late binding has very little to do with how you *create* an object**: **CreateObject** just happens to be able to load a type through a registry lookup, which is rather practical when the compiler can't resolve a type because you haven't referenced the library it's declared in… but if you *are* referencing the library, and then doing something like this:

```
Dim xlApp As Excel.Application
Set xlApp = CreateObject("Excel.Application")
```

…then you are making a registry lookup to locate a type that is *already* readily available: the expression on the right-hand side of that assignment could very easily be bound at compile-time:

```
Dim xlApp As Excel.Application
Set xlApp = New Excel.Application
```

Always use the **New** operator to create instances of types that are known at compile-time (i.e. classes defined in ref-erenced type libraries). But late binding isn't only about types and classes: every single member call you ever write against a **Variant** or **Object**, is late-bound – which means **Option Explicit** can't save you from error 438 here:

```
Dim source As Range
Set source = ActiveWorkbook.Worksheets("Sheet1").Rnage("A1:J10")
```

This code compiles perfectly fine, and yet there's a typo. How did that happen? The VBIDE's *Object Browser* (press F2 anywhere in the VBE) has the answer:

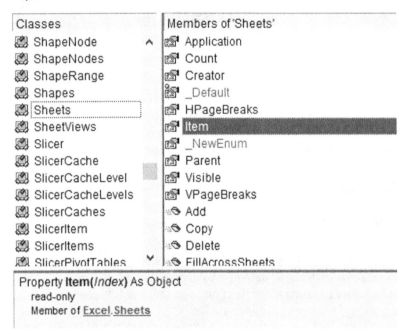

Worksheets("sheet1") is an implicit and indirect call to Sheets.Item, via the hidden [_Default] default member. Item(index) returns an Object. Right-click an empty area in the Object Browser's toolbar and select "Show hidden members" to reveal hidden interfaces and members.

You know a member call is late-bound when you type the dereferencing (dot) operator... and nothing happens: no *IntelliSense*, no *parameter QuickInfo*: moreover, the code will merrily compile with typos.

Because **Worksheets("Sheet1")** returns an **Object**, we have to *cast* this object to an interface that's known at compile-time, like **Worksheet**. But if the **Worksheets** collection only contains **Worksheet** objects, why does its **Item** member return an **Object**? The reason behind this is related to why it's taking a **Variant** parameter, and not only because **Worksheets(1)** is also valid, but also because an array of strings is an equally valid input:

```
Dim sheetNames As Variant
sheetNames = Array("Sheet1", "Sheet3")
Dim surprise As Object
Set surprise = ActiveWorkbook.Worksheets(sheetNames)
Debug.Print TypeName(surprise)
```

Spoiler: this is not a **Worksheet**. Whenever a function or property returns a **Variant** or an **Object**, you lose *IntelliSense* and compiler support – and that's your cue to protect your code against a potential late-bound call gone wrong (in general, error 438), and make an explicit *type cast*.

Note: "casting" is the action of accessing an object through another interface. Unlike many other languages VBA does not have a "cast" operator, so we simply use the **Set** keyword to assign the object reference to an early-bound interface.

Assuming **sheetNames** is some user-provided **Variant**, the below code *casts* the **surprise** object into a **Worksheet** reference. In many ways casting is a lot like changing the color of the lens through which you're looking at an object:

```
Dim surprise As Object
Set surprise = ActiveWorkbook.Worksheets(sheetNames)
Dim sheet As Worksheet
Set sheet = surprise
```

If **surprise** is not a **Worksheet** object, the **Set** assignment fails with a *type mismatch* error at run-time. How is that an improvement from later failing with error 438 "member not found" then? The important word here is "later": the invalid operation was assuming that you were getting a **Worksheet**, and if you're explicit about type casts and strive to keep the code as early-bound as possible, then you get the error the moment when what you're getting is *not* a **Worksheet**. Without a type cast, error 438 is VBA telling you "I can't find that **Range** member you're looking for", when you try to invoke **Worksheet.Range** against that object, perhaps 20 lines underneath, perhaps two or three procedures up the call stack, in code that's completely unrelated to the actual source of the problem.

VBA user classes can't do that, but COM objects are, by default and unless specified otherwise, *extensible*: members can be tacked onto an object at run-time. A good example of this is the late-bound version of `WorksheetFunction` members, extending the `Excel.Application` global object:

```
[A1].Value = Application.Sum([A2:A10])
```

The `Application` class doesn't have a `Sum` member, and yet this code happily compiles, and runs correctly.

> **Note**: Square-bracketed expressions are also late-bound. They are implicit calls to `Application.Evaluate` or `Worksheet.Evaluate` (depending on context) that VBA defers to the host application (Excel). This notation is useful for quick examples and Debug / immediate pane, but should be avoided in code.

Code will fail. And you want it to fail as early as possible. At compile time if you can help it, or as close as possible to the source of the problem otherwise. Casting `Object` and `Variant` to the actual types you mean to work with, as early on as possible, will restore *IntelliSense* / autocomplete and compile-time type checking – making it a very valuable tool to defend against the traps of late-bound member calls.

Perhaps the single best way to guard against weird or unexpected run-time behavior, is to write automated tests that validate and document it. But in order to test something, that something must be *testable*.

Making Code Testable

Modern VBA code is clean, maintainable, extensible, …and *testable*. Not "run the thing and press every button" testable: I mean *automated tests*. Testability is important in any code base, large or small. If you've ever written an Excel user-defined function (UDF) that takes all its worksheet / range dependencies as parameters, then you've written a *pure function* – and pure functions are testable by definition.

Testable code is simply code that you can invoke in a controlled manner and get consistent, predictable results. The outcome is *deterministic*, because a test controls all the *dependencies* of the method being tested.

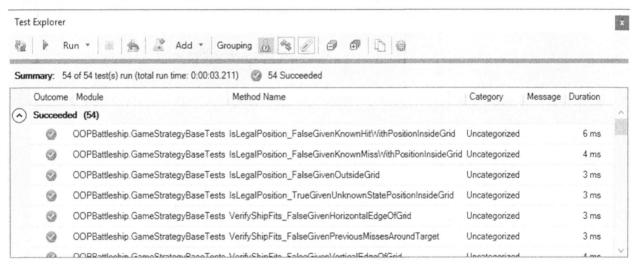

Rubberduck's Test Explorer tool window lists all test methods discovered in the IDE, and exposes commands to add new test modules and new test methods, and run them.

In modern programming, writing unit tests is the industry standard. That means as much as *half* the code written in any project, is test code that's testing whether the other half is working as documented. I'm not saying every VBA project should be full-blown OOP, and I'm not saying every OOP project should have a complete test suite with 80%+ coverage.

I'm saying code that is *testable,* is code for which you *can* write a test that verifiably reproduces the issue described in your latest help desk support ticket (or email from a user), and then *provably* fix it. Code that is decently covered with tests, is code that you can confidently clean up and refactor, without fearing of breaking things: if you change something and it breaks, you'll know exactly what broke just by running the tests.

Each test should be independent of any other tests; tests should be executable in any order, individually or all at once, and always reliably produce the same results. And we can't do that if the method we're trying to test is dependent on things we can't control – like a database, the file system, …or whatever the `ActiveSheet` is.

Abstracting and Injecting Dependencies

Dependencies aren't always obvious: it takes a little bit of eye training to be able to recognize them on sight, but as a rule of thumb the idea that a function or procedure *depends* on something means that it's interacting with any object.

What would be the dependencies of a method like this?

```
Public Function TryDoSomething(ByVal sheetName As String) As Boolean
  Dim sheet As Worksheet
  Set sheet = Application.Worksheets(sheetName)
  '...
End Function
```

As written, the procedure depends on **Application.Worksheets**, and that makes it hard to test automatically *as a unit*, because it's *coupled* with a very specific **Excel.Sheets** object reference that no test can control. Compare to:

```
Public Function TryDoSomething(ByVal sheet As Worksheet) As Boolean
  '...
End Function
```

By taking in a **Worksheet** object reference instead of a **String** worksheet name, we no longer depend on something that the calling code cannot control, we've exposed our *real* dependencies to our callers, and we've moved the responsibility of *getting that worksheet reference* out of the function itself. Ergo, we've single-handedly made the code simpler and better. Avoid depending on anything in global scope. Instead, wrap the global scope in specialized objects (classes) that *encapsulate* the specific state you need to work with – and take an instance of that class as a parameter where you need it.

If many members of a class have similar dependencies, consider promoting the parameters to instance (module) level. The act of providing an object with its dependencies is called *dependency injection*. There are several different ways to inject dependencies into an object, the easiest being *method injection*: each method takes (as parameters) the dependencies it needs to work with. In languages where objects have parameterized constructors, *constructor injection* is ideal. VBA objects don't have parameterized constructors, but we can have parameterized *factory methods* instead – and the result is the same: fully decoupled components that can be individually tested.

We can find an example of what such code looks like by examining the **PlayWorksheetInterface** macro of this Battleship game (see the full source at github.com/rubberduck-vba/Battleship):

```
'@Folder("Battleship")
'@ModuleDescription("Application entry points.")
Option Explicit
Private controller As GameController

Public Sub PlayWorksheetInterface()
  Dim view As Battleship.WorksheetView
  Set view = New Battleship.WorksheetView

  Dim randomizer As IRandomizer
  Set randomizer = New GameRandomizer

  Set controller = New GameController
  controller.NewGame GridViewAdapter.Create(view), randomizer
End Sub
```

Note: the name of the **Battleship.WorksheetView** type is *hiding* (or *shadowing*) the **Excel.WorksheetView** class, which can be confusing if the class type isn't *qualified*. Ideally, another name would be used.

This code is an example of the *Model-View-Controller* pattern which I'm not going to cover here, but if we made a *dependency graph* to show how the different classes and interfaces depend on each other, it would look like this:

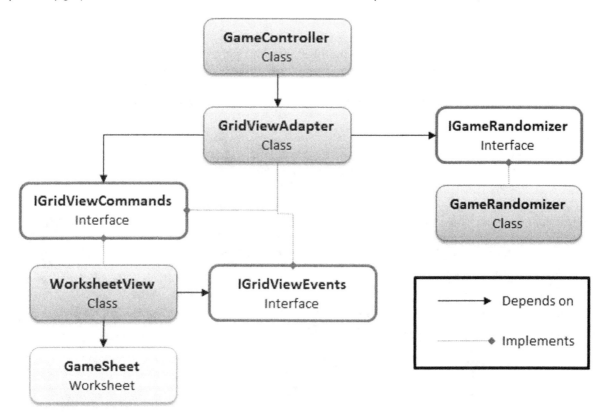

A simplified dependency graph of the types involved highlights how the game logic is abstracting away the worksheet behind interfaces: this proven architecture is flexible enough to make the game, with very little changes, work with a completely different UI (a UserForm, for example).

There's *a lot* going on in that little snippet: the "view adapter" is happy to work with any object that implements the **IGridViewCommands** interface, which is the case for the **WorksheetView** class. It could just as well be injected with a **UserFormView** class that responds to game *controller* commands in its own way, …or anything else that can talk to the view *adapter*.

Separating the **IRandomizer** interface from the game controller logic makes it possible for tests to inject an implementation that any given test can completely control – injecting the randomizer as a dependency means the game logic's response to (pseudo-)random inputs can now be fully deterministically tested: **MercilessStrategyAlmostNeverShootsAtRandom** could absolutely be a nice test for conditional logic like such:

```
If this.Random.Maybe(AlmostNever) Then
  Set position = base.ShootRandomPosition(this.Random, enemyGrid)
ElseIf this.Random.Maybe(Sometimes) Then
  Set position = ScanCenter(enemyGrid)
Else
  Set position = ScanEdges(enemyGrid)
End If
```

By writing a **TestRandomizer** class that implements the **IGameRandomizer** interface, we can test the above logic by "injecting" an instance of the **TestRandomizer** in that class for a test (the real code uses a **GameRandomizer** instance instead). This test-only implementation could have its own instance state, for example it might have properties that return the number of times the **IGameRandomizer.Maybe** method was invoked, with which parameter value; it could also be configurable, so that a unit test could predetermine a sequence of results and make the function always return **True**, or make it return **True** the first 3 times it's invoked, and then systematically return **False** – whatever the tests need it to do.

Nobody will blame you for not writing any unit tests for your VBA code. But code that is *testable*, is code whose dependencies are parameterized, that the caller (test) can control; It's code that generally adheres to the S.O.L.I.D. principles and is written at coherent abstraction levels. It's short, simple procedures with descriptive names, in classes implementing simple interfaces with a clear purpose.

One subheading in a single chapter wouldn't be enough to cover everything there is to say about OOP and the SOLID principles, but we can still review the key ingredients in the secret sauce…

Using Hidden Attributes

Before Rubberduck, leveraging module and member attributes was rather annoying, and thus seldom done: attributes don't appear in the Visual Basic Editor. We have to remove / export the code file, edit the attributes, save the file, then re-import the modified module back into the VBA project. With Rubberduck we can have an IDE add-in do this for us, and reveal a whole new world of possibilities. Consider the @**PredeclaredId** module annotation:

```
'@PredeclaredId
Option Explicit
```

This annotation instructs Rubberduck (and documents to the reader) that the *intent* is for that module to have its hidden **Attribute VB_PredeclaredId** set to **True**, and the add-in uses static code analysis to ensure the annotations and attributes are in sync:

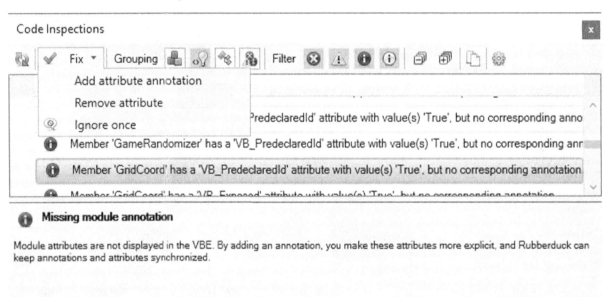

Two automatic fixes are available for the Missing Attribute inspection: remove the annotation or synchronize the module's attributes accordingly. The Missing Annotation inspection works similarly, by suggesting adding an annotation comment to document the presence of a hidden attribute value.

There are a number of annotations that control various attributes' values, notably @**ModuleDescription("…")** and @**Description("…")** annotations – but because learning to use @**PredeclaredId** might very well be the single most life-changing addition to your toolbox since learning to use VLOOKUP in a worksheet, I'll focus on that one; all Rubberduck annotations are documented on the project's wiki (on GitHub).

> **Note:** Every instance of an object gets its own internal ID, so that the VBA runtime can easily locate any given existing reference object quickly. When the **VB_PredeclaredId** attribute of a class module is set to **True**, a project-scoped global object is created automatically, and the name of that class is associated with the predeclared ID. That's how **UserForm1.Show** can work without requiring a **New UserForm1** instance. This "predeclared object" is dubbed the "default instance" of the class.

Default instances are very much a double-edged tool. Well used, they unlock object-oriented language capabilities that very impressively push the boundaries of what VBA code can do. Abused, they are essentially global state in a public module. In other words, default instances make it easy to forget that we're dealing with objects.

Default instances should be stateless. The class itself might be encapsulating and exposing data, but the default instance should never hold any run-time state. Always hold state in **New** instances that you *own* and fully control.

One great use for this "predeclared ID" feature, is to leverage a class' *default instance* to expose a *factory method* – a **Create** function whose only role is to *create* a new instance of the class, initialize it, and return the object to the calling code. The factory method for the **GridViewAdapter** class looks like this:

```
Public Function Create(ByVal view As IGridViewCommands) As GridViewAdapter
 Dim result As GridViewAdapter
 Set result = New GridViewAdapter
 Set result.GridView = view
 Set view.Events = result
 Set Create = result
End Function
```

Parameterized factory methods make a very clean way of initializing objects in VBA; the functionality is similar to having a **CreateSomething** function in a standard module, without the need to have a separate **FactoryMethods** module that can create instances for a bunch of unrelated classes, and without polluting the global namespace with these functions.

Writing a Test

You made your code testable, and now you would like to write a test suite to cover that code – that's great! Know that the VBE will not help you with that. There are all-VBA solutions available online, and other add-ins, but one of the simplest to use is, again, Rubberduck.

Tests have three phases: Arrange, Act, and Assert. In the first part of the test, we setup the dependencies for the class / method we want to test. The *act* part is where we invoke that method; the role of the *assert* step is to determine whether the test passed or not.

This test validates that the **PlayerGrid.TryHit** function returns **AttackResult.Hit** given a **GridCoord** position that holds an enemy ship:

```
'@TestMethod
Public Sub TryHitSuccess_ReturnsHit()
 Dim position As GridCoord
 Set position = GridCoord.Create(1, 1)

 Dim sut As PlayerGrid
 Set sut = New PlayerGrid
 sut.AddShip Ship.Create(ShipType.Battleship, Horizontal, position)

 Assert.AreEqual AttackResult.Hit, sut.TryHit(position)
End Sub
```

The "Arrange" part of this test creates a **PlayerGrid**, places a ship at position (1,1), then verifies what value **TryHit** returns given that position: if the **TryHit** method is modified in any way that makes it no longer return **AttackResult.Hit** (an **Enum** constant value) given an input that's definitely a hit and fully expected to result in a hit, then this test would break, because the "Assert" part would then be failing.

Note: "sut" is a commonly-used identifier referring to the "System Under Test", i.e. the class being tested.

When you create a new Rubberduck *test module*, you get a module-scoped object variable named **Assert**, an instance of a class that implements the **Rubberduck.IAssert** interface: using the **Rubberduck.AssertClass**, you get to *assert* whether an expression **IsTrue**, whether an object reference **IsNothing**, whether two values **AreEqual**, etc.: the role of the "Assert" part of a test is to tell the test engine whether the test passed or not, and the **Rubberduck.IAssert** interface is how Rubberduck exposes this functionality. Ideally, a test should be testing one thing, and have one single reason to fail.

Naming tests precisely, helps with writing tests that are focused on testing the outcome of a specific set of inputs: the form "given {condition} _ {outcome}" seems to work pretty well:

```
'@TestMethod("Test Category")
Public Sub GivenTwoSideBySideHits_GetHitAreaReturnsTwoItems()
```

That test should be inconclusive unless it's setting up two side-by-side hits on a grid; the **PlayerGrid. FindHitArea** method is expected to return two items (grid coordinates) in that situation, and the test should succeed if that's the case, and fail otherwise.

Test methods should be small, easy to read and understand what they're all about and why they would be failing: each class under test should have its own dedicated test module covering as much of the public interface of that class as possible.

> **Note**: test method names can have their own naming conventions. While underscores should absolutely be avoided in public procedure names (especially in class modules), they feel particularly appropriate in a test name as part of a consistent naming scheme.

What about Private Methods?

The private methods of a class are considered its *implementation details*, and should already be invoked by the public methods. If you feel like a class has more responsibilities than it should and some of the private members involve logic that's intricate enough to warrant its own tests, then you can refactor and extract these members to a new class that becomes a dependency of the former one: that new class now has its own public interface that can now be tested. Otherwise, tests shouldn't be bothered with a class' private members.

So... I Can't Change the Code Anymore, or Tests Will Break?

Tests shouldn't break when the implementation details change. A test should break when the code under test no longer fulfills its documented purpose: tests document the behavior of objects – if the specifications didn't change and *what* the code needs to do hasn't changed, then there's no reason your tests should start failing if you modify the code… if you're testing for the right things. The goal of unit testing isn't to cast your entire code in concrete – It's actually quite literally the opposite of that; the goal is to give you the confidence to make any changes you like to your code, and *know* that you didn't break anything doing so.

Does my VBA Project Need to Reference the Rubberduck Type Library?

As with any other library reference, it's best to work early-bound, with a reference to the type library – especially if you're unfamiliar with the API. Before you distribute your project, you can late-bind the library (by declaring the **Assert** variable **As Object**) to avoid broken references and associated compiler errors.

About the MVPs

Jon Acampora is the founder of Excel Campus. His goal is to help you learn to use Excel more efficiently so you can save time with your job, impress your boss, and advance in your career through his articles, YouTube videos, and immersive online training programs. Join him and grab your free gift at ExcelCampus.com/free. When he's not writing macros or building financial models, Jon enjoys spending time with his wife and son at the beach in Southern California.

Liam Bastick is an Excel MVP, financial modeller, Fellow of three accounting institutes and a professional mathematician. He founded SumProduct (www.sumproduct.com) in late 2009, which provides consulting, training, auditing and advisory services in Excel, modelling and the Power BI suite of tools. With over 2,000 blogs and articles to his name, he is an author of several books including An Introduction to Financial Modelling and Divisors. A frustrated comedian, Liam's chequered career includes being a football reporter, a bouncer, an investment analyst and also a successful contestant on some of the nerdiest quiz shows in the world.

Leila Gharani runs her own Excel site at www.XelPlus.com and has an active YouTube channel with many engaging, high quality videos. Most of the videos are Excel tips and tricks based on questions and suggestions she gets from the Excel online community and professionals. If you'd like to create useful tools and get more done, check out Leila's bestselling online courses on her website.

Mike Girvin started the excelisfun channel at YouTube in 2008. Since then he has posted over 3,000 Excel How To Videos with over 600 K Subscribers. As a Highline College Professor since 2002, he posts all of his classes at YouTube with the goal of providing free education to the world. Mike has been an Excel MVP since 2013 and has written a few books about Excel. For fun Mike likes to race BMX bikes and throw boomerangs.

Roger Govier has been an MVP in Excel since 2007. He bought his first computer in 1978 and has worked with the first ever spreadsheet, Visicalc, through all successive versions to the latest Excel. In 1996, Roger set up his own IT Consultancy business, Technology 4 U. He has written many articles and tutorials on the Contextures website run by fellow MVP Debra Dalgleish. https://www.contextures.com/excelfilesRoger.html. Outside of work he enjoys watching Rugby (well, he is Welsh) and Formula 1 motorsport as well as walking with his wife and their two black Labradors around their small farm in Wales where he has his office. Contact him at roger@technology4u.co.uk.

Frédéric le Guen has worked with Excel since 1996 with many different companies to help them to create automation and dynamic dashboards. For years, he has created complex worksheet with the Excel functions and VBA. Then, since 2013, he also works with the new BI tools (like Power Pivot and Power Query) for Big Data. Find him at the YouTube channel ExcelExercice and his website www.excel-exercice.com..

Mathieu Guindon learned VB in the late 90's, but started using VBA in 2004 as part of an office job involving a lot of manual Excel worksheet manipulations. A decade later he was promoting clean-coding best practices on Code Review Stack Exchange and Stack Overflow, where he ranks in the top 0.2% contributors. He founded the Rubberduck open-source VBIDE add-in project with a fellow VBA reviewer, owns rubberduckvba.com and the project's WordPress blog, and continues to oversee and manage the project to this day. Proud father of twins, when he isn't working, helping others with their C# or VBA code, implementing new Rubberduck features, or writing articles revolving around VBA, he likes to spend some quality time with his family.

Ingeborg Hawighorst regards Excel as one of her hobbies. For over ten years she has spent much of her free time answering Excel related questions in online forums and communities. Her professional career revolves around SharePoint and Office 365. When not in front of a screen, Ingeborg likes to work with the right side of her brain, playing cello, drawing and painting. When time allows, Ingeborg blogs at http://teylyn.com.

Tim Heng has over 10 years' experience in developing and reviewing financial models across a range of industries and sectors. He works with clients to develop bespoke modelling solutions for business challenges, using a combination of Excel, VBA, and Power BI and database analytics. Currently he is a Director of Australian consulting firm SumProduct. Tim writes articles for several newsletters published by the Society of Actuaries (US), and has been a regular presenter at conferences, training courses and webinars for Certified Practising Accountants Australia (CPAA) and Chartered Accountants Australia New Zealand (CAANZ).

Wyn Hopkins is a Director at Access Analytic, a Perth-based company delivering Amazing Excel and Power BI solutions.

After qualifying as a Chartered Accountant with PricewaterhouseCoopers in the UK, Wyn moved on to working as an analyst for two UK banks before emigrating to Australia.

Wyn is an experienced Trainer and Excel / Power BI Developer. Since joining Access Analytic in 2007, he has delivered hundreds of amazing solutions for many of Perth's largest organisations.

Ian Huitson works as a Consulting Mining Engineer in Perth, Australia.

Ian has 30+ years experience in hard rock mining as well as data mining and he is passionate about scheduling and budgeting, simulation and mathematics but more importantly their application to solving real world problems.

Ian was a Microsoft MVP (Excel) from October 2013 until June 2019.

You can read more about Ian's Excel work at: https://chandoo.org/wp/about-hui/

To see a gallery of Ian's major Excel contributions please visit: https://www.mining-solutions.com.au/excel

To see what services Ian offers as a Mining Consultant visit Mining Solutions: https://www.mining-solutions.com.au/

Bill Jelen is the host of MrExcel.com and the author of sixty books about Excel. He writes the monthly Excel column for Strategic Finance magazine and has 2200 Excel videos on YouTube. Readers of this book can save 20% on his other books by using coupon code XLMVP at the MrExcel.com Store. When he is not Excelling, you can find him photographing rocket launches near Cape Canaveral with his wife Mary Ellen Jelen.

Tony De Jonker helps companies creating user-friendly Financial Models using the modern Power Tools in Excel and Power BI and has developed more than hundreds of models since the advent of commercial spreadsheets (1985). He teaches his own nuts-and-bolts material based on more than 40 years of work experience as inhouse courses and public courses worldwide in English, Dutch and German. He writes the monthly Excel column for Controller's Magazine since 2005. Tony is the founder of the annual Excel events such as Excel Experience Day, Excel Experts Class and the Amsterdam Excel BI Summit. Find him at http://dejonkerconsultancy.com/

Gašper Kamenšek is an Excel MVP from Slovenia, Trainer, and Consultant at Excel Olympics and owner and Lead Author at Excel Unplugged. He has dedicated his Excel work to the noble goal of helping people enjoy working in Excel through helping them to get better at it as we all know we love doing what we Excel at (no pun intended).

John MacDougall is a freelance consultant and trainer specializing in Excel, Power BI, PowerApps and Flow. He runs a blog (howtoexcel.org) and YouTube channel (youtube.com/c/howtoexcelblog) and you can check out his free ebooks by signing up to his weekly newsletter at howtoexcel.org/newsletter. When he's not consulting or blog-ging, John likes to hang out with friends and family, travel, eat good food or watch MMA.

Dave Paradi has authored nine books and is one of only fifteen people in North America to be recognized by Microsoft with the Most Valuable Professional Award for contributions on Excel and PowerPoint. His focus is on training corporate professionals to visually communicate the messages in their data so they don't overwhelm and confuse executives. Readers of this book can find articles, videos, and other resources at www.CreateExcelCharts.com or www.ThinkOutsideTheSlide.com.

Jon Peltier is founder of Peltier Technical Services, which specializes in development of Excel add-ins and dashboards. Jon writes regular articles on the extensive Peltier Tech blog, where you can find over 600 articles on various topics regarding Excel charting and VBA programming. Jon has been a full-time Excel developer for over 15 years, after a similar time as an R&D metallurgist, working on advanced materials for aircraft and turbine engines. Jon applies his science and engineering approach to his Excel work. When not working in or on Excel, Jon's hobbies include hiking, kayaking, and drinking craft beer.

Jan Karel Pieterse - I am Jan Karel Pieterse, a self-employed Excel and VBA consultant from The Netherlands. I've been working with spreadsheets since 1986 and started using Excel and VBA in 1996. I have received the Microsoft MVP Award many times (each year starting from 2002) for my support of Excel users around the world.

My website https://jkp-ads.com contains many articles about Excel and VBA you cannot find anywhere else and features a couple of industry-standard (free) Excel add-ins.

Ken Puls is the host of Excelguru.ca, and the author of 3 Excel books including the upcoming Master Your Data. He is the co-founder of the world's best Power Query Academy (https://academy.powerquery.training), and spends most of his time flying around the world training people in how to get the most out of Excel.

Oz du Soleil is a 4-time Excel MVP and is best known for his lively, brash, over-dramatic YouTube channel, Excel on Fire. He co-Authored Guerrilla Data Analysis with MrExcel, Bill Jelen. Oz is also a popular instructor on the LinkedIn Learning / Lynda library with courses on Power Query, dynamic arrays, and a few fun courses for Excel beginners. When Oz isn't working on Excel, he's enjoying a good cigar or onstage as a storyteller around his home city of Portland, Oregon in shows like 7 Deadly Sins, Pants on Fire, Risk!, Telltale, Pickathon and The Blacknteurs.

Hervé Thiriez has been a spreadsheet expert since the first Visicalc in 1979. He published the bimonthly "La lettre d'Excel" (24 pages & a floppy disk) from 1990 through 2005. In 2005, he replaced this publication by his blog https://monsieur-excel.blogspot.com/ which is a reference on Excel in French. He developed over 1,000 models for over 100 businesses in over 10 countries.

An MVP since 2014, **Mynda Treacy** started her career as a management accountant in Investment Banking in London. Nowadays, she shares her Excel knowledge with thousands of Excel enthusiasts through her blog, YouTube channel, webinars and weekly Excel newsletters. She also runs online courses in Excel Dashboards, Power Query, Power Pivot and Power BI.

Henk Vlootman is trainer and consultant Excel and Power BI throughout the world in the Dutch or English language since 1992. In Excel or BI conferences Henk acts as chairman, provide keynotes and delivers substantive contributions. Henk writes a monthly blog on Excel for two Dutch financial e-magazines (vakmedianet and Alex van Groningen). Henk is founder and chairman of the foundation of the Dutch Power BI Usergroup and founder and CEO of Quanto, Collective Analytics.

Charles Williams is an Excel, VBA and C++ developer and consultant who spends far too much time working out ways of making Excel and VBA UDFs calculate faster. His website WWW.DecisionModels.com and blog https://fastexcel.wordpress.com/ are primary sources of information about Excel calculation and UDFs. His FastExcel product is widely used to pinpoint the causes of slow Excel calculation in a workbook. Outside of Excel he can often be found sailing his racing dinghies or drinking Pinot Noir.

Index

INDEX